Mastering Appellate Advocacy and Process

Carolina Academic Press Mastering Series
Russell L. Weaver, Series Editor

Mastering Administrative Law
William R. Andersen

Mastering Appellate Advocacy and Process
Donna C. Looper, George W. Kuney

Mastering Bankruptcy
George W. Kuney

Mastering Civil Procedure
David Charles Hricik

Mastering Constitutional Law
John C. Knechtle, Christopher J. Roederer

Mastering Contract Law
Irma S. Russell, Barbara K. Bucholtz

Mastering Corporate Tax
Reginald Mombrun, Gail Levin Richmond, Felicia Branch

Mastering Corporations and Other Business Entities
Lee Harris

Mastering Criminal Law
Ellen S. Podgor, Peter J. Henning, Neil P. Cohen

Mastering Criminal Procedure, Volume 1: The Investigative Stage
Peter J. Henning, Andrew Taslitz, Margaret L. Paris,
Cynthia E. Jones, Ellen S. Podgor

Mastering Elder Law
Ralph C. Brashier

Mastering Employment Discrimination Law
Paul M. Secunda, Jeffrey M. Hirsch

Mastering Evidence
Ronald W. Eades

Mastering Family Law
Janet Leach Richards

Mastering Intellectual Property
George W. Kuney, Donna C. Looper

Mastering Legal Analysis and Communication
David T. Ritchie

Mastering Legal Analysis and Drafting
George W. Kuney, Donna C. Looper

**Mastering Negotiable Instruments (UCC Articles 3 and 4)
and Other Payment Systems**
Michael D. Floyd

Mastering Products Liability
Ronald W. Eades

Mastering Professional Responsibility
Grace M. Giesel

Mastering Property Law
Darryl C. Wilson, Cynthia G. Hawkins DeBose

Mastering Secured Transactions (UCC Article 9)
Richard H. Nowka

Mastering Statutory Interpretation
Linda D. Jellum

Mastering Tort Law
Russell L. Weaver, Edward C. Martin, Andrew R. Klein,
Paul J. Zwier II, Ronald W. Eades, John H. Bauman

Mastering Appellate Advocacy and Process

Donna C. Looper

Adjunct Professor of Law
University of Tennessee College of Law

George W. Kuney

W.P. Toms Professor of Law and the Director of the
James L. Clayton Center for Entrepreneurial Law
University of Tennessee College of Law

Carolina Academic Press
Durham, North Carolina

Library of Congress Cataloging in Publication Data

Looper, Donna C.
  Mastering appellate advocacy and process / Donna C. Looper and George
W. Kuney.
     p. cm. -- (Carolina Academic Press mastering series)
  ISBN 978-1-59460-801-8 (alk. paper)
  1. Appellate procedure--United States. I. Kuney, George W. II. Title. III.
Series.

  KF9050.L66 2011
  347.73'8--dc22

                              2011002483

Carolina Academic Press
700 Kent Street
Durham, NC 27701
Telephone (919) 489-7486
Fax (919) 493-5668
www.cap-press.com

Printed in the United States of America

To J.D., 1997 – 2010, who watched while we wrote.

Contents

Table of Cases   xxi

Table of Statutes and Rules   xxvii

Series Editor's Foreword   xxix

About the Authors   xxxi

Acknowledgments   xxxiii

Introduction   xxxv

Chapter 1 · Appellate Court Systems   3
  Roadmap   3
  I. Federal Courts   3
    a. Overview   3
    b. Federal District Courts   4
    c. United States Courts of Appeal—Circuit Courts   5
      United States Court of Appeals for the First Circuit   7
      United States Court of Appeals for the Second Circuit   8
      United States Court of Appeals for the Third Circuit   8
      United States Court of Appeals for the Fourth Circuit   8
      United States Court of Appeals for the Fifth Circuit   9
      United States Court of Appeals for the Sixth Circuit   9
      United States Court of Appeals for the Seventh Circuit 9
      United States Court of Appeals for the Eighth Circuit   10
      United States Court of Appeals for the Ninth Circuit   10
      United States Court of Appeals for the Tenth Circuit   11
      United States Court of Appeals for the Eleventh Circuit 11
      United States Court of Appeals for the District of
        Columbia Circuit   12
      United States Court of Appeals for the Federal Circuit 12
    d. The United States Supreme Court   12

II. State Courts   14
  a. State Intermediate Appellate Courts   14
  b. State Courts of Last Resort   15
Checkpoints   16

Chapter 2 · Preserving Error for Appeal   19
Roadmap   19
I.   The General Rule Regarding Preservation of Error   19
II. Preservation of Error in the Trial Court   20
  a. Evidentiary Errors   20
  b. Arguments and Conduct of Counsel at Trial   22
  c. Jury Instructions   22
  d. Preserving Issues in Responsive Pleadings and Pre-Trial Motions 23
  e. Post-Trial Motions   24
III. Preservation of Error During the Appeal   25
  a. Record or Appendix on Appeal   25
  b. Briefing the Appeal   26
  c. Oral Argument   26
IV. Exceptions Regarding Preservation of Error   27
  a. Plain or Fundamental Error   27
  b. Subject Matter Jurisdiction   28
  c. Standing   29
A Final Note Regarding Mootness   30
Checkpoints   30

Chapter 3 · Appealability: The Final Judgment Rule and Exceptions 33
Roadmap   33
I.   The Final Judgment Rule   33
II. Exceptions to the Final Judgment Rule   35
  a. The Collateral Order Doctrine   35
  b. Partial Final Judgments under Federal Rule of
     Civil Procedure 54(b)   36
  c. Appeals of Interlocutory Orders under 28 U.S.C. § 1292   38
    1. Orders Regarding Injunctions — 28 U.S.C. § 1292(a)(1)   38
    2. Receivership Orders — 28 U.S.C. § 1292(a)(2)   39
    3. Orders Involving Controlling Questions of Law —
       28 U.S.C. § 1292(b)   39
  d. Class Certification Decisions under Federal Rule of Civil
     Procedure 23(f)   40

    e. Review by Extraordinary Writ (Writ of Mandamus) —
        28 U.S.C. § 1651(a)   41
    f. Pendent Appellate Jurisdiction   42
  III. State Systems   43
  Checkpoints   49

Chapter 4 · Initiating an Appeal   51
  Roadmap   51
  I. Notice of Appeal: Contents and Requirements   52
    a. Basic Requirements — Federal and Many State Court Systems   52
    b. Additional Requirements — Certain State Court Systems   53
  II. Filing the Notice of Appeal   55
    a. Location   55
    b. Time Limits   56
      1. Generally   56
      2. The Federal System   57
      3. Other Jurisdictions — Some Examples   58
      4. Premature Notices of Appeal   59
      5. Relief from the Consequences of Failing to Timely File
         the Notice of Appeal   60
  III. Effect of Filing the Notice of Appeal   63
    a. The Judgment Below — Stays Pending Appeal   63
      1. Money Judgments — Bonding the Appeal —
         Supersedeas Bonds   64
      2. Injunctions   65
    b. Jurisdiction of the Trial Court While the Appeal Is Pending   66
  Checkpoints   66

Chapter 5 · Parties and Non-Parties on Appeal   69
  Roadmap   69
  I. General Rule: Parties That Are Aggrieved   69
    a. Parties   70
    b. Appeals by Non-Parties   70
    c. Intervention   71
    d. Substitution of Parties on Appeal   72
    e. Persons Aggrieved   74
  II. Constitutional Standing and Mootness   76
    a. Standing   76
    b. Mootness — The Mootness Doctrine   77

c. Exceptions to the Mootness Doctrine   78
d. Mootness by Reason of Settlement   79
III. Amicus Curiae   80
Checkpoints   82

Chapter 6 · The Record on Appeal   83
Roadmap   83
I. Purpose   83
II. Contents   84
  a. Generally   84
  b. Documents Filed in the Trial Court: The Clerk's File   84
  c. Record of Oral Proceedings   86
    1. The Transcript   86
    2. When a Transcript Is Unavailable   88
  d. Agreed Statements   88
III. Correcting and Expanding the Record on Appeal   89
  a. General Rule   89
  b. Correcting Errors or Omissions in the Record   89
  c. Judicial Notice   90
  d. Inherent Authority of Appellate Courts to Supplement
     the Record   93
IV. The Appendix   94
  a. Content of the Appendix   96
  b. Form of the Appendix   97
Checkpoints   98

Chapter 7 · Appellate Legal Analysis   101
Roadmap   101
I. Using Fresh Eyes and Focusing on Error   101
II. Tools for Analyzing and Interpreting Statutes   102
  a. Using Tabulation to Explode a Statute   102
  b. Using the Structure and Other Sections of the Same Statute   104
  c. Using Case Law Interpreting a Statute   104
  d. Plain Meaning—The Wording of the Statutory Section at Issue 105
  e. Legislative History   106
  f. Similar Statutes in the Same Jurisdiction   107
  g. Similar Statutes in other States or Jurisdictions   107
  h. Canons of Construction   107
  i. Law Review Articles & Scholarly Commentary   109

III. Reviewing, Using, and Synthesizing Cases 109
  a. Reviewing and Revisiting cases 109
    1. Caption 109
    2. Summaries and Headnotes 110
    3. Disposition 110
    4. Procedural Facts 110
    5. Underlying Facts 110
    6. Issues 110
    7. Statements of Law and their Explanation 111
    8. Application of Law 111
    9. Policy 111
    10. Holding 112
    11. Dicta 112
  b. Using Cases: A Checklist 112
    1. Where Does the Case Come From? 112
    2. Does the Case Deal with the Same Issue as Your Problem
      or Matter? 113
    3. What Laws Does the Court Apply or Articulate? 113
    4. What Does the Court Say about Those Laws? 113
    5. What Are the Facts of the Case? 113
    6. How Does the Court Apply the Laws to the Facts? 113
    7. What Is the Court's Holding—The Court's Decision and
      the Basis for It? 113
    8. Does the Opinion Contain Any Useful Dicta? 114
  c. Synthesizing Multiple Cases—Putting It All Together to
    Advocate a Position 114
    1. Getting Started—Review the Cases Starting with the
      Most Recent 114
    2. After Reading the Cases, Write a Holding for Each 115
    3. Sorting and Grouping 115
    4. Distilling and Synthesizing the Law 115
IV. Final Steps in the Analysis 117
V. Organizing a Persuasive Legal Analysis—IRAC and CRAC Formats 118
Checkpoints 122

Chapter 8 · Appellate Legal Drafting: Techniques and Strategies 125
  Roadmap 125
  I. Three Strategies for Organizing Appellate Legal Drafting 125
    a. Establish the Context before Adding the Details 126

b. Place Familiar Information before New Information   128
c. Make the Structure Explicit   129
II. Paragraphs   130
III. Sentences and Word Choice   131
   a. Where Possible, Always Make Your Subject a Person or
      Entity—Something That Acts—Rather Than a Concept   131
b. Use Plain Language   132
c. Use Fewer Words   132
d. Stamp Out Narration   133
e. Avoid Nominalizations   133
f. Avoid Intrusive Phrases or Clauses   133
g. Choose the Right Word   133
h. Use the Past Tense When Describing Events That Have
   Already Occurred   133
i. Put Yourself in the Position of the Distracted,
   Unfamiliar Reader   134
j. Remember to Keep It Simple   134
IV. The Drafting Process   135
   a. Organizing Preliminary Materials into an Outline—
      Creating an Explicit Structure   135
b. The First Draft   135
c. Revising and Rewriting   136
d. Editing   137
e. Proofreading   137
Checkpoints   138

Chapter 9 • Citation and Quotation on Appeal: Why, When, and How?   141
Roadmap   141
I. Why   141
   a. Overview   141
b. Citations to Legal Authority   142
c. Citations to the Record—The Appendix   144
d. Quotations   144
II. When to Cite or Quote   145
   a. Legal Authority   145
b. Factual Authority—Citations to the Appendix or
   Appellate Record   146
c. Quotations   147

III. How to Cite   148
  a. Legal authority   148
  b. Cites to the Appendix or Appellate Record   153
  c. How to Quote   154
    1. Using Quotation Marks   154
    2. Indicating Omissions or Alterations in a Quote:
      Ellipses and Brackets   155
    3. Citing Original Sources and Indicating Emphasis   156
IV. Conclusion   156
Checkpoints   157

Chapter 10 · Standards of Review and Reversible versus Harmless Error 159
Roadmap   159
I. Introduction   159
II. Standards of Review   160
  a. In General   160
  b. Specific Standards of Review   161
    De Novo: Wrong   161
    Clearly Erroneous: Very Wrong   161
    Substantial Evidence: Very Wrong   162
    Abuse of Discretion: Very, Very Wrong   162
    Other Standards of Review   163
III. Reversible versus Harmless Error   164
  a. In General   164
  b. Errors Requiring Automatic Reversal—Structural Errors
    and Errors Based on Lack of Substantial Evidence   164
  c. Harmless Error Analysis   165
IV. Conclusion   166
Checkpoints   167

Chapter 11 · Drafting Appellate Briefs   169
Roadmap   169
I. The Audience—Intermediate Appellate Courts and Courts of
    Last Resort, Judges, Law Clerks, and Court Attorneys 170
  a. Basics   170
  b. Intermediate Appellate Courts   171
  c. Courts of Last Resort   172
II. Purpose and Goals of an Appellate Brief   173
  a. Basics   173

b. Accomplishing these Goals: Developing and Delivering
    a Message   174
    1. Developing a Message   174
    2. Delivering Your Message   175
III. Appellate Brief Formats and Components   176
IV. Statement of Issues on Appeal   177
V. The Statement of the Case   179
Statement of the Case Drafting and Editing Checklist   182
VI. The Statement of Facts   183
    a. Goals   183
    b. Material Facts in the Record   184
    c. Organizing the Statement of Facts   185
        1. Overall Organization   185
        2. Placement of Individual Facts   186
        3. Treatment and Tone   186
        4. Final Words   187
    d. Appellate Brief Statement of Facts Drafting and Editing
        Guidelines   188
        1. Substance/Analysis   188
        2. Organization   188
        3. Sentence Structure, Word Choice, Tone   189
        4. Paragraph structure   189
        5. Technical Aspects: Proofing, Grammar, Etc.   190
VII. Summary of the Argument   190
VIII. Discussion or Argument: Purpose and Goals   191
IX. Organizing the Discussion Section   192
    a. Basics   192
    b. Main Sections   192
        Ordering Main Sections   192
    c. Subsections   193
X. Statements of the Standard of Review   194
XI. Persuading the Appellate Court   195
    a. Basics   195
    b. Using the CRAC Structure to Persuade   195
        1. C: Conclusion — The Heading   196
        2. R: Rule/Law — Identifying, Explaining, and Illustrating
           the Law   196
        3. A: Application/Analysis   198
        4. C: Conclusion   199
    c. Dealing with Adverse Authority   199

d. Using Policy to Persuade 199
XII. Drafting the Components of the Appellate Brief:
  Order and Timing 201
XIII. Appellate Brief Discussion/Argument Drafting and Reviewing
  Guidelines 202
  a. Substance/Analysis 202
  b. Organization 203
  c. Sentence, Word Choice, and Tone 203
  d. Paragraph Structure 204
  e. Technical: Proofing, Grammar, Bluebook, Etc. 204
XIV. Heading and Topic Sentence Outline 204
XV. Appellate Brief Final Editing Checklist 205
Checkpoints 206

Chapter 12 · Oral Argument 209
Roadmap 209
I. Purpose, Audience, and Goals of Oral Argument 210
  a. Purpose of Oral Argument 210
  b. Audience 210
    1. Generally 210
    2. The Bench — Intermediate Appellate Courts 211
    3. The Bench — Courts of Last Resort 212
    4. Goals of Oral Argument 213
II. Preparing for Oral Argument 213
  a. Goals 213
  b. Knowing the Case 214
    1. Knowing the Law 214
    2. Knowing the Facts 214
    3. Knowing the Context 215
    4. Knowing What You Are Asking the Court to Do and
      the Possible Effects 216
  c. Developing Talking Points 217
    1. What Talking Points Are and How to Use Them in
      Oral Argument 217
    2. Deciding on Your Talking Points 219
  d. The Introduction and Conclusion 221
    1. The Introduction 221
    2. The Conclusion 222
  e. Preparing Your Materials for the Courtroom —
    The Manila File Folder 222

f. Becoming Conversant — Practice 224
g. Knowing the Rules, Procedures, and Format for Oral Argument 225
III. In the Courtroom 226
a. Remain Flexible and Remember Your Goals 226
b. Presenting Your Argument 227
1. The Opening 227
2. Your Main Argument — The Favorable Talking Points 228
3. Concluding 229
4. Rebuttal 230
c. Answering Questions from the Bench 231
1. Welcome Questions and Answer Them Immediately
and Directly 231
2. Handling Questions: A Multi-Step Process 232
3. Answering Particular Questions 234
d. Presentation 239
1. Creating a Good Impression 239
2. Physical Appearance 240
3. Delivery 241
Checkpoints 243

Chapter 13 · Moot Court 247
Roadmap 247
I. Purpose, Audience, and Goals of Moot Court Competitions 248
a. Purpose 248
b. Audience 248
c. Goals 249
II. Getting Started 250
a. Deciding Which Competition to Enter 250
b. Understanding the Rules and Devising a Timeline 251
c. Reviewing and Understanding the Problem 252
d. Learning and Understanding the Context 254
e. Research 254
III. Brief Writing 255
a. Goals 255
1. Generally 255
2. Accomplishing Your Goals 256
b. Working Collaboratively 258
IV. Oral Argument 260
a. Goals 260
b. Preparation 260

c. Practice Rounds   262
d. Handling Questions   263
   1. Hostile Questioning   263
   2. Friendly Questions   264
   3. The Dead Bench   264
e. Courtroom and Competition Demeanor   265
Checkpoints   266

Mastering Appellate Advocacy and Process Checklist   269

Appendix • Sample Appellate Brief and Resulting Order   289

Index   315

Table of Cases

Access Now v. Southwest Airlines, Co., 385 F.3d 1324 (11th Cir. 2004), 26

Ahrenholz v. Bd. of Trs. of Univ. of Illinois, 219 F.3d 674 (7th Cir. 2000), 40

Alabama Power Co. v. I.C.C., 852 F.2d 1361 (D.C. Cir. 1988), 74

American Games, Inc. v. Trade Prods. Inc., 412 F.3d 1164 (9th Cir. 1998), 79

American Textile Mfrs. Inst. v. Donovan, 452 U.S. 490 (1981), 162

Annandale Advocate v. City of Annandale, 435 N.W.2d 24 (Minn. 1989), 71

Arbaugh v. Y & H Corp., 546 U.S. 500, (2006), 24, 28, 29, 77

Arneson v. Jezwinski, 556 N.W.2d 721 (Wis. 1996), 47

ASARCO, Inc. v. Sec'y of Labor, 206 F.3d 720, (6th Cir. 2000), 75

Bank of Herrin v. Peoples Bank of Marion, 473 N.E.2d 1298 (Ill. 1985), 63

BankAmerica Corp. Sec. Litig., 270 F.3d 639, 641 (8th Cir. 2001), 42

Barnes v. Dale, 530 So.2d 770 (Ala. 1988), 27

Beacon Theatres, Inc. v. Westover, 359 U.S. 500, 511 (1959), 42

Bitler v. A.O. Smith Corp., 252 F. Supp. 2d 1123, 1124 (D. Colo. 2003), 90

Blair v. Equifax Check Services, Inc., 181 F.3d 832, 834–35 (7th Cir. 1999), 41

Bolarinwa v. Williams, 593 F.3d 226, 230–31 (2d Cir. 2010), 61

Bowers v. Baystate Technologies, 320 F.3d 1317 (Fed. Cir. 2003), 127, 153

Brecht v. Abrahamson, 507 U.S. 619, 631 (1993), 166

Bridgeport Guardians, Inc. v. Delmonte, 602 F.3d 469, 473 (2d Cir. 2010), 72

Bryant v. Yellen, 447 U.S. 352, 366–68 (1980), 72

Byrd v. Reno, 180 F.3d 298, 300 (D.C. Cir. 1999), 71

Cabalceta v. Standard Fruit Co., 883 F.2d 1553, 1555 (11th Cir. 1989), 94

Caitlin v. United States, 324 U.S. 229, 233 (1945), 33

California v. Rooney, 483 U.S. 307, 311 (1987), 74

Carley v. Wheeled Coach, 991 F.2d 1117 (3d Cir. 1993), 93

Chambers v. Ohio Dept. of Human Services, 145 F.3d 793, 796 (6th Cir. 1998).

Chapman v. California, 386 U.S. 18, 24 (1967), 165, 181, 182

Chemetron II, 212 F.3d at 209–10, 154, 156

Cheney v. U.S. Dist. Court for Dist. of Columbia, 542 U.S. 367, 38 (2004), 42

Church of Scientology Intern. v. Eli Lilly & Co., 778 F. Supp. 661, 666 (S.D.N.Y. 1991), 92

Church of Scientology v. United States, 506 U.S. 9, 18 n. 11 (1992), 71

Cobbledick v. U.S., 309 U.S. 323, 325 (1940), 33

Cohen v. Bd. of Trustees, 867 F.2d 1455, 1465 n. 9 (3d Cir. 1989), 38

Cohen v. Beneficial Indus. Loan Corp., 337 U.S. 541, 546 (1949), 36

Colbert v. Potter, 471 F.3d 158, 165–167 (D.C. Cir. 2006), 94

Cooter & Gell v. Hartmarx Corp., 496 U.S. 384, 400 (1990), 162

Corbin v. Cannon, 838 F. Supp. 561 (M.D. Fla. 1993), 93

Curtiss-Wright Corp. v. General Elec. Co., 446 U.S. 1, 10 (1980), 37

Dairy Queen, Inc. v. Wood, 369 U.S. 472 (1962), 42

Davis v. U.S., 512 U.S. 452, 457–58 & n. * (1994), 81

Deposit Guar. Nat'l Bank v. Roper, 445 U.S. 326, 333 (1980), 69, 74, 75, 76

Detroit Edison Co. v. Nat'l Labor Relations Bd., 440 U.S. 301, 317 (1979), 92

Devlin v. Scardelletti, 536 U.S. 1 (2002), 70

Digital Equip. Corp. v. Desktop Direct, Inc., 511 U.S. 863, 867 (1992), 35

Dilliplaine v. Lehigh Valley Trust Co., 322 A.2d 114 (Pa. 1974), 27

Dilworth v. Riner, 343 F.2d 226, 229 (5th Cir. 1965), 39

Dippin' Dots, Inc. v. Frosty Bites Distrib. LLC, 369 F.3d 1197, 1203–04 (11th Cir. 2004), 92

Drewett v. Aetna Cas. Sur. Co., 539 F.2d 496, 498 (5th Cir. 1976), 97

Eain v. Wilkes, 641 F.2d 504 (7th Cir. 1981), 93

Ebrahimi v. City of Huntsville Bd. of Educ., 114 F.3d 162, 166 (11th Cir. 1997), 37

Electrical. Fittings Corp. v. Thomas & Betts Co., 307 U.S. 241, 242 (1939), 74

Elliott Indus. Ltd. Partnership v. BP American Prod. Co., 407 F.3d 1091, 1103 (10th Cir. 2005), 72

Endress + Hauser, Inc. v. Hawk Measurement Sys. Pty. Ltd., 932 F. Supp. 1147, 1148–50, 64

Environmental Prot. Info. Ctr., Inc. v. Pacific. Lumber Co., 257 F.3d 1071, 1075 (9th Cir. 2001), 74, 75, 76

Federal Election Com'n v. Wisconsin Right to Life, Inc., 551 U.S. 449, 462 (2007), 78

Federal Prescription Serv., Inc. v. American Pharm. Asso., 636 F.2d 755, 758 (D.C. Cir. 1980), 64

Federated Mut. Ins. Co. v. McNeal, 943 So.2d 658, 663 (Miss. 2006), 71

First Nat'l Bank of South Carolina v. United States, 413 F. Supp. 1107, 1110 (D.S.C. 1976), 92

Forney v. Apfel, 524 U.S. 266, 271 (1998), 74

Friends of the Earth, Inc. v. Laidlaw Environmental Services (TOC), Inc., 528 U.S. 167, 189 (2000), 78

Fry v. Pliler, 551 U.S. 112, 114 (2007), 165

Garriga v. Sanitation Dist. No. 1, 2003 Ky. App. LEXIS 305 at *22, n. 26 (Ky. App. 2003) (Ky. Ct. App. 2003), 29, 30, 77

General Elec. Co. v. Joiner, 522 U.S. 136, 143 (1997), 162

Gowen, Inc. v. F/V Quality One, 244 F.3d 64, 66 (1st Cir. 2001), 121

Grant v. Superior Court, 275 Cal. Rptr. 564, 568 (Cal. App. 1990), 64

Graphic Commc' n Int'l Union, Local 12-N v. Quebecor Printing Providence, Inc., 270 F.3d 1, 6 (1st Cir. 2001), 61

Hardy v. Johns-Manville Sales Corp., 681 F.2d 334, 347–48 (5th Cir. 1982), 91

Harris v. Del Taco, Inc., 396 F. Supp. 2d 1107 (C.D. Cal. 2005), 93

Hershey Foods Corp. v. Hershey Creamery Co., 945 F.2d 1272, 1277 (3d Cir. 1991), 38

Hexcel Corporation v. Stepman Co., 239 B.R. 564, 570 (N.D. Cal. 1999), 150, 151

Hilton v. Braunskill, 481 U.S. 770, 776 (1987), 64, 65

Hohn v. United States, 524 U.S. 236, 241 (1998), 82

Holmes Group, Inc. v. Vornado Air Circulation Sys. Inc., 534 U.S. 826 (2002), 12

Hone v. Hanafin, 104 S.W.3d 884, 886 (Tex. 2003), 62

In re C.J., 758 N.E.2d 335, 337 (Ill. App. Ct. 2001), 63

In re Cendant Corp. Sec. Litig., 343 F.3d 658, 662 (3d Cir. 2003), 36

In re Chance Industries, Inc., 367 B.R. 689, 708 (Bankr. D. Kan. 2006), 154, 155

In re City of Memphis, 293 F.3d 345, 346 (6th Cir. 2002), 39

In re Eagle-Pitcher Indus., Inc., 255 B.R. 700, 704 (Bankr. S.D. Ohio 2000), 150

In re *Integra Realty Resources, Inc.*, 262 F.3d 1089, 1107–08 (10th Cir. 2001), 38

In re Marriage of Link, 839 N.E.2d 678, 680 (Ill. App. Ct. 2005), 46

In re Olivia C., 868 N.E.2d 307, 310 (Ill. App. Ct. 2007), 47

In re Orshansky, 804 A.2d 1077, 1090 (D.C. 2002), 71

In re Parullo, 13 B.R. 953 (Bankr. N.D. Ill. 1981), 93

In re Paul, 513 S.E.2d 219, 221 (Ga. 1999), 46

In re School Asbestos Litig., 977 F.2d 764, 777–78, 42

Inland Bulk Transfer Co. v. Cummins Engine Co., 332 F.3d 1007, 1012 (6th Cir. 2003), 93

Intercounty Nat'l Title Ins. Co. of N.Y. v. Intercounty Nat'l Title Ins. Co., 310 F.3d 537, 539–40 (7th Cir. 2002), 36

International Broth. of Elec. Workers v. I.C.C., 862 F.2d 330, 334 (D.C. Cir. 1988), 75

Irons v. Federal Bureau of Investigation, 811 F.2d 681, 683–84 (1st Cir. 1987), 36

Johnson v. United States, 520 U.S. 461, 466–67 (1997), 27, 164

Jones v. Chemetron Corp., 212 F.3 199, 209–210 (3rd Cir. 2000), 151

Jones v. White, 992 F.2d 1548, 1566 (11th Cir. 1993), 93

Kazales v. Minto Leasing, Inc., 61 A.D.2d 1039, 1040 (N.Y.A.D. 1978), 28

Keith v. Volpe, 118 F.3d 1386, 1391 (9th Cir. 1997), 71

Kerr v. United States Dist. Court for Northern Dist. of Cal., 426 U.S. 394, 403 (1976), 42

Lassa v. Rongstad, 718 N.W.2d 673, 694 (Wis. 2006), 47

Lienhart v. Dryvit Sys., Inc., 255 F.3d 138, 144 (4th Cir. 2001), 41

Lowry v. Barnhart, 329 F.3d 1019, 1024 (9th Cir. 2003), 83, 89, 97

Lujan v. Defenders of Wildlife, 504 U.S. 555, 560–61 (1992), 77

Luxton v. North River Bridge Co., 147 U.S. 337, 341 (1893), 33

Maine School Admin. Dist. 35 v. Mr. and Mrs. R., 321 F.3d 9, 17 (1st Cir. 2003), 121

Marino v. Ortiz, 484 U.S. 301, 304 (1988), 70, 71, 72

Marrese v. American Academy of Orthopedic Surgeons, 470 U.S. 373, 379 (1985), 66

Marsh v. Mountain Zephyr, Inc., 50 Cal. Rptr. 2d 493, 498–99 (Cal. App. 1996), 46

Mason v. Mathiasen Tanker Industries, Inc., 298 F.2d 28 (4th Cir. 1962), 92

McBride v. CITGO Petroleum Corp., 281 F.3d 1099, 1104 (10th Cir. 2002), 53

McFarlin v. Conseco Services, LLC, 381 F.3d 1251, 1259 (11th Cir. 2004), 39

McKaskle v. Wiggins, 465 U.S. 168 (1984), 165

Meredith v. Oregon, 321 F.3d 807, 815 (9th Cir. 2003), 43

Michigan v. Mosley, 423 U.S. 96, 104 (1975), 181, 182

Miranda v. Arizona, 384 U.S. 436 (1966), 181

Mitchell v. Forsyth, 472 U.S. 511, 527 (1985), 36

Moses H. Cone Mem. Hosp. v. Mercury Constr. Corp., 460 U.S. 1, 12–13 (1983), 36

Motor Vehicle Mfrs. Ass'n of U.S., Inc. v. State Farm Mut. Auto. Ins. Co., 463 U.S. 29, 43 (1983), 163

Mullane v. Central Hanover Bank & Trust Co., 339 U.S. 306, 314, 70 S. Ct. 652, 94 L. Ed. 865 (1950), 150, 151, 154, 155, 156

Murphy v. Hunt, 455 U.S. 478, 481 (1982), 77, 89

National R.R. Passenger Corp. v. ExpressTrak, L.L.C., 330 F.3d 523, 528 (D.C. Cir. 2003), 43

Neeld v. Nat'l Hockey League, 594 F.2d 1297 (9th Cir. 1979), 92

Neonatology Associates, P.A. v. C.I.R., 293 F.3d 128, 132–33 (3d Cir. 2002), 81

Newton v. Merrill Lynch, Pierce, Fenner & Smith, Inc., 259 F.3d 154, 164 (3d Cir. 2001), 41

Oakville Dev. Corp., v. FDIC, 986 F.2d 611, 613 (1st Cir. 1993), 121

Oliver v. Hallett Const. Co., 421 F.2d 365 (8th Cir. 1970), 93

Ornelas v. United States, 517 U.S. 690, 695 (1996), 161

People v. Moye, 213 P.3d 652, 659 (Cal. 2009), 23

People v. Samuels, 113 P.3d 1125, 1137 (Cal. 2005), 166

People v. Superior Court (Romero), 917 P.2d 628 (Cal. 1996), 104

Perdon Coal Co./United Coal Co. v. Stiltner, 323 S.E.2d 110 (Va. 1984), 26

Pioneer Invest. Services Co. v. Brunswick Asso. Ltd. P'ship, 507 U.S. 380, 388 (1993), 61

Prado–Steiman v. Bush, 221 F.3d 1266, 1274–76 (11th Cir. 2000), 41

Rabbi Jacob Joseph School v. Province of Mendoza, 425 F.3d 207, 210–11 (2d Cir. 2005), 34

Raines v. Byrd, 521 U.S. 811, 817 (1997), 29, 76

Regula v. Delta Family-Care Disability Survivorship Plan, 266 F.3d 1130, 1137–38 (9th Cir. 2002), 34

Reno v. Koray, 515 U.S. 50, 55 n.2 (1995), 81

Riccard v. Prudential Ins. Co., 307 F.3d 1277, 1290 n. 12 (11th Cir. 2002), 53

Ross v. Kemp, 785 F.2d 1467, 1474–75 (11th Cir. 1986), 94

S.E.C. v. Black, 163 F.3d 188, 195 (3d Cir. 1998), 39

S.E.C. v. Forex Asset Management LLC, 242 F.3d 325, 329 (5th Cir. 2001), 71

Samnorwood Indep. School of Dist. v. Texas Educ. Agency, 533 F.3d 258, 265–66 (5th Cir. 2008), 71

Sears v. Hull, 961 P.2d 1013, 1019 (Ariz. 1998), 77

Sears, Roebuck & Co. v. Mackey, 351 U.S. 427, 435–36 (1956), 37

Seminole Tribe of Fla. v. Butterworth, 491 F. Supp. 1015, 1019 (S.D. Fla. 1980), 92

Shelby v. Subperformance Int'l, 435 F.2d 42, 45–46 (1st Cir. 2006), 121

Siedle v. Putnam Invests., Inc., 147 F.3d 7, 10 (1st Cir. 1998), 149, 151, 162

Singh v. DaimlerBenz, AG, 800 F. Supp. 260, 263 (E.D. Pa. 1992), 39

Sosna v. Iowa, 419 U.S. 393, 398 & n. 7, 402 (1975), 78

Stack v. Boyle, 342 U.S. 1 (1945), 36

State v. McAdams, 594 A2d 1273 (N.H. 1991), 27

State v. Sarabia, 875 P.2d 227, 230 (Idaho 1994), 27

Strange v. State, 258 S.W.3d 184 (Tex. App. 2007), 62

Sullivan v. Louisiana, 508 U.S. 275, 281 (1993), 165

Sumitomo Copper Litigation v. Credit Lyonnais Rouse, Ltd., 262 F.3d 134, 139 (2d Cir. 2001), 41

Swinkle v. Illinois Civil Service Com'n, 903 N.E.2d 746 (Ill. App. 2009), 56

Swint v. Chambers County Comm'n, 514 U.S. 35, 35–36 (1995), 35, 43

Therrien v. Target Corp., 617 F.3d 1242, 1249 (10th Cir. 2010), 162, 165

Trans World Airlines, Inc. v. Hughes, 314 F. Supp. 94, 96 (S.D.N.Y. 1970), 64

Trust for Certificate Holders of Merrill Lynch Mortg. Investors, Inc. Mortg. Pass-Through Certificates, Series

1991-cl v. Love Funding Corp., 496 F.3d 171, 173 (2d Cir. 2007), 76

Tumey v. Ohio, 273 U.S. 510 (1927), 165

U.S. Bancorp. Mortgage Co. v. Bonner Mall P'ship, 513 U.S. 18, 25, 29 (1994), 79

United States v. Mundy, 806 F. Supp. 373, 377 (E.D.N.Y. 1992), 92

United States ex rel. Eisenstein v. City of New York, 129 S. Ct. 2230, 2234 (2009), 70

United States v. BioPort Corp., 270 F. Supp. 2d 968, 972 (W.D. Mich. 2003), 93

United States v. Gonzalez-Lopez, 548 U.S. 140, 148–49 (2006), 165

United States v. Gumbs, 283 F.3d 128 (3d Cir. 2002), 92

United States v. Perry, 360 F.3d 519, 526–27 (2004), 72

United States v. U.S. Gypsum Co., 333 U.S. 364, 395 (1948), 161

United States v. Van Hazel, 468 F. Supp. 2d 792 (E.D.N.C. 2006), 93

Valero Terrestrial Corp. v. Paige, 211 F.3d 112, 199 & n. 3 (4th Cir. 2000), 79

Verhoven v. Brunswick School Comm., 207 F.3d 1, 5 (1st Cir. 1999), 121

Vitello v. J.C. Penny Co., 107 F.3d 869, 1997 WL 87248, at *3, n. 1 (4th Cir. 1997), 98

Voices for Choices v. Illinois Bell Tel. Co., 339 F.3d 542, 544 (7th Cir. 2003), 80, 81

Waller v. Georgia, 467 U.S. 39 (1984), 164

Waste Mgmt. Holdings, Inc. v. Mowbray, 208 F.3d 288, 293 (1st Cir. 2000), 41

Welker ex rel. Bradbury v. Teachers Standards and Practices Comm'n, 27 P.3d 1038, 1041 (Or. 2001), 60

Wilkinson v. Fabry, 869 P.2d 182 (Ariz. App. 1992), 56

Wooden v. Missouri Pacific R. Co., 862 F.2d 560 (5th Cir. 1989), 92

Zimomra v. Alamo Rent-A-Car, Inc., 111 F.3d 1495 (10th Cir. 1997), 93

Table of Statutes and Rules

11 U.S.C. 362(a)(2), 65

18 U.S.C. § 700(d), 13

28 U.S.C. § 41, 6

28 U.S.C. § 46(b), 6

28 U.S.C. § 158(b)(1), (5), 5

28 U.S.C. § 158(d)(2), 5

28 U.S.C. § 371, 6

28 U.S.C. § 1253, 13

28 U.S.C. § 1291, 6, 33, 34, 36, 38, 43

28 U.S.C. § 1292, 38

28 U.S.C. § 1292(a)(1), 38, 45

28 U.S.C. § 1292(a)(2), 39, 45

28 U.S.C. § 1292(b), 39

28 U.S.C. § 1292(c)(2), 34

28 U.S.C. § 1294, 5

28 U.S.C. § 1295, 5

28 U.S.C. § 1331, 29

28 U.S.C. § 1332, 29

28 U.S.C. § 1651(a), 41

28 U.S.C. § 1961, 64

42 U.S.C. § 1983, 77

28 U.S.C. § 2342, 5

28 U.S.C. § 2343, 5

Cal. Code Civ. P. § 904.1, 43

Cal. Code Civ. P. § 918(b), 65

Cal. Com. Code § 2207(2), 103

Cal. Pen. Code § 1259, 28

Ga. Code Ann. § 5-6-38(a), 59

Tenn. Code Ann. § 40-14-301-301, 88

U.S. Const. art. I, 4

U.S. Const. art. III, 3, 4, 29

Wis. Stat. § 808.03(2)(a) and (b), 47

Wis. Stat. § 808.04, 59

Wis. Stat. § 808.04(8), 60

Wis. Stat. § 809.30(2)(b), 59

Federal Rules of Appellate Procedure

Rule 1, 23, 37, 41, 57, 72, 73, 80, 87, 95, 111, 174, 191

Rule 2, 23, 24, 47, 57, 59, 86, 105, 120, 174, 196, 226

Rule 3, 24, 33–35, 40, 47, 48, 53, 58, 62, 73, 126, 220

Rule 4, 53, 56–59, 61, 87

Rule 5, 23, 26, 31, 61, 70, 74

Rule 6, 58

Rule 7, 23, 57, 62, 111, 119

Rule 8, 85

Rule 10, 13, 84–87, 90, 95

Rule 11, 205

Rule 12, 23, 24

Rule 14, 65, 87

Rule 15, 23, 62

Rule 18, 134

Rule 19, 23, 24

Rule 23, 35, 40, 41, 50

Rule 24, 23, 71

Rule 25, 73

Rule 26, 62

Rule 28, 24, 33, 49

Rule 29, 79–82

Rule 30, 63, 95

Rule 33, 26, 81

Rule 35, 34, 35

Rule 40, 40
Rule 43, 72–74
Rule 46, 20, 21
Rule 48, 47

Federal Rules of Civil Procedure
Rule 1, 23, 37, 41, 57, 72, 73, 80, 87,
   95, 111, 174, 191
Rule 6, 58
Rule 11, 205
Rule 12, 23, 24
Rule 23, 35, 40, 41, 50
Rule 24, 23, 71
Rule 50, 24, 25, 164
Rule 54, 34, 36, 37, 50
Rule 58, 57, 58
Rule 59, 25
Rule 61, 164
Rule 62, 64, 65
Rule 77, 62
Rule 79, 57, 58

Federal Rules of Criminal Procedure
Rule 29, 79–82
Rule 33, 26, 81

Federal Rules of Evidence
Rule 201, 90, 91

Supreme Court Rules
Rule 3, 24, 33–35, 40, 47, 48, 53, 58,
   62, 73, 126, 220
Rule 5, 23, 26, 31, 61, 70, 74
Rule 10, 13, 84–87, 90, 95
Rule 12, 23, 24
Rule 14, 65, 87
Rule 15, 23, 62
Rule 18, 134
Rule 23, 35, 40, 41, 50
Rule 24, 23, 71
Rule 25, 73
Rule 29, 79–82
Rule 30, 63, 95
Rule 33, 26, 81

Series Editor's Foreword

The Carolina Academic Press Mastering Series is designed to provide you with a tool that will enable you to easily and efficiently "master" the substance and content of law school courses. Throughout the series, the focus is on quality writing that makes legal concepts understandable. As a result, the series is designed to be easy to read and is not unduly cluttered with footnotes or cites to secondary sources.

In order to facilitate student mastery of topics, the Mastering Series includes a number of pedagogical features designed to improve learning and retention. At the beginning of each chapter, you will find a "Roadmap" that tells you about the chapter and provides you with a sense of the material that you will cover. A "Checkpoint" at the end of each chapter encourages you to stop and review the key concepts, reiterating what you have learned. Throughout the book, key terms are explained and emphasized. Finally, a "Master Checklist" at the end of each book reinforces what you have learned and helps you identify any areas that need review or further study.

We hope that you will enjoy studying with, and learning from, the Mastering Series.

Russell L. Weaver
Professor of Law & Distinguished University Scholar
University of Louisville, Louis D. Brandeis School of Law

About the Authors

Donna C. Looper is an Adjunct Professor of Law at The University of Tennessee College of Law, Knoxville, Tennessee, where she teaches Legal Process. She received her J.D. in 1989 from the University of California, Hastings College of Law, and her A.B. in 1984 from Barnard College, Columbia University. She clerked for the Chief Judge of the United States District Court for the Eastern District of Louisiana and then for the United States Court of Appeals for the Ninth Circuit. Before teaching at the University of Tennessee College of Law, Ms. Looper was a Senior Attorney for the California Court of Appeal, Fourth District, Division One and, prior to that, was in private practice in San Diego and San Francisco. She is an author of CALIFORNIA LAW OF CONTRACTS (CEB), MASTERING LEGAL ANALYSIS AND DRAFTING (Carolina Academic Press) and MASTERING INTELLECTUAL PROPERTY (Carolina Academic Press) with her co-author, George W. Kuney. She is admitted to practice law in California and Tennessee and consults in matters nationwide.

George W. Kuney (http://www.law.utk.edu/faculty/kuney/) is a W.P. Toms Distinguished Professor of Law and the Director of the Clayton Center for Entrepreneurial Law at The University of Tennessee College of Law in Knoxville, Tennessee. He holds a J.D. from the University of California, Hastings College of the Law, an M.B.A. from the University of San Diego, and a B.A. in economics from the University of California, Santa Cruz. Before joining the UT faculty in 2000, he was a partner in the Allen Matkins firm's San Diego office. Previously he practiced with the Howard, Rice and Morrison & Foerster firms in his hometown of San Francisco, doing litigation and transactional work largely in the context of business restructuring and insolvency. At the University of Tennessee, he teaches business law courses including Contracts, Contract Drafting, Commercial Law, Property, Debtor-Creditor, Mergers and Acquisitions, Representing Enterprises, and Workouts and Reorganizations. Kuney writes about business, contracts, and insolvency-related topics; advises clients nationwide regarding restructuring, reorganization, and related matters; and conducts training seminars for law firms regarding business law and transactional drafting. He is admitted to practice in California and Tennessee, and consults in matters nationwide.

Kuney is the author of MASTERING LEGAL ANALYSIS AND DRAFTING (with Donna C. Looper, Carolina Academic Press); MASTERING INTELLECTUAL PROPERTY (with Donna C. Looper, Carolina Academic Press), THE ELEMENTS OF CONTRACT DRAFTING (3d ed. West), LEGAL DRAFTING: PROCESS, TECHNIQUES, AND EXERCISES (with Thomas Haggard, 2d ed.West), LEGAL DRAFTING IN A NUTSHELL (with Thomas Haggard, 2d ed. West), *California Contract Law* (with Donna C. Looper, CEB), MASTERING BANKRUPTCY (Carolina Academic Press), MASTERING INTELLECTUAL PROPERTY (with Donna C. Looper, Carolina Academic Press), *Chapter 11-101* (with coauthors, ABI), MASTERING LEGAL ANALYSIS AND DRAFTING (Carolina Academic Press), and a number of articles dealing with contracts, business acquisitions, corporate governance, and reorganization matters.

Acknowledgments

This book would not have been possible without substantial contributions of time and effort on the part of the members of the firms and courts that we have worked for across the country. Any list of those to whom we are indebted for teaching us about legal analysis and drafting is necessarily incomplete. That said, the following individuals have contributed materially to our understanding of legal writing in general and appellate advocacy and procedure in particular and our attempts to teach that skill to law students and lawyers: Barbara J. Cox, Nanna Frye, the Hon. Fredrick J.R. Heebe, the Hon. Alex C. McDonald, the Hon. James A. McIntyre, Carol McCrehan Parker, Mary Ann Darr Wegmann, and our students at Hastings College of Law, California Western School of Law, and The University of Tennessee College of Law. Special thanks and recognition go to Kirby Waddell, University of Tennessee College of Law Class of 2011, for her careful review and thoughtful contributions to the manuscript.

The works of other authors have also influenced our views and must be acknowledged. These include:

Robert J. Martineau, Michael E. Solimine, Kent Sinclair, Randy J. Holland, CASES AND MATERIALS ON APPELLATE PRACTICE AND PROCEDURE, 2d ed. (Thomson West 2005).

Robert H. Klonoff, Gregory Castanias, FEDERAL APPELLATE PRACTICE AND PROCEDURE IN A NUTSHELL (Thomson West 2008).

Bradley G. Clary, Sharon Reich Paulsen, Michael J. Vanselow, VANSELOW's ADVOCACY ON APPEAL, 3d ed. (Thomson West 2008).

Mary Beth Beazley, A PRACTICAL GUIDE TO APPELLATE ADVOCACY, 2d ed. (Aspen 2006).

Alan D. Hornstein, APPELLATE ADVOCACY IN A NUTSHELL, 2d ed. (Thomson West 1998).

Helene S. Shapo, Marilyn Walter, Elizabeth Fajans, WRITING AND ANALYSIS IN THE LAW, 5th ed. (Thomson West 2008).

UCLA Moot Court Honors Program, Handbook of Appellate Advocacy, 3d ed. (Thomson West 1993).

John Korzen, Make Your Argument Make Your Argument: Succeeding in Moot Court and Mock Trial (Kaplan 2010).

William K. Suter, Clerk of Court, Supreme Court of the United States, Guide for Counsel in Cases to be Argued Before the Supreme Court of the United States (2010).

Michael J. Higdon, *Oral Argument and Impression Management: Harnessing the Power of Nonverbal Persuasion for a Judicial Audience*, 57 U. Kan. L. Rev. 631 (2009).

Introduction

Mastering Appellate Advocacy and Process is intended for both upper division law students and practicing attorneys. Our goal in writing this book was to produce a source that comprehensively yet concisely covers all major aspects of an appeal—from preserving error, assembling an appellate record or appendix, through drafting effective appellate briefs and oral argument. We have also included a chapter on moot court, specifically on maximizing one's chances of succeeding in law school's longest running intercollegiate sport.

This book is unique in that it addresses both appellate *advocacy* and appellate *process*—subjects that are usually covered separately in different books, or taught in different courses in law school. We believe that advocacy and process go hand and hand, however. In real life, appellate process is of little moment in the abstract. It becomes relevant when attorneys are involved in an actual case in which they or the other side may pursue an appeal. Also, in real life, approaching appellate advocacy in isolation without knowing and appreciating the process involved is both foolish and dangerous. The best crafted appellate argument in the world will do the client little good if error was not preserved below, if a notice of appeal was not timely filed, if the record is inadequate, etc.

Appellate process begins long before the trial or other disposition in the trial court is concluded. It begins with producing and protecting the factual and legal record in the trial court and clearly communicating to all involved that a ruling on the merits or otherwise against one's client can and will be effectively challenged and reversed on appeal should it issue. In other words, error must be preserved before it may be appealed.

After the proceedings in the trial court have concluded, the appellate process is formally initiated by filing the notice of appeal of a final order or judgment or petition for review of an interlocutory order. This is followed by preparation of the record on appeal, formulation of the statement of the issues, and briefing. These steps, in turn, are followed by oral argument and the appellate court's disposition of the case.

At each juncture there are numerous technical requirements and traps for the unwary. Careful preparation and foresight are critical to effective appellate practice. The aim of this book is to provide a general guide, which, when supplemented by the applicable specific rules of the jurisdiction involved, will guide the novice, whether law student or lawyer, through the process.

The book also explains techniques of advocacy, both in written submissions and in oral argument before the court. It begins with the building blocks of appellate legal analysis and research. Effective appellate advocacy takes looking at the facts and law with a fresh eye, and with a focus on error under the applicable standards of review. Techniques and strategies for compelling appellate legal drafting are reviewed, including organizational principles and using the CRAC (Conclusion, Rule/Law, Application, Conclusion) format to draft persuasively. Drafting the appellate brief itself then is covered extensively, from the various audiences and the processes by which they may review the briefs and decide the appeal, to developing a message or theme to package the arguments, to drafting individual components, to using policy to persuade. In the chapter on oral argument we introduce the talking points method for both conveying your main arguments as well as answering questions from the bench. The focus of all the chapters on advocacy is on *persuading a court to rule your way* as opposed to "winning an argument" or showing up the other side.

The book concludes with a chapter on moot court—where doing well means showing the judgments how much you know and how easily you can explain it all—versus actually persuading them to rule a certain way.

We welcome readers' comments, reactions, and war stories on the subjects covered in this book. dclooper@gmail.com; gkuney@utk.edu.

Donna C. Looper
George W. Kuney
Knoxville, Tennessee
2011

Mastering Appellate
Advocacy and Process

Chapter 1

Appellate Court Systems

Roadmap

- Federal courts consist of the Article III district, circuit, and supreme courts, as well as a number of specialized Article I courts, from which appeals are taken to the Article III courts. The number of judges on each district or circuit court varies, but for all federal circuit courts, appeals are heard in the first instance by three judge panels.

- Procedure in the federal circuit courts of appeal is governed by the Federal Rules of Appellate Procedure (the "FRAP") and by each circuit's local rules.

- The highest federal court is the United States Supreme Court, with nine justices, who hear cases as a single group. The vast majority of appeals to the Supreme Court are discretionary, not as a matter of right, and proceed by petition for a writ of certiorari. The Supreme Court is primarily engaged in deciding important questions of constitutional or other federal law, and cert is rarely granted when the alleged error below is based upon factual error or misapplication of a properly stated rule of law.

- State court systems vary from state to state. Most have intermediate appellate courts and a court of last resort. State appellate court procedures vary widely and may be supplemented by local rules in particular districts.

I. Federal Courts

a. Overview

Article III courts: Article III, Section I of the United States Constitution provides:

> The judicial power of the United States shall be vested in one Supreme Court, and in such inferior courts as the Congress may from time to time ordain and establish. The judges, both of the supreme and inferior courts, shall hold their offices during good behaviour [sic] and shall,

at stated times, receive for their services, a compensation, which shall not be diminished during their continuance in office.

Thus, Article III judges have life time tenure (with "good behavior") during which their compensation cannot be reduced. The hierarchy of Article III courts is as follows:

1. United States Supreme Court;

2. United States Courts of Appeal or "circuit courts;"

3. United States District Courts (general courts of origin or trial courts) and the United States Court of International Trade.

Article I courts: Article 1, Section 8, Clause 9 of the Constitution granted Congress the power "[t]o constitute tribunals inferior to the Supreme Court." Article I judges do not have lifetime tenure, and their compensation can be reduced by Congress. Article I courts include:

• United States Bankruptcy Courts

• United States Court of Appeals for the Armed Forces

• United States Court of Appeals for Veterans Claims

• United States Tax Court

• United States Court of Federal Claims

• United States District Court for the Northern Marinas Islands

• United States District Court for Guam

• United States District Court for the U.S. Virgin Islands

b. Federal District Courts

District courts are the courts of origin or trial courts in the federal system. At the time of this book's publication, there were 94 Article III district courts, with at least one in each state as well as one in the District of Columbia and one in Puerto Rico. In addition there are three Article I territorial district courts for the Northern Mariana Islands, Guam, and the U.S. Virgin Islands. These last three have the same jurisdiction as Article III district courts, but their judges do not have lifetime tenure. All of these district courts are organized into geographical regions or "circuits," and appeals from the district courts are heard by the United States Court of Appeals for the corresponding circuit.

Each of the 94 Article III federal districts also has a separate Article I bankruptcy court. (The Northern Marianas Islands, Guam and the U.S. Virgin Islands do not have separate bankruptcy courts; rather the district courts there have bankruptcy divisions). Appeals from bankruptcy courts are heard by the district court in that district or, in many circuits, also by the Bankruptcy Appellate Panel (BAP), consisting of three bankruptcy judges from another district within the circuit. 28 U.S.C. § 158(b)(1), (5). There is also a discretionary appeal directly to a circuit court from a bankruptcy court for cases involving novel or important issues when certified as appropriate by the bankruptcy court and authorized by the circuit court. 28 U.S.C. § 158(d)(2).

c. United States Courts of Appeal—Circuit Courts

There are thirteen United States Courts of Appeals or circuit courts. The jurisdiction of all the circuit courts except for the Federal Circuit is defined geographically, while the Federal Circuit's jurisdiction is defined by subject matter. The twelve geographic circuit courts hear appeals from district courts within their particular geographic region or circuit. 28 U.S.C. § 1294. Most significantly, the Federal Circuit has nationwide jurisdiction of cases arising under patent law. 28 U.S.C. § 1295. It is important to keep this in mind when filing an appeal, because even if the issues on appeal do not involve patent law, e.g. are purely procedural, if the complaint arises under patent law, the appeal must be filed in the Federal Circuit. The Federal Circuit applies its own law to patent issues, and the law of the circuit in which the originating district court sits as to other issues. (For further discussion regarding appeals in patent cases see George W. Kuney and Donna C. Looper, Mastering Intellectual Property, ch. 4, § 1).

The Federal Circuit also hears appeals from certain specialized courts and federal agencies, listed below. Jurisdiction to review the bulk of agency actions is vested in the 12 geographic circuit courts. *See, e.g.* 28 U.S.C. § 2342. Also, 28 U.S.C. § 2343 provides "The venue for proceeding under this chapter is in the judicial circuit in which the petitioner resides or has its principal office, or in the United States Court of Appeals for the District of Columbia." Thus, much of the agency appeals are heard in the D.C. Circuit. (For further discussion regarding administrative agency appeals *see* 16 Charles Alan Wright, Arthur R. Miller & Edward H. Cooper, Federal Practice & Procedure: Administrative Review §§ 3940-3944).

The number of judges and size of each circuit court varies, with the First Circuit being the smallest and the Ninth Circuit the largest. Congress has authorized the number of active judges per circuit court as follows: First: 6;

Second: 13; Third: 14; Fourth: 15; Fifth: 17; Sixth: 16; Seventh: 11; Eighth: 11; Ninth: 29; Tenth: 12; Eleventh: 12; D.C.: 11; Federal: 12. 28 U.S.C. §41. A judge who has reached the age of 65 and served 15 years as an Article III judge (or reached 66 and served 14 years and so on to 70 years and 10 years of service) is eligible for senior status. 28 U.S.C. §371. Senior judges receive the same amount of compensation they did on active status, have reduced work-loads, and do not "count" toward the number of active judges authorized by Congress. Judges on circuit courts are assisted by law clerks—usually three per judge. Some judges employ permanent law clerks, others hire law clerks for one or two years terms, while some employ a combination of permanent and limited-term clerks.

In all circuit courts, appeals are usually heard and decided by panels of three judges sitting together. 28 U.S.C. §46(b). The assignment of judges to particular panels and assignment of cases to panels normally occurs randomly and is handled by personnel in the clerk's office. *See* http://www.uscourts.gov/journalistguide/appellate_process.html . Upon petition, cases may be reheard en banc—by the entire court, or in the case of the Ninth Circuit, by the Chief Judge plus ten active judges "drawn by lot." Fed. R. App. P. 35; 9th Cir. R. 35-3.

Assuming the order or judgment from the district court is final and juris-diction is proper, appeal to the circuit courts is by right—meaning leave or per-mission to appeal is not required. *See* 28 U.S.C. §1291. This likely contributes to the relatively high volume of cases and high affirmance rates among the cir-cuit courts. *See* http://www.uscourts.gov/judbus2008/contents.cfm; http://www.uscourts.gov/cgi-bin/cmsa2008.pl; Chris Guthrie & Tracey E. George, *The Fu-tility of Appeal: Disciplinary Insights into the "Affirmance Effect" on the United States Courts of Appeals*, 32 FLA. ST. U. L. REV. 357, 358 (2005). Although cir-cuits courts regularly address and decide important matters of federal law, in the majority of cases the focus is on error correction, *i.e.*, whether the correct rule or standard was applied and/or whether it was applied correctly in the court below.

Procedure in the circuit courts is governed by the Federal Rules of Appel-late Procedure (FRAP) and by each circuit court's local rules. Both the FRAP and local circuit rules contain detailed instructions, requirements, and time limits regarding all aspects of processing federal appeals, including filing and perfecting the appeal, motions, briefs, oral argument, and dispositions. Local rules can usually be found on each circuit court's website and should be con-sulted in addition to the FRAP before filing and while working on any circuit court appeal. Note: in all circuit courts the party who has appealed an order or judgment by right is called the "appellant" while the party in opposition is called the "appellee." *See* Fed. R. App. P. 28.

Georgraphic Boundaries of United States Courts of Appeals and United States District Courts

The thirteen circuit courts are listed below along with the cities in which they are based, the number of judges and senior judges serving as of the date of this book's publication, and the district courts and other tribunals from which they hear appeals.

United States Court of Appeals for the First Circuit

Based in Boston, 5 active judges, 3 senior judges

- District of Maine

- District of Massachusetts

- District of New Hampshire

- District of Puerto Rico

- District of Rhode Island

United States Court of Appeals for the Second Circuit

Based in the City of New York, 9 active judges, 12 senior judges

- District of Connecticut
- Eastern District of New York
- Northern District of New York
- Southern District of New York
- Western District of New York
- District of Vermont

United States Court of Appeals for the Third Circuit

Based in Philadelphia, 13 active judges, 9 senior judges

- District of Delaware
- District of New Jersey
- Eastern District of Pennsylvania
- Middle District of Pennsylvania
- Western District of Pennsylvania
- U.S. Virgin Islands

United States Court of Appeals for the Fourth Circuit

Based in Richmond, 11 active judges, 1 senior judge

- District of Maryland
- Eastern District of North Carolina
- Middle District of North Carolina
- Western District of North Carolina
- District of South Carolina
- Eastern District of Virginia
- Western District of Virginia
- Northern District of West Virginia

- Southern District of West Virginia

United States Court of Appeals for the Fifth Circuit

Based in New Orleans, 16 active judges, 5 senior judges

- Eastern District of Louisiana
- Middle District of Louisiana
- Western District of Louisiana
- Northern District of Mississippi
- Southern District of Mississippi
- Eastern District of Texas
- Northern District of Texas
- Southern District of Texas
- Western District of Texas

United States Court of Appeals for the Sixth Circuit

Based in Cincinnati, 15 active judges, 9 senior judges

- Eastern District of Kentucky
- Western District of Kentucky
- Eastern District of Michigan
- Western District of Michigan
- Northern District of Ohio
- Southern District of Ohio
- Eastern District of Tennessee
- Middle District of Tennessee
- Western District of Tennessee

United States Court of Appeals for the Seventh Circuit

Based in Chicago, 10 active judges, 6 senior judges

- Central District of Illinois

- Northern District of Illinois
- Southern District of Illinois
- Northern District of Indiana
- Southern District of Indiana
- Eastern District of Wisconsin
- Western District of Wisconsin

United States Court of Appeals for the Eighth Circuit

Based in St. Louis, 11 active judges, 6 senior judges

- Eastern District of Arkansas
- Western District of Arkansas
- Northern District of Iowa
- Southern District of Iowa
- District of Minnesota
- Eastern District of Missouri
- Western District of Missouri
- District of Nebraska
- District of North Dakota
- District of South Dakota

United States Court of Appeals for the Ninth Circuit

Based in San Francisco, 25 active judges, 21 senior judges

- District of Alaska
- District of Arizona
- Central District of California
- Eastern District of California
- Northern District of California
- Southern District of California

- District of Hawaii
- District of Idaho
- District of Montana
- District of Nevada
- District of Oregon
- Eastern District of Washington
- Western District of Washington

United States Court of Appeals for the Tenth Circuit

Based in Denver, 11 active judges, 9 senior judges,

- District of Colorado
- District of Kansas
- District of New Mexico
- Eastern District of Oklahoma
- Northern District of Oklahoma
- Western District of Oklahoma
- District of Utah
- District of Wyoming

United States Court of Appeals for the Eleventh Circuit

Based in Atlanta;, 11 active judges, 9 senior judges

- Middle District of Alabama
- Northern District of Alabama
- Southern District of Alabama
- Middle District of Florida
- Northern District of Florida
- Southern District of Florida
- Middle District of Georgia

- Northern District of Georgia

- Southern District of Georgia

United States Court of Appeals for the District of Columbia Circuit
Based in D.C., 9 active judges, 4 senior judges

- United States District Court for the District of Columbia

United States Court of Appeals for the Federal Circuit
Based in D.C., 11 active judges, 5 senior judges
Article III courts:

- All United States district courts in patent cases where a cause of action of the *plaintiff* arises under patent law. (Cases in which patent issues arise only in the counter claims are appealed to the geographic circuit court corresponding to the district court in which the action was brought. *Holmes Group, Inc. v. Vornado Air Circulation Sys. Inc.*, 534 U.S. 826 (2002)).

- United States Court of International Trade

Article I courts and other tribunals:

- United States Court of Federal Claims

- United States Court of Appeals for Veterans Claims

- United States Trademark Trial and Appeal Board

- United States Board of Appeals and Interferences of the United States Patent and Trademark Office

- Boards of Contract Appeals (government contracts)

- United States Merit Systems Protection Board (federal employment benefits)

- United States International Trade Commission

d. The United States Supreme Court

The United States Supreme Court is the nation's court of last resort. Primarily, the Court hears cases involving important questions of Constitutional or federal law on writs of certiorari from circuit courts and state courts of last resort. The Court also hears (1) direct appeals from three judge district courts granting or denying an injunction in reapportionment cases or in cases involving certain provisions of the Civil Rights Act of 1964 and the Voting Rights Act of 1965, 28 U.S.C. § 1253, and (2) direct appeals from one judge district courts as specifically provided by Congress, e.g., cases involving desecration of the flag. 18 U.S.C. § 700(d). Such direct appeals to the Supreme Court are rare, however.

Nine justices sit on the Supreme Court. Currently, in order of seniority, they are: Chief Justice John G. Roberts, Jr., Justice John Paul Stevens, Justice Antonin Scalia, Justice Anthony M. Kennedy, Justice Clarence Thomas, Justice Ruth Bader Ginsberg, Justice Stephen Breyer, Justice Samuel A. Alito, Jr., and Justice Sonia Sotomayor. All nine justices hear and decide cases that have been granted writs of certiorari, or "granted cert."

The Supreme Court term runs from the first Monday in October and ends on "the day before the first Monday in October the following year." Sup. Ct. R. 3. The Court takes only a limited number of cases each year (currently, less than 100), and typically does not carry over cases from one term to the next.

The Court grants only a small percentage of the thousands of petitions for writs of certiorari it receives. The criteria or "considerations governing" whether to grant cert are listed in Supreme Court Rule 10. Cert will be granted only for "compelling reasons" generally when a decision of a circuit court or state court of last resort involves an important question of Constitutional or federal law that either (1) conflicts with decisions of other circuit courts, other state courts of last resort, or with decisions of the Supreme Court, or (2) "has not been, but should be, settled by [the Supreme] Court." If there was simply error below, cert is highly unlikely. Rule 10's final paragraph states: "A petition for a writ of certiorari is rarely granted when the asserted error consists of erroneous factual findings or the misapplication of a properly stated rule of law." Supreme Court Rules do not state how many justices must favor cert before the writ will be granted. However, as a matter of long standing tradition the number is four. In contrast to the circuit courts where appeals are a matter of right and the affirmance rate is high, the Supreme Court has reversed the majority of cases it has heard on the merits. *See* Chris Guthrie & Tracey E. George, *The Futility of Appeal: Disciplinary Insights into the "Affirmance Effect" on the United States Courts of Appeals*, 32 FLA. ST. U. L. REV. 357, 358 (2005).

Supreme Court justices are assisted by law clerks, usually 3 per justice. Unlike the circuit courts where some judges have permanent clerks or court attorneys, Supreme Court clerks serve for limited terms — usually one year. Typically, Supreme Court clerks clerked for a circuit, or in some cases a district court, prior to clerking on the Supreme Court.

Procedure in the Court is governed by the Supreme Court Rules. Note: Since cases are usually heard by the Court through the granting of petitions for writ of certiorari, the party seeking review is called the "petitioner" and the party in opposition the "respondent." *See, e.g.,* Sup. Ct. R. 24.

II. State Courts

Appellate court systems vary from state to state. This section discusses the similarities and highlights some of the differences among them.

a. State Intermediate Appellate Courts

Forty states have intermediate appellate courts that hear appeals from the state's courts of general jurisdiction or trial courts. The ten states that have only a supreme court or court of last resort are Delaware, Maine, Montana, Nevada, New Hampshire, Rhode Island, South Dakota, Vermont, West Virginia, and Wyoming. The District of Columbia also has only a court of last resort. Oklahoma has an intermediate appellate court for civil appeals, but not for criminal appeals. There, criminal appeals go directly to the state's court of last resort for criminal cases — the Oklahoma Court of Criminal Appeals. Civil appeals first go directly to the Oklahoma Supreme Court which may chose to send an appeal first to the Court of Civil Appeals. Alabama and Tennessee have separate intermediate appellate courts for criminal appeals and civil appeals. In the vast majority of states, however, criminal and civil appeals are heard in the same intermediate appellate court.

The number of judges sitting on state intermediate appellate courts varies greatly, with Alaska having the fewest with 3, and California having the greatest with just over 100. Some courts are divided geographically and many have multiple divisions. In almost all the states with intermediate appellate courts, appeals are heard and decided by panels of three judges. An exception is Alabama, where its five judge criminal and civil courts of appeals hear and decide cases en banc, with all five judges participating. Many, but not all, state intermediate appellate judges are assisted by either limited-term or permanent law clerks. The focus of state intermediate appellate courts is primarily on error correction, although these courts also hear and decide issue of first impression or sit in the position of making new, or extending existing, law.

Most state intermediate appellate courts have websites setting out their structure, compilation and jurisdiction, and containing or citing to rules of procedure that should be followed in filing and processing an appeal. These websites also post amendments to the rules and other important notices and thus should be checked regularly.

b. State Courts of Last Resort

A state's court of last resort is the final authority on matters of state constitutional, legislative, and common law. All fifty states and the District of Columbia have a court of last resort often called the "Supreme Court." Maryland, New York, and D.C.'s courts of last resort are called the "Court of Appeals." Almost all of the states' courts of last resort review both civil and criminal cases. The exceptions are Oklahoma and Texas. In Oklahoma, civil appeals first go directly to the "Supreme Court" which may refer cases to the Court of Civil Appeals, and then review those cases after the appellate court has heard and decided them. Criminal appeals in Oklahoma go directly to the "Court of Criminal Appeals." In Texas the court of last resort for civil cases is called the "Supreme Court," while the court of last resort for criminal cases is called the "Court of Criminal Appeals."

The number of justices who sit on state courts of last resort varies, but all courts have either 5, 7, or 9 justices who hear and decide cases en banc. Whether an appeal from a final order of judgment is by right or is discretionary with the court varies greatly from state to state. In states without intermediate appellate courts, appeal is usually by right. Also, in states with intermediate appellate courts, some state courts of last resort have direct appellate jurisdiction in certain types of cases, e.g. the Colorado Supreme Court has direct appellate jurisdiction in cases involving the adjudication of water rights, and the Alabama Supreme Court has direct appellate jurisdiction in civil cases in which the amount of damages in dispute is over $50,000. Also, in many states while review is generally discretionary, review is automatic in cases where the death penalty has been imposed.

In addition, state courts of last resort may hear and answer certified questions of state law from other courts, usually federal district or circuit courts, although sometimes from other state courts. Many states have adopted the Uniform Certified Questions of Law Act which sets out the procedures and requirements regarding certified questions.

Thus, whether a state court of last resort's focus is on error correction or on important legal questions depends on the appellate court structure and processes in that state and on the type of case before it.

As with state intermediate appellate courts, most state courts of last resort have websites setting out their structure, compilation, and jurisdiction, and containing or citing to rules of procedures that should be followed in filing and processing an appeal. These websites also post amendments to the rules and other important notices and thus should be checked regularly.

Checkpoints

- The federal appellate system consists of intermediate appellate courts called circuit courts, and the nation's court of last resort, the Supreme Court of the United States.

- There are 13 federal intermediate appellate courts. The United States Courts of Appeal for the First through Eleventh, and D.C., Circuits handle appeals from district courts located in their respective geographic regions, 28 U.S.C. § 41, as well as the majority of appeals from federal government agencies, 28 U.S.C. § 2342. The United States Court of Appeals for the Federal Circuit handles appeals from all district courts in patent cases and appeals from specialized courts such as the Federal Court of Claims, and certain government agencies, such as the International Trade Commission. 28 U.S.C. § 1295.

- The total number of judges appointed to each of the federal circuit courts varies, but in all the circuits, appeals are initially heard and decided by a panel of three judges.

- Where an order is final and jurisdiction is proper, appeal to the circuit courts is by right — prior permission is not needed.

- The majority of orders and judgments appealed to circuit courts are affirmed.

- Procedure in the circuit courts is governed by the Federal Rules of Appellate Procedure and by circuit court local rules.

- The United State Supreme Court is the nation's court of last resort. Its review of cases is, with few exceptions, discretionary — granted by writ of certiorari to decisions involving important questions of federal law that are issued by federal circuit courts or by state courts of last resort. U.S. Const. Art. III, § 2; Sup. Ct. R. 10. Nine justices sit on the Court.

- In comparison to federal circuit courts, the affirmance rate of the United States Supreme court is relatively low — often less than 50%.

- Procedure in the United States Supreme Court is governed by the Rules of the Supreme Court of the United States (http://www.supremecourtus.gov/ctrules/ctrules.html).

- 40 of the 50 States have intermediate appellate courts.

- Of the states with intermediate appellate courts, some have separate courts for civil appeals and criminal appeals, although most state intermediate appellate courts hear both civil and criminal matters.

- The total number of judges sitting on state intermediate courts of appeal varies from state to state, although, as with federal circuit courts, most cases are heard by a panel of three judges.

Checkpoints *continued*

- The focus of state intermediate appellate courts is primarily error correction, *i.e.*, whether the correct law or standard was applied correctly. In contrast, the primary role of state courts of last resort in states with intermediate appellate courts is interpreting or making law, *i.e.*, pronouncing what the law is.

- All states have a court of last resort, often called the "Supreme Court." State courts of last resort consist of either 5, 7, or 9 justices.

- In states with intermediate appellate courts, review by state courts of last resort is discretionary for many cases, but is by right for certain types of cases. Appeal by right varies from state to state.

- State courts of last resort may also decide certified questions from federal courts.

Chapter 2

Preserving Error for Appeal

Roadmap

- Generally, an error must be "preserved" in order to be appealed or otherwise reviewed.

- The general rule is that an issue cannot be raised on appeal unless it was first raised in the court below.

- It is important that the record in the court below reflect that a specific argument or objection was made, that particular evidence was proffered and not admitted, an instruction was requested and refused, or a motion was made and denied, and the like.

- It is also important to preserve error during the appeal itself. Errors or arguments can be waived or forfeited if an inadequate record or appendix is designated, if an argument is not sufficiently briefed, or if it is conceded during oral argument.

- There are exceptions to the general rule regarding preservation of error, including:

  - Plain or fundamental error;

  - Lack of subject matter jurisdiction;

  - Lack of standing.

- Mootness: Even if an issue is preserved at trial, the case may subsequently become moot — which will usually prohibit an appellate court's determination of the issue.

I. The General Rule Regarding Preservation of Error

The general rule is that an issue cannot be raised on appeal unless it was first raised in the trial court or other court of original jurisdiction. In other words, an issue not raised is forfeited. This is because the role of appellate courts is generally limited. Appellate courts *review* decisions and actions of courts of original jurisdiction; they are not meant to be deciders in the first instance. Thus, in general, a trial court or court of original jurisdiction

(1) should be the one to decide an issue in the first instance, and (2) should be afforded an opportunity to correct any error on its part.

The general rule regarding preservation of error is embodied in Federal Rule of Civil Procedure 46, which also eliminated the common law "formal exception" requirement:

> A formal exception to a ruling or order is unnecessary. When the ruling or order is requested or made, a party need only state the action that it wants the court to take or objects to, along with the grounds for the request or objection. Failing to object does not prejudice a party who had no opportunity to do so when the ruling or order was made.

In other words, attorneys should take care to (1) be specific regarding what they want the trial court to do and explicitly state the grounds for their request, and (2) be specific and contemporaneous regarding their objections to actions by the trial court and the grounds for those objections.

Making objections during a hearing or trial often poses a dilemma for attorneys, who fear aggravating the judge or jury. The goal is to be clear, concise and polite, while making sure to preserve the issue in the record. Waiver is rarely if ever excused on the ground that "We did not want to make the judge (or jury) mad."

II. Preservation of Error in the Trial Court

Some of the saddest words that an appellant can hear from the appellate court are "good argument, but it was not preserved below." Although appellate courts have some leeway when dealing with preservation of error, it is best for all involved if counsel in the trial court has taken appropriate action to preserve the error on the record. Methods of preserving different sorts of errors are discussed in the next subsections.

a. Evidentiary Errors

Evidentiary errors occur in either admitting or excluding evidence. To preserve error where evidence is admitted, attorneys should (1) make a timely objection or motion to strike the evidence, and (2) state the ground on which the objection is based. *See* Fed. R. Evid. 103(a)(1). The purpose of these steps is to enable the trial court to make an informed decision and take effective action, as well as to allow the proponent of the evidence to respond to the objection or take corrective action.

An objection or motion to strike should be made as soon as it is apparent that the evidence is inadmissible. Thus, for example, objections made after an exhibit is admitted and published to the jury or after a witness has finished testifying are unlikely to preserve error on appeal. At times, however, it may not be apparent that a question is objectionable until the witness has answered.

General objections—simply stating "objection" or "I object" are usually not enough to preserve the issue for appeal. The attorney must adequately apprize the court of the basis for the objection. If the ground or basis is "apparent from the context," however, the specific ground does not have to be stated. *See* Fed. R. Evid. 103(a)(1). Counsel should err on the safe side and state the ground for an objection even if at the time it appears clear from the context, situation, or line of questioning. This eliminates the need to argue that the ground asserted on appeal was apparent from the context at trial.

If an objection or motion to strike is made on one specific ground at trial, an appellant will generally not be allowed to argue a different ground on appeal. One state, Maryland, does not require counsel to state a specific ground for appeal unless the court asks for one—either on its own initiative or as the result from a request from the evidence's proponent. *See* Md. R. Evid. 2-517, 3-517, 4-323.

Finally, if the trial court orders or otherwise prevents counsel from stating the ground or grounds for an objection, appellate courts are likely to hold that the issue is preserved on appeal. This is similar to the provision of Federal Rule of Civil Procedure 46, which states that failing to object at trial will not prejudice a party who had no opportunity to do so.

In many instances attorneys can anticipate when the other side will proffer potentially objectionable evidence. In those instances, objections are handled before the trial through motions in limine. If the court makes a definitive ruling on a motion in limine, attorneys do not have to reassert the objection at trial. Fed. R. Evid. 301(a). However, as explained in the advisory committee notes to Rule 301, it is counsels' responsibility to clarify whether a ruling on a motion in limine is definitive or provisional. The same is true for rulings made during trial—if those rulings are definitive, objections thereto do not have to be reasserted throughout trial—but it is counsel's responsibility to clarify if there is any doubt.

In order to preserve errors in excluding evidence the "substance of the evidence [must be] made known to the court by an offer of proof, or [be] apparent from the context within which the questions were asked." Fed. R. Evid. 103(a)(2). Thus, counsel seeking to have evidence admitted should take care to make sure the record reflects what the evidence is, e.g., a particular exhibit or the substance of a witness's testimony, and the grounds on which counsel believes it is admissible. As with objections, relying on "context" to preserve error is risky at best.

b. Arguments and Conduct of Counsel at Trial

Trial counsel should also take care to timely object to improper statements or conduct of opposing counsel during opening statements, closing argument, examination of witnesses, and other occasions that might arise. To preserve error on appeal attorneys must make sure that the statements or conduct complained of *and* a timely objection are manifest in the record. This may mean breaking into an opening statement or closing argument even though these are often viewed as an opposing counsel's opportunity to address the jury uninterrupted. However, waiting until the end of these speeches risks waiving the issue on appeal and for trial purposes—*i.e.,* allowing a bell to ring that cannot then be un-rung.

On occasion improper statements or conduct may come from parties, witnesses, people in the gallery, or even court personnel. Again, to preserve error for appeal, trial counsel should make sure that any misstatements or other misconduct as well as the objection to this conduct is part of the record. This is not to suggest that doing so is easy or even without risk of irritating the judge or jury, but a party generally cannot complain on appeal about something that is not part of the record at trial.

c. Jury Instructions

Jury instruction errors involve errors in giving or failing to give particular instructions to the jury. To preserve error regarding a jury instruction that was given, counsel should object on the record as soon as they learn the instruction will be or has been given and state the grounds for the objection. *See* Fed. R. Civ. P. 51. To preserve error regarding a jury instruction the trial court failed to give, counsel should make sure the record reflects that they requested the instruction and that they objected as soon as they learned it would not be given. An objection is not necessary, however, if the trial court made a definitive ruling in the record rejecting the request. In some cases and jurisdictions, certain jury instructions are required by law, and error in failing to give these instructions is preserved even if they were not requested. For example, in California, instructions on lesser included criminal offenses must be given if "the evidence raises a question whether all the elements of the charged offense were present, but not when there is no evidence [that] the offense was less than that charged." *People v. Moye*, 213 P.3d 652, 659 (Cal. 2009).

d. Preserving Issues in Responsive Pleadings and Pre-Trial Motions

Most jurisdictions have specific rules regarding how and when defenses must be raised and preserved. For example, Federal Rule of Civil Procedure 12 provides, *inter alia*:

(b) How to Present Defenses. Every defense to a claim for relief in any pleading must be asserted in the responsive pleading if one is required. But a party may assert the following defenses by motion:

(1) lack of subject-matter jurisdiction;

(2) lack of personal jurisdiction;

(3) improper venue;

(4) insufficient process;

(5) insufficient service of process;

(6) failure to state a claim upon which relief can be granted; and

(7) failure to join a party under Rule 19.

. . . .

(h) Waiving and Preserving Certain Defenses.

(1) When Some Are Waived. A party waives any defense listed in Rule 12(b)(2)–(5) by:

(B) failing to either:

(i) make it by motion under this rule; or

(ii) include it in a responsive pleading or in an amendment allowed by Rule 15(a)(1) as a matter of course.

(2) When to Raise Others. Failure to state a claim upon which relief can be granted, to join a person required by Rule 19(b), or to state a legal defense to a claim may be raised:

(A) in any pleading allowed or ordered under Rule 7(a);

(B) by a motion under Rule 12(c); or

(C) at trial.

(3) Lack of Subject-Matter Jurisdiction. If the court determines at any time that it lacks subject-matter jurisdiction, the court must dismiss the action.

Thus, under Rule 12, the defenses of lack of personal jurisdiction, improper venue, insufficient process, and insufficient service of process must be raised at the very beginning of the litigation or through an amended pleading, if allowed. On the other hand, the failure to state a claim or defense or to join an indispensable party under Federal Rule of Civil Procedure 19(b) may be raised through the time of trial, while lack of subject matter jurisdiction may be raised at any time.

Note: Although motions for failure to state a claim under Rule 12 may be made as late as during trial, they may not be made after trial. *Arbaugh v. Y & H Corp.*, 546 U.S. 500, 507 (2006). In other words, the issue is waived if it is not raised until the post-trial motion stage of the proceedings.

Under federal rules, issues raised prior to trial in a motion for summary judgment may be re-raised before the case goes to the jury by a motion for judgment as a matter of law, and if denied, the motion should be renewed post-trial. Fed. R. Civ. P. 50. See Section e below. Note: Motions for dismissal or summary judgment involving issues of immunity that have been denied are immediately appealable under the collateral order doctrine. See Chap. 3, §II (a).

Finally, it is important to keep in mind that a pre-trial motion will not automatically preserve the issues it raises for appeal. If the motion is denied, the lawsuit continues and the issues and facts may become more developed—in which case those issues can and should be raised again in a later motion. For example, issues raised in a motion to dismiss for failure to state a claim are often revisited in a motion for summary judgment, and later in motions for judgment as a matter of law or the like. See Section e below.

e. Post-Trial Motions

Post-trial motions can be critical in preserving issues for appeal. For example, Federal Rule of Civil Procedure 50, which governs motions for judgment as a matter of law (JMOL), requires a JMOL motion to be made first before the case goes to the jury, when the non-movant "has been fully heard on an issue," Rule 50(a) (formerly known as a 'motion for directed verdict"), and if denied, the motion must be renewed post-trial, within 28 days after the entry of judgment, Rule 50(b) (formerly known as a "motion for judgment notwithstanding the verdict" or "JNOV"). Thus, two successive motions must be made to preserve the claim of error on appeal.

In ruling on a motion for JMOL under Rule 50(b) the court may also elect to order a new trial. In general though, motions for a new trial in federal court are governed by Rule 59. A motion for new trial is not necessary to preserve error on appeal if the error occurred during trial and was otherwise preserved, e.g., by a timely objection to the admission of evidence, conduct of opposing counsel, or jury instructions. In other words, if the issue has already been properly raised with the trial court, it does not have to be re-raised in a motion for new trial. However, if a motion for new trial is the first opportunity to raise an issue, insufficiency of evidence to support the verdict, a motion under Rule 59 *must* be brought in order to preserve that issue for appeal. Note: Counsel should not assume that a motion for new trial will salvage the failure to make a timely objection when, or soon after, the error occurred.

III. Preservation of Error During the Appeal

a. Record or Appendix on Appeal

In general, it is the appellant's job to provide the reviewing court with a record on appeal of the proceedings below that contains the documents, transcripts, and evidence that the appellate court needs to determine the questions of law and fact that make up the appeal. The appellee will have the chance to supplement or counter-designate materials the appellant has omitted. In some systems there is a requirement that the parties work together to produce one joint record or appendix. Counsel must make sure the appellate record or appendix contains the specific ruling or action complained of and shows that an appropriate objection, request, motion, argument, and the like was made and that proper grounds for this relief were presented below.

In some jurisdictions the trial court's clerk's office automatically transfers the entire record to the appellate court, and counsel are required to compile an appendix of particular documents germane to the issues on appeal. In other jurisdictions counsel must designate specific documents in the trial court record to be sent to the appellate court—forming the record on appeal. Also, court reporter's transcripts need to be specifically designated and generated since they are not part of the record maintained in the trial court's clerk's office. There are deadlines for completing these various tasks and counsel need to make sure the appellate court receives all necessary documents and transcripts in a timely manner. For more discussion on the record on appeal and appendices, see Chapter 5.

b. Briefing the Appeal

Even if an issue is preserved in the trial court, it will be deemed abandoned if it is not adequately briefed. This is because (1) appellants control the issues raised on appeal, and (2) appellees must have the opportunity to respond to an argument. The appellee is entitled to rely on the content of an appellant's brief to delineate the scope of the appeal. *See Access Now v. Southwest Airlines Co.*, 385 F.3d 1324, 1330 (11th Cir. 2004). Thus, any issues the appellant wishes the court to address should be "specifically and clearly identified" in the opening brief. Those issues should also be sufficiently addressed and developed so the appellee can respond to them and the court can consider them. Generally, issues raised for the first time in the reply brief or raised only in a footnote will not be considered.

c. Oral Argument

Attorneys have less control over oral argument than they do over the content of their briefs. During oral argument the judges on the panel have ultimate control over the issues they wish to hear addressed and the questions they want answered. Thus, if an issue is adequately raised in the brief, it generally will not be deemed waived if not addressed during oral argument. Note, however, that courts do not always follow this general rule. For example, in the Virginia Supreme Court, any issue that was not discussed or expressly reserved at oral argument was to be deemed abandoned under *Perdon Coal Co./United Coal Co. v. Stiltner*, 323 S.E.2d 110 (Va. 1984), a case that stood until 2010 when it was superseded by Virginia Rule of Appellate Procedure 5.33(e).

Although issues raised in the brief generally are not waived by failing to discuss them at oral argument, such issues can be forfeited by *conceding* them during oral argument. This can occur in the heat of the moment prompted by questioning from the judges on the panel. For example, during an exchange, a judge might say: "Counsel, won't you at least concede that your client had a duty to the appellee?" The attorney may be thinking, "duty is not really my strongest argument, I'd like to get to the standard of care, so maybe I'll give in on duty so I can move to my best argument." However, unless the attorney has thoroughly considered and decided to abandon an issue beforehand, he or she should avoid doing so during oral argument. There is usually no way of knowing for sure how all the members of a panel might decide and issue, and no attorney who did not deliberately intend to concede an issue wants to read in the opinion "counsel conceded at oral argument that...." In the example above, it would be better for counsel to politely decline to concede the issue of duty and then quickly move to the issue of standard of care. (For further discussion on handling questions at oral argument that seek concession from counsel, see Chapter 12, § (c)(3)(C))

IV. Exceptions Regarding Preservation of Error

a. Plain or Fundamental Error

Most, but not all, jurisdictions have a "plain" or "fundamental" error exception that may allow, but does not require, an appellate court to consider an issue that was not raised in the court below. (States rejecting a plain or fundamental error exception include Alabama, New Hampshire, and Pennsylvania. *Barnes v. Dale*, 530 So.2d 770 (Ala. 1988) (rejecting the doctrine of fundamental error in civil cases); *State v. McAdams*, 594 A2d 1273 (N.H. 1991); *Dilliplaine v. Lehigh Valley Trust Co.*, 322 A.2d 114 (Pa. 1974).

Under the federal plain error exception articulated by the Supreme Court, a court may, but need not, consider an issue not raised below where there is (1) an error, (2) that is "plain," meaning clear or obvious under current law, (3) affects substantial rights, and (4) "seriously affects the fairness, integrity or public reputation of judicial proceedings." *Johnson v. U.S.*, 520 U.S. 461, 466–67 (1997); *see also* Fed. R. Crim. P. 52; Fed. R. Civ. P. 51(d)(1). Examples of plain error include (a) a trial judge's participation in plea negotiations; (b) a conviction obtained in blatant violation of the double jeopardy clause of the Fifth Amendment; (c) prison sentences that exceeded the statutory maximum length; (d) orders to pay restitution above the statutory maximum amount; (e) egregious intrusions upon the jury, such as bribing a juror, or prejudicial comments by the bailiff or other court staff, e.g. "The defendant? He's a regular, and as sure as I'm standing here, he's guilty."

Many states have plain or fundamental error exceptions that are broader and more flexible than the federal plain error exception. Although descriptions of fundamental error vary, the standard focuses on whether substantial rights were affected and/or whether there was a miscarriage of justice. Some examples: "Error is fundamental if it goes to the foundation or basis of a defendant's rights or goes to the foundation of the case or takes from the defendant a right which was essential to his defense and which no court could or ought to permit him to waive." *State v. Sarabia*, 875 P.2d 227, 230 (Idaho 1994). "The cases are not a few where, even though an exception not be taken, if the error is of such a fundamental character and the resultant injustice so egregious, that an appellate court will take hold of it in the general exercise of the court's power to reverse and grant a new trial in the interests of justice." *Kazales v. Minto Leasing, Inc.*, 61 A.D.2d 1039, 1040 (N.Y.A.D. 1978). "Upon an appeal taken by the defendant, the appellate court may, without exception having been taken in the trial court, review any question of law involved in any ruling, order, instruction, or thing whatsoever said or done at the trial or prior to or after judgment, which thing was said or done after objection made in and considered by the lower court, and which affected the substantial rights of the defendant. The appellate court may also review any instruction given, refused or modified, even though no objection was made thereto in the lower court, if the substantial rights of the defendant were affected thereby." Cal. Pen. Code § 1259. "Plain errors or defects affecting substantial rights may be noticed although they were not brought to the attention of the trial court." ILCS S. Ct. Rule 615.

Fundamental error has been found based on (a) erroneous and confusing jury instructions; (b) admission of evidence showing the defendant had invoked his right to silence; (c) a jury's inadvertent review of notes belonging to the defendant's attorney that referred to the plaintiff as lying and "playing dumb;" (d) the erroneous dismissal of a juror; (e) the absence of a juror from the court room while the verdict was announced; (f) the erroneous admission of highly inflammatory evidence; and (g) gross misconduct by counsel in closing argument.

b. Subject Matter Jurisdiction

Subject matter jurisdiction refers to the power and authority of a court to hear and adjudicate a particular case or controversy. It is defined by federal and state constitutions and statutes, and is usually based on the type of case or controversy involved, the amount in dispute, and/or the identity of the parties. Subject matter jurisdiction is never waived or forfeited and can be raised at any time in the proceedings. *See* Fed. R. Civ. P. 12(h)(1) ("Whenever it appears by suggestion of the parties or otherwise that the court lacks jurisdiction of the subject matter, the court shall dismiss the action."). In fact, a court has an independent duty to determine that it has subject matter jurisdiction. *See Arbaugh v. Y & H Corp.*, 546 U.S. 500, 514 (2006).

Article 3 of the Constitution defines the subject matter jurisdiction of federal courts as follows:

The judicial power shall extend to all cases, in law and equity, arising under this Constitution, the laws of the United States, and treaties made, or which shall be made, under their Authority; to all cases affecting ambassadors, other public ministers and consuls; to all cases of admiralty and maritime jurisdiction; to controversies to which the United States shall be a party; to controversies between two or more states; between a state and citizens of another State; between citizens of different states; between citizens of the same state claiming lands under grants of different states, and between a state, or the citizens thereof, and foreign states, citizens or subjects.

U.S. Const. Art. 3, § 2, cl. 1.

The most common bases for federal court subject matter jurisdiction are federal question jurisdiction, 28 U.S.C. § 1331, and diversity of citizenship jurisdiction, 28 U.S.C. § 1332. "A plaintiff properly invokes § 1331 jurisdiction when she pleads a colorable claim arising under the Constitution or laws of the United States.... She invokes § 1332 jurisdiction when she presents a claim between parties of diverse citizenship that exceeds the required jurisdictional amount, currently $75,000." *See Arbaugh v. Y & H Corp.*, 546 U.S. at 513 (internal quotations and citations omitted).

States, by constitution or statute, also define the subject matter jurisdiction of their various courts. Certain courts may be authorized to hear certain types of cases or controversies: business courts, probate courts, family law courts, juvenile courts. Often the amount in controversy will determine a court's jurisdiction, e.g., small claims courts. As with federal subject matter jurisdiction, state court subject matter jurisdiction involves a court's power to hear a case. Thus, generally it cannot be waived or forfeited and can be raised at any time in the proceedings.

c. Standing

The federal requirement that a person have standing to bring a claim is based on the "case or controversy" requirement in Article III, Section 2, clause 1 of the Constitution. *Raines v. Byrd*, 521 U.S. 811, 817 (1997) ("No principle is more fundamental to the judiciary's proper role in our system of government than the constitutional limitation of federal-court jurisdiction to actual cases or controversies.").

Because standing is an element of federal subject matter jurisdiction, it cannot be waived or forfeited and can be raised at any time in the proceedings.

Most, but not all, states also consider standing to be a component of subject matter jurisdiction, meaning standing in state courts is an issue that can be raised at any time in the proceedings. *See Garriga v. Sanitation Dist.*

No. 1, 2003 Ky. App. LEXIS 305, at *21, n. 26 (Ky. Ct. App. 2003) (collecting cases); *Compare Sears v. Hull*, 961 P.2d 1013, 1019 (Ariz. 1998) ("we are not constitutionally constrained to decline jurisdiction based on lack of standing").

For further discussion regarding the standing requirement, see Chapter 5, Parties and Non Parties on Appeal, § II(a)

A Final Note Regarding Mootness

The case or controversy requirement in Article III of the federal Constitution, as well as those of most states, prohibits appellate courts from determining an issue after the case has become moot. Thus, even if an error or issue has been preserved in the court below, subsequent mootness will preclude appellate review. The mootness doctrine and its exceptions are discussed in Chapter 5 § II(b).

Checkpoints

- Generally speaking, in order to be addressed on appeal, an error in the trial court must be preserved on appeal. It is up to trial counsel to make sure that both the error and the objection to the error are part of the record.

- For evidentiary errors, complaints about the misconduct of opposing counsel, or jury instructions, counsel should (1) make a timely objection or motion to strike the evidence and (2) state the grounds upon which the objection is made.

- Defenses to causes of action must also be preserved. Some must be raised at every juncture in order to be preserved. Others, like subject matter jurisdiction, are automatically preserved and may be raised at any juncture in the proceedings.

- Post-trial motions can be critical in preserving issues for appeal, especially motions for judgment as a matter of law, which are made first before the case goes to the jury and, if denied, made again after the jury has spoken.

- To preserve the error during the appeal itself, it is necessary to include all supporting material relevant to the error in the record or appendix on appeal and to raise and discuss the error in the appellant's opening brief.

- Generally, if an alleged error is supported by the record on appeal and addressed in the appellant's opening brief, it will not be deemed waived if not addressed in oral argument. However, counsel may forfeit issues by conceding them at oral argument.

Checkpoints *continued*

- There are a few exceptions to the general rule that it is counsel's responsibility to preserve error for appeal. These include the "plain" or "fundamental" error rule, lack of subject matter jurisdiction, and lack of standing.

- Even if an error is preserved at trial, that error will not be reviewed if the case becomes moot. See Chapter 5, § II(b).

Chapter 3

Appealability: The Final Judgment Rule and Exceptions

Roadmap

- Not every decision of a federal trial court is immediately appealable.

- The "final judgment rule" states that, generally, appeals may only be taken from a final judgment or decision that resolves all issues in a case.

- There are exceptions to the final judgment rule that permit what are known as "interlocutory" appeals of collateral orders, injunctions, partial final judgments, class certification orders, and others.

- The states have their own versions of the final judgment rule and its exceptions, as well as processes for review by permission or extraordinary writ.

I. The Final Judgment Rule

The federal courts' final judgment rule requires that all claims and issues presented in a case be decided by the district court before any issue may be reviewed by the court of appeals. The rule is embodied in 28 U.S.C. § 1291, which states, in pertinent part: "The courts of appeals ... shall have jurisdiction of appeals from all final decisions of the district courts of the United States." A final decision or final judgment is often defined as "one which ends the litigation on the merits and leaves nothing for the court to do but execute the judgment." *Caitlin v. United States*, 324 U.S. 229, 233 (1945).

The purpose of the final judgment rule is to avoid piecemeal appeals—successive appeals of individual rulings throughout the course of the litigation. As the Supreme Court stated in *Luxton v. North River Bridge Co.*, 147 U.S. 337, 341 (1893), "The case is not to be sent up in fragments." Avoiding piecemeal appeals serves several interrelated goals, including: promoting the efficient administration of justice, preventing delay, harassment, or costs caused by interlocutory appeals, and safeguarding the independence and autonomy of the district courts. *See Cobbledick v. U.S.*, 309 U.S. 323, 325 (1940).

Thus, an order dismissing some but not all the claims in a complaint is not final and appealable. Or, even if summary judgment is entered dismissing all the plaintiff's claims, that judgment is not appealable if there are counter claims of the defendant remaining. Similarly, a judgment holding a defendant liable but not determining the amount of damages is generally not final and appealable. An exception is a judgment for patent infringement in a civil action that "is final except for an accounting" may be immediately appealed to the Federal Circuit. 28 U.S.C. § 1292(c)(2).

The appealability of an order or judgment is jurisdictional, and the court of appeals has an independent obligation to make a determination of the finality and appealability of the order or judgment before it. *See Andersen v. U.S.*, 298 F.3d 804, 807 (9th Cir. 2002). In some cases the parties will stipulate to the finality of an order in an attempt to make the order immediately appealable. In these situations appellate courts will look to the practical effect of the stipulations. If for all practical purposes the stipulations render the order final—leaving nothing more for the district court to do but execute the judgment and placing all issues in the case before the court of appeal— the court may consider the appeal. *Regula v. Delta Family-Care Disability Survivorship Plan*, 266 F.3d 1130, 1137–38 (9th Cir. 2002), *vacated on other grounds in Delta Family-Care Disability and Survivorship Plan v. Regula*, 539 U.S. 901(2003).

In *Regula*, the issues presented in the plaintiff's motion for summary judgment and the defendant's opposition were identical to the issues that would be presented at trial, and the parties stipulated that the plaintiff could not prevail at trial after the denial of its summary judgment motion; the district court entered judgment in favor of the defendant. The court of appeals determined the judgment was final and that it had jurisdiction to hear the appeal under 28 U.S.C. § 1291.

In addition, where some claims have been dismissed but others remain, plaintiffs may attempt to obtain appellate review by dismissing the remaining claims. If dismissal is with prejudice, courts of appeals generally will hear the appeal; if dismissal is without prejudice, they generally will not. *See Rabbi Jacob Joseph School v. Province of Mendoza*, 425 F.3d 207, 210–11 (2d Cir. 2005). Note: in certain circumstances a district court may enter a final appealable judgment on fewer than all claims under Federal Rule of Civil Procedure 54(b), discussed in Section II(b) below.

In deciding whether an order is appealable, courts of appeal will also determine if an exception to the final judgment rule applies. Exceptions are discussed below.

II. Exceptions to the Final Judgment Rule

a. The Collateral Order Doctrine

The collateral order doctrine allows direct appeal of a small class of decisions that do not terminate litigation, but "in the interest of achieving a healthy legal system," are treated as final and appealable. *Digital Equip. Corp. v. Desktop Direct, Inc.*, 511 U.S. 863, 867 (1992). The doctrine applies only to district court decisions that: (1) are conclusive, (2) resolve important questions completely separate from the merits, and (3) would render such important questions effectively unreviewable on appeal from final judgment in the underlying action. *Id.*

The requirement that a decision be conclusive means the district court ruling must not be tentative or likely to be subject to reconsideration. In other words the order at issue must itself be final. Thus, for example, the collateral order doctrine will not apply where the district court has expressly indicated that its ruling is tentative or will be reconsidered based on further developments or new evidence, or that the motion underlying the ruling may be renewed. *See Swint v. Chambers County Comm'n*, 514 U.S. 35, 35–36 (1995). On the other hand, some types of orders are inherently tentative and subject to reconsideration, such as orders regarding interim awards of costs or attorney fees. Note: Prior to the enactment of Federal Rule of Civil Procedure 23(f), discussed in Section II(d) below, orders regarding class certification were generally considered tentative and not subject to immediate review, so when researching this issue, be aware of this 1998 change and realize that contrary case law before the change should be ignored or viewed with suspicion.

Finally, when an order is not inherently tentative by nature, and the district court has treated the ruling as final, the fact that a district court has the general authority to revise any order or decision before entry of judgment does not defeat conclusiveness for purposes of the collateral order doctrine. *Moses H. Cone Mem. Hosp. v. Mercury Constr. Corp.*, 460 U.S. 1, 12–13 (1983). Otherwise, every district court order would be considered tentative.

The "collateral" requirement of the collateral order doctrine means that the order must decide an issue that is completely separate from the underlying issue. The order must not be a step toward, and must not affect or be affected by, the final judgment—otherwise the order would merge into the final judgment under the final judgment rule. *Cohen v. Beneficial Indus. Loan Corp.*, 337 U.S. 541, 546 (1949). Examples of completely separate, collateral orders are those involving the posting of security as a condition to filing suit, *see id.*, and those involving immunity from suit, *see Mitchell v. Forsyth*, 472 U.S. 511, 527 (1985).

In determining whether an order involves a question that would otherwise be effectively unreviewable, appellate courts assess whether it would be too late to remedy the harm alleged or grant effective relief on an appeal of the final judgment—in other words, whether it would be impossible or impractical to "unring the bell" or "unscramble the egg" after final judgment was entered. Examples are: orders denying bail pending trial, *see Stack v. Boyle*, 342 U.S. 1 (1945); orders requiring the disclosure of privileged or secret information, *see, e.g., In re Cendant Corp. Sec. Litig.*, 343 F.3d 658, 662 n. 5 (3d Cir. 2005) (documents to which attorney client or work product privileges are claimed); *Irons v. Federal Bureau of Investigation*, 811 F.2d 681, 683–84 (1st Cir. 1987) (identity of FBI informants); and orders denying an attorney's motion to withdraw. *Intercounty Nat'l Title Ins. Co. of N.Y. v. Intercounty Nat'l Title Ins. Co.*, 310 F.3d 537, 539–40 (7th Cir. 2002).

In *Digital Equip. Corp.*, the Court stated "the collateral order doctrine is best understood as not an exception to the 'final decision rule' laid down by Congress in § 1291, but as a 'practical construction' of it'"—since immediate appeals of orders meeting those three criteria "do not go against the grain of § 1291, with its object of efficient administration of justice in the federal courts." 511 U.S. at 867–68. Still, the Court stressed that the doctrine is a "'narrow' exception [that] should stay that way and never be allowed to swallow the general rule" allowing only one appeal from one final judgment." *Id.* at 868.

b. Partial Final Judgments under Federal Rule of Civil Procedure 54(b)

Where a case involves multiple claims or parties, Rule 54(b) allows the district court to enter final judgment as to fewer than all the claims or parties if it expressly determines there is no just reason for delay. Rule 54(b) states:

> When an action presents more than one claim for relief—whether as a claim, counterclaim, crossclaim, or third-party claim—or when multiple parties are involved, the court may direct entry of a final judgment as to one or more, but fewer than all, claims or parties only if the court expressly determines that there is no just reason for delay. Otherwise, any order or other decision, however designated, that adjudicates fewer than all the claims or the rights and liabilities of fewer

than all the parties does not end the action as to any of the claims or parties and may be revised at any time before the entry of a judgment adjudicating all the claims and all the parties' rights and liabilities.

There are three requirements under Rule 54(b): (1) there must be more than one claim or party involved in the action; (2) there must be a *final decision* as to the particular claims or parties designated—meaning, as to that claim or party, the decision is conclusive and ends the litigation on the merits, and (3) the district court, acting as a "dispatcher," must determine on the record that there is no just reason for delay—certifying that a final decision as to fewer than all the claims or parties is ready for appeal. *Sears, Roebuck & Co. v. Mackey*, 351 U.S. 427, 435–36 (1956).

The determination that there is no just reason for delay is a matter of discretion with the district court based not only on the equities of each case, but on the "interests of sound judicial administration." *Id.* at 437. An important factor is whether, and how much, the adjudicated claims relate to the remaining unadjudicated claims "so as to prevent piecemeal appeals in cases which should be reviewed only as single units." *Curtiss-Wright Corp. v. General Elec. Co.*, 446 U.S. 1, 10 (1980).

Review of the district court's exercise of discretion has two aspects:

[1] The courts of appeals must, of course scrutinize the district court's evaluation of such factors as the interrelationship of the claims so as to prevent piecemeal appeals in cases which should be reviewed only as single units. [2] But once such juridical concerns have been met, the discretionary judgment of the district court should be given substantial deference, for that court is the one most likely to be familiar with the case and with any justifiable reasons for delay. The reviewing court should disturb the trial court's assessment of the equities only if it can say that the judge's conclusion was clearly unreasonable.

Id. (internal citations and quotations omitted). Appellate courts are unlikely to give a district court "substantial deference," however, where the court has not set out its reasons for concluding there is no just reason for delay. *Ebrahimi v. City of Huntsville Bd. of Educ.*, 114 F.3d 162, 166 (11th Cir. 1997) (collecting and discussing cases).

Even if certification of a partial judgment is unchallenged on appeal, before the court of appeals exercises jurisdiction, the court must satisfy itself that the underlying order was final and conclusive and properly entered under Rule 54(b). The district court's entry of a partial judgment under Rule 54(b) that was proper starts the clock running for purposes of appeal. If the judgment was not proper, e.g. if the decision on which it was based was not a final decision, the time to appeal will generally run from entry of a final judgment in the case under 28 U.S.C. § 1291. *See In re Integra Realty Resources, Inc.*, 262 F.3d 1089, 1107–08 (10th Cir. 2001).

c. Appeals of Interlocutory Orders under 28 U.S.C. § 1292

1. *Orders Regarding Injunctions — 28 U.S.C. § 1292(a)(1)*

Section 1292(a)(1) allows immediate appeals of "[i]nterlocutory orders ... granting, continuing, modifying, refusing or dissolving injunctions, or refusing to dissolve or modify injunctions, except where a direct review may be had in the Supreme Court." The rationale for allowing immediate appeals in these instances is that orders involving injunctions can have an immediate and significant impact on the rights of the parties.

The main issue in section 1292(a)(1) cases is whether an order involves an injunction. For purposes of the statute, an injunction is "[1] directed to a party, [2] enforceable by contempt, and [3] designed to accord or protect some or all of the substantive relief sought by a complaint in more than a temporary fashion." *Cohen v. Bd. of Trustees*, 867 F.2d 1455, 1465 n. 9 (3d Cir. 1989).

Thus, temporary restraining orders generally do not qualify as injunctions. First, they are usually effective for only a brief period of time and are often supplanted by an appealable preliminary or permanent injunction or other denying same. Second, the district court "has not normally had the advantage of a hearing on the facts and the applicable law, [and o]rderly procedure requires that [the] trial [court] be permitted to pass on the question presented before [its] decision is reviewed by a higher court." *Dilworth v. Riner*, 343 F.2d 226, 229 (5th Cir. 1965).

Also, procedural orders that do not "touch on the merits of the claim" do not involve injunctions under section 1292(a)(1) — even though their violation may be punishable by contempt. *Hershey Foods Corp. v. Hershey Creamery Co.*, 945 F.2d 1272, 1277 (3d Cir.1991) (collecting and discussing cases and holding that interlocutory order enjoining a party from prosecuting a related action was not immediately appealable under section 1292(a)(1)).

Note that section 1292(a)(1) *allows* an immediate appeal from orders involving injunctions, but does not *require* one. A party may wait and challenge the order in an appeal from the final judgment. *Chambers v. Ohio Dept. of Human Services*, 145 F.3d 793, 796 (6th Cir. 1998).

2. Receivership Orders— 28 U.S.C. § 1292(a)(2)

Section 1292(a)(2) allows immediate appeals of "[1] interlocutory orders appointing receivers, or [2] refusing orders to wind up receiverships or [3] to take steps to accomplish the purposes thereof, such as directing sales or other disposals of property." Section 1292(a)(2) is narrowly interpreted to apply only to orders falling squarely within one of the three categories of orders specified in the statute. *S.E.C. v. Black*, 163 F.3d 188, 195 (3d Cir. 1998) (holding an award of fees to the receiver is not immediately appealable under section 1292(a)(2)).

3. Orders Involving Controlling Questions of Law—28 U.S.C. § 1292(b)

Section 1292(b) allows a district court to certify interlocutory orders for immediate appeal if the court is "of the opinion [1] that such order involves a controlling question of law [2] as to which there is a substantial ground for difference of opinion and [3] that an immediate appeal from the order may materially advance the ultimate termination of the litigation." If an application is made within 10 days after entry of the order, the court of appeal "may thereupon, in its discretion, permit an appeal to be taken from such order." *Id.*

Generally, a question of law means an "abstract legal issue" involving "the meaning of a statutory or constitutional provision, regulation, or common law doctrine." *Ahrenholz v. Board of Trustees of University of Illinois*, 219 F.3d 674, 677 (7th Cir. 2000) (holding that the issue of whether summary judgment should have been granted was not a question of law for purposes of section 1292(b)). A question of law is controlling "if it could materially affect the outcome of the case." *In re City of Memphis*, 293 F.3d 345, 346 (6th Cir. 2002) (holding that the issue of whether city could use evidence not available to it when the affirmative action plan at issue was enacted was not a controlling legal issue). A substantial ground for difference of opinion generally will not lie if the cases in the circuit are in agreement on the issue or if the issue is clear, straightforward, and uncomplicated. *Id.*; *Singh v. DaimlerBenz, AG*, 800 F. Supp. 260, 263 (E.D. Pa. 1992). Finally, in order to materially advance the termination of the litigation, resolution of the issue on interlocutory appeal must actually speed-up or shorten the litigation, e.g., by avoiding trial. *Ahrenholz*, 219 F.3d at 677; *McFarlin v. Conseco Services, LLC*, 381 F.3d 1251, 1259 (11th Cir. 2004).

It should be noted that interlocutory appeals under section 1292(b) are generally disfavored by the courts of appeal, who do not exercise their discretion very often to hear them. *See Ahrenholz* and *City of Memphis*, *supra* Section II(c)(3).

d. Class Certification Decisions under Federal Rule of Civil Procedure 23(f)

Rule 23 governs class actions in federal courts, and subsection (f), added in 1998, gives courts of appeals discretion to allow immediate interlocutory appeals of orders granting or denying class certification. Rule 23(f) states:

> A court of appeals may permit an appeal from an order granting or denying class-action certification under this rule if a petition for permission to appeal is filed with the circuit clerk within 14 days after the order is entered. An appeal does not stay proceedings in the district court unless the district judge or the court of appeals so orders.

Rule 23(f) does not require the district court to certify or otherwise designate a class certification order as immediately appealable, nor does the rule set out any criteria for the courts of appeals' exercise of discretion in deciding whether to review such orders.

Indeed, the Advisory Committee Notes to Rule 23(f) state: "The court of appeals is given unfettered discretion whether to permit the appeal, akin to the discretion exercised by the Supreme Court in acting on a petition for certiorari." The Notes add, however, that "[p]ermission is most likely to be granted when the certification decision turns on a novel or unsettled question of law, or when, as a practical matter, the decision on certification is likely dispositive of the litigation."

Based on Rule 23(f)'s Advisory Committee Notes, the courts of appeals have developed slightly varying standards determining whether to exercise their discretion to hear an interlocutory appeal under Rule 23(f). Some courts are likely to hear an appeal in these categories of cases:

(1) when a denial of class status effectively ends the case (because, say, the named plaintiff's claim is not of a sufficient magnitude to warrant the costs of stand-alone litigation);

(2) when the grant of class status raises the stakes of the litigation so substantially that the defendant likely will feel irresistible pressure to settle; or

(3) when [an appeal] will lead to clarification of a fundamental issue of law.

Moreover, when the case falls in either of the first two categories, the applicant must also "demonstrate that the district court's ruling on class certification is questionable...."

Waste Management Holdings, Inc. v. Mowbray, 208 F.3d 288, 293 (1st Cir. 2000); *Blair v. Equifax Check Services, Inc.*, 181 F.3d 832, 834–35 (7th Cir. 1999); *see also Newton v. Merrill Lynch, Pierce, Fenner & Smith, Inc.*, 259 F.3d 154, 164 (3d Cir. 2001).

Other courts use a similar five factor test:

(1) whether the certification ruling is likely dispositive of the litigation;

(2) whether the district court's certification decision contains a substantial weakness;

(3) whether the appeal will permit the resolution of an unsettled legal question of general importance;

(4) the nature and status of the litigation before the district court (such as the presence of outstanding dispositive motions and the status of discovery); and

(5) the likelihood that future events will make appellate review more or less appropriate.

Lienhart v. Dryvit Systems, Inc., 255 F.3d 138, 144 (4th Cir. 2001); *Prado-Steiman v. Bush*, 221 F.3d 1266, 1274–76 (11th Cir. 2000).

The Second Circuit has a compressed version of the standard, which it emphasized should be flexible:

[P]etitioners seeking leave to appeal pursuant to Rule 23(f) must demonstrate either (1) that the certification order will effectively terminate the litigation and there has been a substantial showing that the district court's decision is questionable, or (2) that the certification order implicates a legal question about which there is a compelling need for immediate resolution.

Sumitomo Copper Litigation v. Credit Lyonnais Rouse, Ltd., 262 F.3d 134, 139 (2d Cir. 2001)

e. Review by Extraordinary Writ (Writ of Mandamus) — 28 U.S.C. § 1651(a)

Review of an interlocutory order may also be sought through a petition for writ of mandamus under 28 U.S.C. § 1651(a) (the "All Writs Act"). Section 1651(a) provides: "The Supreme Court and all courts established by Act of Congress may issue all writs necessary or appropriate in aid of their respective jurisdictions and agreeable to the usages and principles of law."

A writ of mandamus has been called a "'drastic and extraordinary' remedy [that is] 'reserved for really extraordinary causes.'" *Cheney v. U.S. Dist. Court for Dist. of Columbia*, 542 U.S. 367, 380 (2004) (quoting *Ex parte Fahey*, 332 U.S. 258, 259–60 (1947). The Court in *Cheney* explained: "Although courts have not confined themselves to an arbitrary and technical definition of jurisdiction, only exceptional circumstances amounting to a judicial usurpation of power, or a clear abuse of discretion, will justify the invocation of this extraordinary remedy." 542 U.S. at 380 (internal quotations and citations omitted).

To obtain a writ of mandamus three requirements must be met:

> First, the party seeking issuance of the writ must have no other adequate means to attain the relief he desires,—a condition designed to ensure that the writ will not be used as a substitute for the regular appeals process. Second, the petitioner must satisfy the burden of showing that his right to issuance of the writ is clear and indisputable. Third, even if the first two prerequisites have been met, the issuing court, in the exercise of its discretion, must be satisfied that the writ is appropriate under the circumstances.

Cheney, 542 U.S. at 380–81; *see also Kerr v. United States Dist. Court for Northern Dist. of Cal.*, 426 U.S. 394, 403 (1976).

Examples of situations where writs of mandamus may be granted are where (1) broad discovery orders have been entered against members of the executive branch; *see Cheney*, 542 U.S. at 384–871; (2) where courts have erroneously ordered the disclosure of privileged documents; *see BankAmerica Corp. Sec. Litig.*, 270 F.3d 639, 641 (8th Cir. 2001); (3) where motions for disqualification or recusal have been erroneously denied; *see In re School Asbestos Litigation*, 977 F.2d 764, 777–78; and (4) where courts have erroneously ruled that a party has no right to a jury trial; *see Dairy Queen, Inc. v. Wood*, 369 U.S. 472 (1962); *Beacon Theatres, Inc. v. Westover*, 359 U.S. 500, 511 (1959).

f. Pendent Appellate Jurisdiction

When a court of appeals has jurisdiction to review a particular interlocutory order—e.g. under one of the exceptions discussed above—a party may seek review of another issue in the case that is not otherwise immediately subject to review by asserting "pendent appellate jurisdiction" over that issue.

Pendent appellate jurisdiction is a narrow doctrine that allows courts of appeals "with jurisdiction over one ruling to review, conjunctively, related rulings that are not themselves independently appealable," but only where the related rulings are "inextricably intertwined" with or "necessary to ensure meaningful review of" decisions that are properly before the court on interlocutory appeal. *Swint v. Chambers County Comm'n*, 514 U.S. 35, 50–51 (1995).

This inquiry is often fact specific. For example, in *National R.R. Passenger Corp. v. ExpressTrak, L.L.C.*, 330 F.3d 523, 528 (D.C. Cir. 2003) the court of appeals determined that the district court's grant of an injunction compelling the parties to perform under their leases during arbitration "was 'inextricably intertwined' with, and, in fact, dependent upon, its determination that the parties' dispute was arbitrable." The court noted that "[a]fter determining that the parties' dispute was governed by the arbitration clause in the Operating Agreement, to wit section 6.6, rather than the litigating clause in the Leases, to wit section 30 of the Sublease, the district court enjoined the parties to continue business operations 'as called for by [s]ection 6.6(e)'—a provision found only in the arbitration clause of the Operating Agreement." *Id.*

On the other hand, in *Meredith v. Oregon*, 321 F.3d 807, 815 (9th Cir. 2003), the court determined that that review of district court's decision not to abstain under the *Younger* doctrine was "necessary to ensure meaningful review of" the district court's preliminary grant of a preliminary injunction which was before the court on interlocutory appeal, even though the rulings were not inextricably intertwined. (*Younger* abstention is an equitable doctrine holding that a federal court generally should refrain from interfering with a pending state court proceeding. *Id.* at 815 n. 8).

III. State Systems

States have their own versions of the final judgment rule, along with exceptions, as well as processes for review by permission or extraordinary writ.

As discussed above, in the federal system a final appealable judgment is defined narrowly, 28 U.S.C. § 1291, but there are many exceptions set out in other statutes and procedural rules. In contrast, some states set out in one statute a long, detailed list of orders that are considered final and appealable. These lists include the types of orders that are similar to those that would be appealable as exceptions to the final judgment rule under the federal system. For example, California Code of Civil Procedure § 904.1 "Appealable Judgments and Orders" provides:

(a) An appeal, other than in a limited civil case, is to the court of appeal. An appeal, other than in a limited civil case, may be taken from any of the following:

(1) From a judgment, except (A) an interlocutory judgment, other than as provided in paragraphs (8), (9), and (11), or (B) a judgment of contempt that is made final and conclusive by Section 1222.

(2) From an order made after a judgment made appealable by paragraph (1).

(3) From an order granting a motion to quash service of summons or granting a motion to stay the action on the ground of inconvenient forum, or from a written order of dismissal under Section 581d following an order granting a motion to dismiss the action on the ground of inconvenient forum.

(4) From an order granting a new trial or denying a motion for judgment notwithstanding the verdict.

(5) From an order discharging or refusing to discharge an attachment or granting a right to attach order.

(6) From an order granting or dissolving an injunction, or refusing to grant or dissolve an injunction.

(7) From an order appointing a receiver.

(8) From an interlocutory judgment, order, or decree, hereafter made or entered in an action to redeem real or personal property from a mortgage thereof, or a lien thereon, determining the right to redeem and directing an accounting.

(9) From an interlocutory judgment in an action for partition determining the rights and interests of the respective parties and directing partition to be made.

(10) From an order made appealable by the provisions of the Probate Code or the Family Code.

(11) From an interlocutory judgment directing payment of monetary sanctions by a party or an attorney for a party if the amount exceeds five thousand dollars ($5,000).

(12) From an order directing payment of monetary sanctions by a party or an attorney for a party if the amount exceeds five thousand dollars ($5,000).

(13) From an order granting or denying a special motion to strike under Section 425.16.

(b) Sanction orders or judgments of five thousand dollars ($5,000) or less against a party or an attorney for a party may be reviewed on an appeal by that party after entry of final judgment in the main action, or, at the discretion of the court of appeal, may be reviewed upon petition for an extraordinary writ.

Notice, for example, that orders regarding injunctions and orders appointing a receiver are listed as appealable. § 904.1(a)(6) &(7). These types of orders are addressed under the federal system in 28 U.S.C. § 1292(a)(1) & (2).

Georgia Code § 5-6-34 also sets out a lengthy and detailed list of appealable judgments and orders (orders regarding receivers and injunctions are listed in subsection (a)(4)):

(a) Appeals may be taken to the Supreme Court and the Court of Appeals from the following judgments and rulings of the superior courts, the constitutional city courts, and such other courts or tribunals from which appeals are authorized by the Constitution and laws of this state:

(1) All final judgments, that is to say, where the case is no longer pending in the court below, except as provided in Code Section 5-6-35;

(2) All judgments involving applications for discharge in bail trover and contempt cases;

(3) All judgments or orders directing that an accounting be had;

(4) All judgments or orders granting or refusing applications for receivers or for interlocutory or final injunctions;

(5) All judgments or orders granting or refusing applications for attachment against fraudulent debtors;

(6) Any ruling on a motion which would be dispositive if granted with respect to a defense that the action is barred by Code Section 16-11-173;

(7) All judgments or orders granting or refusing to grant mandamus or any other extraordinary remedy, except with respect to temporary restraining orders;

(8) All judgments or orders refusing applications for dissolution of corporations created by the superior courts;

(9) All judgments or orders sustaining motions to dismiss a caveat to the probate of a will;

(10) All judgments or orders entered pursuant to subsection (c) of Code Section 17-10-6.2; and

(11) All judgments or orders in child custody cases including, but not limited to, awarding or refusing to change child custody or holding or declining to hold persons in contempt of such child custody judgment or orders.

Note: In addition to interlocutory orders set out by statute, courts in California and Georgia employ versions of the collateral order doctrine in order to review qualifying interlocutory orders. *Marsh v. Mountain Zephyr, Inc.*, 50 Cal. Rptr. 2d 493, 498–99 (Cal. App. 1996); *In re Paul*, 513 S.E.2d 219, 221 (Ga. 1999).

More similar to the federal system in form, Illinois, for example, generally allows appeals only from a final judgment, Ill. Sup. Ct. R. 301, and a final judgment is defined as "one that fixes absolutely and finally the rights of the parties in the lawsuit; it is final if it determines the litigation on the merits so that, if affirmed, the only thing remaining is to proceed with the execution of the judgment." *In re Marriage of Link*, 839 N.E.2d 678, 680 (Ill. App. Ct. 2005). Illinois Supreme Court Rule 307 "Interlocutory Appeals as of Right" then sets out a list of exceptions:

(a) **Orders Appealable; Time.** An appeal may be taken to the Appellate Court from an interlocutory order of court:

(1) granting, modifying, refusing, dissolving, or refusing to dissolve or modify an injunction;

(2) appointing or refusing to appoint a receiver or sequestrator;

(3) giving or refusing to give other or further powers or property to a receiver or sequestrator already appointed;

(4) placing or refusing to place a mortgagee in possession of mortgaged premises;

(5) appointing or refusing to appoint a receiver, liquidator, rehabilitator, or other similar officer for a bank, savings and loan association, currency exchange, insurance company, or other financial institution, or granting or refusing to grant custody of the institution or requiring turnover of any of its assets;

(6) terminating parental rights or granting, denying or revoking temporary commitment in adoption proceedings commenced pursuant to section 5 of the Adoption Act (750 ILCS 50/05);

(7) determining issues raised in proceedings to exercise the right of eminent domain under section 20-5-10 of the Eminent Domain Act, but the procedure for appeal and stay shall be as provided in that section.

Note, however, that the Illinois courts have expressly declined to adopt or employ the collateral order doctrine. *See In re Olivia C.*, 868 N.E.2d 307, 310 (Ill. App. Ct. 2007).

Wisconsin has one of the strictest approaches to appeals by right, although it allows appeals by permission in specific circumstances. Wis. Stat. Ann. § 808.03 states:

> **(1) Appeals as of right.** A final judgment or a final order of a circuit court may be appealed as a matter of right to the court of appeals unless otherwise expressly provided by law. A final judgment or final order is a judgment, order or disposition that disposes of the entire matter in litigation as to one or more of the parties, whether rendered in an action or special proceeding....
>
> **(2) Appeals by permission.** A judgment or order not appealable as a matter of right under sub. (1) may be appealed to the court of appeals in advance of a final judgment or order upon leave granted by the court if it determines that an appeal will:
>
> (a) Materially advance the termination of the litigation or clarify further proceedings in the litigation;
>
> (b) Protect the petitioner from substantial or irreparable injury; or
>
> (c) Clarify an issue of general importance in the administration of justice.

Courts in Wisconsin also have not adopted the collateral order doctrine. In *Arneson v. Jezwinski*, 556 N.W.2d 721, 724–25 (Wis. 1996), the court noted that some courts reviewed interlocutory orders denying qualified immunity under the collateral order doctrine. However, the court instead extended its "superintending authority" granted by the state constitution to establish an appeal of right for such orders, determining that "a petition [for review] would always fall within the criteria for leave to appeal under Wis. Stat. § 808.03(2)(a) and (b)." Note that requiring automatic grants of interlocutory appeal pursuant to the Wisconsin Supreme Court's superintending power is generally disfavored. *Lassa v. Rongstad*, 718 N.W.2d 673, 694 (Wis. 2006).

In contrast, New York allows immediate appeals of a wide variety of interlocutory orders. In fact, in New York orders that are not appealable as of right are more the exception than the rule, and any of these orders may be appealed by permission. New York Civil Practice Law and Rule 5701 states:

(a) **Appeals as of right.** An appeal may be taken to the appellate division as of right in an action, originating in the supreme court or a county court:

1. from any final or interlocutory judgment except one entered subsequent to an order of the appellate division which disposes of all the issues in the action; or

2. from an order not specified in subdivision (b), where the motion it decided was made upon notice and it:

(i) grants, refuses, continues or modifies a provisional remedy; or

(ii) settles, grants or refuses an application to resettle a transcript or statement on appeal; or

(iii) grants or refuses a new trial; except where specific questions of fact arising upon the issues in an action triable by the court have been tried by a jury, pursuant to an order for that purpose, and the order grants or refuses a new trial upon the merits; or

(iv) involves some part of the merits; or

(v) affects a substantial right; or

(vi) in effect determines the action and prevents a judgment from which an appeal might be taken; or

(vii) determines a statutory provision of the state to be unconstitutional, and the determination appears from the reasons given for the decision or is necessarily implied in the decision; or

(viii) grants a motion for leave to reargue made pursuant to subdivision (d) of rule 2221or determines a motion for leave to renew made pursuant to subdivision (e) of rule 2221; or

3. from an order, where the motion it decided was made upon notice, refusing to vacate or modify a prior order, if the prior order would have been appealable as of right under paragraph two had it decided a motion made upon notice.

(b) **Orders not appealable as of right.** An order is not appealable to the appellate division as of right where it:

1. is made in a proceeding against a body or officer pursuant to article 78; or

2. requires or refuses to require a more definite statement in a pleading; or

3. orders or refuses to order that scandalous or prejudicial matter be stricken from a pleading.

(c) **Appeals by permission.** An appeal may be taken to the appellate division from any order which is not appealable as of right in an action originating in the supreme court or a county court by permission of a judge who made the order granted before application to a justice of the appellate division; or by permission of a justice of the appellate division in the department to which the appeal could be taken, upon refusal by the judge who made the order or upon direct application.

New York courts do not appear to have expressly adopted, employed, or rejected the collateral order doctrine. Presumably because the doctrine has not been necessary in order to gain review of an interlocutory order in that state.

As demonstrated by these examples, states have a variety of approaches and rules governing the appealability of judgments and orders—with both marked and subtle differences. Thus it is important to familiarize yourself with the rules applicable in the jurisdiction in which you are considering an appeal, and not to automatically assume the order at issue is immediately appealable—or not.

Checkpoints

- Not every decision of a trial court is immediately appealable.

- Under the "final judgment rule" an appeal may be taken only from a "final judgment" or "final decision." 28 U.S.C. § 1291.

- The final judgment rule generally requires that all issues in a case be decided by the trial court before any issue may be reviewed by the court of appeals.

- The final judgment rule avoids piecemeal appeals — separate appeals of separate rulings throughout the course of the litigation.

- Orders that are not final judgments are generally referred to as "interlocutory orders" and appeals from them, when permitted, are often called "interlocutory appeals."

- There are exceptions to the final judgment rule, including:

  - The collateral order doctrine, which allows an appeal from a decision that does not terminate the litigation, but which presents an issue completely separate from the merits of the underlying action that cannot be effectively reviewed in an appeal from the final judgment.

Checkpoints *continued*

- Where there are multiple claims or parties, partial final judgment as to one or more but fewer that all the claims or parties may be entered under Federal Rule of Civil Procedure 54(b).

- Appeals of interlocutory orders regarding injunctions, 28 U.S.C. § 1292(a)(1), and appointing a receiver, 28 U.S.C. § 1292(a)(2).

- Appeals of interlocutory orders involving controlling questions of law under 28 U.S.C. § 1292(b).

- Interlocutory appeals of class certification decisions under Federal Rule of Civil Procedure 23(f).

- Review by extraordinary writ under 28 U.S.C. § 1651(a).

- Pendent Appellate Jurisdiction.

- States have their own versions of the final judgment rule, along with exceptions, as well as processes for review by permission or extraordinary writ. Research on this point in the applicable jurisdiction is essential.

Chapter 4

Initiating an Appeal

Roadmap

- An appeal is initiated by filing a notice of appeal — usually in the trial court or court of original jurisdiction. Although in some states the notice is filed in the appellate court.

- Time limits for filing the notice of appeal are usually strictly enforced.

- Filing a notice of appeal generally will not stay execution of the judgment. Although in some jurisdictions, including the federal system, there is a short automatic stay of certain judgments.

- Execution of a money judgment can be stayed by posting a supersedeas bond in an amount to secure the amount of the judgment plus anticipated post-judgment interest.

- Appellants who cannot afford to post a bond may apply to the trial court for a stay without bond or with a reduced bond. If granted, the trial court will usually impose conditions to attempt to assure the judgment-creditor will be paid if the judgment is affirmed on appeal.

- Non-monetary judgments, e.g., injunctions, generally are not automatically stayed by the posting of a supersedeas bond. Appellants may apply to the trial court for a stay of an injunction pending appeal, however, and as a condition of granting a stay the court may require a bond.

- Filing a notice of appeal in many circumstances will divest the trial court of jurisdiction and vest jurisdiction with the appellate court. However, the trial court usually retains jurisdiction to:

  - Rule on motions for attorneys fees and sanctions;

  - Supervise or ensure compliance with injunctions it entered;

  - Correct clerical errors; *see* Fed. R. App. P. 60.

I. Notice of Appeal: Contents and Requirements

a. Basic Requirements — Federal and Many State Court Systems

In the federal and many state court systems the notice of appeal is a simple, one to two page document whose purpose is simply to notify the other parties as well as the trial and appellate courts that a party intends to seek review of the judgment or order specified. *See* Fed. R. App. P. 3. The notice should:

- Contain the trial court caption and docket number;
- Specify the party or parties that are appealing;
- Designate the order, judgment or part thereof being appealed;
- Name the court to which the appeal is taken;
- Be signed by the attorney (or the party appealing if pro se).

Federal Rules of Appellate Procedure, Form 1 sets out the suggested form for a notice of appeal from a district court:

FORM 1. NOTICE OF APPEAL TO A COURT OF APPEALS FROM A JUDGMENT OR ORDER OF A DISTRICT COURT

United States District Court for the
_____ District of _____

File Number

A.B., Plaintiff }
}
}
v. } Notice of Appeal
}
C.D., Defendant }

Notice is hereby given that _(here name all parties taking the appeal)_, (plaintiffs/defendants) in the above named case, hereby appeal to the United States Court of Appeals for the _____ Circuit (from the final judgment) (from an order (describing it)) entered in this action on the_____ day of_____, 20___.

(s)_____
Attorney _____
Address: _____

Under Federal Rule of Appellate Procedure 3(c)(4), "An appeal must not be dismissed for informality of form or title of the notice of appeal, or for failure to name a party whose intent to appeal is otherwise clear from the notice." In other words, the notice of appeal will be liberally construed. Thus, "a notice of appeal which names the final judgment is sufficient to support review of all earlier orders that merge in the final judgment." *McBride v. CITGO Petroleum Corp.*, 281 F.3d 1099, 1104 (10th Cir. 2002) (collecting and discussing cases). In fact, it is best to designate the entire final judgment generally, rather than specific rulings, orders, or portions of the judgment, which could limit review to only the issues specified. *See Riccard v. Prudential Ins. Co.*, 307 F.3d 1277, 1290 n. 12 (11th Cir. 2002).

A notice of appeal filed pro se is considered to be filed on behalf of the person signing the notice, his or her spouse and minor children, Fed. R. App. P. 3(c)(2), and a notice of appeal filed by a qualified representative of a class includes the whole class — even if the class has not been certified. Fed. R. App. P. 3(c)(3).

b. Additional Requirements — Certain State Court Systems

Many states only require simple notices of appeal — the same or similar to that described in Federal Rule of Appellate Procedure 3. However, some states require the notice to set out additional information or details, or require additional documents with more detailed information, be filed with the notice of appeal. Thus, it is important for attorneys always to be aware of — i.e., to actually look up — the up-to-date rules applicable in the jurisdiction in which they intend to pursue their appeal.

For example, Colorado Appellate Rule 3(d) contains a lengthy list of requirements:

(d) Contents of the Notice of Appeal in Civil Cases (Other Than District Court Review of Agency Actions and Appeals From State Agencies). The notice of appeal shall set forth:

(1) A caption that complies in form with C.A.R. 32 [regarding typeface and paper size]. In the caption:

(A) The case title in compliance with C.A.R. 12(a) [regarding payment of docketing fees];

(B) The trial court from which the appeal is taken;

(C) The trial court judge;

(D) The party or parties initiating the appeal; and

(E) The trial court case number.

(2) A brief description of the nature of the case including:

(A) A general statement of the nature of the controversy (not to exceed one page);

(B) The judgment, order, or parts being appealed and a statement indicating the basis for the appellate court's jurisdiction;

(C) Whether the judgment or order resolved all issues pending before the trial court including attorneys' fees and costs;

(D) Whether the judgment was made final for purposes of appeal pursuant to C.R.C.P. 54(b);

(E) The date the judgment or order was entered (if there is a question of the date, set forth the details) and the date of mailing to counsel;

(F) Whether there were any extensions granted to file any motion(s) for post-trial relief. If so, the date of the request, whether the request was granted and the date to which filing was extended;

(G) The date any motion for post-trial relief was filed;

(H) The date any motion for post-trial relief was denied or deemed denied under C.R.C.P. 59(j); and

(I) Whether there were any extensions granted to file any notice(s) of appeal. If so, the date of the request, whether the request was granted and the date to which filing was extended.

(3) An advisory listing of the issues to be raised on appeal;

(4) Whether the transcript of any evidence taken before the trial court or any administrative agency is necessary to resolve the issues raised on appeal, the name of the court reporter, and the approximate length of any transcript of testimony anticipated to be filed in this action;

(5) As to filings in the Court of Appeals only, state whether or not a preargument conference is requested;

(6) The names of counsel for the parties, their addresses, telephone numbers, and registration numbers;

(7) An appendix containing a copy of the judgment or order being appealed, the findings of the court, if any, the motion for new trial,

if any, and a copy of the trial court's order granting or denying leave to proceed in forma pauperis if appellant is filing without docket fee pursuant to C.A.R. 12(b); and

(8) A certificate of service, in compliance with C.A.R. 25 showing service of a copy of the notice of appeal (with attachments) on the trial court and all other parties to the action in the trial court.

In most states the level of detail that is required in Colorado's notice of appeal is not required until later in the appeal process when a "docketing statement" is filed to aid the appellate court in processing the appeal. Some states, however, require a docketing statement to be filed with the notice of appeal. *See* Ala. R. App. P. 3(e) (requiring the notice of appeal be accompanied by a docketing statement that sets forth the basis for appellate court jurisdiction, describes the nature of case, and lists the potential issues on appeal and the length of the trial, if any).

In some states the additional information required in the notice of appeal pertains to the record on appeal or to reporters' transcripts. For example, in Indiana the notice of appeal should contain a request for the trial clerk court to assemble the entire record and a designation of all portions of the reporter's transcript "necessary to present fairly and decide the issues on appeal." Ind. R. App. P. 9(f). Similarly, in Oregon the notice must contain a designation of the portions of the transcript to be prepared as well as the exhibits to be included in the record in addition to the trial court's file. Or. R. App. P. 2.05(6). In Virginia, the notice of appeal must state "whether any transcript or statement of facts, testimony, and other incidents of the case will be filed" and if the notice must be accompanied by a certificate stating that the transcript has been ordered from the court reporter. Va. Sup. Ct. R. 5A:6(b), (d)(4).

For further discussion regarding the record on appeal see Chapter 6.

II. Filing the Notice of Appeal

a. Location

An appeal is initiated by filing the notice of appeal—usually in the trial court or court of original jurisdiction. *See* Fed. R. App. P. 3(a)(1). This is the court that entered the final judgment or appealable order and that has custody of the documents and exhibits that were filed in the case. The majority of state court systems also require the notice of appeal to be filed in the trial court. However, in a few states, e.g., Alaska, Colorado, Michigan, New Hampshire, and Oregon, the notice of appeal is filed in the appellate court. Alaska R. App. P. 204(b); Colo. App. R. 3(a); Mich. Ct. R. 7.101(c)(1); N.H. Sup. Ct. R. 7(2); O.R.S. § 19.240(3).

In the federal system, notices of appeal that are mistakenly, but timely, filed in the appellate court instead of the district court are considered valid — the appellate court clerk is directed to note the date the notice was filed and transmit the notice to the district court. Fed. R. App. P. 4(d). Many states have adopted a similar rule and consider the appeal valid if timely filed in an incorrect court. *See, e.g.,* Fla. R. App. P. 9.040(b); Miss. R. Ct. 4(a); Nev. R. App. P. 4(e); Vt. R. App. P. 4; *Wilkinson v. Fabry,* 869 P.2d 182 (Ariz. App. 1992) (holding that a notice of appeal timely but incorrectly filed in the appellate court or in the wrong trial court can be effective to confer jurisdiction on the appellate court).

In some states, however, a notice of appeal that is timely but is filed in the incorrect court is not effective to initiate an appeal. *See Swinkle v. Illinois Civil Service Comm'n,* 903 N.E.2d 746 (Ill. App. 2009) (appellate court held it had no jurisdiction over an appeal where the notice was timely filed in the appellate court but not filed in the trial court until after the time to file an appeal had expired).

Having to resort to "mistaken filing" exceptions is suboptimal. Thus, before attorneys file a notice of appeal it is important that they confirm in which court the notice should be filed, and then ensure that it is, in fact, timely filed there. It may seem inconceivable that an attorney would mistakenly file a notice of appeal, for example, in a different trial court than the one that heard the case. With electronic filing, however, that can happen with the push of a button.

b. Time Limits

1. Generally

Time limits for filing a notice of appeal are often considered "jurisdictional" — meaning that if the notice of appeal is not filed within a specified time limit, the appeal must be dismissed. Although in some jurisdictions, including the federal system, relief for failing to timely appeal is available under limited circumstance. See Section b(5) below.

Often the notice of appeal must be filed within a specified number of days (typically anywhere from 10 to 180) after the entry of the judgment or order being appealed. Timely filing the notice of appeal can present many challenges for counsel because the time within which a notice of appeal varies from jurisdiction to jurisdiction and can depend on:

• the type of case,

- the identity of the parties,

- whether another party has filed a notice of appeal,

- the processes used in entering the judgment and notifying the parties, and

- the existence of post trial motions.

Thus, it is very important that attorneys know and understand the current rules applicable in the jurisdiction in which they intend to pursue their appeal. A very good overview of the filing and timing requirements for notice of appeal in each state and federal jurisdiction is found in C. Flango & D. Rottman, *Appellate Court Procedures* (Williamsburg, Va.: National Center for State Courts, 1998). However, this overview is no substitute for checking the actual, governing procedural rules as amendments occur, albeit infrequently, in most jurisdictions.

2. The Federal System

Federal Rule of Appellate Procedure 4 governs time limits for filing an appeal in federal court. In civil cases the time limit for filing the notice of appeal is within 30 days after the entry of the judgment or order, unless the United States or its officer or agency is a party, in which case, the time limit for all parties is 60 days. Fed. R. App. P. 4(a)(1). If one party files a notice of appeal, any other party may file a notice of appeal within 14 days after the first notice was filed, or within the regular applicable time period after the entry of judgment set out in Rule 4(a)(1)—whichever period ends later. Fed. R. App. P. 4(a)(3).

Also, if post-trial motions are timely filed (1) for judgment as a matter of law, (2) to amend or make additional findings, (3) for attorneys fees (if the trial court extends the time for appeal), (4) for a new trial, (5) to alter or amend the judgment, or (6) for relief from judgment, the time to file an appeal starts running from the entry of the order disposing of the last remaining motion. Fed R. App. P. 4(a)(4).

Rule 4(a)(7) addresses the meaning of *entry*:

(7) Entry Defined.

(A) A judgment or order is entered for purposes of this Rule 4(a):

(i) if Federal Rule of Civil Procedure 58(a) does not require a separate document, when the judgment or order is entered in the civil docket under Federal Rule of Civil Procedure 79(a); or

(ii) if Federal Rule of Civil Procedure 58(a) requires a separate document, when the judgment or order is entered in the civil docket under Federal Rule of Civil Procedure 79(a) and when the earlier of these events occurs:

• the judgment or order is set forth on a separate document, or

• 150 days have run from entry of the judgment or order in the civil docket under Federal Rule of Civil Procedure 79(a).

Note that counsel may check the dockets of federal district courts through the Public Access to Court Electronic Records (PACER) service found at pacer.gov, and should look specifically for terms like "judgment entered" or "entry of judgment" and the corresponding date.

In federal criminal cases the time limit for a defendant to file an appeal is 10 days after entry of the judgment or order being appealed or 10 days after the filing of the government's notice of appeal—whichever is later. In contrast, when the government is entitled to appeal its notice of appeal may be filed up to 30 days after entry of the judgment or order being appealed or the filing of a notice of appeal by any defendant—whichever is later. Fed. R. App. P. 4(b)(1).

If the defendant makes a timely post-trial motion (1) for judgment of acquittal, (2) for a new trial, or (3) for arrest of judgment, the notice of appeal from a judgment of conviction must be filed within 10 days after the entry of the order disposing of the last such remaining motion, or within 10 days after the entry of the judgment of conviction, whichever period ends later. Fed. R. App. P. 4(b)(3).

Rule 4(b)(6) succinctly defines entry for criminal cases: "A judgment or order is entered for purposes of this Rule 4(b) when it is entered on the criminal docket." Counsel may access the criminal dockets of district courts though PACER.

3. Other Jurisdictions—Some Examples

Time limits for filing the notice of appeal and their triggering events also vary among the state court systems.

For example, in California civil cases the triggering event is usually service of notice of the entry of judgment: A notice of appeal must be filed within 60 days after notice of entry of judgment or a file stamped copy of the judgment is served. If neither is served, the time limit for filing the notice of appeal is 180 days from the entry of judgment. Cal. R. Ct. 8.104. The appeal deadline is also extended in the event of a motion for new trial, to vacate the judgment, for judgment notwithstanding the verdict, for reconsideration, generally to 30 days after service of notice denying the motion. Cal. R. Ct. 8.108(b)–(d). In criminal cases the notice of appeal must be filed by either party, the defendant or the People, within 60 days after the judgment is rendered or the order being appealed from is made. Cal. R. Ct. 8.308.

In Wisconsin civil cases the notice of appeal must be filed within 45 days of entry of a final judgment or order appealed from—if written notice of the entry of a final judgment or order is given within 21 days of the final judgment or order. If written notice is not given, the time limit is 90 days from entry of the judgment or order. Wis. Stat. § 808.04. In criminal cases, to initiate an appeal, the defendant must file a "notice of intent to pursue postconviction or postdisposition relief" within 20 days after the date of sentencing or other final adjudication. Wis. Stat. § 809.30(2)(b).

On the other hand, in Georgia, for both civil and criminal cases, the time limit for filing the notice of appeal is 30 days from the entry of judgment, unless a motion for new trial or a motion for judgment notwithstanding the verdict is filed, in which case, the time limit is 30 days from entry of the order ruling on the motion. Ga. Code Ann. § 5-6-38(a). Similarly, in Illinois the time limit for filing the notice of appeal in both civil and criminal cases is 30 days after the entry of the final judgment appealed from or if a motion directed against the judgment is timely filed, within 30 days after the entry of the order disposing of the motion. Ill. Sup. Ct. R. 303(a), 606(b).

As this section makes clear, the rules governing initiation of an appeal, although similar in their general format across jurisdictions, vary considerably in their specifics. As a result, one must take pains to research and verify the process and procedure in the particular jurisdiction involved. Especially in those places where proper initiation of an appeal is considered "jurisdictional," failure to correctly do so can be of enormous prejudice to one's client and can easily lead to malpractice claims against the attorney and firm involved.

4. Premature Notices of Appeal

Sometimes notices of appeal are filed prematurely, e.g., before the judgment is entered, before notice of entry of the judgment is served, or before a post-trial motion is ruled upon. In many jurisdictions a premature notice of appeal is treated as timely filed on or immediately after the date of the entry of judgment or the disposition of the post-trial motion.

For example, Federal Rule of Appellate Procedure 4(a)(2) provides that "[a] notice filed after the court announces a decision or order—but before entry of the judgment or order—is treated as filed on the date of and after the entry." Similarly, "[i]f a party files a notice of appeal after the court announces or enters a judgment—but before it disposes of any [post-trial] motion listed in Rule 4(a)(4)(A)—the notice becomes effective to appeal a judgment or order, in whole or in part, when the order disposing of the last such remaining motion is entered." Fed. R. App. P. 4(b)(i). *See, e.g.,* Cal. R. Ct. 8.101(e) ("(1)

A notice of appeal filed after judgment is rendered but before it is entered is valid and is treated as filed immediately after entry of judgment. (2) The reviewing court may treat a notice of appeal filed after the superior court has announced its intended ruling, but before it has rendered judgment, as filed immediately after entry of judgment"); Ill. Sup. Ct. R. 303(a)(1) ("A notice of appeal filed after the court announces a decision, but before the entry of the judgment or order, is treated as filed on the date of and after the entry of the judgment or order."); Tenn. R. App. P. 3(d) ("A prematurely filed notice of appeal shall be treated as filed after the entry of the judgment from which the appeal is taken and on the day thereof"). Wash. R. App. P. 5.2(g) (A notice of appeal or notice for discretionary review filed after the announcement of a decision but before entry of the decision will be treated as filed on the day following the entry of the decision"); Wis. Stat. § 808.04(8) ("If the record discloses that the judgment or order appealed from was entered after the notice of appeal or intent to appeal was filed, the notice shall be treated as filed after that entry and on the day of the entry.").

In some jurisdictions, however, a premature notice of appeal is ineffective to confer jurisdiction on the appellate court and the appeal will be dismissed. This can have dire consequences when counsel do not realize that their premature notice of appeal was ineffective until *after* the time to appeal has expired.

For example in *Welker ex rel. Bradbury v. Teachers Standards and Practices Comm'n*, 27 P.3d 1038, 1041 (Or. 2001), the Oregon Supreme Court held: "A notice of appeal filed before the time to appeal begins to run is jurisdictionally defective." The court then vacated the decision of the intermediate court of appeals as void for lack of jurisdiction, because the notice of appeal had been prematurely filed. In Massachusetts, a notice of appeal filed before disposition of a post-trial motion judgment notwithstanding the verdict, to amend or make additional findings of fact, to alter or amend a judgment, or for a new trial "shall have no effect. A new notice of appeal must be filed within the prescribed time measured from the entry of the order disposing of the motion ." Mass. R. App. P. 4(a).

5. *Relief from the Consequences of Failing to Timely File the Notice of Appeal*

Although time limits for filing the notice of appeal are often thought of as mandatory and jurisdictional, in some jurisdictions and in limited circumstances, it is possible for parties and their counsel to gain relief from the consequences of failing to timely file the notice of appeal. The process and criteria for granting such relief vary by jurisdiction. Some examples:

In the federal system, the district (trial) court may grant relief from failure to timely file the notice of appeal in two categories of cases: (1) in both civil and criminal cases, where the party shows excusable neglect or good cause, Fed. R. App. P. 4(a)(5) & (b)(4); or (2) in civil cases, where the party did not receive notice of entry of the judgment or order being appealed within 21 days after entry. Fed. R. App. P. 4(a)(6).

In the first category, the district court may extend the time to file a notice of appeal if the party moves for an extension within thirty days after the time to appeal has expired and "shows excusable neglect or good cause." Fed. R. App. P. 4(a)(5) & (b)(4). According to the Advisory Committee Notes to Rule 4, the excusable neglect standard applies where there is some fault on the part of the movant that would need to be excused, while the good cause standard applies where the is no fault on the part of the movant. In the case law, however, there is some overlap between the standards.

For example in *Bolarinwa v. Williams*, 593 F.3d 226, 230–31 (2d Cir. 2010) the court concluded both (1) that the appellant showed good cause for failing to timely appeal the dismissal of her petition for habeas corpus because she was waiting for a letter establishing her history of mental illness, and (2) that she could be excused for believing she had to justify her appeal through this letter at the same time she gave notice of it, "given statutory requirement that a habeas petitioner seeking appellate review of the denial of her petition must make a substantial showing of the denial of a constitutional right."

Excusable neglect is a flexible standard. As the Supreme Court stated in *Pioneer Investment Services Co. v. Brunswick Associates Limited P'ship*, 507 U.S. 380, 388 (1993), "Congress plainly contemplated that the courts would be permitted, where appropriate, to accept late filings caused by inadvertence, mistake, or carelessness, as well as by intervening circumstances beyond the party's control." The court also discussed factors to be considered when determining if relief was appropriate:

> [W]e conclude that the determination is at bottom an equitable one, taking account of all relevant circumstances surrounding the party's omission. These include ... the danger of prejudice to the [nonmoving party], the length of the delay and its potential impact on judicial proceedings, the reason for the delay, including whether it was within the reasonable control of the movant, and whether the movant acted in good faith.

Id. at 395.

Of these factors, the reason for delay is usually given the most weight. *Graphic Commc'n Int'l Union, Local 12-N v. Quebecor Printing Providence, Inc.*, 270 F.3d

1, 6 (1st Cir. 2001). Moreover, courts are often reluctant to find excusable neglect "when a party's or counsel's misunderstanding of clear law or misreading of an unambiguous judicial decree is the reason for the delay in filing the notice of appeal." *Id.*

The second "lack of notice" category of grounds for relief allows the district court to "reopen" the time to file an appeal for a further 14 days, "but only if all the following conditions are satisfied:

> (A) the court finds that the moving party did not receive notice under Federal Rule of Civil Procedure 77(d) of the entry of the judgment or order sought to be appealed within 21 days after entry;
>
> (B) the motion is filed within 180 days after the judgment or order is entered or within 7 days after the moving party receives notice under Federal Rule of Civil Procedure 77(d) of the entry, whichever is earlier; and
>
> (C) the court finds that no party would be prejudiced.

Fed. R. App. P. 4(a)(6). Remember that in the federal system, motions to extend or open the time to appeal are directed to the district court, not the court of appeal.

In contrast, in Texas it is the appellate court that has the discretion to extend the time to file a notice of appeal, provided that the appellant, within 15 days after the deadline for filing the notice of appeal, files (1) the notice of appeal in the trial court, and (2) a motion to extend in the appellate court. Tex. R. App. P. 26.3. Texas appellate courts appear to have a liberal approach to granting extensions under Rule 26.3 — as long as the 15 day deadline is met.

First, a motion to extend "is implied when an appellant, acting in good faith, files an appeal notice within Rule 26.3's 15 day period." *Hone v. Hanafin,* 104 S.W.3d 884, 886 (Tex. 2003). Moreover, the appellant must have only a "reasonable explanation" for failing to timely file a notice of appeal, which means "any plausible statement of circumstances indicating that failure to file within the [specified] period was not deliberate or intentional, but was the result of inadvertence, mistake or mischance." *Id.* (holding appellant's belief that appeal was timely filed was a reasonable explanation). Note, however, that where the notice of appeal is filed after Rule 26.3's 15 day deadline (even shortly after) the appellate court has no jurisdiction to hear the case and will dismiss the appeal. *Strange v. State,* 258 S.W.3d 184 (Tex. App. 2007).

Similarly, in Illinois the appellate court may grant an extension of time to appeal upon a "showing of reasonable excuse" for failure to timely file the notice of appeal. Ill. Sup. Ct. R. 303(e). The motion must be filed within 30 days after the regular deadline to file the notice. *Id.* Reasonable excuse is "intended as a lenient standard" and includes illness of counsel, an honest mistake of counsel, delay in the mail, a snowstorm, and many others." *Bank of Herrin v. Peoples Bank of Marion*, 473 N.E.2d 1298, 1300 (Ill. 1985). In contrast to Texas, in Illinois, a motion to extend will not be implied when a notice to appeal is filed after the regular time to appeal but within Rule 303(e)'s 30 day period and a late filed appeal without a motion to extend will be dismissed . *In re C.J.*, 758 N.E.2d 335, 337 (Ill. App. Ct. 2001) (appellate court lacked jurisdiction over appeal one day after the time to appeal had expired where no motion to file late notice of appeal was filed).

In California appeal deadlines are among the most "jurisdictional." Absent +"the occurrence or danger of an earthquake, fire, or other public emergency, or by the destruction of or danger to a building housing a reviewing court," Cal. R. Ct. R. 8.66(a), "no court may extend the time to file a notice of appeal. If a notice of appeal is filed late, the reviewing court must dismiss the appeal." Cal. R. Ct. R. 8.104(b).

Even if extensions to file a notice of appeal exist in the jurisdiction, attorneys should take pains to avoid having to resort to special provisions, exceptions, or discretion of the courts in order to initiate their appeal. This means ensuring that they file their notice of appeal from the correct and final order or judgment in the right court, and at the right time.

III. Effect of Filing the Notice of Appeal

a. The Judgment Below—Stays Pending Appeal

It can come as a surprise to new attorneys that generally the filing of a notice of appeal will not suspend or prevent execution of the judgment or order appealed from. *See, e.g.,* Fed. R. Civ. P. 62(c) & (d). This means that steps may be taken to collect money or seize property awarded in a judgment and that injunctive relief will go into effect unless a stay pending appeal is obtained.

However, some jurisdictions, including the federal system, do provide a brief automatic stay that prevents immediate enforcement of the judgment. *See, e.g.,* Fed. R. Civ. P. 62(a) (providing for an automatic 14-day stay of enforcement of judgments—other than judgments in actions for injunctions or receiverships, or in judgments directing an accounting in patent cases).

1. Money Judgments — Bonding the Appeal — Supersedeas Bonds

In most jurisdictions, enforcement of judgments for money or property will be stayed upon the posting of a bond — usually called a "supersedeas" bond. The purpose of a supersedeas is "to protect the judgment won in the trial court from becoming uncollectible while the judgment is subjected to appellate review. A successful litigant will have an assured source of funds to meet the amount of the money judgment, costs and post judgment interest after postponing enjoyment of a trial court victory." *Grant v. Superior Court*, 275 Cal. Rptr. 564, 568 (Cal. App. 1990).

Thus, the amount or method for determining the amount of a supersedeas bond (often set by statute or rule of court) usually includes the amount of the judgment, plus post-judgment interest. *See* Cal Code. Civ. P. 917.1(d) (amount of the judgment "together with any interest which may have accrued pending the appeal and entry of the remittitur, and costs which may be awarded against the appellant on appeal"); N.D. Ill. L.R. 62.1 ("amount of the judgment plus one year's interest at the rate provided in 28 U.S.C. § 1961, plus $500 to cover costs"). Alternatively the amount of the bond is expressed as a percentage of the judgment. *See* Pa. R. App. P. 1731(a) (bond to equal "120% of the amount found due by the lower court and remaining unpaid").

In some instances, particularly with large money judgments, the losing party is unable to post a supersedeas bond. In some jurisdictions, including the federal system, appellants may apply to the trial court for a stay with a reduced bond, with alternative security, or without a bond. The issue in these motions is whether and how the judgment can be otherwise protected. *See Endress + Hauser, Inc. v. Hawk Measurement Systems Pty. Ltd.*, 932 F. Supp. 1147, 1148–50 (S.D. Ind. 1996). Alternative security can include letters of credit, security interests in the appellant's property, stock pledges, and pledges of accounts receivable. *Id.* A bond might also be reduced upon an adequate showing by the appellant that it will maintain a net worth sufficient to secure the remainder of the judgment. *Id.*; *Trans World Airlines, Inc. v. Hughes*, 314 F. Supp. 94, 96 (S.D.N.Y. 1970).

Finally, in some cases a stay pending appeal is granted without requiring any bond or alternative security. This may occur where the appellant has a net worth many times greater than the judgment, *Federal Prescription Service, Inc. v. American Pharmaceutical Assoc.*, 636 F.2d 755, 758 (D.C. Cir. 1980), or, in certain cases, where the appellant makes a showing that would have been sufficient to obtain a stay of an injunction under Federal Rule of Civil Procedure 62(d), *Hilton v. Braunskill*, 481 U.S. 770, 776 (1987); *Endress + Hauser, Inc*, 932 F. Supp. at 1148–50. See Section III(a)(2), below.

Note that not all jurisdictions afford courts discretion to stay a money judgment without the posting of a bond. *See, e.g.,* Cal. Code Civ. P. §918(b) ("If the enforcement of the judgment or order would be stayed on appeal only by the giving of an undertaking [bond], a trial court shall not have power, without the consent of the adverse party, to stay the enforcement thereof pursuant to this section for a period which extends for more than 10 days beyond the last date on which a notice of appeal could be filed.").

Finally, an option for appellants who cannot afford to post a bond and cannot otherwise obtain a stay is to file for protection under the Bankruptcy Code because enforcement against the judgment will be prevented by the automatic stay under 11 U.S.C. §362(a)(2).

2. Injunctions

Unlike money judgments, injunctions usually are not automatically stayed by the posting of a supersedeas bond. The 14 day automatic stay under Federal Rule of Civil Procedure 62(a) also does not apply to injunctions. Instead, appellants must first apply to the trial court for a stay pending appeal, and the court may then require the posting of a bond or other security as a condition of granting the stay. For example, Federal Rule of Civil Procedure 62(c) provides: "While an appeal is pending from an interlocutory order or final judgment that grants, dissolves, or denies an injunction, the court may suspend, modify, restore, or grant an injunction on terms for bond or other terms that secure the opposing party's rights."

Courts generally consider four factors in deciding whether to grant a stay pending appeal:

> (1) whether the stay applicant has made a strong showing that he is likely to succeed on the merits; (2) whether the applicant will be irreparably injured absent a stay; (3) whether issuance of the stay will substantially injure the other parties interested in the proceeding; and (4) where the public interest lies.

Hilton v. Braunskill, 481 U.S. 770, 776 (1987).

However, courts take different approaches to this test. Some courts balance the factors—treating no single factor as determinative—but giving great weight to certain factors such as likelihood of success on the merits and irreparable harm. Others treat the 4 factors more like elements[1] and require the appellant to es-

---

1. For discussion regarding the difference between factors and elements see George Kuney and Donna Looper, *Mastering Legal Analysis and Drafting,* 4–5 (Carolina Academic Press 2009).

tablish each factor before considering the next. *See* John Logata, *The Emerging Standards for Issuing Appellate Stays*, 45 Baylor L. Rev. 809 (1993).

b. Jurisdiction of the Trial Court While the Appeal Is Pending

"In general, filing of a notice of appeal confers jurisdiction on the court of appeals and divests the district court of control over those aspects of the case involved in the appeal." *Marrese v. American Academy of Orthopedic Surgeons*, 470 U.S. 373, 379 (1985). Thus, if the appeal is of a collateral order, the trial court would still have jurisdiction of matters not on appeal. *See id.* (noting that an appeal from a judgment of criminal contempt based on noncompliance with a discovery order did not transfer jurisdiction over the entire case to the court of appeals). See Ch. 3 § II(a), regarding the collateral order doctrine.

Moreover, even if the appeal is of the final judgment in the case, the trial court usually retains limited jurisdiction to, for example, supervise or ensure compliance with injunctions it entered, rule on motions for attorney fees, costs and sanctions, and correct clerical or technical errors. *See, e.g.,* Fed. R. Civ. P. 60.

Checkpoints

- The first step in initiating an appeal is preparing the notice of appeal. The contents of the notice of appeal are usually simple. *See* Fed. R. App. P. 3. The notice should:
    - Contain the trial court caption and docket number;
    - Specify the party or parties that are appealing;
    - Designate the judgment or order that is being appealed;
    - Name the court to which the appeal is taken; and
    - Be signed by the attorney or the party appealing if pro se.
- Many state court notices of appeal involve similar basic information, although some states have additional requirements.
- An appeal is initiated by filing a notice of appeal — usually in the trial court or court of original jurisdiction. Although in some states the notice is filed in the appellate court.
- Time limits for filing the notice of appeal are usually strictly enforced.
- The time within which a notice of appeal must be filed varies not only by jurisdiction, but by type of case, identity of the parties, and the process used in entering the order or judgment and notifying the parties.
- Some, but not all, jurisdictions provide that premature notices of appeal shall be deemed timely filed.

Checkpoints *continued*

- In some jurisdictions, including the federal system, relief may be granted for failing to timely file — but only in limited circumstances.

- Filing a notice of appeal generally will not stay execution of the judgment.

- Although in some jurisdictions, including the federal system, there is a short automatic stay of certain judgments.

- Execution of a money judgment can be stayed by posting a supersedeas bond in an amount to secure the amount of the judgment plus anticipated post-judgment interest. Fed. R. App. P. 62(d).

- Appellants who cannot afford to post a bond may apply to the trial court for a stay without bond or with a reduced bond. If granted, the trial court will usually impose conditions to attempt to assure the judgment-creditor will be paid if the judgment is affirmed on appeal.

- Non-monetary judgments, e.g., injunctions, generally are not automatically stayed by the posting of a supersedeas bond.

- Appellants may apply to the trial court for a stay of an injunction pending appeal, however, as a condition of granting a stay the court may require a bond. Fed. R. App. P. 62(c). Courts consider four factors in deciding whether to grant a stay of injunctive relief:

    (1) whether the stay applicant has made a strong showing that he is likely to succeed on the merits;

    (2) whether the applicant will be irreparably injured absent a stay;

    (3) whether issuance of the stay will substantially injure the other parties interested in the proceeding; and

    (4) where the public interest lies.

- Filing a notice of appeal in many circumstances will divest the trial court of jurisdiction and vest jurisdiction with the appellate court. However, the trial court usually retains jurisdiction to:

    - Rule on motions for attorneys fees and sanctions;

    - Supervise or ensure compliance with injunctions it entered; and

    - Correct clerical errors; *see* Fed. R. App. P. 60

Chapter 5

Parties and Non-Parties on Appeal

Roadmap

- Generally, only parties to an action that qualify as "persons aggrieved," original parties, substituted parties, or intervenors, have standing to appeal a decision.

- To have standing to appeal, one must have had standing to sue. Standing is part of "case or controversy" requirement in Article III, Section 2, clause 1 of the Constitution.

- Broadly speaking, appellate courts are not permitted to decide cases or issues that have become moot. There are a limited number of exceptions to this rule.

- Interested third parties that are not parties to an action may participate in an appeal as amicus curiae (friend of the court) if permitted to do so by the appellate court.

I. General Rule: Parties That Are Aggrieved

The general rule is that only parties to an action may appeal a judgment or an order in that action. Indeed, federal and state rules regarding initiating appeals require that the notice of appeal specify the party or parties appealing the judgment or order. *See, e.g.,* Fed. R. App. P. 3(e). (Notices of appeal are discussed in Chapter 4 § I(a) & (b)). In addition, the party or parties appealing usually must be "aggrieved." As the Supreme Court has explained: "Ordinarily, only a party aggrieved by a judgment or order of a district court may exercise the statutory right to appeal therefrom. A party who receives all that he has sought generally is not aggrieved by the judgment affording the relief and cannot appeal from it." *Deposit Guar. Nat'l Bank v. Roper,* 445 U.S. 326, 333 (1980).

a. Parties

"The rule that only parties to a lawsuit, or those that properly become parties, may appeal an adverse judgment, is well settled." *Marino v. Ortiz*, 484 U.S. 301, 304 (1988). The Supreme Court has strictly defined "party" as "one by or against whom a lawsuit is brought." *United States ex rel. Eisenstein v. City of New York*, 129 S. Ct. 2230, 2234 (2009) (quoting Black's Law Dictionary 1154 (8th ed. 2004)). This would include parties originally named, parties that are added by plaintiffs in amended complaints, *see, e.g.,* Fed. R. Civ. P. 15, and parties that are added by defendants by impleader or cross-claim, *see, e.g.,* Fed. R. Civ. P. 14. Persons may properly become parties on their own only by intervening in the action— "the requisite method for a nonparty to become a party to a lawsuit." *Marino v. Ortiz*, 484 U.S. 301, 304 (1988). (Intervention is discussed in Section I(c), below.

The Supreme Court has been resistant to exceptions or expansions of the rule limiting appeals to named and intervening parties. For example, in *Marino v. Ortiz*, the Court refused to allow a group of white police officers to appeal a consent decree approving the settlement of a racial discrimination class action brought by minority officers. *Id.* The Court acknowledged that the judgment affected the interests of the white officers, but noted the white officers were not original parties to the action, and although they presented their objections to the settlement at a hearing before the district court, they did not seek to intervene in the action prior to judgment or for purposes of appeal. *Id.*

b. Appeals by Non-Parties

In *Devlin v. Scardelletti*, 536 U.S. 1 (2002), the Supreme Court created a narrow exception to the rule limiting appeals to named and intervening parties, holding that unnamed class members who timely object to approval of a class action settlement may bring an appeal without first intervening. The Court stated "[w]hat is most important to this case is that nonnamed class members are parties to the proceedings in the sense of being bound by the settlement." *Devlin*, 536 U.S. at 10 (2002). The Court distinguished *Marino v. Ortiz*, 484 U.S. 301 (1988), *supra*, noting in that case the white police officers were not members of the class of minority officers that had brought the racial discrimination action and "[a]lthough the settlement affected them, the District Court's decision did not finally dispose of any right or claim they might have had because they were not members of the class." *Devlin*, 536 U.S. at 9.

Some federal circuits have also developed more flexible balancing tests for determining whether a non-party may appeal. These tests have two or three factors, a key factor being whether the non-party participated in the lower court proceedings. *See Keith v. Volpe*, 118 F.3d 1386, 1391 (9th Cir. 1997) (non-parties allowed to "appeal a district court order where: (1) the appellant participated in the district court proceedings even though not a party, and; (2) the equities of the case weigh in favor of hearing the appeal"); *S.E.C. v. Forex Asset Management LLC*, 242 F.3d 325, 329 (5th Cir. 2001) (courts examine "whether [1] the non-party actually participated in the proceedings below, [2] the equities weigh in favor of hearing the appeal, and [3] the non-party has a personal stake in the outcome ").

Many states have adopted similar flexible tests for determining whether a non-party may appeal. For example, in Minnesota one may become a party and appeal a judgment by participating in the lower court proceedings and having an interest in the outcome—even if he or she has not been named or intervened in the lawsuit. *Annandale Advocate v. City of Annandale*, 435 N.W.2d 24, 27 n. 1 (Minn. 1989) (in newspaper's action to obtain investigative report concerning the discharge of a police chief, the chief could appeal an order releasing portions of the report despite not being named as a party or intervening in the action; the chief "was party by virtue of his participation in the lower court proceedings and his obvious interest in the outcome."). In *Federated Mut. Ins. Co. v. McNeal*, 943 So.2d 658, 663 (Miss. 2006), the Mississippi Supreme Court followed the Fifth Circuit's test articulated in *S.E.C. v. Forex Asset Management LLC* , 242 F.3d 325, 329 (5th Cir. 2001), *supra*, in allowing an appeal by an insurance company who was not named and did not intervene in the underlying lawsuit but who participated and had an interest in the proceedings. The court noted that no one had objected to the insurance company's participation in the trial court or pursuit of the appeal. *See also In re Orshansky*, 804 A.2d 1077, 1090 (D.C. 2002) (applying similar test).

Finally, non-parties are generally allowed to appeal individual orders specifically directed at them. *See, e.g., Church of Scientology v. United States*, 506 U.S. 9, 18 n. 11 (1992) (discovery order directed at a disinterested third party is immediately appealable); *Samnorwood Indep. School Dist. v. Texas Educ. Agency*, 533 F.3d 258, 265–66 (5th Cir. 2008) (non-parties have standing to appeal injunctions purporting to bind them or adversely affect their interests); *Byrd v. Reno*, 180 F.3d 298, 300 (D.C. Cir. 1999) (non-party to a proceeding can obtain immediate review of a civil contempt order).

c. Intervention

Intervention is the means by which a non-party becomes a party to a proceeding and may then appeal a final adverse order or judgment. *Marino v. Ortiz*, 484 U.S. 301, 304 (1988). For example, Federal Rule of Civil Procedure 24(a) provides for intervention as of right where one "claims an interest relating to the property or transaction that is the subject of the action, and is so situated that disposing of the action may as a practical matter impair or impede the movant's ability to protect its interest, unless existing parties adequately represent that interest." Also, a court "may permit anyone to intervene who has a claim or defense that shares with the main action a common question of law or fact" (known as permissive intervention). Fed. R. Civ. P. 24(c). For further information regarding intervention, *see* DAVID CHARLES HRICIK, MASTERING CIVIL PROCEDURE, Chapter 20, Intervention (Carolina Academic Press 2008).

Courts have allowed intervention after entry of judgment for purposes of appeal and even during the pendency of appeal, but a strong showing must be made and the interveners must meet Constitutional standing requirements. *See Bryant v. Yellen,* 447 U.S. 352, 366–68 (1980); *United States v. Perry,* 360 F.3d 519, 526–27 (2004) (victim of defendant in securities fraud case allowed to intervene to appeal the release of her judgment lien against the defendant); *see also Elliott Indus. Ltd. Partnership v. BP America Production Co.,* 407 F.3d 1091, 1103 (10th Cir. 2005) (allowing unnamed member of putative class who met the requirements of intervention as of right to intervene during the appeal because it intended to raise and address challenges to subject matter jurisdiction that no other party would). Constitutional standing is discussed in Section II(a), below.

A non-party whose motion to intervene is denied may immediately appeal that order. *Marino v. Ortiz,* 484 U.S. 301, 304 (1988); *Bridgeport Guardians, Inc. v. Delmonte,* 602 F.3d 469, 473 (2d Cir. 2010).

d. Substitution of Parties on Appeal

Substitution of parties on appeal is generally allowed upon the death of an original party, where an original party is incapable of proceeding, or upon the succession or replacement of a party who was a public officer. For example, Federal Rule of Appellate Procedure 43 provides:

Rule 43. Substitution of Parties

(a) Death of a Party.

(1) *After Notice of Appeal Is Filed.*

If a party dies after a notice of appeal has been filed or while a proceeding is pending in the court of appeals, the decedent's personal representative may be substituted as a party on motion filed with the circuit clerk by the representative or by any party. A party's motion must be served on the representative in accordance with Rule 25. If the decedent has no representative, any party may suggest the death on the record, and the court of appeals may then direct appropriate proceedings.

(2) *Before Notice of Appeal Is Filed — Potential Appellant.*

If a party entitled to appeal dies before filing a notice of appeal, the decedent's personal representative — or, if there is no personal representative, the decedent's attorney of record — may file a notice of appeal within the time prescribed by these rules. After the notice of appeal is filed, substitution must be in accordance with Rule 43(a)(1).

(3) *Before Notice of Appeal Is Filed — Potential Appellee.*

If a party against whom an appeal may be taken dies after entry of a judgment or order in the district court, but before a notice of appeal is filed, an appellant may proceed as if the death had not occurred. After the notice of appeal is filed, substitution must be in accordance with Rule 43(a)(1).

(b) Substitution for a Reason Other Than Death.

If a party needs to be substituted for any reason other than death, the procedure prescribed in Rule 43(a) applies.

(c) Public Officer: Identification; Substitution.

(1) *Identification of Party.*

A public officer who is a party to an appeal or other proceeding in an official capacity may be described as a party by the public officer's official title rather than by name. But the court may require the public officer's name to be added.

(2) *Automatic Substitution of Officeholder.*

When a public officer who is a party to an appeal or other proceeding in an official capacity dies, resigns, or otherwise ceases to hold office, the action does not abate. The public officer's successor is automatically substituted as a party. Proceedings following the substitution are to be in the name of the substituted party, but any misnomer that does not affect the substantial rights of the parties may be disregarded. An order of substitution may be entered at any time, but failure to enter an order does not affect the substitution.

Rule 43(b) allows substitution of parties in cases other than death when "need[ed]." This generally means "when a party is incapable of continuing the suit, such as where a party becomes incompetent or a transfer of interest in the company or property involved in the suit has occurred." *Alabama Power Co. v. I.C.C.*, 852 F.2d 1361, 1366 (D.C. Cir. 1988).

e. Persons Aggrieved

Generally, only one who is "aggrieved" may appeal a judgment or order. As stated above: "A party who receives all that he has sought generally is not aggrieved by the judgment affording the relief and cannot appeal from it." *Deposit Guar. Nat'l Bank v. Roper*, 445 U.S. 326, 333 (1980). This means that "a party is 'aggrieved' and ordinarily can appeal a decision 'granting in part and denying in part the remedy requested.'" *Forney v. Apfel*, 524 U.S. 266, 271 (1998).

On the other hand, if a party receives an entirely favorable judgment but disagrees with the grounds on which it was based, with the court's reasoning, with statements in the opinion, or the like, that party is usually not considered aggrieved and cannot appeal the judgment. The oft stated reason for this rule is that appellate courts "review[] judgments, not statements in opinions." *California v. Rooney*, 483 U.S. 307, 311 (1987) (judgment that the state's search warrant was valid was entirely in the state's favor; thus, the state was not an aggrieved party and could not appeal the judgment to challenge portions of the ruling stating some of the evidence offered in support of the warrant was obtained illegally).

There are ways, however, in which a recipient of a favorable judgment may be considered aggrieved and may thus appeal. The "three established prudential routes" involve "reformation of judgment, future economic loss or collateral estoppel." *Envtl. Prot. Info. Ctr., Inc. v. Pac. Lumber Co.*, 257 F.3d 1071, 1075 (9th Cir. 2001).

First, "a party may seek reformation of a favorable decree ... that contains discussion of issues "'immaterial to the disposition of the cause.'" *Id.* (quoting *Elec. Fittings Corp. v. Thomas & Betts Co.*, 307 U.S. 241, 242 (1939)). The term "decree" means judgment, thus the offending discussion of immaterial issues, i.e., dicta, must appear on the face of the judgment as opposed to in the opinion or ruling leading to the judgment. *Envtl. Prot. Info. Ctr.*, 257 F.3d at 1075. Most judgments are succinct, however, and simply state that judgment is awarded in favor of a particular party or parties and/or that the complaint is dismissed. *Id.*

Second, "a winning party will be considered aggrieved by a favorable judgment if future economic loss will result to the party on account of adverse collateral rulings." *Envtl. Prot. Info. Ctr.*, 257 F.3d at 1076; *see, e.g., Deposit Guar. Nat'l Bank v. Roper*, 445 U.S. 326, 326 (1980) (holding that district court's judgment in favor of the named plaintiffs in a putative class action did not prevent them from appealing the denial of class certification because class certification would spread the costs of the litigation). The future economic loss must be certain or imminent, however, and cannot be based on the mere possibility that expenses may be incurred in litigating the issue again at a later date. *Envtl. Prot. Info. Ctr.*, 257 F.3d at 1076.

For example, in *International Broth. of Elec. Workers v. I.C.C.*, 862 F.2d 330, 334 (D.C. Cir. 1988), the Interstate Commerce Commission (ICC) asserted jurisdiction to review an arbitrator's decision favorable to an aggrieved employee over the objection of the International Brotherhood of Electrical Workers ("IBEW"). The ICC upheld the arbitrator's decision, and IBEW petitioned the court to reverse the ICC's ruling that it had jurisdiction to review arbitration judgments settling disputes over the interpretation, application, or enforcement of labor protective conditions. The court held that even though IBEW was a prevailing party in the individual proceeding, it had standing to appeal the ICC's jurisdictional ruling because that ruling meant that IBEW "will be forced to litigate future arbitration awards before the ICC." On the other hand, in *ASARCO, Inc. v. Secretary of Labor*, 206 F.3d 720, 723–24 (6th Cir. 2000), ASARCO, a zinc mine operator, sought review of a decision of an administrative law judge vacating a citation against ASARCO, but holding that "single-shift sampling" was, in principle, a permissible method of determining compliance with dust safety standards. The court held ASARCO, a prevailing party, did not have standing to appeal — that the future economic loss exception was not applicable because any future loss was speculative. The court noted: "The only damage to ASARCO is, perhaps, the cost it *may* incur in repeating the litigation of the single-sampling issue in the future, *if* it is cited for a violation, *if* the citation rests on a single-shift sample, and *if* the citation is upheld by an ALJ."

Third, a party may appeal a favorable judgment if an "adverse collateral ruling can serve as the basis for collateral estoppel in subsequent litigation." *Envtl. Prot. Info. Ctr., Inc. v. Pac. Lumber Co.*, 257 F.3d 1071, 1076 (9th Cir. 2001). The collateral estoppel exception is rarely effective in practice because generally, "[d]eterminations which are immaterial to the judgment below have no preclusive effect on subsequent litigation." *Id.* In other words collateral rulings usually cannot be the basis for collateral estoppel.

Thus, although reformation, future economic loss, and collateral estoppel are the "established prudential routes" by which a party may appeal a favorable judgment, they are limited in scope.

Even if these established exceptions are inapplicable, however, appellate courts usually have discretion to review adverse rulings on appeal from a favorable judgment "in the appropriate case." *Deposit Guar. Nat'l Bank v. Roper*, 445 U.S. 326, 334 (1980).

For example, in *Envtl. Prot. Info. Ctr., Inc. v. Pac. Lumber Co.*, 257 F.3d 1071, 1077 (9th Cir. 2001), the district court granted Pacific Lumber Company's motion to dismiss as moot, the action brought by the Environmental Protection Information Center, Inc., and entered judgment in Pacific Lumber's favor. However, the district court filed an order after the case had become moot that outlined its reasons for granting a preliminary injunction in favor of the plaintiff. Pacific Lumber appealed this order, and the Environmental Protection Information Center argued it did not have standing to appeal since the judgment was entirely in Pacific Lumber's favor. The Ninth Circuit noted that none of the established exceptions applied, but that "the district court's decision to flout the dictates of Article III and render an opinion in spite of knowing the cause was moot did render Pacific Lumber an "aggrieved party."

Also, many appellate courts allow prevailing parties to file a protective, conditional cross-appeal "to insure that any errors against [their] interests are reviewed so that if the main appeal results in modification of the judgment [their] grievances will be determined as well." *Trust for Certificate Holders of Merrill Lynch Mortg. Investors, Inc. Mortg. Pass-Through Certificates, Series 1991-c1 v. Love Funding Corp.*, 496 F.3d 171, 173 (2d Cir. 2007).

II. Constitutional Standing and Mootness

a. Standing

The federal requirement that a person have standing to bring a claim is based on the "case or controversy" requirement in Article III, Section 2, clause 1 of the Constitution. *Raines v. Byrd*, 521 U.S. 811, 817 (1997) ("No principle is more fundamental to the judiciary's proper role in our system of government than the constitutional limitation of federal-court jurisdiction to actual cases or controversies.").

An essential element of the case or controversy requirement is that plaintiffs must establish that they have standing to sue. This means plaintiff must show "that their claimed injury is personal, particularized, concrete, and otherwise judicially cognizable." *Id.* In other words, (1) the plaintiff must suffer an "injury in fact"; (2) "there must be a causal connection between the injury and the conduct complained of"; and (3) "it must be likely, as opposed to merely speculative, that the injury will be redressed by a favorable decision." *Lujan v. Defenders of Wildlife*, 504 U.S. 555, 560–61 (1992) (holding environmental groups lacked standing to challenge a regulation of the Secretary of the Interior that required other agencies to confer with him under the Endangered Species Act only with respect to federally funded projects in the United States and on the high seas).

Because standing is an element of federal subject matter jurisdiction, it cannot be waived or forfeited and can be raised at any time in the proceedings. *See Arbaugh v. Y & H Corp.*, 546 U.S. 500, 514 (2006). Most, but not all, states also consider standing to be a component of subject matter jurisdiction, meaning standing in state courts is an issue that can be raised at any time. *See Garriga v. Sanitation Dist. No. 1*, 2003 Ky. App. LEXIS 305 at *22, n. 26 (Ky. Ct. App. 2003) (collecting cases). *But see Sears v. Hull*, 961 P.2d 1013, 1019 (Ariz. 1998) ("we are not constitutionally constrained to decline jurisdiction based on lack of standing.").

b. Mootness — The Mootness Doctrine

The case or controversy requirement in Article III of the federal Constitution, as well as those of most states, prohibits appellate courts from determining an issue after the case has become moot.

A case becomes moot "when the issues presented are no longer live or the parties lack a legally cognizable interest in the outcome." *Murphy v. Hunt*, 455 U.S. 478, 481 (1982) (internal quotations omitted). An issue is no longer "live" when an appellate determination can have no practical effect. This often occurs when a stay pending appeal is denied or otherwise not obtained and actions occur that cannot be undone, *i.e.*, "the egg cannot be unscrambled." This is common in the bankruptcy context when a sale of assets is approved and the assets sold, or when a plan of reorganization is confirmed and implemented immediately thereafter.

In *Murphy v. Hunt*, supra, Hunt filed a complaint under 42 U.S.C. § 1983 challenging a provision of the Nebraska state constitution limiting pre-trial bail in cases of first degree sex offenses. The Court held "Hunt's claim to pre-trial bail was moot once he was convicted." The court explained: "The question was no longer live because even a favorable decision on it would not have entitled Hunt to bail. For the same reason, Hunt no longer had a legally cognizable interest in the result in this case. He had not prayed for damages nor had he sought to represent a class of pretrial detainees." 455 U.S. at 481–82.

The "legally cognizable interest" requirement under the mootness doctrine has been compared to the standing requirement (discussed in Section II(a) above), but it is less strict because it is subject to exceptions, whereas the standing requirement is not. To have standing, plaintiffs must have a legally cognizable interest when they file their claims. In order to avoid a case becoming moot this interest must continue throughout the proceedings, *unless* one of the exceptions to the mootness doctrine is present (see below).

c. Exceptions to the Mootness Doctrine

There are three important exceptions to the mootness doctrine. First, cases that are "capable of repetition yet evading review" are not moot. The exception applies where "(1) the challenged action is in its duration too short to be fully litigated prior to cessation or expiration; and (2) there is a reasonable expectation that the same complaining party will be subject to the same action again." *Federal Election Comm'n v. Wisconsin Right to Life, Inc.*, 551 U.S. 449, 462 (2007). In that case, Wisconsin Right to Life, seeking to run ads close to election days, challenged a provision the Bipartisan Campaign Reform Act of 2002 prohibiting "electioneering communications" and prescribing blackout periods for advertisement. The Court held that the case was not mooted by the passing of the election cycle at issue in the complaint, noting that the case "fit comfortably within the established exception to mootness for disputes capable of repetition, yet evading review." *Id.*

Second, a case is not rendered moot by "a defendant's voluntary cessation of a challenged practice" unless "subsequent events made it absolutely clear that the allegedly wrongful behavior could not reasonably be expected to recur." *Friends of the Earth, Inc. v. Laidlaw Environmental Services (TOC), Inc.*, 528 U.S. 167, 189 (2000). Furthermore, the "heavy burden of persua[ding] the court that the challenged conduct cannot reasonably be expected to start up again lies with the party asserting mootness." *Id.* If this showing were not required, "the courts would be compelled to leave the defendant free to return to his old ways." *Id.* (internal quotations and citations omitted).

Third, a class action is not rendered moot if the named representative had standing when the complaint was filed and when the class was certified, but then ceases to have a stake and be a member of the class. *See Sosna v. Iowa*, 419 U.S. 393, 398 n. 7, 402 (1975). In *Sosna*, the named representative in an action challenging Iowa's one year residency requirement for divorce no longer had a stake in the action and ceased to be a member of the class once she obtained a divorce in another state. However, the Court held this did not moot the case because there was still a live controversy between the respondents and the members of the class.

d. Mootness by Reason of Settlement

A common way in which cases become moot is settlement by the parties. Once parties have entered into a settlement, the case is no longer live, and the parties no longer have a stake or interest in the outcome.

Whether a case becomes moot by "happenstance," or settlement — in which the losing party "has voluntarily forfeited his legal remedy" — becomes an issue in determining whether to vacate the judgment. *U.S. Bancorp. Mortgage Co. v. Bonner Mall P'ship*, 513 U.S. 18, 25, 29 (1994). Where federal cases become moot for reasons other than settlement, the ordinary practice is for the appellate court to "vacate the judgment below and remand with a direction to dismiss." *Id.* at 22. However, the Supreme Court held in *Bonner Mall* that "mootness by reason of settlement does not justify vacatur of a judgment under review" absent "exceptional circumstances" which "do not include the mere fact that the settlement agreement provides for vacatur." *Id.* at 29.

This rule poses difficulties for settling parties because the losing party will often want the judgment and any adverse opinions to be vacated, e.g., to avoid collateral estoppels or to eliminate adverse precedent. The individual interest of a party, however, is juxtaposed to the public's interest, since "[j]udicial precedents are presumptively correct and valuable to the legal community as a whole." *Id.* at 26.

The approach and interpretation of "exceptional circumstances" varies by circuit. See Kathleen Scanlon, *A Case for Judicial Accountability: When Courts Add a Settlement Detour on the Traditional Appellate Path*, 17 OHIO ST. J.: ON DISP. RESOL. 379 (2002) (addressing issues created by appellate mediation programs and settlement-related vacatur case law). There is also a split in the circuits regarding whether a district court may vacate *its own* prior judgment in absence of exceptional circumstances. *Compare Valero Terrestrial Corp. v. Paige*, 211 F.3d 112, 199 n. 3 (4th Cir. 2000) (adopting the exceptional circumstances test for district courts); *American Games, Inc. v. Trade Prods. Inc.*, 142 F.3d 1164, 1169–70 (9th Cir. 1998) (holding district courts may "balance the equities" rather than requiring a showing of exceptional circumstances in deciding whether to vacate their own judgments when a case has become moot on appeal due to settlement). The rules of the different states regarding vacatur of judgments where cases have become moot due to settlement also vary.

Thus, it is important for counsel (1) to keep in mind that vacatur of the judgment as the result of settlement may likely not be automatic, and (2) to familiarize themselves with any steps that must be taken to secure vacatur prior to or at least during settlement negotiations.

III. Amicus Curiae

A non-party may also seek to participate in an appeal as an amicus curiae or "friend of the court." Originally amici curiae functioned almost exclusively in that role—as neutral, independent assistants of the court. Now, however, most amici curiae have some interest in the litigation, often representing some industry or public interest group. Indeed, amici are often required to identify their interest in the case in seeking to file an amicus brief. *See* Fed. R. App. P. 29(b)(1) (motion for leave to file amicus brief "must ... state (1) the movant's interest").

Generally, an amicus brief may be filed only by leave of court or with the consent of all the parties. The exception to this rule is that the United States, its officers and agencies, as well as states and the District of Columbia may file an amicus brief without leave or consent . *See* Fed. R. App. P. 29(a)(1). Rule 29 does not set out specific criteria for granting leave to file an amicus brief. A motion for leave must only state the movant's interest and "the reason why an amicus brief is desirable and why the matters asserted are relevant to the disposition of the case." Fed. R. App. P. 29(b). However, the Advisory Committee Notes to Rule 29 state:

> An amicus curiae brief which brings relevant matter to the attention of the Court that has not already been brought to its attention by the parties is of considerable help to the Court. An amicus curiae brief which does not serve this purpose simply burdens the staff and facilities of the Court and its filing is not favored.

Fed. R. App. P. 29(b)(1998) Amendment Advisory Committee Notes.

Courts differ in their views and acceptance of participation by amici curiae. Judge Posner of the Seventh Circuit espouses a restrictive approach, noting:

> [J]udges have heavy caseloads and therefore need to minimize extraneous reading; amicus briefs, often solicited by parties, may be used to make an end run around court-imposed limitations on the length of parties' briefs; the time and other resources required for the preparation and study of, and response to, amicus briefs drive up the cost of litigation; and the filing of an amicus brief is often an attempt to inject interest group politics into the federal appeals process.

Voices for Choices v. Illinois Bell Tel. Co., 339 F.3d 542, 544 (7th Cir. 2003).

Judge Posner described the decision to permit the filing of an amicus brief as "a matter of 'judicial grace'" and set forth the following criterion: "whether the brief will assist the judges by presenting ideas, arguments, theories, insights, facts, or data that are not to be found in the parties' briefs." *Voices for Choices*, 339 F.3d at 544–45. He stated further that "[t]he criterion is more likely to be satisfied in a case in which a party is inadequately represented; or in which the would-be amicus has a direct interest in another case that may be materially affected by a decision in this case; or in which the amicus has a unique perspective or specific information that can assist the court beyond what the parties can provide." *Id.* Judge Posner noted, however, that in his experience the vast majority of amicus briefs were merely repetitive of the arguments in the brief of the party the amicus was supporting. *Id.*

Conversely, Justice Alito, then a judge on the Third Circuit Court of Appeal, advocated a liberal approach to permitting the filing of amicus curiae briefs. In *Neonatology Associates, P.A. v. C.I.R.*, 293 F.3d 128, 132–33 (3d Cir. 2002), Judge Alito stated that Rule 29(b)'s criteria, which he described as "(a) an adequate interest, (b) desirability, and (c) relevance," should be interpreted broadly. He opined that a restrictive approach may create "a perception of view point discrimination" and "may also convey an unfortunate message about the openness of the court." *Id.* at 133. Judge Alito also expressed doubt that a restrictive approach to granting leave to file amicus brief would lighten the work load of the courts, noting:

> [T]he time required for skeptical scrutiny of proposed amicus briefs may equal, if not exceed, the time that would have been needed to study the briefs at the merits stage if leave had been granted. In addition, because private amicus briefs are not submitted in the vast majority of court of appeals cases, and because poor quality briefs are usually easy to spot, unhelpful amicus briefs surely do not claim more than a very small part of a court's time.

Id. Accordingly, he concluded that the "court would be well advised to grant motions for leave to file amicus briefs unless it is obvious that the proposed briefs do not meet Rule 29's criteria as broadly interpreted." *Id.*

Amicus curiae briefs can be particularly useful in (1) explaining the wider impact of a particular decision on persons, groups, or entities other than the parties; (2) providing empirical factual or background information—statistics, studies, comparisons and the like; or (3) providing expertise regarding an industry, practice, procedure or subject relevant to the litigation that is not possessed by the parties or the court.

Generally, appellate courts will not entertain issues raised in an amicus brief that were waived or not raised by the parties, or that were decided by the court below. *See Reno v. Koray*, 515 U.S. 50, 55 n.2 (1995); 132 L.Ed. 2d 46 (1995); Davis v. United States, 512 U.S. 452, 457–58 n. * (1994). On the other hand, when a party changes its position on an important issue in alignment with the opposing party, a court is likely to appoint an amicus curiae to brief and argue the opposing view. *Hohn v. United States*, 524 U.S. 236, 241(1998) ("since Hohn and the Government both argue in favor of our jurisdiction, we appointed an amicus curiae to argue the contrary position.").

Note that Rule 29(c) regarding the contents of amicus curiae briefs was recently amended to require amicus briefs to disclose whether counsel for a party authored the brief in whole or in part and whether a party or a party's counsel contributed money with the intention of funding the preparation or submission of the brief. The purpose of this amendment was "to deter counsel from using an amicus brief to circumvent page limits on the parties' briefs." Fed. R. App. P. 29(c), 2010 Amendment Advisory Committee Notes.

Checkpoints

- Generally, only parties to an action that qualify as "persons aggrieved," either original parties, substituted parties, or intervenors, have standing to appeal a decision. There is an exception for members of a class that have objected to a class action settlement below.

- To have standing to appeal, one must have had standing to sue. Standing is part of "case or controversy" requirement in Article III, Section 2, clause 1 of the Constitution.

- Constitutional standing requires that the plaintiff's "claimed injury [be] personal, particularized, concrete, and otherwise judicially cognizable." *Raines v. Byrd*, 521 U.S. 811, 817 (1997).

- If a case becomes moot while on appeal, generally it will be dismissed. A case becomes moot when the issues are not "live" because an appellate ruling can have no practical effect or the parties no longer have a stake in the outcome. Perhaps the most common cause of mootness is settlement of the case by the parties, in which case the judgment below and any adverse opinions may be, but are not always, vacated.

- There are three exceptions to the mootness doctrine: (1) cases involving conduct or issues that are capable of repetition yet evade review, (2) when a defendant voluntarily ceases the conduct at issue but may reasonably be expected to engage in that conduct in the future, and (3) when a class action plaintiff/appellant ceases to have a stake and be a member of the class—substitution of another class member cures the mootness problem.

- Interested third parties that are not parties to an action may participate in an appeal as amicus curiae (friend of the court) if permitted to do so by the appellate court.

Chapter 6

The Record on Appeal

Roadmap

- The record on appeal usually consists of the documents filed in the trial court and a record of oral proceedings and provides the background and foundation for the appellate court's decision.

- Any asserted error must appear, and be preserved, in the record.

- Generally, in deciding the appeal, the appellate court may consider only what was in the trial court record. Errors and omissions, however, may be corrected.

- Appellate courts may take judicial notice of facts outside the record that are not subject to reasonable dispute.

- Appellate courts generally have inherent power to supplement the record with information not reviewed by the trial court and not subject to judicial notice, but it is very rarely used.

- The appendix, an abbreviated form of the record, is used in many jurisdictions for the convenience of the court.

I. Purpose

The record on appeal should enable the appellate court to thoroughly and accurately review the judgment or order below. The record provides the background and context for the appellate court's review and, most importantly, the foundation on which the court will base its decision.

In order for an appellate court to review an asserted error in the trial court, the error must appear in the record and, absent limited exceptions, be preserved by the appellant — as manifest in the record. (Preservation of error is discussed in Chapter 2). Also, in deciding if there was error below, the appellate court should have the same facts, documents, evidence, and other information that was presented in the trial court. In the same vein, the appellate court generally may not consider material that was not brought before the trial court. *See Lowry v. Barnhart*, 329 F.3d 1019, 1024 (9th Cir. 2003); Alaska R. App. P. 210 ("Except as otherwise ordered by the appellate court, the record does not include documents or exhibits filed after, or electronic records or transcripts of proceedings occurring after, the filing date of the notice of appeal).

II. Contents

a. Generally

The appellate record generally consists of a record of written documents filed in the trial court, as well as a record of oral proceedings — often the reporter's transcript. For example, Federal Rule of Appellate Procedure 10(a) states: "The following items constitute the record on appeal: (1) the original papers and exhibits filed in the district court; (2) the transcript of proceedings, if any; and (3) a certified copy of the docket entries prepared by the district clerk." In addition, many jurisdictions allow the parties to file an "agreed statement" in lieu of the record on appeal.

b. Documents Filed in the Trial Court: The Clerk's File

In all jurisdictions the record on appeal includes various documents that were filed in the trial court and considered part of the clerk's file. Which of these documents become part of the appellate record varies from jurisdiction to jurisdiction, however.

In federal courts the record on appeal includes the entire trial court clerk's file, described as "the original papers and exhibits filed in the district court." Many states have a similar rule, *see, e.g.*, Alaska R. App. P. 210 ("The record on appeal consists of the entire trial court file, including the original papers and exhibits filed in the trial court ."); Del. Sup. Ct. R. 9 ("An appeal shall be heard on the original papers and exhibits which shall constitute the record on appeal."); Mass. R. App. P. 8 ("The original papers and exhibits on file, ... a certified copy of the docket entries prepared by the clerk of the lower court shall constitute the record on appeal in all cases"); N.D. R. App. P. 10 ("The original papers and exhibits filed in the trial court, ... and a certified copy of the docket entries prepared by the clerk of the trial court constitute the record on appeal in all cases").

Some states require the appellate record to contain more than the documents and exhibits filed with the trial court. For example, Hawaii requires the record on appeal to contain "(1) the documents filed in the court or agency appealed from; (2) written jury instructions given, or requested and refused or modified over objection; (3) exhibits admitted into evidence *or refused*." Hawaii R. App. P. 10(a) (emphasis added). In Utah, the record on appeal includes the entire trial court clerk's file as well as "the index prepared by the clerk of the trial court." Utah R. App. P. 11(a).

Some states specify documents in the trial court clerk's file that should be omitted from the record on appeal unless designated by one of the parties. *See, e.g.,* Ala. R. App. P. 10(a) ("(a) *Omitted Parts of Record.* The record on appeal, in both civil and criminal appeals, shall not contain the following, unless some particular question is raised with respect thereto and decided in the trial court and unless specifically designated by a party: (1) subpoenas or summons for any witness or the order therefor, nor for any defendant where there is an appearance for such defendant; (2) motion and order of continuance; (3) commission to examine a witness or certificate of a commissioner to a deposition or affidavit made to obtain such commission; (4) pretrial discovery material that is not made a part of the trial court's proceedings."); Fla. R. App. P. 9.200(a) ("Except as otherwise designated by the parties, the record shall consist of the original documents, all exhibits that are not physical evidence, and any transcript(s) of proceedings filed in the lower tribunal, except summonses, praecipes, subpoenas, returns, notices of hearing or of taking deposition, depositions, and other discovery.").

Other states rules specify certain documents that must be part of the record and then allow the parties to designate additional documents. For example Colorado Court Rule 10(a), "Composition of the Record on Appeal," provides:

> The final pleadings which frame the issues in the trial court; the findings of fact, conclusions of law and judgment; the judgment entered upon any jury verdict, the jury verdict, and answers by the jury to any special interrogatories; motions for new trial and other post-trial motions, if any, and the trial court's ruling; together with any other documents which by designation of either party or by stipulation are directed to be included shall constitute the record on appeal in all cases.

In a similar vein, California Rule of Court 8.122 requires the record on appeal to contain:

- The notice of appeal;

- Any judgment appealed from and any notice of its entry;

- Any order appealed from and any notice of its entry;

- Any notice of intention to move for a new trial, or motion to vacate the judgment, for judgment notwithstanding the verdict, or for reconsideration of an appealed order, with supporting and opposing memoranda and attachments, and any order on such motion and any notice of its entry;

Any party may also designate:

- Any other document filed or lodged in the case in superior court;

- Any exhibit admitted in evidence, refused, or lodged; and

- Any jury instruction that any party submitted in writing and the cover page required by rule 2.1055(b)(2) indicating the party requesting it, and any written jury instructions given by the court.

Finally, in some states the content of the record on appeal is left primarily to the discretion of the parties — within some parameters. *See* S.C. Ct. R. 209 (a party "shall serve ... a Designation of Matter to be Included in the Record on Appeal which shall set forth with specificity those parts of the transcript, pleadings, orders, exhibits, or other materials which he proposes to include in the record on appeal.... A party shall not include any matter in his Designation which is not relevant to the appeal."); W. Va. R. App. P. 8 (providing for appellant and respondent, in turn, to designate "matter relevant to the issues presented by the appeal.").

c. Record of Oral Proceedings

1. The Transcript

A record of oral proceedings, e.g. trial or hearings, traditionally has been made stenographically by a certified court reporter. More recently, oral proceedings are also recorded digitally or electronically. In either case, this record may be transcribed at the request of a party — creating a "reporter's transcript" or "certified transcript." If oral proceedings are relevant to an issue on appeal — particularly the case where the appellant contends "a finding or conclusion is contrary to the evidence" — the appellant is generally required to designate and order a transcript of those proceedings to be included in the record on appeal. *See, e.g.* Fed. R. App. P. 10(b)(2); Ariz. R. Civ. App. P. 11(b)(1); Ala. R. App. P. 10 (b)(2); Fla. R. App. P. 9.200(b)(1); Mass. R. App. P. 8 (b)(1); N.C. R. App. art. II, 7(a)(1); Utah R. App. P. 11(e)(1), (2); Vt. R. App. P. 10 (b)(1), (2).

The federal and various state systems have specific procedural rules regarding designation of the transcript by appellants and counter designation by appellees, including notice requirements, time limits, payment of costs, etc. Thus, in every appeal it is important for counsel to look up and carefully follow the most recent version applicable in their jurisdiction. For example, Federal Rule of Appellate Procedure 10(b) provides:

(b) The Transcript of Proceedings.

(1) Appellant's Duty to Order. Within 14 days after filing the notice of appeal or entry of an order disposing of the last timely remaining motion of a type specified in Rule 4(a)(4)(A), whichever is later, the appellant must do either of the following:

(A) order from the reporter a transcript of such parts of the proceedings not already on file as the appellant considers necessary, subject to a local rule of the court of appeals and with the following qualifications:

(i) the order must be in writing;

(ii) if the cost of the transcript is to be paid by the United States under the Criminal Justice Act, the order must so state; and

(iii) the appellant must, within the same period, file a copy of the order with the district clerk; or

(B) file a certificate stating that no transcript will be ordered.

(2) Unsupported Finding or Conclusion. If the appellant intends to urge on appeal that a finding or conclusion is unsupported by the evidence or is contrary to the evidence, the appellant must include in the record a transcript of all evidence relevant to that finding or conclusion.

(3) Partial Transcript. Unless the entire transcript is ordered:

(A) the appellant must—within the 14 days provided in Rule 10(b)(1)—file a statement of the issues that the appellant intends to present on the appeal and must serve on the appellee a copy of both the order or certificate and the statement;

(B) if the appellee considers it necessary to have a transcript of other parts of the proceedings, the appellee must, within 14 days after the service of the order or certificate and the statement of the issues, file and serve on the appellant a designation of additional parts to be ordered; and

(C) unless within 14 days after service of that designation the appellant has ordered all such parts, and has so notified the appellee, the appellee may within the following 14 days either order the parts or move in the district court for an order requiring the appellant to do so.

(4) Payment. At the time of ordering, a party must make satisfactory arrangements with the reporter for paying the cost of the transcript.

In most jurisdictions appellants are required to designate and order relevant portions of the transcript within a limited number of days after filing the notice of appeal, or, in some states, when the notice of appeal is filed. *See, e.g.,* Fed. R. App. P. 10(b)(1) (within 14 days); Ala. R. App. P. 10(b) (within 7 days); Cal. R. Ct. 8.121 (within 10 days); Ind. R. App. P. 9(f) (when the notice of appeal is filed). Such strict time limits are necessary because transcribing records of oral proceedings can be a time consuming process and a court reporter or certified transcriber is likely to have orders for transcripts in many different cases.

2. When a Transcript Is Unavailable

In some cases a transcript of oral proceedings will be unavailable. This can occur when the stenographic, digital, or electronic recording has been lost, damaged, or destroyed, or where proceedings were not recorded in the first place, *see, e.g.,* Tenn. Code Ann. § 40-14-301-301 (requiring that court reporters be present to record proceedings in criminal proceedings only — not civil). If this is the case, the appellant may prepare a statement of the evidence or proceedings from the best available means, including the appellant's recollection. The appellant must serve the statement on the appellee, who may then make objections or propose amendments to the appellant's statement. Any disputes regarding the contents of the statement will be settled by the trial court. *See* Fed. R. App. P. 10(c); Ala. R. App. P. 10(d); Ariz. R. Civ. App. P. 11(c); Colo. App. R. 10(c); Fla. R. App .P. 9.200(b)(4); Ill. Sup. Ct. R. 323 (c); Minn. R. Civ. App. P. 110.03; N.D. R. App. P. 10 (f); Ohio R. App. P. 9(C); Pa. R. App. P. 1923; Tenn. R. Ct. 24(c); Vt. R. App. P. 10(c); Wy. R. App. P. 3.03; Utah R. App. P. 11(g).

d. Agreed Statements

In lieu of the record on appeal, many jurisdictions allow the parties to file an "agreed statement" that simply shows how the issues presented in the appeal arose and were decided by the trial court. An agreed statement should include "only those facts averred and proved or sought to be proved that are essential to the [appellate] court's resolution of the issues." Fed. R. App. P. 10 (d); *see also, e.g.,* Ala. R. App. P. 10(e); Ariz. R. Civ. App. P. 11(d); Cal. R. Ct. 6(a); Colo. App. R. 10(d); Kan. Sup. Ct. R. 3.05; Mass. R. App. P. 8(d); N.D. R. App. P. 10(g); Ohio R. App. P. 9(D); Pa. R. App. P. 1924; S.D. Codified Laws § 15-26A-55; Utah R. App. P. 11(f); Vt. R. App. P. 10(d). If the statement is "truthful" it will be approved by the trial court, which may make any additions or corrections it deems appropriate. *See, e.g.,* Fed. R. App. P. 10(d). The statement, along with any corrections or modifications, will then be transmitted to the appellate court.

III. Correcting and Expanding the Record on Appeal

a. General Rule

Generally, in deciding an appeal the appellate court may consider only what was in the trial court record—this means evidence and documents that were considered or offered in the trial court, as wells as transcripts or other memorializations of the oral proceedings. As the court explained in *Lowry v. Barnhart*, 329 F.3d 1019, 1024 (9th Cir. 2003):

> This limitation is fundamental. As a court of appeals, we lack the means to authenticate documents submitted to us, so we must be able to assume that documents designated part of the record actually are part of the record. To be sure, the fact that a document is filed in the district court doesn't resolve all questions of authenticity, but it does ensure that both opposing counsel and the district court are aware of it at a time when disputes over authenticity can be properly resolved. Litigants who disregard this process impair our ability to perform our appellate function.

Trial and appellate courts may, however, correct errors or omissions in the record. Appellate courts may also take "judicial notice" of certain facts that were not part of the record, as well as "exercise inherent authority to supplement the record in extraordinary cases." *Id.* Finally, appellate courts must consider matters outside the record that render a case moot, *id.*,—meaning "the issues presented are no longer live or the parties lack a legally cognizable interest in the outcome." *Murphy v. Hunt*, 455 U.S. 478, 481 (1982). For discussion of the mootness doctrine, see Chapter 5, §II(b)–(e).

b. Correcting Errors or Omissions in the Record

After the record on appeal has been prepared,[1] both parties have the opportunity and responsibility to review the record and determine that it is com-

---

1. The federal and state systems have detailed rules regarding the process and responsibility for preparing the record. In many jurisdictions the trial court clerk is responsible for preparing the clerk's file, with the appellant being responsible for monitoring the preparation and ensuring it is timely filed. In other jurisdictions the appellant is responsible for preparing the record. For a taxonomy of the processes, responsibilities, and deadlines for

plete and correct. If material is missing from the record or is misstated or otherwise inaccurate, the record may be supplemented or corrected (1) by stipulation of the parties or (2) by motion in the trial or appellate court. For example, Federal Rule of Appellate Procedure 10(e) provides:

(e) Correction or Modification of the Record.

(1) If any difference arises about whether the record truly discloses what occurred in the district court, the difference must be submitted to and settled by that court and the record conformed accordingly.

(2) If anything material to either party is omitted from or misstated in the record by error or accident, the omission or misstatement may be corrected and a supplemental record may be certified and forwarded:

(A) on stipulation of the parties;

(B) by the district court before or after the record has been forwarded; or

(C) by the court of appeals.

Correcting or modifying the record on appeal may be as simple as adding a document to the clerk's file that was mistakenly omitted, e.g., a complaint or other pleading. More difficult situations arise when the record of oral proceedings is incomplete or even, at times, unintelligible. *See, e.g., Bitler v. A.O. Smith Corp.*, 252 F. Supp. 2d 1123, 1124 (D. Colo. 2003) (court noted: "The audiotape transcript contains hundreds of instances in which the proceedings were inaudible to the transcriber. Indeed, on the very first page of audiotaped transcript, the transcriber notes that '[t]here appear to be no microphones turned on except the Judge's and the speakers are barely audible.'").

c. Judicial Notice

In the federal and most state systems, appellate courts may take judicial notice of facts outside the record that are not subject to reasonable dispute. Federal Rule of Evidence 201 addresses judicial notice of facts extrinsic to the record, and provides in pertinent part:

---

preparing the record on appeal as well as the consequences for failing to do so in all the federal and state court systems, *see* C. Flango & D. Rottman, *Appellate Court Procedures* (Williamsburg, Va.: National Center for State Courts, 1998).

(b) *Kinds of facts.* A judicially noticed fact must be one not subject to reasonable dispute in that it is either (1) generally known within the territorial jurisdiction of the trial court or (2) capable of accurate and ready determination by resort to sources whose accuracy cannot reasonably be questioned.

(c) *When discretionary.* A court may take judicial notice, whether requested or not.

(d) *When mandatory.* A court shall take judicial notice if requested by a party and supplied with the necessary information.

(e) *Opportunity to be heard.* A party is entitled upon timely request to an opportunity to be heard as to the propriety of taking judicial notice and the tenor of the matter noticed. In the absence of prior notification, the request may be made after judicial notice has been taken.

(f) *Time of taking notice.* Judicial notice may be taken at any stage of the proceeding.

The majority of states have adopted a version of Rule 201 and allow courts to take judicial notice in similar circumstances. *See* 21B. CHARLES ALAN WRIGHT & KENNETH W. GRAHAM, JR., FEDERAL PRACTICE & PROCEDURE: EVIDENCE § 5101.2 (2d ed. 2010).

A fact must essentially be indisputable before a court may take judicial notice of it. "[J]udicial notice applies to self-evident truths that no reasonable person could question, truisms that approach platitudes or banalities." *Hardy v. Johns-Manville Sales Corp.*, 681 F.2d 334, 347–48 (5th Cir. 1982) (holding the lower court erred in taking judicial notice that asbestos causes cancer because that proposition "is inextricably linked to a host of disputed issues — e.g., can mesothelioma arise without exposure to asbestos, is the sale of asbestos insulation products definitely linked to carcinoma in the general population, was this manufacturer reasonably unaware of the asbestos hazards in 1964."). In other words, "[t]he rule of judicial notice 'contemplates there is to be no evidence before the jury in disproof.'" *Id.* at 348 (quoting Fed. R. Evid. 201, Advisory Committee Note g (1975).)

A fact may be indisputable because it is "either (1) generally known within the territorial jurisdiction of the trial court or (2) capable of accurate and ready determination by resort to sources whose accuracy cannot reasonably be questioned." Fed. R. Evid. 201(b).

Examples of facts that were held to be generally known are:

- That color indicates a particular flavor of ice-cream, e.g., pink indicates strawberry and brown indicates chocolate. *Dippin' Dots, Inc. v. Frosty Bites Distribution, LLC*, 369 F.3d 1197, 1203–04 (11th Cir. 2004).

- That "an expensive vehicle such as a Porsche is especially vulnerable in New York City." *United States v. Mundy*, 806 F. Supp. 373, 377 (E.D.N.Y. 1992).

- That bingo is largely a senior citizen pass time. *Seminole Tribe of Fla. v. Butterworth*, 491 F. Supp. 1015, 1019 (S.D.Fla.1980), *aff'd*, 658 F.2d 310 (5th Cir. 1981).

- "The sensitivity of any human being to disclosure of information that may be taken to bear on his or her basic competence." *Detroit Edison Co. v. Nat'l Labor Relations Bd.*, 440 U.S. 301, 317 (1979) (dealing with disclosure of test scores).

- That ice hockey is a very rough physical contact sport. *Neeld v. Nat'l Hockey League*, 594 F.2d 1297 (9th Cir. 1979).

- That credit cards play a vital role in American society. *First Nat'l Bank of South Carolina v. United States*, 413 F. Supp. 1107, 1110 (D.S.C.1976), *aff'd*, 558 F.2d 721 (4th Cir. 1977).

- That a person may slip on a stairway, due to extremely slippery conditions, with such force that his hand may be loosened from handrail. *Mason v. Mathiasen Tanker Industries, Inc.*, 298 F.2d 28 (4th Cir. 1962).

On the other hand, these facts were held not to be generally known:

- That nearly all government contracts in the United States Virgin Islands are federally funded. *United States v. Gumbs*, 283 F.3d 128 (3d Cir. 2002).

- That there is a public controversy surrounding the drug Prozac. *Church of Scientology Intern. v. Eli Lilly & Co.*, 778 F. Supp. 661, 666 (S.D.N.Y. 1991).

- That, in the late 1950s, working in a cloud of silicon dust without respiratory gear could cause severe lung diseases. *Wooden v. Missouri Pacific R. Co.*, 862 F.2d 560 (5th Cir. 1989) (this fact was held to be not generally known in the late 1950s).

Examples of facts capable of accurate and ready determination by resort to sources whose accuracy cannot reasonably be questioned are:

- Public records and government documents, including those available from "reliable sources on the Internet." *United States v. BioPort Corp.*, 270 F. Supp. 2d 968, 972 (W.D. Mich. 2003).

- That the distance between the plaintiff's residence and allegedly inaccessible restaurant was 573.66 miles. *Harris v. Del Taco, Inc.*, 396 F. Supp. 2d 1107 (C.D. Cal. 2005).

- Provisions of an ordinance concerning daily usage fees on car rentals from airport. *Zimomra v. Alamo Rent-A-Car, Inc.*, 111 F.3d 1495 (10th Cir. 1997).

- That a county sheriff did not hold his position until after a specified date. *Corbin v. Cannon*, 838 F. Supp. 561 (M.D. Fla. 1993).

- That the zip code prefix of 603 would put the location of the addressee in or near Oak Park, Illinois. *In re Parullo*, 13 B.R. 953 (Bankr. N.D. Ill. 1981).

- That on Oct. 7, 1966, in Little Rock, Arkansas, sundown was at 5:45 P.M. Central Standard Time. *Oliver v. Hallett Const. Co.*, 421 F.2d 365 (8th Cir. 1970).

Examples of facts that were found not capable of accurate and ready determination by resort to sources whose accuracy cannot reasonably be questioned are:

- The reliability of the horizontal gaze nystagmus (HGN) test, including the purported causal connection between exaggerated HGN and alcohol ingestion. *United States v. Van Hazel*, 468 F. Supp. 2d 792 (E.D.N.C. 2006).

- That motor vehicles with a high center of gravity have greater tendency to roll over. *Carley v. Wheeled Coach*, 991 F.2d 1117 (3d Cir. 1993).

- That Israel routinely tortures prisoners. *Eain v. Wilkes*, 641 F.2d 504 (7th Cir. 1981).

d. Inherent Authority of Appellate Courts to Supplement the Record

Appellate courts generally have inherent power to supplement the record with information not reviewed by the trial court. Such power is rarely exercised, however, and only in extraordinary circumstances. *See Inland Bulk Transfer Co. v. Cummins Engine Co.*, 332 F.3d 1007, 1012 (6th Cir. 2003); *Jones v. White*,

992 F.2d 1548, 1566 (11th Cir. 1993). Whether to supplement the record is evaluated on a case by case basis, and may involve these factors:

> (1) whether "acceptance of the proffered material into the record would establish beyond any doubt the proper resolution of the pending issue," (2) whether remand of the case would be contrary to the interests of justice and judicial economy; (3) whether the inherent judicial powers of the court in habeas corpus actions dictate supplementation.

Cabalceta v. Standard Fruit Co., 883 F.2d 1553, 1555 (11th Cir. 1989) (quoting *Ross v. Kemp*, 785 F.2d 1467, 1474–75 (11th Cir.1986)).

In *Cabalceta v. Standard Fruit Co.*, for example, the court supplemented the record with information concerning the citizenship of the defendant corporation for purposes of diversity jurisdiction. The court stated: "Since the court is considering the existence of subject matter jurisdiction, a consideration of all relevant information is necessary to make an informed and final decision." 883 F.2d at 1555. *Ross v. Kemp* involved a state habeas corpus claim in which the appellate court allowed the record to be supplemented with jury lists that state officials had purposely failed to disclose in earlier proceedings. 785 F.2d 1467. In *Colbert v. Potter*, 471 F.3d 158, 165–67 (D.C. Cir. 2006), the court supplemented the appellate record with an original United States Post Office "Domestic Return Receipt" that demonstrated that the action was not timely filed. In the proceedings below, only a copy of the back of the receipt was filed. The court noted:

> Certainly, we could have remanded this case to the District Court with instructions to obtain and review the front side of the original Domestic Return Receipt. However, remand for such a ministerial task, which this court easily can perform itself, would serve no good purpose and would ultimately amount to a waste of judicial resources.

Id. at 166.

IV. The Appendix

Generally, the appendix is an abbreviated form of the record consisting of documents from the clerk's file and portions of the reporter's or certified transcript that pertain to the specific issues to be decided on appeal.[2] A well cho-

---

2. Note that in some jurisdictions the parties may choose to prepare and file an appendix in lieu of designating a record to be prepared by the trial court clerk. *See, e.g.,* Cal. Ct. R. 8.124.

sen, well prepared appendix focuses judges, court attorneys, and law clerks on documents pertinent to the appeal and makes those documents easily accessible. The appendix is usually filed with, or shortly after, the appellate briefs.

The various jurisdictions as well as individual courts have specific rules regarding the form and content of appendices that counsel must review and follow in each case. For example, Federal Rule of Appellate Procedure 30 provides, *inter alia*:

Rule 30. Appendix to the Briefs

(a) Appellant's Responsibility.

(1) Contents of the Appendix.

The appellant must prepare and file an appendix to the briefs containing:

(A) the relevant docket entries in the proceeding below;

(B) the relevant portions of the pleadings, charge, findings, or opinion;

(C) the judgment, order, or decision in question; and

(D) other parts of the record to which the parties wish to direct the court's attention.

(2) Excluded Material.

Memoranda of law in the district court should not be included in the appendix unless they have independent relevance. Parts of the record may be relied on by the court or the parties even though not included in the appendix.

(3) Time to File; Number of Copies.

Unless filing is deferred under Rule 30(c), the appellant must file 10 copies of the appendix with the brief and must serve one copy on counsel for each party separately represented. An unrepresented party proceeding in forma pauperis must file 4 legible copies with the clerk, and one copy must be served on counsel for each separately represented party. The court may by local rule or by order in a particular case require the filing or service of a different number.

(b) All Parties' Responsibilities.

(1) Determining the Contents of the Appendix.

The parties are encouraged to agree on the contents of the appendix. In the absence of an agreement, the appellant must, within 14 days after the record is filed, serve on the appellee a designation of the parts of the record the appellant intends to include in the appendix and a statement of the issues the appellant intends to present for review. The appellee may, within 14 days after receiving the designation, serve on the appellant a designation of additional parts to which it wishes to direct the court's attention. The appellant must include the designated parts in the appendix. The parties must not engage in unnecessary designation of parts of the record, because the entire record is available to the court. This paragraph applies also to a cross-appellant and a cross-appellee.

(d) Format of the Appendix.

The appendix must begin with a table of contents identifying the page at which each part begins. The relevant docket entries must follow the table of contents. Other parts of the record must follow chronologically. When pages from the transcript of proceedings are placed in the appendix, the transcript page numbers must be shown in brackets immediately before the included pages. Omissions in the text of papers or of the transcript must be indicated by asterisks. Immaterial formal matters (captions, subscriptions, acknowledgments, etc.) should be omitted.

(e) Reproduction of Exhibits.

Exhibits designated for inclusion in the appendix may be reproduced in a separate volume, or volumes, suitably indexed. Four copies must be filed with the appendix, and one copy must be served on counsel for each separately represented party. If a transcript of a proceeding before an administrative agency, board, commission, or officer was used in a district-court action and has been designated for inclusion in the appendix, the transcript must be placed in the appendix as an exhibit.

a. Content of the Appendix

Counsel must strike a balance between being under-inclusive and over-inclusive in the appendix. This requires a clear and thorough understanding of the issues on appeal, the arguments the attorney intends to make, arguments she or he anticipates from the other side, and the facts and documents relating to those issues and arguments. This would include documents such as pleadings and rulings that provide background and context regarding an issue, as well as documents and transcripts that support or undermine particular arguments. It helps to keep in mind that every underlying or procedural fact referred to in an appellate brief should be accompanied by a citation to a document or portion of a transcript in the appendix that supports it.

Sometimes appendices are under-inclusive because counsel have focused so much on documents supporting their arguments that they omit basic contextual documents such as the complaint or other pleadings, or charging documents, e.g., indictments, and intermediate court orders. On the other hand, sometimes counsel focus so exclusively on legal argument, statutes and case law, that they neglect supporting facts and documents in the record. Unfortunately, some appendixes are under-inclusive because counsel are simply unprepared, overwhelmed, or have shoddy work habits.

Most counsel would rather err on the side of being over inclusive in the appendix. An over-inclusive appendix does not present problems where only a few documents are concerned. Indeed, if counsel give careful consideration to the contents of an appendix and decide specifically to include a document rather than omit it—they are being prudent. Problems arise however, when counsel give little thought to the appendix and simply include most or all of the documents in the clerk's file. This burdens the court with pages and pages of irrelevant material that must be sifted through to reach the documents that are actually pertinent. *See Drewett v. Aetna Cas. Sur. Co.*, 539 F.2d 496, 498 (5th cir. 1976) (granting the appellant's motion to tax costs where the appellee, after reviewing the appellant's designation of documents to be included in the appendix, counter designated "everything else in the record below."). On the other hand, sometimes appendices are over inclusive because counsel have deliberately added material that was not part of the record below, rather than asking to court to take judicial notice or supplement the record. This practice is frowned upon by appellate courts and likely to lead to sanctions. *See Lowry v. Barnhart*, 329 F.3d 1019, 1025 (9th Cir. 2003) (the court noted in assessing sanctions that "[s]adly, this is not the first time a party has graced us with so-called "excerpts of record" that have never before seen the light of courtroom day.").

b. Form of the Appendix

The form of the appendix will usually be spelled out specifically by appellate and local court rules. These rules will address the table of contents, the order in which documents should appear, pagination requirements, how pages should be bound, and the like. The goal of these rules is to ensure the appendix is easy to follow and use. It is the attorney's responsibility to become familiar with the current rules and to follow those rules religiously. This means building in ample time to prepare and assemble the documents.

Unfortunately the appendix is treated as an afterthought by some counsel—to the dismay of the courts. The appendix was particularly awful in *Vitello v. J.C. Penny Co.*, 107 F.3d 869, 1997 WL 87248, at *3, n. 1 (4th Cir. 1997). The court commented:

In ascertaining the facts, we had to look to the record and expected to rely on the joint appendix as setting forth the relevant portions of the record. After all, the joint appendix is supposed to assist an appellate court by being a compilation of those portions of the record necessary to decide the appeal; however, the appendix prepared in this case was far from helpful. Mechanically, it was a mess— too many pages were put in a volume so that the volumes fell apart. Page numbers were largely unreadable so the court was reduced to counting each page of the appendix itself in order to find something referred to by joint appendix page in the briefs. The index to the appendix was useless, referring to "transcript of evidence" rather than identifying the trial testimony by witness. The joint appendix totaled more than 1,000 pages and yet failed to contain the complaint and other crucial portions of the record. In short, the joint appendix was a disaster that utterly failed to comply with the letter or spirit of Fed. R. App. P. 30.

Id.

Checkpoints

- The record on appeal usually consists of the documents filed in the trial court and a record of oral proceedings.

- The record on appeal provides the background and foundation for the appellate court's decision.

- Any asserted error must appear, and be preserved, in the record.

- Generally, in deciding the appeal, the appellate court may consider only what was in the trial court record. Errors and omissions, however, may be corrected.

- Appellate courts may take judicial notice of facts outside the record that are not subject to reasonable dispute.

- A fact may be indisputable because it is "either (1) generally known within the territorial jurisdiction of the trial court or (2) capable of accurate and ready determination by resort to sources whose accuracy cannot reasonably be questioned." Fed. R. Evid. 201(b).

- Appellate courts generally have inherent power to supplement the record with information not reviewed by the trial court and not subject to judicial notice, but it is very rarely used.

Checkpoints *continued*

- The appendix, an abbreviated form of the record, is used in many jurisdictions for the convenience of the court.

- A well chosen, well prepared appendix focuses judges, court attorneys, and law clerks on documents pertinent to the appeal and makes those documents easily accessible.

- The appendix is usually filed with, or shortly after, the appellate briefs.

Chapter 7

Appellate Legal Analysis

Roadmap

- It is important for an appellate attorney to analyze the legal and factual issues surrounding the appeal with fresh eyes, which often means revisiting basic techniques and building blocks of legal analysis — tools that might have gotten lost in the flurry of trial proceedings and motion practice below.

- Tools for analyzing and interpreting statutes include using tabulation to make the statute into a checklist, analyzing the statute's structure, considering applicable case law, using the "plain meaning" rule, reviewing legislative history, looking at similar statutes in other jurisdictions, using the canons of construction, and reading journal articles and other commentary.

- In preparing for the appeal, review and revisit the relevant cases, actively, with the purpose of determining what statements of law the courts issuing these decisions used and how they applied them to the facts before them.

- The goal of legal analysis is to produce a synthesized understanding of the law, including statutes and case law, and how they are applied; take care not to lapse into sequential statutory and case analysis.

- The basic structure for all legal analysis is IRAC (issue, rule, analysis, conclusion) or its advocacy-crafted cousin CRAC (conclusion, rule, analysis, conclusion).

I. Using Fresh Eyes and Focusing on Error

There can be a tendency for lawyers on either side of an appeal to assume the legal analysis of the situation was complete as of the trial or other dispositive hearing, except for updating the cases used in the proceedings below. This is especially true if the lawyers on appeal are the same ones who handled the case in the original proceedings. A challenge in planning and preparing an appellate brief is to review the facts, statutes, cases, and other authorities with fresh eyes focusing on potential error, or its absence.

While new issues generally cannot be raised on appeal, with a fresh look and an open mind, it is possible to improve the arguments in your favor and further undermine your opponents' positions. Thus, counsel for appellees or respondents should not assume that, because they prevailed below, the same arguments made the same way will prevail on appeal. Similarly, counsel for appellants should not assume or hope that unlike the trial court, an appellate court will "get" or "appreciate" the same arguments made below, made in the same way, or worse, simply made longer. Rather than a de novo retrial, an appeal is focused on identifying error—legal or factual—and meeting the requirements of the standard of review.

In any instance, legal analysis is a system of breaking things down—be they rules, factors, statutes, cases, facts, etc. and then fitting the parts together into a cohesive whole that advances your position. A fresh look for appellate counsel often means revisiting basic techniques and building blocks of legal analysis—tools that can get lost in the flurry below.

II.   Tools for Analyzing and Interpreting Statutes

In some cases the meaning and interpretation of a particular statute is central to the appeal. In others cases a statute may be involved, but is treated almost as wallpaper—existing in the background with little attention paid to it or its language. In every case involving a statute it behooves appellate counsel to review the particular section and the statutory scheme it is a part of, as well as the following tools.

a.   Using Tabulation to Explode a Statute

Statutes that are properly drafted constitute a checklist of sorts. Thus when reviewing the statue involved in your appeal, use a pen or pencil or on-screen track changes feature so that you can explicitly divide the statute into elements (requirements) and factors (things to be considered), insert numbers and letters to tabulate these features, and pay close attention to words like "and" and "or" to determine how many requirements, options, and considerations there are under the statute. Reformatting a statute in tabular form on your word processor or on paper, focusing on these factors and elements, rather than looking at a large block of text is essential in taking a fresh look at the statute. By exploding the statute or statement of law into its constituent parts, you can identify each element or factor, and then analyze each of them in light of a given set of facts.

Take Restatement (Second) of Contracts section 24, which operates like a statute and defines what constitutes an "offer":

An offer is the manifestation of willingness to enter into a bargain, so made as to justify another person in understanding that his assent to that bargain is invited and will conclude it.

Even this simple block of text will benefit by being reformatted in tabular form so that it resembles a checklist:

An offer is:

(a) the manifestation of

(b) willingness to enter into a bargain,

(c) so made as to justify another person in understanding that:

  (i) his assent to that bargain is invited and

  (ii) will conclude it.

For another example, take a sub-section of the UCC as enacted in California dealing with what additional terms in an acceptance or confirmation of an order mean. The statute was exploded in the drafting process:

California Commercial Code § 2207(2)

The additional terms are to be construed as proposals for addition to the contract. Between merchants such terms become part of the contract unless:

(a) The offer expressly limits acceptance to the terms of the offer;

(b) They materially alter it; *or*

(c) Notification of objection to them has already been given or is given within a reasonable time after notice of them is received.

This sub-section opens with a statement that additional terms (in an acceptance or confirmation, discussed in § 2207(1)) are deemed to be merely proposals for addition to the contract. If the parties are not merchants, this is as far as the statute takes us—the additional terms are proposals, nothing more. Some additional acts of acceptance would be needed before they became part of the parties' contract.

This first sentence is followed by a second one that creates a presumption, *if the parties are merchants*, that the additional terms will be included in the contract unless one of three conditions is met. Merchants are defined by the commercial code in § 2104, and this definition will, thus, control whether the condition is met and whether the second sentence of § 2207 has any applicability. The three conditions that overcome the presumption of incorporation of the additional terms into the contract are phrased in the alternative, joined with an "or," which means that only one of them needs to be met to overcome the presumption.

Thus, the first and most important step in analyzing and interpreting statutes is to explode them into their component elements (requirements) and factors (things to be considered) creating a checklist that you can understand and explain to others.

b. Using the Structure and Other Sections of the Same Statute

Do not review your statute in a vacuum; be sure to revisit the statutory scheme that it is a part of—the body of related statutes—to understand the structure of the whole. Often complex statutes or bodies of statutes will have logical divisions, perhaps first stating the scope of the enactment, and perhaps even the legislative intent or policy reasons for enacting the statute or statutory scheme, then providing definitions of key terms, then containing positive provisions, standards, and rules; then exceptions and exemptions. All of these features can be used to understand the context of the specific statute at issue and to construe it appropriately under the circumstances. One of the important dangers of modern electronic research is that legal research databases (Lexis, Westlaw, etc.) generally display sections of a statute in isolation rather than in the serial format of a statute book where, at most, the sections are separated by official comments or case annotations.

Appellate counsel should also examine how the same or similar words in other sections or subsections have been used. Have these words been interpreted by the courts? If so, should that interpretation also apply to the words as used in the statute involved in your appeal? There is a strong tendency in the law to give words in similar statutes and rules the same meaning to promote uniformity. For example, in People v. Superior Court (Romero), 917 P.2d 628 (Cal.1996), the California Supreme Court rejected the People's argument that the words "prior offense" in § 667 (c)(2) of California's "Three Strikes" legislation meant "prior felony conviction." The court stated that this interpretation "makes no sense in context. Throughout the Three Strikes law, when the Legislature intended to refer to a previous conviction of an offense, as it did in many instances, it properly used the word 'conviction.' [citing Pen. Code] § 667, subds. (d), (d)(1), (d)(2), (d)(3), (e), (e)(1), (e)(2), (f)(1), (f)(2), (g)."

c. Using Case Law Interpreting a Statute

Case law interpreting a statute is an obvious tool of statutory construction. In preparing an appeal, counsel will certainly Sheppardize or otherwise update the statute and cases used in the lower proceedings. In addition, counsel should review—with a fresh eye—the cases used below. Courts and cases deal with statutes in numerous ways, and it is possible that portions of opinions that were skimmed or glossed over by counsel in the proceedings below will take on new significance. For example, courts may:

1. Determine if a statute is *valid*. Does it conflict with a higher authority? Does a state statute conflict with the state's constitution or the United States' Constitution? Does a regulation or ordinance conflict with a higher ranked statute? Do rules from an appellate court case conflict with a rule or rules articulated in a Supreme Court case?

2. Determine *whether* a statute applies or *which* statute applies.

3. *Interpret* a statute—determine what its terms mean, what is required, permitted, or forbidden under what circumstances.

4. *Apply* the statute to the facts before them and determine the outcome.

See also Section III, below, "Reviewing, Using, and Synthesizing Cases."

d. Plain Meaning—The Wording of the Statutory Section at Issue

Another tool of statutory interpretation is the so-called "plain meaning" rule: Are the words of the statute clear and unambiguous? If so, then courts say that one should look no further and simply apply the terms of the statute in their plain and ordinary fashion. The plain meaning rule often comes into play when an appellate court has not interpreted the terms of the statute that are at issue. Or your position may be that the trial court's interpretation is contrary to the statute's plain meaning. Plain meaning is a useful tool, but appellate counsel should be alert and beware. It can be easy for courts to announce that the "meaning is plain" or that a proposed interpretation is "contrary to the plain meaning." The problem, of course, is that "plain meaning" is in the eye of the beholder.

For example, consider a procedural rule allowing enforcement of a judgment that is triggered when all appeals of a civil judgment are complete and opportunities for further appeals have been exhausted. Imagine that this rule was passed in the 19th century, when appeals to the United States Supreme Court were a matter of right if a federal issue had been preserved. Imagine further that it is now the 21st century and that, since the late 20th century, parties have no appeal of right to the United States Supreme Court. All that remains is the potential for discretionary review via a petition for a writ of certiorari. One of the parties to your client's dispute has exhausted its appeals but has petitioned for review by certiorari. Is the procedural rule triggered so that the judgment can be enforced before the petition for certiorari is ruled upon? One view is that the meaning of the rule is plain, all appeals are complete, so the judgment is collectable. The other view would be that events subsequent to the rule's enactment have changed matters and the meaning of the rule is not so plain. How should a court rule in the absence of any other information using the plain meaning rule? Answers may vary.

Also, some counsel can be seduced by the seeming mechanical nature of the plain meaning rule. This can lead them to embrace the fiction that, if you they convince a court that the meaning of statutory language is "plain," the court cannot look to extrinsic evidence such as legislative history to interpret the statute. Understand: If a court wants to, it will look at legislative history, no matter how plain the meaning. Whether the court will do anything with what it finds in that history, or whether it will expressly state that it has examined that history in its written opinion, is a different matter. But it takes more than a simple chant of "plain meaning" to put blinders on a court.

Raising a compelling plain meaning argument requires complete and thorough understanding of the statute, as well as any case law dealing with the statute. This should enable you to make an argument that is clear, concise, and easy to grasp. Nothing is less compelling than a murky, convoluted argument that a proposed meaning is "plain."

e. Legislative History

Legislative history consists of documents and records created by the various parts of the legislature that enacted the statute. It includes statements of legislators regarding why they were in favor of a bill or why they opposed it, as well as different versions of a bill as it progressed through the legislative process. A good piece of legislative history can tip the balance in a question of how a statute should be interpreted when its meaning is less than plain and there are no judicial precedents on point.

Take care not to put too much stock in legislators' statements in legislative history, however. For every statement you find that you think supports your position, there may be just as many that support the opposite. Moreover, the statements of legislators can be written up and inserted in the Congressional Record after enactment and need never have been uttered to another person, much less made before a packed house of Congress. However, courts may give greater weight to analyses by a neutral staff professional, for example digests of bills by California's Legislative Counsel.

Legislative history also includes the various versions of the bill as it went through committees. Check to see what words were added or subtracted. This sort of analysis can bear fruit and is, perhaps, the most reliable form of legislative history that exists as it reflects the results of an actual deliberative process in the legislature.

Related to legislative history, also examine the state of the law before the statute was enacted. What was the historical context at the time of enactment? Does the section at issue codify a case? Overrule a case? Codify a case with changes? Each of these observations can be used to promote or undermine an interpretive argument regarding a statute.

f. Similar Statutes in the Same Jurisdiction

If courts in your jurisdiction have not addressed the statute involved in your case, they may have addressed a similar statute. Examine what courts have said regarding similar words or elements, and ask if this reasoning can or should be applied by analogy to your client's case. For example, after enacting three strikes statutes, many states enacted two strikes statutes, and then even one strike statutes. In these states, case law interpreting terms and provisions in established three strikes legislation would be useful in interpreting similar terms or provisions in the new two strikes and one strike legislation.

g. Similar Statutes in other States or Jurisdictions

In a similar vein, if courts in the jurisdiction have not interpreted the same or a similar statue, courts in other jurisdictions may have interpreted similar statutes. Especially in the case of uniform acts or restatements, often the opinions of courts in jurisdictions that were early adopters of the statute or principle can be very persuasive to courts in jurisdictions that are later adopters. Most judges would prefer not to reinvent the wheel, especially if doing so may subject them to reversal on appeal, and showing them how some other authoritative body has performed the analysis of the statute and applied it can be very persuasive.

h. Canons of Construction

The canons of construction are rules of statutory interpretation stated in the abstract. They include principles like "prefer the specific authority over the general" or the "last in time" rule which prefers more current statutes over older ones. The central, stated goal of all of these rules is to determine the "intent of the legislature." These canons are so general, however, that there are often more than one that might apply to a particular statutory provision, often in contradictory ways. As a result, it is often observed that the canons are seldom dispositive tools of legal analysis and are often used selectively to provide justification for an interpretation that has been decided upon for other reasons. Thus, while useful, they are seldom dispositive.

Some statutes contain their own rules of interpretation, such as a specification that the singular shall include the plural and the masculine gender shall include the feminine. *See*, for example, Title 1, Chapter 1, United States Code. Some of the other canons from the common law, which many states have codified, are listed below, with brief explanation:

- *The Plain Meaning Rule.* If a statute's meaning is plain on its face, then one should not look beyond the four corners of the statute in interpreting it. Exceptions to this rule are found when an ambiguity can be found or when application of the rule would lead to absurd results.

- *The Rule of Strict Construction.* Often strict or narrow construction of statutes is said to be appropriate for statutes in derogation of the common law and statutes that deprive a court of jurisdiction.

- *The Rule of Liberal Construction.* Liberal or broad construction of remedial statutes is often said to be appropriate so as to give effect to their remedial intent.

- *Expressio Unis Est Exclusio Alterius.* To express one thing is to exclude another.

- *Ejusdem Generis.* When a sentence lists specific things and the list ends with phrases such as "etc.," "and the like," and "and others," the concluding general phrase should be limited by the listed specifics to things similar to those listed.

- *Noscitur a Sociis.* A word is known by its associates. In other words, interpret words in their context. This rule is particularly applicable to choosing the meaning of a homonym to be applied in a particular situation.

- *The Rule of Last Modification.* A qualifying phrase will modify only the immediately preceding word or phrase. (To avoid its application, place your qualification before the list, not after.)

- *Specific Language Trumps General Language.*

- *A Document Must Be Read as a Whole.*

- *Construe a Document Against its Drafter.*

- *Adopt a Construction that Favors Validity of a Contract or Statute.*

- *Adopt a Construction that is Consistent with Public Policy.*

i. Law Review Articles & Scholarly Commentary

A student, professor, or expert in the field may have written a note, article, or treatise on the subject that your statue involves. In these cases, it can be useful to refer to the note, article, or treatise for its suggested analysis. These sources, especially law review articles, may be useful both for what they contain as well as the conclusions that they reach—their footnotes collect authorities and can save you hours of research time. The article itself may also advocate a position favorable to your appeal and provide useful policy arguments or empirical support.

III. Reviewing, Using, and Synthesizing Cases

Appellate counsel should of course update the authorities used below as well as conduct independent research to ensure they are well versed in the law applicable to the issues on appeal. The result may be no new authorities, just a few, or a list of them. The next step is to review any new authorities, as well as revisit the "old" and put them together into a cohesive, persuasive whole.

a. Reviewing and Revisiting cases

The following subsections discuss considerations relevant to particular sections or features of judicial opinions and suggestions for approaching them.

1. Caption

Experienced counsel may tend to skip over a case's caption. Instead, quickly note the court rendering the decision and the date, and then run through this checklist: (1) which jurisdiction does the opinion come from—is it the same as the jurisdiction your matter is in? (2) what level is the deciding court?—trial, appellate, or a supreme court or other court of last resort, (3) is the opinion designated as not for publication or otherwise restricted for precedential or citation purposes? (4) is the opinion binding and, if so, upon which courts in what jurisdiction? For discussion on binding versus nonbinding authority and the hierarchy of authority, see Chapter 10, Section II.

2. Summaries and Headnotes

These portions of a published opinion are added by the legal publisher and are not part of the court's decision. As a result, they cannot be cited to or relied upon. However, they are useful tools in identifying the issues addressed and their location in the case.

3. Disposition

At the outset, check what the disposition was, e.g., was the decision below affirmed, reversed, or vacated? This will give you perspective as you read. Courts often put things differently depending on whether they are affirming, reversing, modifying, or vacating and remanding. It is helpful to know where the court is heading before it gets there.

4. Procedural Facts

Most opinions set forth the procedural history of the case. Do not skip over this section. Instead review it strategically, noting:

(1) What type of action is being appealed, e.g., a judgment after a jury verdict, default judgment, summary judgment, or evidentiary order;

(2) How the court below ruled or what the jury found;

(3) Who won, who lost, who is appealing; and

(4) On what grounds (if stated).

5. Underlying Facts

Most opinions contain a statement of facts, which explains the underlying story of the case on which the opinion's legal analysis is based. Since statements of fact can be quite lengthy, do not get bogged down on the first reading. Attempt to categorize these facts as relevant, irrelevant, similar, or different from the client's case. Often the important facts become apparent in the court's analysis or discussion section as they are used to reach conclusions. Thus, it is often best to go back and reread the statement of facts after you have finished the discussion section.

6. Issues

Look for any recitation of the issues by the court. Often, especially in more modern opinions, the court will set out the issues after its statement of the facts. Or, optimally, a court will do this at the beginning of the opinion in its introductory paragraph.

7. Statements of Law and their Explanation

The law or rule section of an opinion may (1) determine whether particular laws are valid, (2) determine which or what laws apply; (3) interpret laws; and/or (4) explain laws, e.g., how they work or why they are important.

Statements of the law can be slippery characters. Often opinions involving very specific situations contain general statements of the law that are perfectly appropriate for the case itself but are inaccurate when taken out of context and applied to different, even if somewhat analogous, facts. Think of laws as statements of what is required, permitted, or forbidden in particular circumstances, or what legally results from particular events or actions. Alternatively, think of them as listing what is required or considered in determining whether a legal result occurs, e.g., whether someone is liable for a criminal or civil sanction. Statements of the law are also set out as definitions, tests, or standards, with elements or factors or both. Explanations of laws often contain additional subsidiary or corollary laws.

8. Application of Law

When the court "applies the law," i.e., discusses the facts of the case before it and why and how they meet or fail to meet the applicable laws, pay careful attention to facts the court indicates are significant. Remember that an opinion is a document drafted to support a ruling. What is included, omitted, emphasized, or downplayed is significant. Your goal is to identify the facts that are important in the court's analysis and resolution of the issues.

Not all opinions will have an application section, however. Sometimes they are not necessary, for example where a court determines that a particular law is invalid or does not apply to the issue. However, other times, the court may set out the facts and the law and then announce its conclusion, without "showing its work." If that is the case, you will need to do your own application and determine which facts were significant to the court's analysis and why.

9. Policy

In setting out or applying the law, a court may describe its reasoning in terms of the *policies* that the law is meant to promote. For example, statutes of limitations are meant to promote the timely adjudication of most disputes while memories and evidence are relatively fresh and to encourage law enforcement to promptly investigate and prosecute crimes. These goals are important for the efficient and accurate administration of justice. With particularly heinous crimes like first degree murder, this policy may be outweighed by other considerations such as the need to incarcerate, punish, or rehabilitate murderers, and, thus, there is no statute of limitations in any of the United States for first degree murder. Focus on policy discussions and evaluate how these statements might help or hurt the matter you are working on. Often policy discussions are, or are later characterized as, dicta (see below).

10. Holding

The holding is the court's decision on the issue along with the essential supporting facts or reasons. If the opinion has an application section, note what specific facts the court cites in coming to its conclusion. In appellate briefs, it is useful to provide holdings as part of citations, in parentheticals — *Smith v. Jones*, _____ Rptr. _____ (Court, date) (holding that _____, when _____). Citations with parentheticals can be a very efficient and effective form of shorthand that captures the case name, citation, holding and essential facts in two to three lines of text.

11. Dicta

Dicta, or, more fully, "obter dicta" — Latin for "things said in passing" — consist of statements included in an opinion that are not necessary to the court's holding. These statements go beyond the facts and circumstances before court and are not essential to its determination. Dicta can be very useful, however, in giving examples of how a rule or standard might or might not be met. To spot dicta, look for phrases like "for example," "such as" or "this is not a case where _____." These comments, while not binding in a technical sense as precedent, are often powerful indicators of a court's or a particular judge's attitude toward the issue discussed and how he or she might rule if faced with those facts or issues.

b. Using Cases: A Checklist

The following is a checklist of consideration for appellate counsel to consider when deciding how a case might be used on appeal.

1. Where Does the Case Come From?

All cases are not created equal. Is the case from the same state or jurisdiction as your matter? Which level of court decided the case—

trial, appellate, or court of last resort? When was the case decided—was it after the law(s) at issue took effect?

In terms of hierarchy: the most recent case from the highest court in the pertinent jurisdiction is accorded the most weight. Then less recent cases from the highest court in the jurisdiction, assuming they are still good law and have not been overruled by later cases, or superseded by statute. Next are recent cases from appellate courts in the jurisdiction. Cases from outside the pertinent jurisdiction, other than cases from the United States Supreme Court, are not binding, although they may provide persuasive authority *if* the court chooses to consider them.

2. *Does the Case Deal with the Same Issue as Your Problem or Matter?*

A similar issue? If so, how similar is it?

3. *What Laws Does the Court Apply or Articulate?*

4. *What Does the Court Say about Those Laws?*

Anything to help explain them or why they are important, or to explain why they apply? Any policy statements—e.g. why the law is important, the purposes served?

5. *What Are the Facts of the Case?*

Are they similar to the ones in your problem or matter? How? Are they different? How?

6. *How Does the Court Apply the Laws to the Facts?*

What does the court say when it evaluates the facts based on the laws? What is its reasoning? Does it highlight certain types of facts as being important? Does it further explain any of the rules? Are there any helpful policy statements?

7. *What Is the Court's Holding—The Court's Decision and the Basis for It?*

How does the court decide the issue? How does the court describe the basis for its decision? Set forth the holding in a parenthetical, i.e., in one or two lines put in parentheses after the case citation. Depending on the client and their situation, it may be best to describe a holding so that it applies broadly or generally, e.g., *Smith v. Jones* (mandatory arbitration agreement in employment contract held unenforceable). At other times it is best to describe a holding in detail, so that it appears confined to specific facts, e.g., *Smith v. Jones* (mandatory arbitration agreement in employment contract held unconscionable and thus unenforceable, where it (a) lacked mutuality, (b) imposed pre-arbitration resolution procedure controlled by employer, and (c) severely limited time within which employee could request arbitration).

8. Does the Opinion Contain Any Useful Dicta?

The court may make statements that are not necessary to its holding, but that are helpful to your cause. Particularly look for when the court gives examples. Some of these can be very useful, especially when the court gives examples of how a rule or standard would or would not be met: "On the other hand, if the defendant had been carrying a knife he would have been guilty...."

c. Synthesizing Multiple Cases—Putting It All Together to Advocate a Position

Sometimes even experienced counsel will lapse into "sequential case analysis" in their briefs– listing summaries of cases that appear relevant, leaving the reader to fit them together. Quality legal analysis, however, is much more than just a "report" on a string of individual cases that deal with an issue. It should be a synthesized analysis of the laws and their application to particular facts. Fitting cases together so that they make good legal sense and advocate a position is essential to effective appellate advocacy. This entails (1) distilling the legal principles from multiple cases (both familiar and new) and explaining, (i.e., advocating) what they are and how they relate to each other, and (2) applying those principles to the facts to promote a particular result.

1. Getting Started—Review the Cases Starting with the Most Recent

For each main issue on appeal, review the applicable cases in the order of newest to oldest. It is likely that the later courts will have at least partially synthesized the cases already—meaning ideally, they will have distilled legal principles from prior cases, fit them together, and explained them. This is a starting point, and should give an indication of the significant issues, laws, and cases and how they evolved. Caution though: the courts might have missed things, made mistakes, or even intentionally obfuscated portions of prior cases — so read critically at all times.

2. After Reading the Cases, Write a Holding for Each

For each case, write out the holding on each issue addressed using a short parenthetical, e.g. *Smith v. Jones* (bar owner liable for bartender's assault on a patron because bartender's duties included maintaining the peace, and thus it was foreseeable he would need to use force dealing with unruly patrons). Think of these case names and holdings as building blocks and pieces that can be moved around on your analysis chart described below.

3. Sorting and Grouping

After reading the cases, newest to oldest and writing a holding for each, you should have an idea of the various issues or sub-issues involved. At this stage it is often useful to start a chart with the issues set out as categories. The next step is to sort the cases by issue. For each issue or category, note the relevant cases. Some cases may involve more than one issue and will be listed in multiple categories. Then for each issue, group the cases by result: cases that met the overall standard or requirements and those that did not. For example, if an issue is whether an offer was made, sort the cases into two groups: those that held there was an offer, and those that held there was not.

By sorting the cases with their holdings by issues and sub-issues and then grouping them by result, you will more easily recognize patterns, trends, and factors that point to a particular result. You will also more easily recognize any commonalities between the cases.

4. Distilling and Synthesizing the Law

The essential function of synthesizing cases is distilling or extracting the laws from multiple cases and fitting them together so that you can explain the laws to promote your position to the court. To start, review the charts you made in sorting and grouping cases — you will see what cases address the different issues and sub-issues in your matter. Then review each case separately and take down the statements of law made by the court and what the court says about them — how the court explains the laws. Statements of law, of course, come in many forms, e.g., a list of requirements or considerations, tests, definitions, descriptions of standards, or rules of construction. Explanations of laws also often contain additional statements of law.

Once you have isolated the statements of law and explanations in a case, note for each issue which of the statements of law are elements and which are factors. Elements are requirements. They must be present for a certain result to occur. Factors are indicators or considerations that may, or should, be taken into account in determining whether a standard has been met. Factors are types or categories of facts that point to a particular result, but do not mandate it. Remember not to mix up elements and factors or use the terms interchangeably. Often a court will identify factors in the law section of an opinion, e.g. "Factors include ..." Or when a court states "Important consideration are...." or "We look to whether [a description of various types of facts]," it is likely the court is describing factors. Unfortunately, courts may also use the terms elements and factors interchangeably.

After you have extracted the statements of laws on the pertinent issues from each case and determined their character, you are ready to put them together. For each issue, first look for statements of law that are repeated in the cases that overlap. These are likely your broad or overarching rules. If you detect any differences in wording or terms, review the cases and whether the differences make a difference. Did a court announce a change in the law or explain why it used the specific words it did? Did the different words yield different results? You may not be able to tell in the beginning of your analysis, but make an inquiry. Next, look for more specific or subsidiary rules that apply in more limited circumstances. These might be set out as definitions or tests or factors that further explain the broader, more general rules.

Once you have assembled the statements of law for each issue and sub-issue, return to your charts and in each category write down the statements of law in order of broad/overarching ones to more narrow specific ones, along with the case(s) from which the statements came. Sometimes the statements of law will nest together easily, with broad statements of the general law, then lists of elements with specific tests and or factors for each. Other times, there will be "holes" of little or no statements of law on certain sub-issues. You will also find that statements of law may appear to contradict each other and cannot be neatly reconciled. Your goal is to set out and explain the law in a way that (1) promotes your position, and (2) your reader will easily understand—even if it is complicated.

Also, when a case contains a list of factors, the court has helped synthesize them already. Other times you will have to synthesize factors yourself. To do this, for each case, note the type of facts the court considered significant in coming to its conclusion. Check first in the application section, where the court discusses whether the facts meet the rules, test, or standards it had set out and explained. If the opinion does not have an application section—in other words, the court simply announces its decision after setting out the rules — reread the statement of facts in the opinion and sort out the facts that appear most significant to you. This is also where your sorting and grouping chart of case names and holdings is useful — review it and looks for trends and similarities and differences in the facts of the cases that met the tests or standards and those that did not.

This process may seem tedious, but with time it should become second nature. It is important that you go through the process so that the judge, court attorney, or law clerk who is considering your brief does not have to do so.

IV. Final Steps in the Analysis

Effective appellate advocacy requires thorough and sophisticated knowledge of the law and authorities and how they affect your facts. There is no substitute for sound research, analysis, and preparation. With that foundation you will be able to:

(1) Recognize strong points and arguments and make the most of them;

(2) Understand and overcome or minimize weaknesses in your positions;

(3) Understand the hierarchy of your authorities and use them to your best advantage, and

(4) Organize your arguments persuasively and coherently.

All these accomplishments combine to further persuade a court to rule your way.

After you have reviewed and analyzed any statute involved, as well as reviewed, revisited and synthesized the cases (old and new), you will have a good idea of which cases and authorities you will use in your brief. Make sure that you have thorough and comfortable knowledge of their holdings and important facts, as well as any laws, tests, factors, and the like, they contain. Complete and sophisticated knowledge of how the cases and other authorities help or hurt your cause is essential in drafting good appellate briefs.

Before starting the drafting process, for each issue and subissue, determine which:

- cases you will use to set out your basic laws or tests;

- cases have compelling language that you will want to quote or paraphrase;

- cases have facts that you want to use to analogize or distinguish the facts in your case;

- cases are useful simply because the court ruled the same way you want the trial court to rule. It is likely that the same case or cases will be useful in more than one category. These cases go to "the top of the heap" and will be featured in your argument.

If there are cases you thought you might use that did not make any of these categories, put them aside. It is likely you will not use them in your discussion. Do not throw them away yet, because a use for them may be triggered as you draft your arguments. What is important is that you start with a plan regarding which cases you are going to use and why. This will focus your writing and prevent you from cluttering up your memorandum with extraneous discussion and case citation.

Also examine and rank the cases you think are harmful because:

- they set forth rules that are detrimental to your cause;

- they have damaging language that you can imagine the other side quoting; or

- their facts and holding could undermine your theory of the case.

Here, too, the same case or cases might satisfy more than one category. These go to the top of the "must legally assail and/or factually distinguish" heap. Resist the urge to ignore or dismiss cases that might be damaging, because the opposing side certainly will not.

Finally, all cases and authorities are not created equally. Be clear on where in the hierarchy of authority each falls. First note whether the case or other authority is controlling (binding) — does it come from an appellate or court of last resort in the trial court's jurisdiction? Is a statute or ordinance from the state or county in which the trial court is situated? Authority that is not controlling (binding), e.g., cases and statutes from other jurisdictions and secondary sources such as treatises, is merely optional. Optional authority is sometimes referred to as "persuasive authority" — which is a misnomer, because optional authority is only persuasive if the court decides it is. Then for each section and subsection, rank the controlling authorities among themselves, e.g., cases from courts of last resort in the jurisdiction are ranked higher than appellate court cases.

V. Organizing a Persuasive Legal Analysis — IRAC and CRAC Formats

In organizing and presenting legal analysis, two formats predominate:

IRAC: Issue, Rule, Application, Conclusion

CRAC: Conclusion, Rule, Application, Conclusion

The IRAC or CRAC format will form the basis of discussion on issues and sub-issues in memoranda, briefs, opinions, and almost any other form of legal drafting that predicts, advocates, or defends an outcome. The two are variants of each other. IRAC is used for more neutral sounding analysis while CRAC is used for analysis with more of an advocacy slant, e.g., appellate briefs.

Attorneys may learn IRAC and CRAC in law school, use them in taking exams, and then shelve these techniques as practicing lawyers. This is unfortunate, because the IRAC and CRAC structure are usually the best ways to deliver information in a way that a wide assortment of readers can most easily understand. Appellate counsel may assume the CRAC is too simple for the complex issues their briefs must tackle. Yet it is this simplicity in basic structure that makes the CRAC such an effective advocacy tool—enabling the drafter to break down complicated issues and explain them in a series of manageable parts. Keep in mind that your audience—courts, judges, court attorneys, and law clerks—can only be persuaded by arguments they readily understand.

The Persuasive IRAC or CRAC

For each issue and subissue:

C: Identify the issue by stating the conclusion you want the court to make.

First set out the conclusion in the heading for the issue or subissue. Then elaborate on this conclusion in the topic sentence of the paragraph immediately below the heading and cite supporting authority. Do not worry about sounding repetitive. Some readers skip over headings, and thus the heading and the topic sentence should be able to stand alone.

R: Identify, Explain, and Illustrate the Rules–the Law to Promote Your Position:

In the CRAC format, the topic sentence of the first rule paragraph will contain the conclusion you are advocating, along with the fundamental reason in support, followed by a citation to you strongest authority. Then set out and explain the applicable laws, in a logical, easy-to-follow order that promotes your position. Usually this means beginning with the most important or basic law and then moving from general to specific and broad to narrow. Often in explaining law, you will set forth additional laws. For example, you may set forth the general law, "An employer is liable for the acts of its employee that are within the course and scope of employment." You will then explain what is meant by "course and scope of employment" setting out tests or standards for each with elements or factors. In other words, you will explain a general law with more narrow, specific laws. Identifying factors is also part of explaining the law.

Your discussion will seem merely theoretical unless you illustrate the laws by including specific factual examples from the cases—showing when the rules, standards, tests you set out and explained were met and when they were not.

Remember to set out, explain, and illustrate the rules so as to advance your side. However, do not ignore—but rather, bury and/or diminish the import of—rules, factors or cases that you know the other side will rely on.

Finally, (1) every law, explanation, or case you refer to in the Application section must first be set out in the Rule section, and (2) do not discuss the client's facts in the rule section. This last one can be challenging for many advocates, who want to apply the laws as they go. For the reader, however, this results in piecemeal analysis that is much harder to follow. Thus, present, explain, and illustrate all the applicable laws first, then when you are done, apply them.

A: Application of the Law to the Facts of the Case:

Begin the application section with the conclusion you want the court to reach—that the facts or circumstances at issue meet or fail to meet the basic or most important law set out in the rules section, followed by a citation to your strongest case(s). Then, in order of broad to narrow, strongest to weakest:

(1) *Tell* the court why the facts meet or fail to meet the rules you've set out and explained, with citations to supporting cases. These are your "assertions."

(2) *Show* the court how the facts meet or fail to meet the rules you've set out and explained by comparing and contrasting them to the cases cited in the Rule section—be sure to pin cite to these cases as you discuss them. Also distinguish and diminish any authorities you know the other side will rely on. The goal is to show the court that your conclusions and assertions are sound and well supported.

Do not introduce or refer to any new rules, explanations, factors, cases, or facts in the Application section. They must be first introduced in the Rule section or the Statement of Facts. In other words, if a rule, explanation, factor, case, or fact is important enough to use in an application section, the reader should already be familiar with it.

Think of the Application as the "tell and show" section.

C: Conclusion

Tell the court again the conclusion you want it to make and why, with a cite to your essential case(s).

Here is an example of a CRAC from a successful brief written by the authors, appealing the trial court's refusal to allow access to court documents:

The District Court Erred in Finding Moot the Motion to
Intervene and Dissolve or Modify the Stipulated Protective Order

This Court reviews the question of mootness de novo. *Maine School Admin. Dist. 35 v. Mr. and Mrs. R.*, 321 F.3d 9, 17 (1st Cir. 2003); *Verhoven v. Brunswick School Comm.*, 207 F.3d 1, 5 (1st Cir. 1999). A matter becomes moot "[o]nly if it were indisputable that no form of relief could be provided." *Gowen, Inc. v. F/V Quality One*, 244 F.3d 64, 66 (1st Cir. 2001); *see also Mr. and Mrs. R.*, 321 F.3d at 18 (cases filed under the Individual with Disabilities Education Act do not become moot when the child's eligibility for services ends as long as a claim based on past deprivation of services remains). Changed circumstances that make it impossible to grant relief would render a matter moot. *Oakville Dev. Corp., v. FDIC*, 986 F.2d 611, 613 (1st Cir. 1993) (matter became moot where the foreclosure sale that the plaintiff sought to enjoin had occurred and the title to the property passed to third party). A settlement may also render a matter moot. *Shelby v. Subperformance Int'l Inc.*, 435 F.2d. 42, 45–46 (1st Cir. 2006) (appeal rendered moot where a settlement resolved of all the controverted issues between the parties).

Here, the district court erred in finding moot Kuney's motions to intervene and to dissolve or modify the Stipulated Protective Order (Docket No. 547, Appendix, Tab 2, p. 10). *Mr. and Mrs. R.*, 321 F.3d at 18. None of the circumstances that might render a matter moot are present. *Id.* There have been no changed circumstances that would make it impossible to grant Kuney the relief sought, which is intervention and modification of the stipulated protective order. *Oakville Dev. Corp.*, 986 F.2d at 613. Unlike in *Oakville*, where the property at issue had been sold to a third party at a foreclosure sale, here, the documents Kuney seeks access to still exist and are available to Kuney if the proposed stipulated order is entered. *Id.* Nor is the matter rendered moot due to settlement. *Shelby*, 435 F 2d. at 45–46. Kuney and Bean did negotiate a settlement modifying Stipulated Protective Order, which was embodied in the proposed stipulated order. However, the district court denied Kuney's motion to enter the proposed stipulated order; the order has not been entered and the Stipulated Protected Order remains unmodified. Accordingly, the matter is still in controversy and effective relief can be granted. *Gowen*, 244 F.3d at 66.

Checkpoints

- It is important for an appellate attorney to analyze the legal and factual issues surrounding the appeal with fresh eyes.

- A fresh look for appellate counsel often means revisiting basics techniques and building blocks of legal analysis — tools that can get lost in the flurry of trial proceedings or motion practice below.

- Tools for analyzing and interpreting statutes include:

  - Using tabulation to explode a statute into its constituent parts so that you can identify each element and factor and how they relate.

  - Viewing the section at issue using the structure and other sections of the same statute. In other words do not read and analyze the section in isolation.

  - Case law interpreting the statute. Often the applicable statute has been interpreted by the courts. Cases may (a) determine if a statute is *valid*, (b) determine *whether* a statute applies or *which* statute applies, (c) *interpret* a statute, or (d) *apply* a statute. Resist the urge, however, to go directly to reading cases, skipping the first two steps of statutory interpretation. Have a solid understanding of the statute and what it means first.

  - The plain meaning rule — the wording of the statute at issue. Beware of the plain meaning rule, however, because whether a meaning is plain or what meaning is plain is usually subject to debate.

  - Legislative history — documents and records created by the various parts of the legislature that enacted the statute. It includes statements of legislators, different versions of the bill as it progressed through the legislative process, and analyses by committees and legislative staff professionals.

  - Similar statutes in the same jurisdiction that have been addressed by the courts. If courts have not addressed the section at issue, they may have addressed similar ones.

  - Similar statutes in different jurisdictions that have been addressed by those courts.

  - Canons of construction — rules of interpretation stated in the abstract. Remember, more than one may apply with conflicting results.

  - Law review articles and scholarly commentary. Court may use comments from experts in a field to aid in interpreting statutes. Law review articles are also useful for the authorities collected in their footnotes.

- A fresh look entails reviewing any new authorities, as well as revisiting the "old," and putting them together into a cohesive, persuasive whole.

Checkpoints *continued*

- Cases often contain (1) a caption, (2) a summary and headnotes, (3) the disposition, (4) procedural facts, (5) underlying facts, (6) an indication of the issues being addressed, (7) statements of the law and their explanation, (8) an application of the law, and (9) the holding, which is the court's decision on the issue along with the essential supporting facts or reasons.

- Cases may also contain statements of policies that the law is meant to promote, and dicta — statements included in the opinion that are not necessary to the court's holding. Look for dicta that give examples of how a rule or standard might or might not be met.

- In reading a case strategically for how it affects the client and the client's situation use this checklist:

  - Where does the case come from and what level of court decided it?

  - Does the case deal with the same or similar issue as your problem or matter?

  - What laws does the court apply or articulate?

  - What does it say about those laws?

  - What are the facts of the case?

  - How does the court apply the laws to the facts?

  - What is the court's holding? Depending on the client's situation, is it better to describe the holding so that it applies broadly or narrowly?

  - Does the case contain any useful dicta?

- In legal analysis you will need to (1) *distill* the legal principles from multiple cases and explain what they are and how they relate to each other, and (2) *apply* those principles to the facts of your client's situation and advocate the outcome.

- In dealing with multiple cases, use this process:

  - Read the cases in the order of most recent to oldest. It is likely that later courts will have synthesized (at least partially) the cases for you — meaning they will have distilled the legal principles from prior cases, fit them together, and explained them.

  - For each case, write out its holding on each issue in a short parenthetical.

  - Sort and group the cases. Create a chart that sets out the issues as categories, then sort the cases based on which issue(s) they address. Then for each issue/category, group the cases by result: those that met the overall standard or requirements and those that did not. Once your chart is complete look for patterns, trends, or factors that point to a result.

Checkpoints *continued*

- Distill and synthesize the legal principles from the cases. Once you have sorted, grouped, and charted the cases, reread them individually and take down the statements of law and what the court says about them for each issue. Then determine which of the statements of law are elements, and which are factors. Then for each issue fit the statements of law from each case together in as logical and cohesive whole as possible. This usually means going from general statements of law to more specific statements and from broad statements of law to more narrow statements.

- Organize and present your legal analysis using the CRAC (Conclusion, Rule/Law, Application, Conclusion), which is designed to deliver information in a way that is thorough, comprehensive, persuasive, and easy for the reader to understand.

Chapter 8

Appellate Legal Drafting: Techniques and Strategies

Roadmap

- The key to good appellate legal drafting is ensuring the audience can easily understand and follow your analysis and arguments.

- There are three key strategies for organizing appellate legal drafting:

    (1) establishing context before details,

    (2) placing familiar information before new information, and

    (3) making your structure explicit.

- Paragraphs are essential building blocks of appellate legal drafting. Paragraphs begin with a topic sentence that identifies the subject or point of the paragraph. Then each sentence must relate to the topic sentence and to the sentences around it.

- Sentences in appellate legal writing should be as clear, direct, and concise as possible. The goal is for your readers to quickly and easily understand them.

- The appellate drafting process is a multistep process involving:

    (1) organizing your preliminary materials into a workable outline,

    (2) writing the first draft,

    (3) revising and rewriting,

    (4) editing, and

    (5) proofreading.

- Do not expect to produce a quality appellate brief in one draft or the day before it is due.

I. Three Strategies for Organizing Appellate Legal Drafting

Some attorneys assume that appellate legal drafting should be long and complicated—that readers on the appellate level will appreciate more "sophisticated" arguments (which, in actuality, are often merely more convoluted). Instead, the attorney's goal in appellate legal drafting is to organize complex information so that the readers, be they judges, court attorneys, or law clerks, will understand it as easily and clearly as possible. This means taking complicated issues, breaking them down, and making it easy for readers to understand your analyses and agree with your conclusions.

There are three basic strategies for organizing complex information:

(1) establish the context before adding the details,

(2) place familiar information before new information, and

(3) make your structure explicit.

a. Establish the Context before Adding the Details

Be sure to give readers enough context or background information to easily understand the various details you supply—including how those details fit and why they are important. By the time you are ready to draft your brief, you will have analyzed all of the facts and issues and become thoroughly familiar with them. Remember that your readers are not. Thus, for example, before explaining the specific prongs of a test, set out the basic law for which the test was designed. Otherwise, your readers will not easily understand the specifics and why you are discussing them.

To ensure readers have enough background and context to understand the details, remember these drafting principles:

(1) state the general before the specific,

(2) state the broad before the narrow, and

(3) state the rule before the exception.

Setting the context in an appellate brief often starts with the jurisdictional statement (if required), which states the basis for the court's authority to decide the matter, or the statement of the case, which describes the order or judgment appealed from and the grounds for reversal or affirmance. In drafting either of these sections, keep in mind that this is the best opportunity to establish the context for the appeal from your client's perspective.

In the statement of facts, the beginning paragraphs should describe the situation underlying the controversy, e.g., the transaction, event, altercation, or injury, as well as the parties and important players. Here is an example of context paragraphs in the Statement of Facts taken from a successful brief written by the authors, appealing the trial court's refusal to allow access to court documents:

STATEMENT OF FACTS

This case and ensuing appeals led to the landmark decision by this Court in *Bowers v. Baystate Technologies*, 320 F.3d 1317 (Fed. Cir. 2003), which has had far reaching ramifications for copyright and contract law and has attracted the attention of scholars and other commentators due to its importance in the software and other industries. (Docket No. 560, Kuney's reply to Bean's opposition to motion to dissolve or modify protective order, Appendix, Tab 13, p. 148.)

Kuney is a Professor of Law at the University of Tennessee College of Law and the Director of the College's Clayton Center for Entrepreneurial Law. He is writing a detailed account of this important case, its appeals, and the chapter 11 and 7 bankruptcy cases that followed. He seeks access to the documents set forth in the proposed stipulated order—trial exhibits and documents filed with the District Court and designated on appeal—to use with the text and to ensure the accuracy and thoroughness of his scholarship. (Kuney Decl. ¶ 2, Appendix, Tab 5, p. 41.) Not only are the source documents needed to support the text of Kuney's book, but the documents themselves are also intended as concrete examples that will allow students to examine the actual documents that are being summarized in the text. The book will be published in both hard copy and digital form; the digital version will contain links to the underlying documents referenced.

When discussing the law, present the broad legal principles first, and then give the rationale, elements, factors, tests, and other details. When applying the law, make sure the readers are already familiar with the rules, standards, and cases you use, and remind them as necessary. Thus, when making or developing a point, make sure your readers know from the beginning what the point is, why it is important, and how it fits into the analysis. You are familiar with the material, but they are not. You know what points you are making; be sure your readers will also—without any work on their part. Using the CRAC structure in your briefs will help you accomplish this. It is especially important to begin your application section with your overall conclusion on the issue or sub-issue and then explain, or tell, why and show how that conclusion is sound and well supported. "Tell" by making assertions or predictions supported by authority; and "show" by comparing and contrasting your facts with the facts of the cases you have used in the law section. Adhering to this method will help you ensure that the points you make are explicit to your readers.

Similarly, do not make or expect your readers to connect the dots, add 2 and 2 together, or complete the analysis for you. Some attorneys assume that at the appellate level, if they "lay the information out there" it "will be obvious" or readers will "make the connection" or come to the same conclusion as the drafter. Not so. Know that your readers will be unfamiliar with what you are writing about and that you are competing for their time and attention. You need to clearly state the issue, give your conclusion, and do the analysis—telling and showing them why and how your conclusion is sound and well supported. Imagine yourself holding a mallet when you draft and revise—you should be hammering points home for the readers.

b. Place Familiar Information before New Information

Placing familiar information before new information is similar in purpose to providing context before details—ensuring easy comprehension by those reading your brief.

The first step is to first make sure you familiarize your readers with important information you will use and build on later in the document. Thus, in drafting appellate briefs adhere to the CRAC structure. Any law, law-explanation, or case you use or refer to in the application section must first be set forth in the rule/law section. Similarly, any fact you use or refer to an application section should first be set forth in the statements of facts. If a law, law-explanation, case, or fact is important enough to use in your analysis, the reader should already be familiar with it. Also, do not "allude" to a law, rule, or standard that you have not yet addressed. The English literature practice of "foreshadowing" has no place in drafting appellate briefs.

Second, make sure your readers understand how a piece of new information—be it a fact, a law, a standard, an element, a factor, an explanation, a reason, or a policy—emerges from and connects with the information the readers have already consumed. You might assume it is obvious or that readers on the appellate level will see the connection or relationship. Do not assume. Show your readers how the new information connects with the old. Use transition words, e.g., "similarly," "moreover" "conversely," as well as sentences that explicitly guide the reader: "Even if Smith ran the stop sign (which he did not), this did not cause the accident."

Some useful transitional words:

To add or build on material:

Moreover
Furthermore
Also
In addition
Similarly
Likewise

To indicate or introduce alternatives or differences:

Conversely
On the other hand
However
But
Yet
Still
Nevertheless
Although
Though

To indicate a result:

Thus
Therefore
Hence
Accordingly
As a result
Consequently

c. Make the Structure Explicit

An explicit, easy-to-follow structure is very important in constructing an appellate brief. This is another reason to embrace the CRAC structure. Thus, do not organize as you go, or simply follow the same structure of the brief you are responding to. Have a clear idea of how you need to deliver the information so that your readers can easily understand it. Make sure your thoughts and points do not appear scattered or random.

Do not just retrace the path you took when you were initially analyzing the issue. Often in the initial stages you will begin with the details and experiment and fit them together to build to a conclusion. In preparing or revising your first draft of a legal document, however, put your conclusion first and then explain why and how that conclusion is sound and well supported. In other words, "turn your analysis on its head." Also be sure to eliminate stray wanderings, recursive loops, and paths that resulted in dead ends. Readers are not interested in the writer's musings on the issue or the amount of thought the writer put into producing the document. They want conclusions, set forth explicitly then well explained and supported.

Statements of facts might be logically organized chronologically, by issue or subject, or by witness. Rule sections should be organized starting with the most important laws, and go from general to specific laws, from broad to narrow laws. Application sections should begin with a topic sentence stating the overall conclusion, followed by supporting reasons in order of strongest to weakest. Avoid producing work product that makes your analysis sound like: "and another thing, and another, one more, oh here's another point...." This may be difficult in the early stages of the drafting process because you may not be sure which of your reasons are strongest, or which points are most important. This is why it may take several drafts to produce a well organized, compelling, convincing brief.

Finally, in all legal drafting make your organization explicit by making good use of clear and informative headings, as well as topic and transitional sentences.

II. Paragraphs

Many attorneys give little thought to paragraphs or paragraph structure. The well-written and organized paragraph is key to appellate legal drafting, however. Indeed, paragraphs are the essential building blocks of the appellate brief. Think back to what you learned in grade school and middle school about paragraphs — and what you may have forgotten or underutilized since then.

Paragraphs have three essential requirements:

1. *Paragraphs must begin with a topic or transitional sentence that clearly identifies the point, the main idea, the subject of the paragraph.*

The paragraph's first sentence must clearly inform the reader what that paragraph is about. Thus, topic sentences of paragraphs in the statement of facts should indicate the type of facts addressed, e.g., "Mr. Jones suffered serious injuries in the accident." Paragraphs regarding the law should begin with the basic or most important law regarding the issue or sub-issue, e.g., "Generally, minors' contracts are voidable at the election of the minor."

In applying the law, the topic sentence should contain your overall conclusion on the issue or sub-issue, e.g., "Steven may void the contract he entered into when he was fifteen." Many times, however, writers will build up to a conclusion that they put at the end of the paragraph. This is backwards—do not bury your lead. Make the conclusion your topic sentence and then show why and how it is correct and well supported.

2. *Every sentence in the paragraph must relate to the topic or transitional sentence—to the subject or point you identified there.*

In reviewing your paragraphs, check each sentence against your topic sentence. If you have written sentences that do not relate to the topic or transitional sentence, it may be that you should break the paragraph up into two or more paragraphs, or perhaps you should revise your topic or transitional sentence.

3. *Every sentence in the paragraph must relate to the sentences around it.*

This is accomplished by (1) arranging the sentences in a logical sequence, for example chronological order, general to specific, broad to narrow, order of importance—most important, to strongly supporting to also-supporting; and (2) using transition words that signal how the sentence relates, e.g., similarly, likewise, moreover, conversely, however, on the other hand.

Finally, check your paragraphs for length. Save the one or two sentence paragraph for the rare occasion when it can be used for effect or flourish. Check to see if the sentences should be combined with or folded into other paragraphs, or if the very short paragraph should be developed more. Also check for paragraphs that are longer than ¾ of a page. Ask yourself if these should be broken into more than one paragraph connected by transitional sentences. Beware of the paragraph that tries to do too much or contains more information than the reader can easily assimilate.

III. Sentences and Word Choice

Sentences in legal writing should be as clear, direct, and concise as possible. Always look for ways to use fewer words and to eliminate unnecessary words. The following are tools to accomplish this goal:

a. Where Possible, Always Make Your Subject a Person or Entity—Something That Acts—Rather Than a Concept

This will help prevent your sentences from becoming unwieldy. So, for example, state: "The jury [entity as subject] is not likely to convict Ms. Philips" rather than "The possibility of the jury's convicting Ms. Philips [concept as subject] is remote." Attorneys often must make a conscious effort to do this, because the law is often discussed in terms of concepts. However, at the root of these concepts are people. For example, adverse possession is a legal concept, but in order to acquire title by adverse possession a person must *do* certain things and *act* in certain ways. Negligence is a legal concept, but in order to be liable for negligence a person must *act* or *fail to act* in particular circumstances.

In other words, make your subject concrete and put the action in the predicate. Thus, generally avoid the passive voice as it obscures the action and sounds weak and uncertain. The exception to this rule is that it is a good idea to use the passive voice when one is seeking to conceal an actor's identity or it is unknown.

Generally yes: *Officer Pitcain made mistakes while investigating the crime by _____.*

Generally no: *Mistakes were made in the investigation.*

On the other hand, if you are representing Officer Pitcain, you would likely want to obscure the subject and would use passive voice. Thus, if you use the passive voice, make it a conscious choice.

b. Use Plain Language

Avoid legalese and words or phrases you or the average person would normally not use. This can be difficult for experienced lawyers who are used to reading legalese or less than accessible writing. Your readers, however—be they judges, court attorneys, or law clerks—will appreciate straightforward, easy-to-grasp words and sentences. Thus, even if you have an expansive, sophisticated vocabulary, resist the urge to use an uncommon or complicated word if a simpler word will do. A primary goal in legal drafting is to ensure that readers easily understand the words.

On the other hand, *do* use legal terms of art—those that communicate a concept particular to the law—where appropriate. For example "The defendant moved for summary judgment" versus "The defendant opposed the lawsuit." In avoiding legalese, be sure not to use slang or overly casual terms. Finally, you should not use contractions, e.g., write "you are" instead of "you're." Some readers will think contractions are fine, but others will see them as errors and a sign of poor drafting. You are drafting to please a wide audience across a whole spectrum of biases.

c. Use Fewer Words

In legal drafting, you are competing for the readers' time and attention; therefore, do not use more words than necessary to clearly and accurately communicate the information. Many of the tools in this section will help you to use fewer words. In addition, you should check your sentences specifically for unnecessary words or "chaff" and delete them. For example, "in the event that" should be replaced with "if; " "for the reason that" should be replaced with "because."

d. Stamp Out Narration

Eliminate any words or sentences that simply narrate the process of your or the court's analysis, e.g., "This issue was addressed by the Illinois Supreme Court" or "Guidance is found in the case law." Instead, state the rule, requirement, test or standard and cite the case(s). The citation "supports" — or holds up — the preceding statement.

e. Avoid Nominalizations

Unbury your verbs. For example: "We represented Ms. Philips" rather than "We provided representation to Ms. Philips." "She fixed the flat tire and flushed the radiator" rather than "She performed repair services on the vehicle."

f. Avoid Intrusive Phrases or Clauses

Do not interrupt yourself with subordinate dependent clauses (the descriptions that are set off by commas in the middle of the sentence). Either make them into their own sentence, move them to the beginning or end of the sentence, or eliminate them entirely. In other words, subjects should be close to verbs, and verbs close to objects.

g. Choose the Right Word

Make sure you use the right word. For instance, courts rule, hold, or conclude, but they do not feel or argue. Also make sure the word you use actually is a word, e.g., "irregardless" is not a word. If you are unsure if you are using the correct word in the correct way, look it up.

h. Use the Past Tense When Describing Events That Have Already Occurred

This includes underlying facts and rulings in cases: "In *Smith v. Jones* the court held the plaintiff did not have standing." "Mr. Black stated in his interview...." Use the present tense, however, for events or circumstances that are ongoing: "He exercises five times a week." "According to *Smith v. Jones*, Rule 18 applies whenever parties seek to amend their pleadings."

i. Put Yourself in the Position of the Distracted, Unfamiliar Reader

Are any of your sentences too long or hard to follow? Three lines on the page is stretching the limit. Take a hard look at sentences over two and a half lines, and sentences under two-thirds of a line (for choppiness). In reviewing long sentences, ask if you can use fewer words and clearly communicate the same idea; if you can, do so. If not, it is likely you have packed too much content into one sentence and should break it up into two or more sentences. Also, use enumeration—(1), (2), (3) for example—to aid the reader in keeping track of requirements in a legal rule, even if you do not use fully tabulated (exploded) format to present it. In reviewing short sentences check for tone—do they appear abrupt or choppy? Also see if very short sentences should be combined with sentences around them—for tone and to avoid repetition of words. Finally, if you think a reader might have to read a sentence more than once to fully understand what it means, you should revise the sentence.

j. Remember to Keep It Simple

Use short words found in everyday speech that best express your intended meaning (but avoid slang). Avoid Latin and other forms of legalese that are opaque and pompous. Some key rules about word choice are listed below:

- Avoid elegant variation—using a word and its synonyms. Use one word for each concept and use the same word each and every time you refer to that concept.

- Beware of pronouns. Use them only if their antecedent (the thing they refer to) is unmistakable. Cure unclear pronoun references by using the noun itself or a defined term.

- Do not use "aforesaid," "hereinabove," and similar ancient-sounding words.

- As much as possible, use "the," "this," or "that" rather than "said" or "such."

- Do not use "he/she." Rather, attempt to use gender-neutral terms by making the subject plural, e.g. "they."

Sometimes attorneys resist using the tools described in this section because they think they should not have to "dumb down" their writing for the appellate court. They need to abandon this attitude. Legal drafters should do everything needed to make their documents easy to follow and readily accessible to readers. Appellate court dockets are often full of cases and each case is full of briefs. You want yours to be the brief that makes the court's decision-making easier, not harder.

IV. The Drafting Process

Drafting an appellate brief is a multistep process: (1) organizing your preliminary materials into a workable outline, (2) writing the first draft, (3) revising and rewriting, (4) editing, and (5) proofreading. Attorneys need to build in time for each step as well as time away from the document. They are often procrastinators, however, telling themselves they work best under pressure, etc. Not so—rushing an appellate brief almost always leads to an inferior work product.

a. Organizing Preliminary Materials into an Outline— Creating an Explicit Structure

Before you begin drafting the brief, organize your materials into a workable outline. The form and complexity of the outline will depend on the complexity of the issues and your working, thinking, and drafting styles. In all cases, though, you should put your preliminary materials in order and create an explicit structure for the document. The structure may change as you draft and revise, but you should begin with one. Once you have organized your thoughts and created a structure—the framework for your document—you need to start drafting. Do not get bogged down in the organizing step of the process or use it to put off actually writing.

b. The First Draft

The first draft is where you get your thoughts and ideas down and where you test them. In the first draft a significant amount of legal analysis occurs as you write and think through the issues. Writing forces you to think critically. Conclusions or assumptions you may have made in the research or preparation stage may not write up when it comes time to explain or defend them, or in drafting you may come to different conclusions. You may also discover gaps in your preparation or analysis. Thus it is important to begin the first draft early in the process and well before the document's due date. The most important part of the process of the first draft is to get it done. The first draft will not be a masterpiece and you should not try to make it one. At this stage do not overly concern yourself with sentence structure, word choice or even paragraph structure, all of which you can fix later. Just write.

You do not need to start with the beginning of a document. You might start with a section or issue that seems easiest, then, as you get warmed up, you can tackle other sections. If you find yourself getting bogged down or frustrated with a section, step back and examine why. It could be that some of your preliminary analysis or conclusions are faulty or do not make good sense when put down on paper. You may need to think through issues again. That is part of the first draft process. If you have tested your assumptions and analysis, but are still bogged down in a section, move to another part of the document. Sometimes all you need is time away to regain perspective. Remember, your goal with the first draft is not perfection; it is getting it done so that you can start revising and rewriting, the most critical stage of the process.

c. Revising and Rewriting

After you finish your first draft, put it away for at least a day if possible. Although you will have revised and rewritten as you produced the first draft, you did so from the perspective of the writer organizing and putting thoughts down on the page. You need fresh eyes for the revising and rewriting stage of the drafting process, which is where you turn your draft into a quality document. Some attorneys make the mistake of becoming too attached to their drafts. In the revising and rewriting stage you must detach yourself and approach the document from the perspective of the readers—judges, court attorneys, or law clerks.

First assess the brief's structure and content—does it address all issues and sub-issues involved in a logical way? A good way of testing this in memos and briefs is to create a heading and topic sentence outline, explained in Chapter 11, Section XIV. After you have made any revisions needed to ensure that the document logically addresses all issues and sub-issues, set it aside for a day, if possible. The next step is assessing how *well* they are addressed. This involves critically reviewing any CRACs, paragraphs, clauses, provisions, or sentences and rewriting them as necessary. Have you adhered to the CRAC structure in addressing all issues and sub-issues? Also test paragraphs and individual provisions: Are they logically arranged and easy to follow? Do they follow the three requirements discussed above for effective paragraphs? After paragraphs, move to sentence structure and word choice; use the ten tools described in Section III to test and revise your sentences so they are clear, direct, and easy to understand.

Revising and rewriting is a critical, multi-step process. It will take longer than you think to produce a thorough, yet direct and concise brief. That is why you should start the first draft as early as possible, and block out more time than you think you will need to revise and rewrite.

d. Editing

After you are satisfied with your revisions of the brief, set it aside again. The next step is editing—reviewing the brief from the readers' perspective for flow and easy understanding. Revising and rewriting can be an arduous process; editing should not be. Think of it as touching-up as opposed to making full scale repairs. Check your sentences and words to make sure they are as clear and concise as possible and that they are logically arranged. Ask yourself, "Can I say this in fewer words?" A good technique is to read the brief aloud, which forces you to put yourself in the place of the readers. Poor phrasing or confusing sentences that seem fine on screen or paper often reveal themselves when read aloud. Editing is an important stage in making sure your brief is easily accessible to the reader. However, be sure not to get bogged down in this stage, e.g., rewriting the same sentence over and over, changing a word, then changing them back, and so on. It is possible to overwork a document and lose perspective.

e. Proofreading

When you are satisfied that you have a high quality, thorough, and easy to follow brief, put it away for at least a day. In the final proofing stage, *print out the document* and examine it strictly for errors—punctuation, grammar, capitalization, missing words that were dropped in the revising or editing process, incorrect words that spell check did not recognize, e.g., "trial" versus "trail." Proofreading and editing should be kept as separate steps. When editing you will miss proofing errors or even create them, because your focus is different. Some proofreading techniques are reading the document aloud, reading with a straight edge so that you only see one line at a time, and reading the document backwards, from the end to the beginning. Some attorneys underestimate the importance of the proofreading stage and do not leave enough time to do a thorough job. This is a big mistake. Documents with proofing errors look shoddy and tell the readers that you do not care, even if you do.

Checkpoints

- The key to good appellate legal drafting is ensuring that the audience can easily understand and follow it.

- The three key strategies to organizing appellate legal drafting are:

  - establish the context before discussing the details;

  - place familiar information before new information and show how new information emerges from or relates to familiar information;

  - make the structure explicit.

- The well-written and organized paragraph is the building block of good appellate legal drafting.

- Paragraphs have three essential requirements:

  - Paragraphs begin with a topic or transition sentence that identifies the point, main idea, or subject of the paragraph.

  - Every sentence in the paragraph must relate to the topic or transitional sentence.

  - Every sentence in the paragraph must relate to the sentences around it. This is accomplished by arranging the sentences in a logical sequence, and by using transition words that signal how the sentences relate, e.g., similarly, moreover, however.

- Sentences in appellate legal drafting should be clear, direct and concise, and quick and easy to understand. Some tools for accomplishing this:

  - Where possible, always make your subject a person or entity that can *act*, rather than a concept. In other words, make the subject concrete and put the action in the predicate.

  - Use plain language — avoid legalese and words that might not be quickly and easily understood by the average reader.

  - Use fewer words — no more than necessary to clearly and accurately deliver the information or convey your point.

  - Stamp out narration — eliminate words or sentences that narrate the process of your analysis, e.g. "Guidance is found in several cases."

  - Avoid nominalizations — unbury your verbs, e.g., write "We represented Ms. Jones" rather than "We provided representation to Ms. Jones."

  - Avoid intrusive phrases or clauses — do not interrupt the main point of your sentences. Subjects should go close to verbs and verbs close to objects.

  - Chose the right word — the one that is correct and most accurate.

  - Use the past tense for events that have already occurred.

Checkpoints *continued*

- Put yourself in the position of the distracted, unfamiliar reader and check if any of your sentences are too long or not easy to follow. Ideally sentences should be between three quarters of a line and two and a half lines.

- Keep it as simple as possible.

- Appellate legal drafting is a multi step process involving these steps:

  - Organizing your materials into and outline. Before beginning to draft, organize your thoughts and materials into an explicit structure. The structure may change as you draft and revise the document, but it is important to begin with one.

  - Writing the first draft. The first draft is where you get your thoughts and ideas down and where you test them. Writing forces you to think critically. The most important things about the first draft are to just write and get it done.

  - Revising and rewriting. This stage involves distancing yourself from the draft and approaching it as a *reader*. Assess the document's structure and content—does it address all issues and sub issues in a logical way? Then assess how *well* you have addressed the issues and sub issues. This involves critically reviewing any CRACs, paragraphs, clauses, provisions, or sentences and rewriting them as necessary, with the unfamiliar reader in mind.

  - Editing. After your have revised your draft, the editing process involves fine tuning the document for flow and ease of understanding so that it is easily accessible to readers.

  - Proofreading. Once you are satisfied that you have a high quality brief, put it aside. Then print it and go over it with a fine tooth comb ensuring that there *no errors*. Do not combine the editing and proofing steps. Suggested techniques include reading the document aloud and reading with straight edge so that you see only one line at a time. Proofing errors make the brief look shoddy and the drafter look bad.

Chapter 9

Citation and Quotation on Appeal: Why, When, and How?

Roadmap

- Citations in appellate briefs are used to identify and attribute the sources used by attorneys in preparing the document and to show the readers where to find those sources.

- Quotations are used to communicate the exact words of the original source, should be accompanied by a citation, and should be used selectively.

- Every statement, explanation, and illustration of the law in the brief should be accompanied by a citation to the statute, case, or other legal authority on which it is based.

- Every statement of fact, description of fact, or allusion to fact in the brief should be accompanied by a citation to evidence in the record that establishes that fact.

- Your brief will be judged in part by the quality and correctness of your citation form.

I. Why

a. Overview

Citations in appellate briefs show the readers that your arguments and supporting facts are well supported—both by legal authority and documents in the appellate record. These citations should also enable your readers to quickly and easily locate those legal and factual sources. In sum, the purposes of citations in appellate briefs are to:

(1) identify and attribute the sources used in preparing the brief, and

(2) show readers exactly where to find those sources.

Quotations are used to communicate the exact words of original sources, and are accompanied by citations to those sources. Quotations should be used selectively, for emphasis, or when the particular language is significant to the issues, e.g. the language of a statute or contract provision.

b. Citations to Legal Authority

Citations to legal authority are used to support statements, explanations, and illustrations of the law and to identify the sources from which they come so that the readers can find and review that authority for themselves. Citations to legal authority are also used in the application sections of the CRAC format in supporting predictions and assertions and in comparing and contrasting the facts in the underlying case with those in the cases used to explain and illustrate the law. The goal is to show the readers that your legal analyses and discussions are sound and well supported. Thus it is important to provide citations that identify each authority as well as the specific pages supporting your statements.

Legal authority includes primary authority such as constitutions, statutes, cases, rules of procedure, administrative regulations, and ordinances. Primary authority are *sources* of law. Legal authority also includes secondary authority such as treatises, legal periodicals, encyclopedias and dictionaries, law review articles, and websites containing reports and statistical data. Secondary authority comments on the law, but is not a source of the law. Sometimes considered "in between" these primary and secondary sources is legislative history, including legislative counsel digests, legislative committee reports, and statements of legislators' comments in the legislative record.

Legal authority is not created equally—there is a hierarchy. Within primary authority, there is binding (also called mandatory) authority and optional (also called persuasive) authority. Binding authority must be followed by the court in which your case is pending.

Binding primary authority includes the United States Constitution, the constitution and statutes of the state or jurisdiction in which the court is situated, and case law rendered by the United States Supreme Court and higher courts in the jurisdiction of the court in which your case is pending.

Optional primary authority is just that—optional. A court may choose to consider it, or not. Optional primary authority comes from a state or jurisdiction other than one in which the court is situated, i.e., constitutions, statutes, or cases from another state or, on the federal side, case law from another circuit. Additionally, cases from courts of the same level within the jurisdiction are optional authority. Thus, an intermediate appellate court in one part of the state is usually not bound by a decision of an intermediate appellate court in another part of the state, or even by one of its own decisions—although the doctrine of stare decisis may prevail to accomplish the same result as if it were binding. Thus, generally, such decisions by the same or equal level courts are likely to be highly persuasive.

For example, a California appellate court would be bound by cases decided by the United States Supreme Court and the California Supreme Court, but cases decided by California appellate courts (even the court itself) would be optional—although persuasive. Similarly, a federal circuit court located in Illinois would be bound by cases decided by the United States Supreme Court, and, for questions of purely state law, by the Illinois Supreme Court. Cases from the United States Court of Appeals for the Seventh Circuit (which includes Illinois) would be optional but generally quite persuasive; cases from other circuit courts would also be optional and the degree of their persuasiveness would vary depending on the circuits and issues involved.

Secondary authority such as legal treatises and law review articles is always optional. Its persuasiveness depends on the quality and reputation of the sources and their authors or editors. When a secondary authority is relied upon in a judicial opinion, its status is elevated. For example, if a court defines a term in a case using a quotation from Black's law Dictionary, that particular definition, as incorporated into the judicial opinion, becomes primary authority on that matter.

Legislative history is secondary authority in that it is not a source of the law. However it often does more than comment on the law—it can provide insight and evidence regarding what the law means, its purpose, how it should be interpreted and the like. Thus, although it is optional authority, courts can be highly persuaded by legislative history. See Chapter 7, Section II (e) for further discussion regarding legislative history.

Primary Authority
(Sources of Law)

Binding Primary Authority
- Constitutions
- Statutes
- Regulations
- Court rules
- Case law from a higher court in the state, jurisdiction, or federal circuit in which the court at issue is situated.

Optional Primary Authority
- Constitutions from other jurisdictions
- Statutes from other jurisdictions
- Regulations, rules from other jurisdictions
- Case law in a state or jurisdiction other than the one in which the court at issue is situated, or case law from an equivalent level court in the same jurisdiction or federal circuit as the court at issue.

Secondary Authority—Always Optional

- Legal Treatises,
- Legal Encyclopedias,
- Legal Dictionaries,
- Law Review Articles and the like.

Legislative History—Optional but Often Persuasive

Documents and records created by the various parts the legislature that enacted the statute, including:

- Statements of legislators regarding why they were in favor of a bill or why they opposed it;
- Different versions of a bill as it progressed through the legislative process; or
- Reports and analyses by committees and staff members such as legislative counsel.

c. Citations to the Record—The Appendix

Most appellate courts require an appendix—an abbreviated form of the record consisting of documents from the clerk's file and portions of the reporter or other certified transcript that pertain to the issues on appeal. Citations to the appendix or the record support the procedural and substantive facts referred to in the brief and allow readers to easily locate the documents that contain those facts. Except in rare circumstances, appellate courts may only consider material that was in the trial court record. Thus it is essential that any reference to a procedural or substantive fact in the brief be accompanied by a clear appendix or record citation to the specific pages of the supporting document. A well chosen, well prepared appendix combined with an appellate brief with clear and ample appendix citations focuses judges, court attorneys, and law clerks on documents pertinent to the appeal and makes those documents easily accessible. For more discussion on the appellate appendix, see Chapter 6, Section IV.

d. Quotations

Quotations are used when it is important to communicate the exact words of a source. For example, the particular wording of a statute or contractual provision, a controlling standard or definition set out in a case, or the exact statement of a party or witness if it is important to your position or analysis. Quoting the exact words of a source adds emphasis to both the words and the source. Thus, quotations are always accompanied by a citation to their source—whether legal authority, or factual authority found in the record or an exhibit. The citation should also include the specific page(s) that contain the words quoted.

II. When to Cite or Quote

a. Legal Authority

Many attorneys undercite legal authority. They may assume that once they have cited an authority there is little need to cite it again or worry that the flow of the legal discussion and analysis will be interrupted by citations. Readers, however, will expect thorough citation in appellate briefs and will expect attorneys to identify, with regularity and particularity, the legal authorities on which their positions and analyses are based. Readers will skip over the citations when verification of a statement is not important to them and hone in on them when it is. A missing citation makes these readers wonder if there is any support for the proposition stated other than the author.

Many times attorneys will have synthesized cases and developed a statement or explanation of the law that is based on their analysis of cases, but not explicitly articulated in those cases. In those instances, the statement or explanation of the law should be accompanied by a citation to the legal authorities from which it is *derived*. Readers of briefs are usually not interested in what might appear to be an attorney's own ideas devoid or independent of legal authority, so be sure to show what authority supports each of your statements and explanations.

Every illustration of the law should also be accompanied by a citation. Thus, when using the facts and holding of a case as an example, provide a citation that will allow readers to go to the exact page(s) of that case for verification or further illumination.

Also cite to legal authority to support any conclusions or assertions made in your briefs. This includes the application/analysis of any CRAC used in the discussion or argument section, as well as in any summaries, statements of the case, or final conclusions. These citations show that any conclusion or assertion you have made is legally supported and allow the readers to review the sources themselves. Some attorneys undercite in the application/analysis portion their CRAC because they have recently cited the same authority in the rule/law portion. However, if drafters do not include cites to support their conclusions or assertions in the application/analysis, readers are forced to refer back and attempt to find the supporting authority themselves.

Similarly, when discussing the facts of your case in the application/analysis portion of any CRAC, link these facts specifically with the facts of the cases you have used in the rule/law portion to illustrate the law. In other words, compare and contrast the facts of your case with the facts in those cases and cite to those cases. This shows the readers how and why the particular client facts are legally significant. For example:

> Mr. Smith's use of the adjoining property was open and notorious, satisfying the first requirement for acquiring title by adverse possession. *Parker*, 100 P. 3d at 358. A reasonable land owner would have been put on notice of Mr. Smith's use. *Morningside*, 122 P.3d at 122. Mr. Smith cleared land, built a partial fence and a smokehouse on the adjoining property—similar to the claimant in *Parker*, 100 P. 3d at 359, who staked boundaries, blazed trails, marked boundaries and built a small camping shelter on the property.

In the above paragraph readers are not forced to go back to the rule/law section to figure out which authority supports the drafter's two assertions. They also do not have to go back to remind themselves what happened in the *Parker* case to understand why the facts discussed by the drafter are legally significant.

b. Factual Authority—Citations to the Appendix or Appellate Record

Attorneys should provide citations to the appendix (or in some jurisdictions the appellate record) any time they reference procedural or substantive facts. The statement of the case and the statement of facts sections of an appellate brief usually contain the most citations to the appendix or record. Attorneys should also provide citations to the appendix or record in the discussion or argument section when they are quoting from factual sources, and other times when they wish to emphasize particular facts.

An appeal's pertinent procedural history is generally set forth in the statement of the case—the purpose of which is to tell the appellate court what is being appealed and to describe the nature of the action, the parties, and how and why the matter has come before the court. Thus, every procedural act and document described should be followed by a cite to the appendix or record so that the judge, court attorney, or law clerk working up the case can easily locate the pleading or other document detailing the action. For an example of a statement of the case with citations to the record see Chapter 11, Section V.

Absent exceptional circumstances, the statement of facts in an appellate brief may contain only the facts and evidence that were presented to the court or jury below. Thus, any fact set forth or described must be accompanied by citations to the appendix or record that enables the persons working up the appeal to look up and review the original the source. Citations to the appendix or record enable the reader to confirm that the matter described was actually presented to the trial court or jury, and to verify the attorney's accuracy in describing those facts.

Many facts that have been set out in the statement of the case and the statement of facts will be repeated in the discussion or argument section of the brief. Providing appendix cites for each of these facts risks cluttering up the text. When quoting, however, it is important to provide an appendix citation to the document as well as the exact pages that contain the quote. Readers should be able to quickly and easily verify the source and accuracy of the quote without having to refer back to the statement of the case or statement of facts. Similarly, any facts referenced in the discussion or argument section that are essential to your analysis or position should be accompanied by an appendix cite to the specific source document and page(s).

c. Quotations

Attorneys should use quotations selectively to communicate a source's exact words. It is often important to quote the exact words of the controlling statute or contract provision. Similarly, if a particular test or standard is described clearly and concisely in a case, it is a good idea to quote that specific test or standard. The same holds true with clear definitions articulated by courts. Also, there will be times when it is best to quote a person's specific words in the brief if they are important in your analysis — for example, whether a person's statements amounted to an offer or an acceptance. Also, at times a person's exact words will create a more powerful impression than a paraphrase. For example:

> *The defendant told police "Yeah, I shot him — right between the eyes. So what?"*

as opposed to

> *The defendant acknowledged shooting the victim.*

Attorneys should avoid, however, drafting statements of facts that are merely a string of quotes because this often leads to long, repetitive text that readers will tend to skim or skip over. Similarly, attorneys should avoid drafting discussions of the law that are essentially a series of quotes from the cases strung together. This is often an indication that the drafter has not done sufficient synthesis and analysis. Also, long strings of quotes often appear disjointed and are cumbersome for readers to wade through.

If you have tried to paraphrase a source but your words are still quite close to the original, you should instead quote the source's words and note any omissions or changes you have made using ellipses and brackets (described below). A very close paraphrase erroneously implies that another person's words are yours and can be considered misleading.

Attorneys will sometimes mistakenly quote words used in a headnote that are not actually found in the case itself. Since headnotes are not part of the court's opinion, they should not be quoted as if they were. Doing so implies these are words of the court, which is inaccurate. On the other hand, repeating the exact words of a headnote without quotation marks inaccurately implies that these words are the attorney's. The solution is to come up with different and, ideally, better, words to use.

Some drafters will put quotations marks around their own words in an attempt to emphasize them. This stems in part from the spoken practice of pantomiming quotation marks when making a sarcastic or euphemistic reference. Although sometimes hard to resist, you should not do this in an appellate brief. When you feel that you must emphasize your own words, for this or another purpose, use italics; and, above all, resist the urge to over emphasize—effective prose communicates its message well without the technique.

Finally, use quotation marks to define terms that you will use throughout your brief for which you want a short, standardized term, i.e., the Asset Purchase Agreement between Melody Partners LLC and Rancho Promotions, Inc., dated June 7, 2010 (the "APA").

III. How to Cite

a. Legal authority

In most jurisdictions court rules specify acceptable cite forms for memoranda and briefs—usually *The Bluebook: A Uniform System of Citation* and occasionally a style manual particular to the state, e.g., the *California Style Manual.* In law school, students are usually assigned *The Bluebook* or the *Association of Legal Writing Directors (ALWD) Citation Manual* with which to learn the most common rules of citation. Following either will result in citations that look substantially the same. Mastering proper citation form and the rules of citation is like mastering a new language—it takes practice and the more you use it, the easier it becomes. Throughout their practice, however, attorneys will need to use the index of *The Bluebook* or *ALWD Citation Manual* to find out how to cite a particular source.

Two things to keep in mind regarding citation in appellate briefs: (1) your legal drafting and analysis will be judged in part by the quality and correctness of your cite form, and (2) the goal in citation to legal authority is to clearly convey enough information concisely so that the readers can easily identify the source and look it up themselves.

Some of the recurrent rules in citing legal authority, particularly cases, are discussed below.

1. *Information contained in a case citation*

A case citation contains a number of components that convey information to the reader, primarily:

1. the case name;

2   the reporter(s) containing the case as well as the reporter's volume number, the first page of the case, and the particular page(s) that contain the information the drafter has referred to (the "pin cite" or "pinpoint citation");

3. the court that decided the case; and

4. the year of the decision.

For example:

1   2   3   4

Siedle v. Putnam Investments, Inc., 147 F.3d 7, 10 (1st Cir. 1998).

The reporter is the Federal Reporter, Third Series, volume 147. The case begins on page 7, and page 10 contains the pertinent information referred to by the drafter, e.g., the holding, a test, or a set of facts. This information allows the reader to look up the case either in hard copy or on-line. The deciding court was the United States Court of Appeals for the First Circuit, and the year the case was decided was 1998. This information tells the reader about the weight of authority—the level of the deciding court, its geographic jurisdiction, and how recent the case is.

Readers will know the citation language shorthand and will grasp all this information quickly. Thus, there is no benefit to leaving out any of this information when citing the case for the first time. Unfortunately, some attorneys do—either through mistake, inadvertence, or ignorance. The result is more work for the readers, who for example, will have to page or scroll through a case looking for the relevant page if a pin-cite is left out.

Note: The Carolina Academic Press Mastering Series does not follow *The Bluebook* form, as citations in this book include italicized case names. In the examples of case citations that follow, italicized case names are proper *Bluebook* form because they represent citations in legal documents. The case name is set forth in italics. Although the examples from *The Bluebook*'s "blue pages" — also called "practitioner style pages" — underline case names, attorneys in the 21st century, armed with a personal computer, laser printer, and a word processor, should use italics. Previously, case names were underlined in memoranda and briefs because most typewriters could not produce italics. That is not the case now with computers. Also, using italics makes for a cleaner, more professional looking document in general.

   2.   *Citation sentences and clauses.*

   Generally, a citation or citations are set forth in a separate citation sentence following the sentence of text. For example:

> Adequate notice lies at the heart of due process. *Mullane v. Central Hanover Bank & Trust Co.*, 339 U.S. 306, 314, 70 S. Ct. 652, 94 L. Ed. 865 (1950).

There is a period after the word "process" and then two spaces and a new sentence containing the citation to *Mullane*.

   Sometimes citations are contained in clauses that are inserted into the textual sentence. For example, if a sentence contains two propositions and one case supports one proposition and a different case supports the other:

> This motion is made on the grounds that (1) the Asset Purchase Agreement between the Debtor and the Successor, by its terms, does not apply to products liability claims arising after the sale, *In re Eagle-Pitcher Industries, Inc.*, 255 B.R. 700, 704 (Bankr. S.D. Ohio 2000), and (2) as a matter of law, sales under section 363(f) of the Bankruptcy Code do not extinguish causes of action for personal injuries that occur after the sale, *Hexcel Corporation v. Stepman Co.*, 239 B.R. 564, 570 (N.D. Cal. 1999).

   In the above example, each citation clause is inserted right after the portion of the text it supports, preceded by a comma. The problem with using citations clauses like this is that the result is a long and cluttered sentence. It would be best to break up this example into two sentences, each supported by separate citation sentence:

> This motion is made on two grounds. First, the Asset Purchase Agreement between the Debtor and the Successor, by its terms, does not apply to products liability claims arising after the sale. *In re Eagle-Pitcher Industries, Inc.*, 255 BR 700, 704 (Bankr. S.D. Ohio 2000). Sec-

ond, as a matter of law, sales under section 363(f) of the Bankruptcy Code do not extinguish causes of action for personal injuries that occur after the sale. *Hexcel Corporation v. Stepman Co.*, 239 B.R. 564, 570 (N.D. Cal. 1999).

3.   *The sequence of multiple cases in one citation sentence.*

Many times attorneys will want to show that more than one case supports the proposition or other information contained in the textual sentence. The rules regarding the order in which to list those cases reflect the hierarchy of authority discussed in Section I (b), *supra*. This order is based on the court that decided the case and the date of the decision. Cases from the pertinent jurisdiction come before cases from outside the jurisdiction and secondary authorities (law review articles, etc.). Then, within the pertinent jurisdiction, cases from courts of last resort come before cases from intermediate appellate courts, which come before cases from trial courts. Within each court level, cases are arranged from newest to oldest.

Thus, the most recent case from the highest court would come first in the citation sentence. An older Supreme Court case would come before a more recent appellate court case:

> *Mullane v. Central Hanover Bank & Trust Co.*, 339 U.S. 306, 314, 70 S. Ct. 652, 94 L. Ed. 865 (1950); *Jones v. Chemetron Corp.*, 212 F.3d 199, 209–10 (3rd Cir. 2000).

Often attorneys will have good reason to list multiple cases in a different order than called for in *The Bluebook*, for example if an appellate court case is more on point, while the cases from the court of last resort supports the more general proposition. They may do this, but they must insert the signal "*see*" or "*see also*" before the higher ranked case in order to continue to comply with the rules of citation:

> *Jones v. Chemetron Corp.*, 212 F.3d 199, 209–10 (3rd Cir. 2000); *see also Mullane v. Central Hanover Bank & Trust Co.*, 339 U.S. 306, 314, 70 S. Ct. 652, 94 L.Ed. 865 (1950).

Multiple authorities within citation sentences are separated by semi colons as if they were closely-related independent clauses.

4.   *Short citation forms*

Short citation forms save space. They are not required and should not be used for the first citation to an authority. Some examples:

Full citation:

> *Siedle v. Putnam Investments, Inc.*, 147 F.3d 7, 10 (1st Cir. 1998).

Partial case name and reporter short form:

> *Siedle*, 147 F.3d at 10.

A textual reference using the partial case name and reporter short form:

> In *Siedle*, the court rejected this argument. 147 F.3d at 10.

When citing to the same case previously cited with no intervening cites:

> *Id.*—Where citing to the same page as that pin cited in the previous cite.

> *Id.* at 11.—Where citing to a different page than the one pin cited in the previous cite.

The period in "*Id.*" is italicized. Also of note, using a partial case name followed by just a page number, e.g., *Siedle* at 11, is not a proper short form citation, and, for many readers, this will mark you as a hack.

The full cite contains the most information, followed by the partial name and reporter short form. Each of these cite forms gives the reader the information needed to look up the case and find the exact relevant page(s). Using the short form *Id.* requires readers to refer back in the document to find this information. This is not a problem if they do not have to look very long or hard. However, if readers would have to go back to another section or turn the page to find the information necessary to look up the case, it is best to use the partial name and reporter short form.

There must be no ambiguity regarding which case *Id.* refers to. Therefore, if the previous citation sentence contains more than one case, *Id.* may not be used.

When drafting, do not convert citations to short forms until the last draft. The danger in doing so is that the authorities may be deleted or reordered during the revision process and what was once a perfectly proper short form is now inappropriate because no earlier full citation is present or a lonely *Id.* remains referring back to where a primary authority is no longer present.

5. *Citations to other sources*

The Bluebook and the *ALWD Citation Manual* also contain detailed rules and explanations regarding citations to myriad other sources including constitutions, statutes, federal rules, legislative history, treatises, law review articles, and electronic databases. Attorneys should consult the index of either of these manuals before citing to any of these sources. The indexes are detailed and may contain the exact source you intend to cite.

b. Cites to the Appendix or Appellate Record

There is no equivalent to *The Bluebook* or the *ALWD Citation Manual* governing citation to the appendix or appellate record. However the rules of court or other procedural rules in various jurisdictions may set out requirements or guidelines, and counsel should always check for these rules in preparing the appellate brief. Attorneys should clearly (1) identify the source supporting each procedural or substantive fact they describe, (2) show where to locate that source and the exact pages containing or supporting the facts described, and (3) adopt a consistent citation form throughout the document. Often this means longer descriptions in the beginning followed by abbreviations and defined terms.

An example from an appellate brief drafted by the authors:

> On February 21, 2007, Kuney filed his motions to intervene and to dissolve or modify a stipulated protective order entered in 1998 (Stipulated Protective Order) in order to use documents related to the case in a textbook on law and business. (Docket No. 547, Appendix of the Appellant George W. Kuney (Kuney App.), Tab 2, p. 10.) Kuney served the motions to intervene and dissolve or modify the Stipulated Protective Order on all parties to *Baystate Technologies, Inc. v. Bowers*, No. 91-40079, and the appeal, *Bowers v. Baystate Technologies.*, Inc., 320 F.3d 1317, as well their successors and all attorneys involved. (Docket No. 551, Notice of Motion and Motion filed February 21, 2007, Kuney App., Tab 2, p. 10.) Robert Bean (Bean), who is not party to the stipulated protective order, filed the only opposition to the motion. (Docket No. 555, Bean's Opposition filed March 21, 2007, Kuney App., Tab 8, p. 129.) Thereafter, Kuney and Bean entered into a settlement providing that Kuney could use the jury exhibits and the confidential and nonconfidential appeal appendixes filed in *Bowers v. Baystate Technologies, Inc.*, 320 F.3d 1317 (Fed. Cir. 2003), Case No. 01-1108-11109. (Docket No. 557, proposed stipulated order signed by Kuney and Bean's counsel, Kuney App., Tab 10, p. 140.) The terms of this settlement are set forth in a proposed stipulated order filed with the District Court on April 2, 2007. (Docket No. 557, Kuney App., Tab 10, p. 140.) No action was taken by the District Court regarding Kuney and Bean's settlement and the proposed stipulated order, however.

Notice that, unlike citations to legal authorities, the citations to the appendix or record are set off in parentheses. A reason for this is to clearly distinguish appendix or record cites from the text. Since citations to legal authorities often include italics, this, rather than parentheses, distinguishes them from the text. Also, the abbreviation "p." is used to denote page numbers in the documents. Often cites to documents in the appendix or record will include abbreviations for pages "p.", clauses "cl.", sections "§", and paragraphs "¶" to clearly identify portions of the document cited.

If there are concerns regarding page limitations, attorneys must use their best judgment in deciding how much information to include in the appendix or record cites. At a minimum, readers must be directed to the exact pages in the appendix of record that contain or support the facts referenced, e.g.: (Kuney App., pp. 21–22).

For more examples of citing to the appendix or record, see Chapter 11, Section V.

c. How to Quote

The Bluebook and the *ALWD Citation Manual* also contain rules regarding quotations. We have included some of the more recurrent rules below.

1. Using Quotation Marks

In general, when you use the exact words of another source, put quotation marks (" ") around those words and put punctuation marks inside the quotation marks: "Under fundamental notions of procedural due process, a claimant who has no appropriate notice of a bankruptcy reorganization cannot have his claim extinguished in a settlement pursuant thereto." *Chemetron II*, 212 F.3d at 209–10.

If you need to quote within a quote, put single quotation marks around the internal quote: "The purpose behind requiring notice to creditors is to provide them the 'opportunity to be heard' which is 'the fundamental requisite of due process of law.'" *In re Chance Industries, Inc.*, 367 B.R. 689, 708 (Bankr. D. Kan. 2006) (quoting *Mullane v. Central Hanover Bank & Trust Co.*, 339 U.S. 306, 314, 70 S. Ct. 652, 94 L.Ed. 865 (1950)).

However, if the quote is fifty words or more, the words are set forth in a single spaced, justified, indented block quotation, and external quotation marks are omitted:

The court in *Chance Indus., Inc.* further explained the constitutional inadequacy of notice by publication to potential future claimants:

Some of the future claimants may not be living persons at the time the notice is given, so they are not necessarily capable of seeing it. If they are alive and actually see the notice, they could not recognize themselves as affected in any way by the bankruptcy case and will, therefore, take no action to ensure their interests are represented. The purpose behind requiring notice to creditors is to provide them the "opportunity to be heard" which is "the fundamental requisite of due process of law." Such a notice by publication is an exercise in futility as applied to creditors who are not only unknown to the debtor, but are also unknown to themselves. It cannot possibly define the requirements of the Due Process Clause.

367 B.R. at 708 (quoting *Mullane v. Central Hanover Bank & Trust Co.*, 339 U.S. 306, 314 70 S. Ct. 652, 94 L.Ed. 865 (1950)).

Use block quotes sparingly, since many readers tend to skim or skip over them. If you do block quote, introduce or follow it with a sentence that explains the point or substance of the quote.

2. *Indicating Omissions or Alterations in a Quote: Ellipses and Brackets*

If you alter a quote from what appears exactly in the source document, you need to indicate omissions with ellipses and any changes to words or letters with brackets.

Three periods separated by a space in between each constitute a typical ellipsis and indicate that you have omitted a word or words from the quote ("..."). There should be a space before and after the ellipsis: "The defendant shot ... the victim in the hip." If you omit the last words of a sentence you need a four period ellipsis — the first three represent the ellipses, and the fourth is the period at the end of the sentence: "But Franklin, the defendant, shot James Cook in the hip...."

If you omit an entire paragraph, indicate this omission by putting a three dot ellipses centered on a separate line in between the quoted paragraphs.

When you make changes to words of a quote, by adding or changing words, letters, or case (e.g., upper case to lower case) you indicate those changes by putting your version inside brackets. Examples:

"[T]he defendant shot [the victim] in the hip."

This indicates that the drafter left out the first part of the sentence in the original quote and thus had to capitalize the "T." Also, the drafter changed the original sentence to replace "James Cook" (see above) with "the victim."

3. Citing Original Sources and Indicating Emphasis

Every quotation must be followed by a pin citation to its source. If the quote contains an internal quotation, the source for that quotation should generally also be pin cited in an explanatory parenthetical: *In re Chance Industries, Inc.*, 367 B.R. 689, 708 (Bankr. D. Kan. 2006) (quoting *Mullane v. Central Hanover Bank & Trust Co.*, 339 U.S. 306, 314, 70 S. Ct. 652, 94 L.Ed. 865 (1950)).

You would not need an explanatory parenthetical if the court in *Chance* had merely cited to *Mullane* as opposed to having quoted language from that case. An alternative is to note in the parenthetical to the lead case (here, *Chance Industries*) that you have not included the internal quotation or accompanying citation with the parenthetical: (internal quotations and citations omitted).

You may emphasize words in quotations that were not emphasized in the original source, but you must note this added emphasis in an explanatory parenthetical: "Under fundamental notions of procedural due process, a claimant who has no appropriate notice of a bankruptcy reorganization *cannot* have his claim extinguished in a settlement pursuant thereto." *Chemetron II*, 212 F.3d at 209–10 (emphasis added).

If the original source has emphasized words in a sentence or sentence that you quote, you do not have to explain that the emphasis was in the original source, but many attorneys often do to make this clear — adding the explanatory parenthetical: (emphasis in original).

IV. Conclusion

This chapter has summarized the basics of why, when, and how to cite to legal authorities and the appendix or record. Although some attorneys view these rules as technical and even small minded, they are fundamental to legal drafting. Failure to follow them will mark you as disorganized and will increase the workload of those reviewing your brief. Best practice is to cite, fully and correctly, as you draft the brief. Leaving citation or bluebooking to the last minute means creation of extra work and a frantic attempt to complete the task before a deadline. Citing correctly as you go provides an audit trail for your work and analysis and produces better documents in less time and, thus, for less money.

Checkpoints

- Citations in legal documents are used to
  - identify and attribute the sources used by drafters in preparing the document and
  - show the readers where to find those sources.
- Quotations are
  - used when communicating the exact words of the original source,
  - should be accompanied by a pin citation, and
  - should be used selectively.
- Citations to legal authority are used to support all statements, explanations, and illustrations of the law and to identify the sources from which they come so that readers can look up those sources for themselves.
- Citations to legal authority are also used in the application portion of the CRAC format in
  - supporting any conclusions or assertions, and
  - comparing and contrasting the underlying facts with those in the cases used in describing the law.
- A key goal in citing legal authority is to show that your legal analyses, discussions, predictions, and assertions are sound and well supported.
- Legal authority is not created equally. There is a hierarchy.
- First there is primary authority, such as constitutions, statutes, and cases. Primary authorities are sources of law.
- Within primary authority there is:
  - Binding (sometimes called mandatory) primary authority, which must be followed by the court your case is in. Binding primary authority includes the Constitution of the United States, the constitution and statutes of the jurisdiction or state in which the court is situated, and case law rendered by the United States Supreme Court, and higher courts in that state or jurisdiction.
  - Optional (sometimes called persuasive) primary authority, which the court may chose to consider or not. Optional primary authority comes from a state or jurisdiction other than the one in which the court at issue is situated. It also includes case law within the same jurisdiction or state rendered from courts on the same level as the court at issue.
- Then there is secondary authority—authorities that are not a source of the law but which comment on and/or describe the law. Secondary authority is always optional, and its persuasiveness depends on the quality and reputation of the source.

Checkpoints *continued*

- Secondary authority includes:
    - Treatises, legal periodicals, encyclopedias and dictionaries, and law reviews.
    - Legislative history.
- In most jurisdictions court rules will specify acceptable cite forms for legal authority; often the default format is *The Bluebook*.
- The goal of citation to legal authority in an appellate brief is to clearly provide enough information concisely so that readers can easily identify and look up the source.
- Citations to the appendix or record are used to support statements and references to procedural and substantive facts in appellate briefs, and allow readers to identify, review, and verify any procedural or factual event described in the brief.
- Absent exceptional circumstances, the statement of facts in an appellate brief may contain only facts and evidence that were presented to the court or jury below.
- When using another source's words, put quotation marks around those words.
- If you have tried to paraphrase a source, but your words are very close to the original, you should quote the source's words and put any changes in brackets, and note omitted words with ellipses.
- Do not put quotation marks around your own words.
- Your legal drafting and analysis will be judged in part by the quality and correctness of your citation form.

Chapter 10

Standards of Review and Reversible versus Harmless Error

Roadmap

- Appellate review involves determining if there was error below and its effect on the case.
- Standards of review define the amount of deference the appellate court will accord the lower court in determining if there was error.
- The four basic standards of review are
  - De Novo (the decision below must merely be wrong).
  - Clearly Erroneous (the decision below must be very wrong).
  - Substantial Evidence (the decision below must be very wrong).
  - Abuse of Discretion (the decision below must be very, very wrong).
- If the appellant successfully convinces the court that, under the standard of review, there was error below, the court then determines if the error requires reversal of the judgment or order below.
- Certain errors, such as (1) structural errors and (2) errors based on insufficiency of the evidence, require automatic reversal.
- Otherwise the court will engage in a harmless error analysis to determine whether and how much the error affected the result at the hearing or trial.
- Thus, it is possible to win the battle (convince the court there was error) and lose the war (fail to convince the court that the error requires reversal).

I. Introduction

Appellate review involves determining (1) if there was error below, and (2) if so, whether the error requires reversal.

The first step involves evaluating the decision below based on the applicable standard of review. Standards of review define the amount of deference the appellate court will accord the lower court in determining if there was error. In other words, the standard of review prescribes how wrong the lower court's decision must be in order to be found in error. With some decisions, it is enough merely to show the decision was wrong; with others, the decision must be "clearly wrong," while for others, the decision must have been an "abuse of discretion," etc. Thus, the standard of review provides the context in which the issues on appeal are evaluated and will determine what arguments are made, as well as how they are structured.

Determining whether there was error below is only one part of the appellate court's decision making process. If the court finds error, it must next determine whether the error requires the judgment or order to be reversed — in other words, whether the error is reversible or harmless. This inquiry involves evaluating whether and how the error affected the result and the rights of the parties.

II. Standards of Review

a. In General

Despite the many articulations of the standards of review that are discussed below, the human mind generally only applies two: deferential and non-deferential review. Deferential review is generally applicable to factual determinations and matters within the trial court's discretion. This makes sense as the court, jury, or agency below is the body that received the evidence and made its factual findings accordingly. A reviewing court is not in a position to have enough information to reliably review every nuance of the proceedings below. Similarly, the deferential standard of abuse of discretion is reserved for decisions particularly within the trial judge's province, such as courtroom management matters.

Non-deferential review is a different story. Non-deferential review is usually applicable to questions of law. In these situations, because the issue is purely legal in nature, the appellate court is in just as good a position as the court below to pass on these issues.

However, even when the standard of review is non-deferential, at the intermediate appellate court level there is often an unwritten presumption of correctness in favor of the trial court. This presumption is generally not present or not as strong in the case of discretionary review of cases in courts of last resort.

b. Specific Standards of Review

Keeping in mind that there are probably really only two basic standards of review in practice—deferential and non-deferential—spread along a spectrum, here are the most commonly articulated standards of review:

(1) De Novo (Wrong);

(2) Clearly Erroneous (Very Wrong);

(3) Substantial Evidence (Very Wrong);

(4) Abuse of Discretion (Very, Very Wrong).

De Novo: Wrong

Under the de novo standard, the appellate court reviews the question anew, on its own, with no deference given to the lower court's decision on the matter. The court need only find that the decision below was incorrect. The appellate court is under no constraints and may freely substitute its judgment for that of the lower court. This no-deference standard is also sometimes referred to as "plenary" or "independent" review.

The de novo standard of review typically applies to questions of law, for example, the proper interpretation of a statute or the determination of whether a statute is constitutional. Also, in some jurisdictions, including the federal system, mixed questions of law and fact in which the questions of law predominate are generally reviewed de novo. *See Ornelas v. United States*, 517 U.S. 690, 695 (1996). In those instances, a mixed question of law and fact involves applying a rule or standard to established facts. *Id.* at 696–97 (de novo standard of review applies to question of whether an officer had reasonable suspicion to make an investigatory stop—a mixed question of law and fact).

Typical statements of this standard of review are: "This is a question of law which we review de novo" or "We independently review whether *x* applies to juveniles."

Clearly Erroneous: Very Wrong

Under this standard a finding of the lower court "shall not be set aside unless clearly erroneous." Fed. R. Civ. P. 52(a)(6). "A finding is 'clearly erroneous' when although there is evidence to support it, the reviewing court on the entire evidence is left with the definite and firm conviction that a mistake has been committed." *United States v. U.S. Gypsum Co.*, 333 U.S. 364, 395 (1948). Thus, as long as a finding is plausible, it will not be set aside, even if the appellate court would have reached a different result had it considered the matter itself. *Cooter & Gell v. Hartmarx Corp.*, 496 U.S. 384, 400 (1990) ("In practice, the 'clearly erroneous' standard requires the appellate court to uphold any district court determination that falls within a broad range of permissible conclusions").

The clearly erroneous standard applies to findings of fact made by the trial court in the federal court system and in many state court systems. Typical enunciations of this standard of review are "Although we might have found differently, we cannot say that the trial court's findings are clearly erroneous" or, "We review the trial court's findings for clear error."

Substantial Evidence: Very Wrong

Under the substantial evidence standard, appellate review is limited to determining, in the light most favorable to the prevailing party, if any substantial evidence supports the decision below. "Substantial" does not mean the weight or preponderance of evidence. Rather, substantial evidence is, essentially, adequate or sufficient evidence. *See Therrien v. Target Corp.*, 617 F.3d 1242, 1249 (10th Cir. 2010) ("Substantial evidence is something less than the weight of the evidence, and is defined as such relevant evidence as a reasonable mind might accept as adequate to support a conclusion, even if different conclusions also might be supported by the evidence); *see also American Textile Mfrs. Institute, Inc. v. Donovan*, 452 U.S. 490, 522 (1981) ("[W]e have defined substantial evidence as 'such relevant evidence as a reasonable mind might accept as adequate to support a conclusion.' ").

The substantial evidence standard applies to findings of fact made by a jury in the federal court system and in most state court systems. The standard also applies in certain cases to findings of fact made by administrative agencies in the federal system, and in many state jurisdictions to findings of fact made by the trial court.

Abuse of Discretion: Very, Very Wrong

"[D]eference … is the hallmark of abuse-of-discretion review." *General Elec. Co. v. Joiner*, 522 U.S. 136, 143 (1997). This standard is difficult but not impossible to meet, and often is met in situations where the court below did not do its job in the eyes of the reviewing court. For example, "a district court may abuse its discretion by ignoring a material factor that deserves significant weight, relying on an improper factor, or even if it mulls over the proper mix of factors, by making a serious mistake in judgment." *Siedle v. Putnam Investments,*

Inc., 147 F.3d 7, 10 (1st Cir. 1998). In the *Siedle* case, the trial court rescinded an order sealing the record "after a brief colloquy with counsel," without writing a decision or otherwise stating its reasons. The appellate court reversed, stating "In this instance, we discern no evidence that the district court identified and balanced the interests at stake, or that the court endeavored to determine whether any information contained in Siedle's filings actually fell within the ambit of the attorney client privilege. In the circumstances at hand, these omissions amounted to an abuse of discretion." In other words, the court below had not done its job.

This abuse of discretion standard often applies to sanctions, courtroom management issues, protective or sealing orders, or decisions regarding whether or not to admit certain evidence.

Other Standards of Review

Apart from the four usual standards of review discussed above that permeate the federal and many state court systems, various jurisdictions have their own enunciations of their standard of review. As with any standard of review, when faced with one that is new or unfamiliar, it is important to understand its nuances, both as the standard is stated and as it is applied — remember to watch what courts *do* as well as what they *say*.

For example, Tennessee appellate courts' "review of findings of fact by the trial court in civil actions shall be de novo upon the record of the trial court, accompanied by a presumption of the correctness of the finding, unless the preponderance of the evidence is otherwise." Tenn. R. App. P. 13(d). There appears to be a lot of wiggle room in the wording of this standard, which may afford the appellate court more flexibility should it choose to use it and deniability should it choose not to do so. On one hand, the trial court's findings of fact are to be reviewed "de novo upon the record," while on the other hand there is a "presumption of correctness" — but the appellate court may conclude that the evidence preponderates the other way.

Another example is the arbitrary and capricious standard used in reviewing decisions made by federal agencies pursuant to their rule-making authority. Under this standard, "a reviewing court may not set aside an agency rule that is rational, based on consideration of the relevant factors and within the scope of the authority delegated to the agency by the statute." *Motor Vehicle Mfrs. Ass'n of U.S., Inc. v. State Farm Mut. Auto. Ins. Co.*, 463 U.S. 29, 43 (1983). So, under this standard, agency decision making is insulated from reversal unless the agency (a) did not consider all relevant factors, (b) acted irrationally, or (c) acted outside its Congressional authority.

It is important in each appeal to correctly articulate the standard used in the jurisdiction. Not only might it make a substantive difference, even if it is only a matter of "semantics," articulating a different standard than the one actually applicable to the matter on appeal will reflect poorly on the drafter and his or her brief.

III. Reversible versus Harmless Error

a. In General

If the appellant successfully convinces the appellate court that there was error under the applicable standard of review, the court then determines if the error requires reversal of the judgment or order below. Whether an error is reversible or harmless depends on whether and how it affected the outcome of the case and the right of the parties. For example, Federal Rule of Civil Procedure 61, entitled "Harmless Error," states:

> Unless justice requires otherwise, no error in admitting or excluding evidence — or any other error by the court or a party — is ground for granting a new trial, for setting aside a verdict, or for vacating, modifying, or otherwise disturbing a judgment or order. At every stage of the proceeding, the court must disregard all errors and defects that do not affect any party's substantial rights.

Similarly, Federal Rule of Criminal Procedure 50(a) states: "Any error, defect, irregularity, or variance that does not affect substantial rights must be disregarded."

b. Errors Requiring Automatic Reversal — Structural Errors and Errors Based on Lack of Substantial Evidence

Some types of errors require reversal because by their very nature they are so serious or fundamental that they will have affected the outcome of the case or substantial rights. In these cases, appellate courts do not conduct a separate harmless error analysis.

These errors, often called "structural errors" require automatic reversal because they render a trial fundamentally unfair or the verdict fundamentally unreliable. For examples of errors involving fundamental unfairness, *see United States v. Gonzalez-Lopez*, 548 U.S. 140, 148–49 (2006) (erroneous disqualification of criminal defense counsel denied defendant of his Sixth amendment right to counsel of one's choice); *Johnson v. United States*, 520 U.S. 461 (1997) (complete denial of counsel); *McKaskle v. Wiggins*, 465 U.S. 168 (1984) (denial of self-representation at trial); *Waller v. Georgia*, 467 U.S. 39 (1984) (denial of public trial); *Tumey v. Ohio*, 273 U.S. 510 (1927) (biased trial judge). Regarding fundamental unreliability, an erroneous jury instruction that misdescribed the prosecution's burden of proving guilt beyond a reasonable doubt was held to require automatic reversal because "it vitiate[d] all the jury's findings" leaving a reviewing court "to engage in pure speculation—its view of what a reasonable jury would have done." *Sullivan v. Louisiana*, 508 U.S. 275, 281 (1993).

If the court determines the error is structural, it will automatically reverse the judgment below. The term automatic is a bit misleading to the extent it implies that this is a quick and easy process. On the contrary, structural error analyses and arguments are often complex.

Additionally, when an appellate court finds error under the substantial evidence standard reversal is usually automatic. A finding of error under this standard generally means there is no evidence in the record that is adequate to support the conclusion below. *See Therrien v. Target Corp.*, 617 F.3d 1242, 1249 (10th Cir. 2010). In that case the finding of the error itself is enough to determine that it has directly and significantly prejudiced the outcome of the case.

c. Harmless Error Analysis

With most errors, the appellate court will engage in a harmless error analysis to determine whether and how much the error affected the result at the hearing or trial. The tests used to determine if an error requires reversal or is merely harmless vary depending on the type of error and the case.

For example, on direct appeal, if the error relates to a right protected by the United States Constitution in a criminal matter, the error must be "harmless beyond a reasonable doubt." This means the government "must prove beyond a reasonable doubt that the error did not contribute to the verdict obtained"; otherwise, the judgment must be reversed. *Chapman v. California*, 386 U.S. 18, 24 (1967) (prosecutor's repeated references to the defendant's failure to testify and combined with jury instruction that adverse inferences could be drawn from her failure to testify were not harmless beyond a reasonable doubt).

On the other hand, in collateral review of constitutional errors, e.g. through habeas corpus proceedings, the prejudicial effect of the error is determined under the more lenient "substantial and injurious effect" standard. *Fry v. Pliler*, 551

U.S. 112, 114 (2007). "Under that standard, an error is harmless unless it 'had substantial and injurious effect or influence in determining the jury's verdict.'" *Id.* at 116 (quoting *Brecht v. Abrahamson*, 507 U.S. 619, 631 (1993) (which held that the prosecutor's improper but infrequent comments regarding the defendant's post-Miranda silence for purposes of impeachment did not have substantial and injurious effect or influence in determining jury's verdict)).

Also, more lenient standards are likely to be applied to non-constitutional errors in state cases. For example, in California state cases involving errors of state law, reversal is required only where "it is reasonably probable the verdict would have been more favorable to the defendant absent the error." *People v. Partida*, 122 P.3d 765, 772 (Cal. 2005); *see, e.g., People v. Samuels*, 113 P.3d 1125, 1137 (Cal. 2005) (holding that any error in admitting character evidence was harmless "in light of the prosecution's extensive case against defendant.").

IV. Conclusion

It is important to keep in mind the two-step review process when drafting an appellate brief.

First, the court determines whether there was error under the applicable standard of review. Counsel should correctly articulate the standard of review in their briefs and oral argument and directly and specifically address how that standard is met for every error that they allege requires reversal.

If it finds error that meets the standard of review, the court then considers whether the error requires reversal, which depends on what type of error was committed. With structural error or errors based on insufficient evidence, reversal is largely automatic. In other cases, the court conducts a harmless error analysis under varying standards — depending on the type of error committed and the jurisdiction involved. Thus it is possible to win the battle (convince the court there was error below), but lose the war (fail to convince the court that the error requires reversal).

Checkpoints

- Appellate review involves determining if there was error below and its effect on the case.

- Standards of review define the amount of deference the appellate court will accord the lower court in determining if there was error.

- Although there are many different articulations of standards of review, the human mind generally applies one of two: either deferential or non-deferential to the decision or action below.

- The four basic standards of review are:

  - De Novo (the decision below must merely be wrong).

  - Clearly Erroneous (the decision below must be very wrong).

  - Substantial Evidence (the decision below must be very wrong).

  - Abuse of Discretion (the decision below must be very, very wrong).

- There are many other permutations and articulations of standards of review among the jurisdictions, and it is important to articulate the correct standard.

- If the applicable standard of review is not satisfied, the decision or action below will be upheld.

- If the appellant successfully convinces the court there was error below, the court then determines if the error requires reversal of the judgment or error below.

- Certain errors, such as (1) structural errors and (2) errors based on insufficiency of the evidence, require automatic reversal.

- Otherwise the court will engage in a harmless error analysis to determine whether and how much the error affected the result at the hearing or trial.

- Thus, it is possible to win the battle (convince the court there was error) and lose the war (fail to convince the court that the error requires reversal).

Chapter 11

Drafting Appellate Briefs

Roadmap

- The purpose of an appellate brief is to persuade a court to reverse or affirm a judgment or order below. An appellate brief should not attempt to retry the case.

- The audience for the appellate brief will be an intermediate appellate court or a court of last resort. Both these courts include more than one decision maker (judges or justices) and you will need to persuade a majority of them to reverse or affirm.

- An appellate brief should show:

  - that there was or was not error below — that the decision below was incorrect or correct under the applicable standard of review; and

  - that the error requires reversal because the error was not harmless, or does not require reversal because the error was harmless.

- An appellate brief is comprised of separate components, usually prescribed by local rules of procedure. Typical components include a statement of issues on appeal, tables of contents and authorities, statement of the case, statement of facts, summary of the argument, discussion or argument with headings and subheadings, and a conclusion.

- The issues on appeal should specifically identify the alleged error or lack of error below. Often whether an error was harmless or reversible is not identified as a separate issue on appeal since it is generally always an issue.

- The statement of the case should set out the relevant procedural history of the case and should also contain the essential reasons why the decisions below should be reversed or affirmed. Accurate citations to the record for each fact or document are essential.

- The statement of facts should tell an accurate story that will make readers want to adopt your legal positions and that gives them enough information to be able to do so. Accurate pinpoint citations to the record for each fact are essential.

- The purpose of the discussion or argument is to show readers how to rule in your client's favor and why they should do so. This involves making your points as clearly as possible, which usually means organizing complex information so that readers can understand it as easily as possible. It also involves showing why your positions are the better alternative as compared with the other side's positions.

- The conclusion section of an appellate brief is usually a short reiteration of the request for the relief you seek.

I. The Audience—Intermediate Appellate Courts and Courts of Last Resort, Judges, Law Clerks, and Court Attorneys

a. Basics

The purpose of an appellate brief is to persuade the court to reverse or affirm the judgment or order below. The party appealing from the judgment or order is usually called the "appellant" especially if the appeal is by right, e.g. an appeal of a final judgment to an intermediate appellate court. However, if a party must petition for review or certiorari in order to have a judgment or order reviewed, that party is often called the "petitioner." The party opposing the appeal is usually called the "appellee" or the "respondent." Check local rules to make sure you refer to your client with the correct term.

The audience for appellate briefs will be an intermediate appellate court or a court of last resort. The focus and role of each are somewhat different. The focus of an intermediate appellate court is chiefly on error correction. Courts of last resort also correct errors, but in addition, make policy, make new law, and extend or clarify existing law much more than intermediate courts. Many courts of last resort with a wholly or largely discretionary review function, like the United States Supreme Court, state that they do not take cases merely to correct an error in the case at bar. Rather, in addition to an allegation of error below, these courts are looking for questions of policy or splits of authority that require consideration and resolution.

Unlike the trial court, in both intermediate appellate courts and courts of last resort the audience for your brief will include more than one decision maker (at least three), and you will need to persuade a majority of them to reverse or affirm the decision below. Thus, keep in mind that some of your audience may lean favorably toward your position from the outset, some may be hostile, and some may be neutral—and it is often the neutral decision makers who will cast the deciding vote(s).

b. Intermediate Appellate Courts

The vast majority of appeals are to intermediate appellate courts. At the intermediate level, cases are usually heard and decided by a three-judge panel. (For further discussion regarding the structure and compilation of the federal and state intermediate courts see Chapter 1, Sections I(c) and II(a).)

One judge on the panel is usually assigned as the "writing judge," and this person and a law clerk or court attorney will be the primary audience for the brief. In most cases, you will not know who the writing judge is until the opinion is issued, however. The other two judges on the panel (and perhaps their law clerk or court attorney) will also review your brief. The writing judge will change if the other two judges do not agree with his or her analyses or conclusions regarding the appeal. In that case, one of the other two judges on the panel will become the writing judge and will issue the opinion, which the initial writing judge may join or dissent from in whole or in part.

The writing judge on the intermediate appellate level will likely spend more time reading the brief than a trial judge spends reviewing a memorandum in support of or in opposition to a motion. The person who will probably spend the most time with your brief, however, is the judge's law clerk or the court attorney who is charged with working up the appeal. Working up an appeal involves reading the briefs, reviewing the record on appeal, researching and analyzing the law, and then preparing a bench memorandum or a draft an opinion for review by the judges on the panel. (Some non-writing judges also ask their law clerks or court attorneys to review and write short in-chambers memos on the other cases assigned to the panel.) The law clerks or court attorneys for appellate judges will probably have and take more time to review your brief than those assisting trial judges, but your case will be one of many that they are working on. Thus, you will still want to be as concise and direct as possible. This means working hard on your drafting to ensure your organization is easy to follow and that your points and arguments are easy to grasp—even, or especially, if they are complex.

Since the focus and function of intermediate appellate courts is primarily on error correction, the appellate briefs should concentrate on whether the correct law was applied and whether it was applied correctly. Hence, arguments should generally focus on what the correct law *is* rather than what the correct law *should be*. Policy arguments may help support arguments regarding which law is correct or how a law is correctly applied, but they should not be your primary support.

Sometimes an intermediate appellate court will be in the position of making new law or clarifying existing law, e.g. where a statutory scheme is new or recently amended. Also, some intermediate appellate courts are more inclined and in a better position to make policy, e.g. United States Courts of Appeals. In general, though, the primary focus of the appellate brief in an intermediate appellate court will be whether, under existing law, there was error below.

Also keep in mind that intermediate courts of appeal are much more likely to affirm the judgment or order of the trial court than reverse it. Indeed, one study indicates that in the past decade, the affirmance rate in the United States Courts of Appeals was approximately 90%. Chris Guthrie & Tracey E. George, *The Futility of Appeal: Disciplinary Insights into the "Affirmance Effect" on the United States Courts of Appeals*, 32 Fla. St. U. L. Rev. 357, 358 (2005).

c. Courts of Last Resort

If the appeal is heard by a court of last resort, e.g. the United States Supreme Court or a state supreme court, your brief will be read by as many as nine decision makers (usually referred to as "justices") as well as their law clerks or court attorneys. The number of justices sitting on courts of last resort varies, e.g. the United States Supreme Court has nine, the California Supreme Court has seven, and the Tennessee Supreme Court has five. (For further discussion regarding the structure and compilation of the federal and state courts of last resort see Chapter 1, Sections I(d) and II(b).)

In some courts a writing justice may be tentatively assigned before the case is heard; in others the writing justice is decided after the matter is heard and the judges have conferred. It is much more likely that the law clerks or court attorneys of each justice will review and work up each and every cases that will be decided regardless of who might be tentatively be assigned as the writing justice. In any event, it is certain that your brief will have a significantly larger audience when before a court of last resort than an intermediate appellate court. Also, if review is discretionary, it is guaranteed that a certain number of justices have concluded that the issues presented are significant. Note, though, that not all appeals to courts of last resort are discretionary. For example, the Colorado Supreme Court has direct appellate jurisdiction in cases involving the adjudication of water rights, and the Alabama Supreme Court has direct appellate jurisdiction in civil cases in which the amount of damages in dispute is over $50,000. Also, in many states review by the highest court is automatic in cases where the death penalty has been imposed.

Since courts of last resort have a more expanded role than intermediate appellate courts, they will entertain and, indeed, expect policy arguments to aid them in determining the law, making new law, and clarifying existing law. Justices and their law clerks or court attorneys will also have and take more time reviewing your brief. However, it remains important to make your points and arguments as clearly as possible. You will still need to show whether or not there was error and why. Policy arguments involve demonstrating why your position is the better one among choices. In order for policy arguments to be effective, drafters must first convince the court that their basic legal positions are sound and well supported. (For further discussion regarding policy arguments see Section XI(d), below.)

Generally, courts of last resort are not as likely to affirm as intermediate appellate courts, probably because if it is a matter of discretionary review, they primarily take cases that a significant number of the judges or justices are inclined to reverse, preferring to deny review to those that they would otherwise summarily affirm. In fact, during the same period that the United States Court of Appeals affirmed 90% of their cases, the United States Supreme Court *reversed* 64% of its cases. Chris Guthrie & Tracey E. George, *The Futility of Appeal: Disciplinary Insights into the "Affirmance Effect" on the United States Courts of Appeals*, 32 Fla. St. U. L. Rev. 357, 358 (2005).

II. Purpose and Goals of an Appellate Brief

a. Basics

The purpose of an appellate brief is to persuade the court to reverse or affirm the judgment or order below. An appellate brief should not attempt to retry the case below.

Thus, if you are representing the appellant, your goals in drafting the brief are to convince a majority of the judges or justices deciding the case that:

(1) there was error below—that the decision below was incorrect under the applicable standard of review, that is, *it was incorrect to the appropriate degree*, and

(2) that the error requires reversal—that the error *matters* because it sufficiently affected the result or the rights of the parties. In other words, it must be reversible or prejudicial and not harmless error.

When representing the appellee or respondent, your goals in drafting the brief are to convince a majority of the judges or justices deciding the case that:

(1) there was no error below—that, at minimum, the decision at issue *was not incorrect to the appropriate degree*, and

(2) even if there was error, that error was harmless — that it does not warrant reversal because it did not sufficiently affect the result or the rights of the parties.

The standards of review and standards for determining whether an error was prejudicial or harmless will dictate much of the content and organization of an appellate brief. Thus understanding the applicable standards and using them to your best advantage are crucial in drafting a brief that will have the best chance of persuading a court to reverse or affirm the decision below. For further discussion on standards of review and reversible versus harmless error, see Chapter 10.

b. Accomplishing these Goals: Developing and Delivering a Message

Ideally, to convince an appellate court to affirm or reverse the decision below your brief should (1) make the court want to rule in your favor, and (2) make it easy for the court to do so. Remember, the purpose of an appellate brief is to *persuade* the court to act in a certain way. Persuading is more than simply winning an argument or proving that you are right. Think: sales and marketing versus arguing and rhetoric. Both sets of skills are pertinent.

1. Developing a Message

Drafters of appellate briefs to both intermediate appellate courts and courts of last resort should develop a theory or theme through which to package and market their arguments. This is the message you send to the court that justifies your position and motivates the court to rule your way. Your message provides the framework for the discussion and focuses your drafting. A compelling message can be described in just one or two lines — similar to a slogan or tag line in advertising. Only instead of "Coke: it's the real thing" it could be "The plaintiff not only assumed the risks, he embraced them," or "The police did not just fail to honor the defendant's right to silence, they undermined it."

Messages are not pulled out of thin air. They evolve through research, review, and synthesis of cases and other authorities. To develop an effective message, first focus on the judgment or order being appealed. If you represent the appellant, ask: How is it vulnerable? What are the essential weaknesses and flaws that you think warrant reversal? How do they relate to each other? How might one link them? If you conclude there is only one ground for reversal, how do you best describe it so it will quickly and easily resound with readers? If you represent the appellee, what shields the judgment or order from attack or makes it irreversible? Since you will already know the appellant's grounds for appeal, ask: What are the flaws or weaknesses in those grounds? Is there a fundamental flaw that permeates them?

As you research, review, and analyze the law and facts, look for common threads and strengths that emerge, and be thinking of how your case should be packaged. When you start your first draft, have an idea of your theory or theme and test it in the drafting process. This will help focus your writing and keep you alert to alternative, possibly more compelling, messages.

2. Delivering Your Message

First, just going through the process of developing a message will help you to package and organize your arguments, and will focus your drafting and help deliver your message. Your mission is to file a cohesive brief that, *as a whole*, persuades the court to reverse or affirm the decision below, rather than a brief that constitutes an assortment of arguments.

Delivering your message and making the court want to rule in your favor involves using each component of the brief to accurately sell your positions. (The typical components of an appellate brief and how to best use them to your advantage are discussed below in Section III.) Drafting the statement of facts, for example, means telling a story supported by citations to the record or appendix that is both easy to follow and leaves the most favorable impression possible. The discussion or argument section should show how and why the law, facts, and any underlying policies compel a ruling in your favor. You would focus on the strengths of your position, as well as address and dispel or minimize difficulties or weaknesses, e.g. cases, facts, or arguments that the other side will use. Ignoring weaknesses or difficulties will undermine your position. If you do not address them, the court will hear about them only from your adversary.

Making it easy for the court to rule in your favor will help make the court want to do so. Although it is not always possible to provide one, courts of any level are usually drawn to clear, simple solutions. In other words, a persuasive brief solves problems rather than creates them. Present your message and make your points as clearly and concisely as possible. This means spending extra time to make complex arguments appear as simple as possible and editing out unnecessary sentences and words. In other words, you need to work harder to make it easier for your readers. Also make sure your briefs are easy to read visually — that the font size is large enough, that the headings are clear and concise, and that there is enough white space between paragraphs. Proofing errors are also a distraction and make a document difficult to read.

Finally, an overarching goal for both appellant's and appellee's counsel is to draft a brief that the appellate court adopts in whole, or in large part, as its own opinion in the case. This demonstrates that the drafter has persuaded the court and made it very easy for the court to rule in her client's favor by adopting her positions.

III. Appellate Brief Formats and Components

Always check the most recent rules of the court in which the appeal is pending before drafting your brief. Most appellate court rules state exactly the format required for opening briefs, responding briefs, and reply briefs. These rules will include the sections required in each brief, as well as length and type face requirements. It is particularly important to know the page or word limitation before starting to draft the brief so that you are sure to come within it. Below is a list and summary of typical appellate brief components; then in the sections following, individual components are discussed in detail.

Typical Appellate Brief Components

Statement of Issues on Appeal. This section identifies the legal questions presented in the appeal. First and foremost, make sure the issues are clear. We recommend using the "whether (legal question), when (essential facts)" format for setting out issues on appeal.

Tables. These contain the table of contents and authorities cited in the brief. Fill in the page numbers last or code all headings and citations for your word processor's automatic table creation utility. Refer to your appellate rules of court for the order in which to list the authorities.

Statement of the Case. This is where you set out the pertinent procedural history of the case, telling the appellate court what is being appealed, the nature of the action, what happened below, the parties involved, and why the matter has come before the court. Also, it is often your first opportunity to state your reasons why the judgment should be reversed or affirmed—in setting forth or responding to the grounds for appeal.

Statement of Facts. This is where you set out the relevant facts that were heard or considered by the court or jury in rendering a decision. You are limited to evidence in the record and must provide cites to appellate record for every fact you describe. Some jurisdictions require the statement of the case (procedural facts) and the statement of facts to be set forth in one section usually called "The Statement of the Case." If this is the case, the procedural facts should come first to establish context and background.

Summary of the Argument. The summary of the argument provides the road map for the brief and is where drafters deliver their message—their theory, theme, or pitch—for reversal or affirmance of the judgment or order. First tell the court what you want it to do—affirm or reverse—and the grounds for that action. Clearly and concisely state the legal and factual basis for your appeal or response, citing the most important legal authorities.

Discussion/Argument with Headings and Subheadings. The discussion section forms the heart of the appellate brief. This is where you show the court in detail how to rule in your favor and why it should. Showing the court how to rule in your favor involves presenting your points clearly and showing that your positions are sound and well supported. Showing the court why it should rule in your favor involves convincing the court that your points and positions are not only sound, but also that they are the best way to resolve the issues (or at least that they are better than the opposite side's). Headings flag the issues in a way that summarizes and advances the main point made in each section.

Conclusion. In this section drafters briefly remind the court of what they want it to do (affirm or reverse) and, if court rules allow, the main reasons in support.

IV. Statement of Issues on Appeal

The Statement of Issues on Appeal describes the issues the court is being asked to address and decide.

If you represent the appellant, the issues on appeal should identify the individual grounds on which you believe the judgment or order below should be reversed. If the same attorneys that handled the case at the trial level are handling the appeal (and this is often a mistake as new counsel can bring an unbiased eye to the record), their initial reaction may be that there are myriad of errors or that the court or jury "got it wrong." It is important, however, to isolate the issues and errors that are likely to result in reversal because the case cannot be retried on appeal. This requires examining the record objectively with the various applicable standards of review and harmless error standards in mind.

In other words, drafters must first identify a specific *error*. Then they need to examine the likelihood that that error will mandate a reversal. This involves assessing the type of error involved and the applicable harmless error standard. For example, it may be clear that a court erred in admitting certain evidence, but whether this error would require reversal depends on the strength or impact of this evidence compared to all the other properly admitted evidence. Did the court erroneously admit your client's confession, or did it allow equivocal hearsay testimony from one of many witnesses?

Counsel for the appellant should then phrase the grounds on which they are appealing the judgment or order as issues on appeal. For each ground, set out the legal question the court must decide to find error, along with the factual context. Appellants generally control the issues to be decided on appeal since the issues reflect the grounds for appeal.

Counsel for appellees are not bound by the appellants' choice of wording. Rather appellees' counsel will state the issues on appeal so as to advance their reasons for affirming the judgment or order. What is essential for both appellants' and appellees' statements of the issues is that the issues be set out clearly, specifically, and not in a conclusory fashion.

Whether any error is reversible or harmless does not have to be set forth in the issues on appeal. However, if counsel for the appellant or appellee wants to emphasize this as an issue or advocate a particular standard they should add it to the statement of issues.

Statements of issues on appeal are much like questions presented in a formal office memorandum. They set out the legal question for the court to decide along with the essential facts that raise the question. We recommend using the "Whether/When" format: Whether (a legal result occurs), when (essential facts). The question should appear neutral, but think: what ruling do you want the court to make and what *concise* facts support the ruling?

An example of a Statement of Issue on Appeal from Appellant's counsel:

> Whether a confession is inadmissible on the ground that the defendant's Sixth Amendment right to counsel was violated when police continued questioning him after he stated "I'm thinking I should speak to my attorney."

The first, "Whether," part of the statement of issue contains the ruling the appellant wants the court to make along with the legal ground therefore, and the second, "when," part of the statement contains the essential facts that raise the issue.

Appellee's counsel may phrase the issue this way:

> Whether a confession is admissible under the Sixth Amendment where police ceased questioning the defendant after he stated, "I want to talk to my attorney."

Both statements of the issue identify for the court that the legal issue is whether the defendant's confession was properly admitted under the Sixth Amendment pertaining to the right to counsel. However, the counsel for the appellant and counsel for the appellee have focused on different facts that they considered essential to resolving the issue: appellant's counsel on what happened when the suspect *initially mentioned* an attorney, and appellee's counsel on what happened when the suspect later stated he *wanted to speak* with his attorney.

Also, neither statement of the issue is conclusory. Conclusory statements occur when the facts are described in such a way that a particular answer is mandated. In other words, do not overstate by answering your own question; do not assume the very point that you are trying to make.

Examples of conclusory statement of issues on appeal:.

> Appellant: Whether a confession is inadmissible when the police violated the defendant's Sixth Amendment's right to counsel by continuing to interrogate him after he invoked his right to counsel. (If the statement is posed this way, the answer has to be yes in favor of the appellant).

> Appellee: Whether a defendant's confession is admissible under the Sixth Amendment where the police honored his right to counsel once he invoked that right. (If the statement is posed this way, the answer has to be yes in favor of the appellee).

Both questions are conclusory because the central issue is whether and when the defendant invoked his right to counsel.

Also, resist the urge to cram in so many supporting facts that the statement of issue becomes long and muddled. If this happens, your readers will stop reading and skip over it.

If you are having trouble formulating your statement of issues on appeal, put that task aside and revisit it after you have drafted other portions of the brief such as the statement of the case or discussion/argument section.

V. The Statement of the Case

The statement of the case in an appellate brief sets forth the relevant procedural history of the case. Its purpose is to tell the appellate court what is being appealed and to describe the nature of the action, the parties, and how and why the matter has come before the court. The statement of the case is often the first opportunity for drafters to deliver their message—to set forth their essential reasons why the decision below should be reversed or affirmed. Thus, although the statement of *facts* should be free of legal conclusions or argument, in the statement of the *case,* you may and should advance your legal positions in describing the grounds for appeal or stating the reasons the decision should be affirmed.

Statements of the case in both appellants' and appellees' briefs should begin with a description of the decision being appealed from, e.g., a conviction of first degree murder after a jury trial, a summary judgment dismissing appellant's personal injury suit, an order denying certification of a class action, and the like. If representing the appellant, include the date the judgment or order was entered, state when the notice of appeal was filed, and set forth the grounds on which you are appealing the decision. Appellants need to set forth the relevant dates to show the appeal was timely filed.

If you are representing the appellee, you may follow your description of the decision being appealed with the reasons it should be affirmed or, if the statement of the case is relatively short, you may set out the reasons to affirm at the end — try it both ways and choose. The appellee does not have to repeat the appellants' grounds for appeal, nor is it necessary to include the dates the judgment was entered or the notice of appeal filed unless you are challenging the appellate court's jurisdiction based on failure to file a timely notice of appeal.

Next, this is the typical order for setting forth the additional information in the statement of the case:

1. Briefly describe the nature of the action if it is not already clear from the description of the decision being appealed;

2. In chronological order, set out the pertinent acts and pleadings that led up to the decision, e.g. the filing of a motion to exclude the appellant's statement to police, the opposition to the motion, and the hearing on the motion;

3. Set out the court's ruling or decision and its basis (if given), or the jury's verdict. (Often it is unnecessary to repeat the jury's verdict if it is set forth in the beginning of the statement in describing the judgment being appealed); and

4. If representing the appellant, briefly elaborate on the reasons the decision should be reversed. If representing the appellee, set forth the reasons the decisions should be affirmed, or elaborate, as necessary, on the reasons you gave in the beginning of the statement of the case.

For each procedural act described and document filed, provide a cite to the appellate record so that the judge, law clerk, or court attorney working up the case can easily locate the pleading or other document detailing the action. Also, in the statement of the case, define terms for the parties and other persons or entities you refer to frequently in the brief.

Statements of the case vary in length and complexity depending on what happened procedurally in the court or courts below. In some cases the proceedings are simple and straightforward. In others they may be complex and contain the source of the reversible error.

The following are examples of simple preliminary statements in an appeal of a judgment of conviction of first degree murder after a jury verdict. The issue is the admission of statements the appellant made to police.

Appellant's version:

On March 15, 2010, Appellant Steven Turner ("Mr. Turner") was convicted of murder in the first degree after a jury verdict. (Joint Appendix "JA" 78). Mr. Turner filed a notice of appeal on April 12, 2010. (JA 81). He appeals his conviction on the grounds the court erroneously admitted his statements to police that were obtained in violation of his right to silence under the Fifth amendment and *Miranda v. Arizona*, 384 U.S. 436 (1966). Prior to trial, Mr. Turner moved to exclude statements he made to police on the grounds they were improperly obtained while he was in custody and after he invoked his right to silence. (JA 17). The government opposed the motion. (JA 19). After a hearing on the matter (JA 28), the trial court denied Mr. Turner's motion to exclude concluding that the statements were voluntary and thus admissible (JA 29). The statements were admitted into evidence at trial and considered by the jury. (JA 67).

Mr. Turner maintains on appeal that the trial court erred in admitting his statements to police because "voluntariness" is not the standard for admissibility of statements obtained from persons who are in police custody and have invoked their right to silence. Rather, after a person has invoked his right to silence under *Miranda*, police must "scrupulously honor" his right to cut off questioning. *Michigan v. Mosley*, 423 U.S. 96, 104 (1975). Police failed to scrupulously honor Mr. Turner's right to cut off questioning, rather, they undermined it. This error requires reversal of Mr. Turner's conviction because Appellee cannot prove that admission of these damaging statements did not contribute to the jury's verdict. *Chapman v. California*, 386 U.S. 18, 26 (1967).

Appellee's version:

Appellant has appealed his conviction by jury of first degree murder in the stabbing death of Shawn Martin ("Mr. Martin"). (Joint Appendix "JA" 76–78). Appellant was indicted for first degree murder after stabbing Mr. Martin in the back and through the heart. (JA 3).

Prior to trial, Appellant moved to exclude statements he made to police from evidence at trial. (JA 17). The People opposed this motion. (JA 19). The trial court, after holding an evidentiary hearing (JA 28) and considering the moving and opposition papers as well as the oral argument from counsel, denied the motion (JA 29). After a six-day jury trial, the jury found Appellant had committed first degree murder. (JA 100–110).

Appellant's conviction should be affirmed because his statements were given freely and voluntarily in compliance with the Fifth Amendment. *Michigan v. Mosley*, 423 U.S. 96 104 (1975); *Miranda v. Arizona*, 384 U.S. 436 (1966). Moreover, any error in admitting the statements was harmless: The evidence at trial against appellant was overwhelming and the statements were merely cumulative and did not contribute to the verdict. *Chapman v. California*, 386 U.S. 18, 26 (1967).

Both appellant's and appellee's statements of the case are accurate and supported by citations to the record in the form of the joint appendix, but their messages are different. Appellant's statement focuses in on the police officers' conduct and the admission of appellant's statements at trial. Appellee's focus is more diffused—on the nature of the crime, all that the court considered before ruling on the motion, and the length of the trial. The treatment of appellant's ground for appeal is almost matter of fact—implying "all is fine."

In sum, use the statement of the case both to explain the pertinent procedural history to the appellate court, and to deliver your message. The statement of the case is often the first opportunity to package and market your positions, be sure to make the most of it.

Statement of the Case Drafting and Editing Checklist

1. Does the statement of the case begin with the specific decision or action being appealed, e.g., a particular judgment or final order? Does the appellant's statement include the date the judgment or order was entered?

2. In the appellant's brief, is the description of the action or decision being appealed followed by the grounds for appeal? The appellee may choose to state the reasons the decision should be affirmed here or at the end of the statement of the case.

3. Does the statement of the case briefly describe the nature of the case?

4. Does the statement of the case set out the pertinent parties, persons, and entities and define a term for each?

5. Does the statement of the case set out the pertinent pleadings, hearings, and other acts that led up to the decision with citations to the record for each?

6. Does the statement of the case state the rulings or decisions below and the basis therefore, if given?

7. In the appellant's brief does the statement of the case then briefly elaborate on the grounds/reasons the judgment or order should be reversed? In the appellee's brief, does the statement of the case then set forth the reasons the order or judgment should be affirmed, or elaborate, as necessary, on the reasons given in the beginning?

8. Is the statement of the case easy to follow: does it clearly explain what is being appealed, the nature of the case, the pertinent parties and other players, and how and why the matter has come before the appellate court?

9. Does the statement of the case effectively deliver the drafter's message — the essential reasons the judgment or order should be reversed of affirmed?

10. Is the statement of the case free from any grammatical, punctuation, formatting, or proofing errors?

VI. The Statement of Facts

a. Goals

In the statement of the case, you described the procedural posture of the matter and stated your essential reasons why the decision below should be reversed or affirmed. Thus, when readers turn to the statement of facts, they will probably know the nature of the case, the parties, and your basic legal positions. Your goal in drafting the statement of facts is to tell a clear, accurate story that will make readers want to adopt your legal positions and that gives them enough information to be able to do so.

While readers at the trial court level may have been vaguely familiar with the case, readers on the appellate level will usually know nothing about the case except for what you and your opponent tell them and what they find in the record. Appellate court readers must be able to easily understand from the statement of facts what the case is about and what facts surround the issues on the appeal. They can only be persuaded by a story they can follow.

Keep your message in mind as you draft and package the statement of facts. This will focus your drafting and help you tell an accurate story that is both easy to understand and persuasive.

Show versus tell: The statement of facts should lay out the specific details that will lead readers to the conclusion you want them to reach. It is much more powerful if they feel they have reached the conclusion themselves than if you tell them what to conclude. Thus, be sure not to describe facts such that they become legal conclusions, e.g., "When the plaintiff put on her skis, she assumed the risk that she might be injured by fellow skiers," or "The defendant voluntarily waived his right to silence, and then spoke to the police." Save these types of statements for the discussion or argument section. In the statement of facts concentrate on telling an accurate, compelling story or painting a picture for the court.

We use the term "compelling" in context. Your underlying facts may not be riveting; they may be technical, tedious, or, even, in the abstract, dull. Or your client may not be seen as sympathetic, for example, if you represent BigCo in a serious personal injury case in which you are moving for summary judgment based on the expiration of the statute of limitation. Your goal is still to tell the story so that the facts (1) are as easy to follow and as accessible as possible and (2) promote your message.

Finally, keep in mind the overarching goal of having the court adopt your brief in large part as their opinion — this should help keep you on track in drafting a statement of facts that is easy to follow, accurate, and tells the story in a compelling, professional way.

b. Material Facts in the Record

Absent limited exceptions, only facts in the record may be included in the statement of facts in an appellate brief. This means only the facts that were proffered, presented to, heard, or considered by the court or jury below can be described in the statement of facts. Thus, for example, a witness must have testified to a fact at trial, or a document containing a fact must have been presented to the court as an exhibit in order for those facts to be used in the statement of facts. In addition, every fact set out in the statement of facts must be accompanied by a citation to the record or the appendix (an abbreviated record designated by the parties) that enables the persons working up the appeal to look up and verify a witnesses' testimony or review the document containing the facts described. The record on appeal and appendices are discussed in detail in Chapter 6.

On appeal you should have a good idea of the material facts in the record — those that pertain to the issues on appeal. These are facts that support or undermine the appellant's grounds for appeal or that support or undermine the appellee's reasons for affirming the decision below. Also, each side will want to include any background or shading facts that help convey the drafter's message.

Finally, any fact referred to in the discussion/argument section must be included in the statement of facts. If a fact is important enough to be used in an argument, the reader should first learn about it in the statement of facts.

c. Organizing the Statement of Facts

The statement of facts should be organized to promote your goal of telling a clear, accurate story that will make readers want to adopt your legal positions. This means a statement of facts that is easy to follow and that emphasizes favorable facts and minimizes or diffuses unfavorable facts. You should not omit unfavorable facts from the statement of facts. Not only is this misleading, but you can be sure that any facts unfavorable to your side will be included and emphasized in your opponent's brief. Drafters emphasize favorable facts and deemphasize unfavorable facts through (i) the overall organization of the statement of facts, (ii) placement of individual facts, and (iii) tone and treatment of individual facts.

1. Overall Organization

Tell the story in the order you want to tell it—the order that best conveys your message and places your positions in the most favorable light. This means a logical and persuasive order. A common, easy-to-follow sequence is chronological order. Other logical arrangements are by issue or subject, by witness, or from general to specific. Often in appellate briefs, different sets of facts relate to different issues, and it, thus, makes sense to organize the statement of facts by issue, and then chronologically arrange the pertinent facts within each issue. Which issue you begin with depends on your message and the impression you want the readers to have.

For example, in the appeal of the murder conviction addressed in the discussion of statements of the case above, there are two sets of underlying facts: (1) facts (evidence presented to the court) pertaining to police obtaining the suspect's statements, which are relevant to whether the trial court erred in admitting those statement, and (2) facts (evidence presented to the jury) pertaining to the underlying crime, which are relevant to whether any error in admitting the statements was reversible or harmless.

Counsel representing the appellant would probably begin with the facts regarding the police obtaining their client's statements and emphasize any police misconduct. Their goal would be to focus the readers' attention on the actions of the police.

Counsel representing the appellee would probably begin with a description of the underlying crime using and citing evidence other than the appellant's statements and follow with the appellant's arrest and questioning by the police. Not only is this order chronological, it emphasizes the appellant's crime—which was stabbing the victim to death—and all the evidence against the appellant other than his statements.

Where facts are organized by issue or subject, it is usually best to break them up with short subheadings that describe the issue or subject the facts pertain to. Headings serve as useful sign posts and help make a longer or complex statement of facts easier to follow and easier on the eyes.

Note: The statement of the case should have already set out the nature of the case as well as the parties. However, the first paragraph in the statement of facts should still establish the context for the story that best delivers the drafter's message. In the above example, the appellant would make the context the police interrogation, while the appellee would make the context the underlying crime.

2. Placement of Individual Facts

Drafters also promote their message in smaller scale organization by placing favorable facts in positions of emphasis, e.g., at the beginning of a section, paragraph or sentence, or at the end with a solid build up. They deemphasize damaging facts by placing them in the middle of the narrative or the middle of paragraphs or sentences. Sometimes, unfavorable facts can be de-emphasized by being joined or juxtaposed with favorable facts. However, be sure to test these sentences for overall impression to make sure favorable facts are not undermined in doing so.

Always, at a minimum, set forth all the facts the court will need to rule in your favor. This requires a thorough understanding of your theory of the case and the applicable law, including any tests, elements, requirements, or factors. Make sure you have corresponding facts for each.

3. Treatment and Tone

Emphasize favorable facts by using the active voice, concrete subjects, and active predicates when describing them. In other words, employ all the sentence writing techniques described in Chapter 8, Section III regarding clarity and getting and keeping the reader's attention.

On the other hand, distance and minimize unfavorable facts with the passive voice. Sentences containing unfavorable facts can and should be dull—accurate but not commanding attention. Avoid, however, couching unfavorable facts in confusing sentences that a reader may have to read more than once to understand. This will call attention to the unfavorable facts.

Favorable facts should be set forth in vivid, specific terms that convey as much meaning as possible, without going overboard, e.g., "the stabbing" versus "the incident." Specific concrete words are more effective than adjectives and adverbs. They also take up less space. You may use your own words to characterize facts, as long as those words are accurate. On the other hand, short, specific quotations are also an effective way of emphasizing favorable facts. Your goal is to tell a compelling story without going too far and appearing overwrought or overly dramatic. We suggest using a "might readers roll their eyes at this?" test for assessing this. If they would, cut that material from the brief.

In treating unfavorable facts, use words that are as bland and general as possible, without being inaccurate. This is the time to use terms like "incident," "matter," etc. Also avoid terms that are used in cases that are unfavorable to your side. It is possible to be too artful in the placement and treatment of unfavorable facts, however. For example, burying an unfavorable fact so deeply that the drafter appears to be hiding something, like a fatal flaw in their position. Or describing a fact with so bland or vague a term that it becomes absurd, e.g., referring to a fatal stabbing as a "contact."

Finally, always maintain a professional tone in treating favorable and unfavorable facts. Do not stray into the realm of pulp fiction or appear to be belittling or arguing with the other side. This will undermine your position and prevent a court from ever adopting your statement of facts in its opinion. Thus, always remember that you are telling a story to and painting a picture for the court, not arguing with the other side.

4. Final Words

In the statement of facts, you are telling a story—a true one. It must be accurate and contain all legally material facts, but how you tell it depends on whose story it is and the message you want to send the court. Your statement of facts should both set up your analysis and make the court want to rule your way.

We discussed the "roll the eyes test" for going overboard and appearing dramatic or absurd. On the other side of the coin is the "eyes glazed over test." Passing this test means doing all that you can to simplify technical or complicated facts so they become accessible and easy to grasp. Also avoid simply summarizing the transcript or using a repetitious question and answer format. Similarly, do not pack your statement of facts with quotations, especially block quotations, as readers tend to skip over them. Use only your best quotes for special emphasis and/or to support a compelling statement or characterization you have made. Expect that the appellate court or its staff will read the transcript. Your goal is for the court to read it with your narrative in mind. This is the case even if the appeal presents primarily questions of law in a court of last resort. The statement of facts will give the appeal context, and how you tell the story will still leave an impression with your readers.

d. Appellate Brief Statement of Facts Drafting and Editing Guidelines

Examine the statement of facts for the following:

- Substance/Analysis

- Organization

- Sentence Structure, Word Choice, Tone

- Paragraph Structure

- Technical — Proofing, Grammar, Bluebook, etc.

1. Substance/Analysis

Does the statement of facts include all legally material facts as well as helpful or compelling factual background or shading of the facts? Does it contain all facts necessary to rule in your client's favor? Have any facts pertaining to any relevant legal issue, element, or factor been omitted?

Does the statement of facts provide enough information and context for an unfamiliar reader to understand what the case is about and what happened?

Does the statement of facts promote your message — your theory or theme for reversing or affirming the judgment or order?

Does the statement of facts set up your analysis in the discussion or argument section? Is every fact you refer to in the discussion or arguments section set forth in the statement of facts?

Does the statement of facts provide clear citations to the appellate record or appendix for every fact set forth, described, or alluded to?

2. Organization

Overall, is the story you have told as easy to follow and as compelling as the underlying facts allow?

First, make sure you have set out the facts, including background facts so that the reader will understand what the underlying case is about and what happened. Then confirm that you have told the story in the order that best promotes your message. Do you begin with facts that create the initial impression you want your readers to have? Are favorable facts put in positions of emphasis—at the beginning of the section, paragraph or sentence, or at the end with a solid "build up?" Check to see if unfavorable facts are deemphasized or diffused—placed in the middle of the section, paragraphs, or sentences, or effectively joined or juxtaposed with favorable facts.

If complex, have you broken the statement of facts up with short, descriptive subheadings to aid the reader in finding topics and to provide some relief for the eyes?

3. Sentence Structure, Word Choice, Tone

First check for sentences that are confusing or hard to read and understand. This is a detraction for both favorable and unfavorable facts. (Indeed, when dealing with an unfavorable fact, you do not want the reader to have to read your sentence more than once.) Then check to see if favorable facts are described using compelling, specific, and descriptive words in sentences with concrete subjects and active predicates. This also goes for favorable/unfavorable rulings and reasons. Are unfavorable facts deemphasized by use of the passive voice, and flat, general terms?

Check that the tone is compelling, yet professional. Is it subtle in its partisanship? Detractions would be an overly emotional, angry, combative, smug, or partisan tone; or conversely, a tone that is too flat and seemingly uninvolved. Any tone that suggests the lawyer putting herself in the place of the court or commanding the court is detraction as well. Apply the "Will my readers roll their eyes" test for treatment of both favorable and unfavorable facts.

4. Paragraph Structure

The guidelines for critiquing paragraphs in the statement of facts are the same as with all legal writing only with an eye toward emphasizing favorable facts and deemphasizing unfavorable ones. Paragraphs should begin with a topic or transitional sentence. Every sentence in the paragraph should (1) relate to the topic/transitional sentence, and (2) relate to the sentences around it. The second requirement is accomplished by arranging the sentences in a logical progression, and, often, by using good transition words that signal where you are going with the sentence, e.g. thus, accordingly, moreover, conversely, nevertheless.

Also check for effective placement of emphasis of favorable facts, and effective de-emphasis of unfavorable facts within the paragraphs.

As always, distractions include paragraphs without clear topic or transition sentences; sentences that do not relate to the topic identified; paragraphs that are choppy or disconnected because the sentences are not arranged smoothly and/or because transition words are needed.

5. Technical Aspects: Proofing, Grammar, Etc.

This category involves attention to detail. Attorneys should make time to proofread their appellate briefs thoroughly. A document that has proofing and citation errors is distracting to readers and reflects poorly on the drafter and his or her positions and arguments.

Some points on the technical editing checklist:

- Check for "widows and orphans"—opening and ending lines of paragraphs that are stranded alone on their own page. There should always be at least two sentences of a paragraph on a page. If not, change the page break.

- Check that pages are numbered consecutively.

- Examine the font size used. 12 point is standard, although 14 point is becoming increasingly the norm for federal appellate courts for ease of reading.

- Check margins (at least one-inch around); use defined terms where appropriate.

- Finally, check that you have strictly complied with all requirements of local appellate court rules.

VII. Summary of the Argument

Most appellate courts allow, and many require, that the discussion or argument portion of the brief begin with a summary of the argument. Drafters should always include one if allowed. The summary provides a roadmap for the rest of the brief. It will help readers to better follow the discussion section and it will deliver your essential message before readers tackle the details.

Begin the summary with a request for the relief you want and explain briefly and plainly why you're entitled to it. On appeal this means asking for the judgment or order below to be reversed or affirmed and stating the grounds, e.g. "The judgment should be reversed/affirmed because (1) _____ and (2) _____." This is your essential pitch—what the court should do and why. Also be sure to include citation to the strongest authorities supporting each ground. Then, in the same order as you do in the discussion or argument section, set out your essential supporting reasons for each ground with citations to authority. Difficulties or weaknesses are usually not addressed in the summary of the argument unless they are central to one or more of your positions.

It is often best to draft the summary of the argument after you have drafted and revised the main discussion/argument. At that point you will have tested your arguments and points and will have a good idea of the most important supporting reasons and authorities.

VIII. Discussion or Argument: Purpose and Goals

The purpose of the discussion or argument section in the appellate brief is to persuade a majority of the members of the court to reverse or affirm the judgment or order below. You are challenging or defending a decision or action that has already occurred — not starting with a clean slate. Thus, the discussion section should focus on identifying or refuting reversible error. This often means addressing what feels like just the tip of the iceberg and leaving out a variety of things you believe the court or the other side did wrong below. This is one of the reasons appellate courts require a statement of issues on appeal — to focus the attorneys on the issues that matter.

The goals of the discussion section in appellate briefs are to show the court *how* to rule in your favor and *why* it should. Showing the court how to rule in your favor involves making your points as clearly as possible, which usually means organizing complex information so that the readers can understand it as easily as possible. Although readers on the appellate level will generally have more time to spend with the briefs than readers at the trial court, you are still competing for your readers' time and attention. See Chapter 8 for methods of accomplishing this, including (1) putting context before details, (2) going from broad to narrow and general to specific, (3) linking new information with familiar information, and (4) having an explicit structure.

When drafting the discussion section, envision the opinion you would like the court to issue and *draft it like that*. The best thing that can happen to the drafter of an appellate brief is to find that their brief has been turned into the opinion issued by the court — make it easy for them to do this by drafting an easy-to-follow, legally sound, persuasive brief.

The structure of the discussion section of an appellate brief is based on the CRAC format (Conclusion, Rule/Law, Application, and Conclusion), which is designed to deliver information in the most straightforward manner. In some appeals, particularly those to courts of last resort, the emphasis is on the rule/law portion. For example, a decision regarding (1) which law applies, (2) the interpretation of existing law, (3) the articulation of a new law, or (4) the extension or reining in of the law, may dictate or heavily influence the resolution of the issue. In these situations, the application section will be short and straightforward. Do not leave it out, however—be sure to concisely connect the dots for the readers so they don't have to do so themselves.

Issues on appeal may be factually intensive, as well. For example, whether an error in admitting certain evidence at trial is reversible depends on the harmless error standard applied and all the other evidence admitted at trial as compared to the evidence admitted in error. This will often entail a thorough, detailed application section. See Section XI(b), below for discussion regarding using the CRAC structure to persuade an appellate court.

IX. Organizing the Discussion Section

a. Basics

An explicit, easy-to-follow structure is critical in delivering your message. You want the court to accept, and ideally adopt, your positions, and, before a court can do that, it must easily understand them. Thus you must lead the court from point A to point B in a straightforward manner, not take it through a maze. This means organizing your main sections and subsections in logical and persuasive order and identifying them with concise, compelling headings.

Thus, before you start to draft the appellate brief, decide what your main arguments are and have a plan regarding what order to put them in. Also have an idea which argument should be divided into subsections and in what order those subsections should go. This may change as you draft and revise, but it is important to start with a structure in mind. Then make that structure explicit with headings, subheadings, CRAC, well-organized paragraphs, sentences, and appropriate transitions.

b. Main Sections

Each separate issue on appeal becomes a main section in the discussion section of the brief. Often reversible versus harmless error gets its own main section at the end of the brief.

Ordering Main Sections

The discussion in appellate briefs should begin with any threshold issues. These are issues that must be decided before the court can reach the merits of the appeal. Examples include whether one of the parties had standing to bring suit, whether there was personal jurisdiction over the parties at trial, or whether a matter is appealable.

After any threshold issues, the strongest argument with the greatest consequence should come next. This is the argument that is most likely to persuade a court to grant the entire relief requested, i.e. an outright reversal or affirmance. Thus, the discussion usually begins with the section that contains the drafter's strongest and most persuasive arguments and reasons for reversing or affirming the decision below, then the section with the next strongest arguments and reasons, and so on.

Your strongest argument is the one that delivers your message most effectively. It contains the highest ranking and most on-point cases and makes the most of your facts. Which section contains the most persuasive arguments may be obvious as you review the decision or action below, the record, and the authority cited to and relied on by the court. Sometimes this hierarchy may not be clear until you have tested your arguments in the drafting and revision stages. It is important, though, to start with an idea of the strongest arguments and where they should come in the discussion.

If you have more than one section that you think contain arguments of equal strength, lead with the one that is most consequential—the one that would give you the most relief. Thus, a section pertaining to an error that would require automatic reversal of the entire judgment would come before an alleged error subject to a harmless error analysis or one that would lead to reversal of only a portion of the judgment. For similar reasons, drafters rarely lead with the strongest if that argument will have little consequence, e.g. an argument that would result in the appellant's lengthy criminal sentence being reduced by one month, or that would result in a small change in the award of damages. These types of low consequence arguments usually go toward the end of the brief.

Finally, sometimes, despite the general rules or ordering arguments, above, drafters must lead with arguments other than their strongest. This would be the case for example, when the strongest argument is dependent on first establishing another element or requirement. Or a court may not be able to understand the stronger argument unless it is preceded by a simpler argument that helps set the context for the stronger, but more detailed and complicated argument.

c. Subsections

Each separate issue on appeal may have sub-issues that merit discussion, i.e., that each gets its own CRAC and a subheading. If, for example, several elements of a test must be established to show that a court did or did not commit error, each element deserves its own subsection where it can be separately addressed. Or for clarity's sake you may need to divide a complex argument with several types of legal support into subsections, each with its own CRAC and subheading. Division of an argument into subsections may be obvious from the beginning. Or, while you are drafting the discussion, you may find that you need to break up a long argument into subsections.

In general, if a matter merits a paragraph or more of discussion of the law, followed by a paragraph or more application of the law to your facts, it should become a subsection and get its own heading and a separate CRAC. On the other hand, be careful not to subdivide your argument unnecessarily or excessively. Too many subsections and headings can break up the flow of an argument. Also, a short subsection may look skimpy or flimsy on its own, which could undermine the overall point you are making.

If you use subsections, do not have a main argument with just one subsection under it. A single, standalone subsection is not a subsection at all.

Ordering your subsections requires balancing clarity with strength. Ideally, the subsection with the strongest arguments goes first. If this interrupts the flow or logic of the main argument, or if your strongest argument is dependent on one in another subsection, the strongest material may have to come later in the discussion. For example, it may make the most sense for readers to address the elements of a three-part test in serial order. A discussion that is quickly and easily understood is most important. In order to be persuaded by an argument, a court must first understand it.

If a main section contains subsections, it is usual to put a mini summary argument after the main section heading and before the first subheading that sets forth your overall conclusion on the main argument, supported by your conclusion for each of the subsections, in the order you discuss them, with citations to authority for each.

X. Statements of the Standard of Review

Each main section of the discussion should contain a statement of the standard of review that applies to the type of error addressed. If the standard of review is undisputed, this portion can and should be short: State the standard and include a citation to authority, then briefly describe what it is. If representing the appellant, describe the standard using terms found in case law in which the standard was met and cite those cases. If representing the appellant, describe cases in which the standard was not met and cite those cases. Often, the same standard of review will be described slightly differently depending on whether the court concluded it was met or not.

Sometimes the standard of review on an issue will be contested, in which case this portion will require its own CRAC. C—Conclusion: set forth the standard you want the court to adopt. R—Rule/Law: Set forth and explain the two different standards including the type of issues and situations to which they apply and why, and A—Application/Analysis: tell why and show how the error at issue is the type that requires or merits the standard of review you advocate.

XI. Persuading the Appellate Court

a. Basics

Persuading the appellate court involves showing that your positions and arguments are (1) sound and well supported by authority, and (2) the better choice.

First and foremost, persuading the court involves drafting arguments that are clear and easy to follow. Even when the argument is complex, your job is to make it as easy as possible for the readers to grasp. Courts are reluctant to implement solutions they do not readily understand. Showing the appellate court that your positions are sound and well supported requires thorough and sophisticated knowledge of the law and authorities and how they affect your case so that you (1) recognize strong points and arguments and make the most of them, (2) understand and overcome or minimize potential weaknesses in your positions, and (3) understand the hierarchy of your authorities and use them to your best advantage.

Showing the court that your positions and arguments are the better choice often starts with exposing and exploiting the weaknesses in the other side's arguments and showing they are incorrect, unsound, or not well supported. In other words, you demonstrate that your position is better because it is correct and sound, while your opponent's is not.

b. Using the CRAC Structure to Persuade

Some attorneys forget or abandon the CRAC (Conclusion, Rule/Law, Application, Conclusion) structure when drafting appellate briefs. This is a mistake because the CRAC structure is the best way to deliver complex information in a way that is most easily understood by a wide audience. Readers and decision makers can only be persuaded by arguments they understand, and the easier and argument is understood, the more persuasive it is.

Thus, discussion or argument section of the brief should be comprised of CRACs, each of which help deliver your message to the court and persuade it to rule in your favor. Each main argument without subsections is addressed using a CRAC, and each subsection within a main argument gets its own CRAC.

1. C: Conclusion — The Heading

Each section and sub-section of the brief is preceded by a heading that concisely sets forth the conclusion you want the court to reach on the issue or sub-issue. The headings in an appellate brief should identify and advance the main point of the section or subsection for the reader. Phrasing the heading in the form of a conclusion makes it persuasive. Drafters should resist the urge to cram their arguments and supporting reasons in headings because this usually makes the headings long and unwieldy. Also, readers tend to skip over lengthy headings — those with more than 3 lines. If you can set forth your conclusion and fundamental reason in support in less than 3 lines, do so. Otherwise you are better off saving the fundamental reason for the topic sentence that immediately follows the heading.

Your headings should be formatted so that they are easy to read. Traditionally main point headings have been set single spaced using all caps, which can be difficult to read. Also single spaced, underlined text appears cramped and is often difficult to read. Using italics is usually better. In other words, beware of cluttering up your headings with too many word processing tools — e.g., the bold, all-caps, underlined heading.

Headings are a good way to test the logic and flow of the discussion section. Indeed, they form the table of contents and serve as an outline for the discussion. After you have drafted them, arrange your headings in order in a separate document, headings with subheadings, etc. Do the headings make sense when read together? Would an unfamiliar reader be able to easily grasp your basic arguments from reading the headings? Does it appear that your strongest sections and your strongest arguments come first and go in descending order? Do the headings easily and effectively deliver your message?

Finally, if you are having difficulty drafting a heading, skip it and move on to explaining and applying of the law on the issue or sub-issue. After you have finished, the exact conclusion you want the court to reach will become much clearer and can form the basis of your heading for that section.

2. R: Rule/Law — Identifying, Explaining, and Illustrating the Law

Begin every rule/law section with a topic sentence that sets forth the conclusion you want the court to reach and the fundamental reason why, accompanied by a cite to the strongest supporting authority. This may feel repetitive to the heading, but probably will not be if your heading is of manageable length. By including a citation to authority, you are backing up the conclusion with law. The topic sentence elaborates on the heading, without becoming bogged down in details. The goal is to be simple and compelling. Use concrete, descriptive words, and the active voice.

Next set out and explain the law, standards, tests and/or factors in a way that supports your argument. For every law, include a pin cite to the authority from which it came. Similarly, every explanation of the law should be followed by a pin citation to the authority from which it came or on which it is based. This shows readers you are not making things up and enables them to quickly look up the case or other authority for themselves. Quote where you think the language is particularly compelling, but limit block quoting as readers often skip over them. If you do block quote, it may be useful to include a summary of the block quote either immediately before or after it to ensure that its content is communicated effectively even to those who skip block quotes.

Be sure to illustrate the law and explanations with examples from the cases. Illustrating the law means including specific factual examples from cases that show how a particular requirement was met or not met or to show when a factor or series of factors was or were present, or not. Specific facts and holdings are necessary to show how a law works in practice. Without them, the law section will be merely abstract. Placement of illustrations depends on the laws being explained. Sometimes the rules and laws will relate easily so that you can explain them together in one paragraph and follow that paragraph with a paragraph of case examples. Other times you will need to illustrate as you go, meaning certain laws will need to be illustrated before moving to explaining others.

As you explain and illustrate the rules so as to advance your side, it is important not to ignore law, explanations, or cases on which the other side will rely. Ignoring them will not make them go away. Your goal is to diminish their impact. This means preemptively distinguishing them on their facts or assailing them legally. (See subsection c, below for discussion regarding dealing with adverse authority).

Every law, explanation, or case that you refer to in the application section of your CRAC must first be set out in the rule/law section. Do not discuss the facts until the application section. Readers have a hard time following a piecemeal or serial analysis in which the drafter states a law and applies it; states another law and applies it, etc. Instead, set out, explain, and illustrate all the laws applicable to an issue or sub-issue, then apply them.

3. A: Application/Analysis

Begin each application section with an overall assertion of whether facts in your case meet or fail to meet the basic law you have set forth in the rule/law section, with a pin cite to your strongest authority. In this topic sentence, you are telling the court specifically the result you would like it to reach based on the law and facts. Thus, make your overall conclusion specific: "The court has personal jurisdiction over the defendant" rather than general: "The defendant meets the above tests and factors."

Then, in order of broad to narrow, strongest to weakest:

A. *Tell* the court why the facts in your case meet or fail to meet the laws you have set out and explained with pin cites to supporting authorities (these are your "assertions"), e.g., "The defendant had numerous and systematic contacts with Texas, including monthly business trips, leasing a summer home, and renting a post office box." *See McDermott v. Cronin*, 31 S.W. 2d 617 (Tx. Ct. App. 2000) (defendant established minimum contacts with the forum by using a Texas mailing address on both correspondence and contracts).

B. *Show* the court how the facts in your case meet or fail to meet the laws you have set out and explained by comparing and contrasting them to facts of the cases cited in the rule/law section of your CRAC. Here you will show the court how your facts are (1) the same or similar to cases that held in your favor, and (2) unlike the facts of cases that did not. Remember, a good contrast can be just as persuasive as a comparison. Be sure to pin cite to these cases as you discuss them and the facts of your case. This shows that the specific facts you are highlighting are legally significant, and enables the reader to go to the exact page and find the facts of the case you are comparing or contrasting. The goal in the application section is to show the court that your conclusions and assertions are sound and well supported by the law and the facts.

Avoid a mechanical application of the various laws, tests, factors, etc. in the order they are set out in the cases. Look at your facts and decide which are the most compelling. Perhaps several combine into a central theme. Highlight these facts or the theme and show they meet or violate a rule or requirement as explained in the cases. This is the time when you can use some of the descriptive words you concluded were too over the top for your statement of facts. You still want a professional tone, however—you do not want to appear overwrought.

Note: Some appeals are rule-driven—a legal question, whether or which rule applies, or how a rule should be interpreted, largely dictates the result. In these cases, your application section should be short and straightforward, but do not leave it out. Be sure to concisely connect the dots for the readers so they don't have to do so themselves.

4. C: Conclusion

Unless the application section is very brief, wrap up each CRAC discussion by restating the conclusion you want the court to reach—beginning with a transition word such as Therefore, Accordingly, and the like, and followed by a citation to your strongest supporting authority.

For an example of a discussion of an issue in the CRAC format taken from one of the authors' appellate briefs, see Chapter 7 § V.

c. Dealing with Adverse Authority

You will need to address adverse cases in the controlling jurisdiction. Deal with adverse authority by distinguishing it on its facts, and/or assailing it legally, which may involve showing its reasoning was flawed, that the court misinterpreted prior case law, that it was decided before a change in the law, or that the case is an outlier—that few other courts have cited it or ruled the same, etc. There are many reasons a case may be "wrong." A good lawyer and drafter is able to identify these reasons and explain them coherently.

In general, first try to distinguish a case on its facts, because courts are more apt to distinguish a case than to say it is wrong if they can do so. This means showing how its facts are different than those in your client's case and why that is significant. But do not be afraid, if you have grounds, to show how and why a case is legally incorrect.

Try to minimize the impact of an adverse case by putting it in the middle of your argument rather than at the beginning or the end. Avoid ending your argument on a low note. Finally, when you take up the adverse case or other authority in your discussion, deal with it as swiftly as possible.

d. Using Policy to Persuade

Your audience will include at least several decision makers, and you should assume that one or more may consider that the positions of either side of the appeal are tenable. Thus, showing that your positions are the *better* choice will involve making what are often referred to as "policy arguments." Unfortunately this term often leads attorneys to approach such arguments too abstractly, writing at length and using lofty terms and phrases. This should not be the case. Policy arguments are concrete but larger reasons why the court should adopt a tenable legal position. They show the court that your position advances a particular societal goal and/or that the other side's position will undermine this goal or cause societal harm.

Examples of policy goals include: furthering the underlying purpose of the statute or legislation at issue, promoting the efficient administration of the courts, encouraging safety, promoting freedom of alienation and property rights, and the like. Potential harms could be unknown, unintended consequences; foreclosing access to the courts; creating a "slippery slope;" creating a disincentive to free market behavior; and the like.

Our point is that potential policy arguments are numerous and varied. Your mission as the drafter is to explore the various goals your positions may promote, and the potential harms the other side's positions may cause, and find the ones that best package your message, that best advance your purpose in persuading the court to affirm or reverse. This involves having solid knowledge and understanding of both positions and the authorities supporting them. Look for potential policy arguments in case law — in majority opinions, concurrences, and dissents (earlier dissents can become later majority opinions), and legislative history, particularly legislative comments to statutes. Once you have decided on the policy arguments you think you will use, research them further, finding law review articles or cases in other jurisdictions that further explain or promote them.

Sometimes attorneys will find an oft-stated policy their position would promote and simply chant it in their discussion or argument, e.g., "This question is better left to Legislature." This is not enough. Rather, drafters should acquire sophisticated knowledge regarding the policies they use in their arguments so that they can (1) clearly identify them and explain them, (2) show why and how they are valuable, and (3) explain exactly how their position furthers those policies, or how the other side harms them. Unsurprisingly, it is often best to approach this process using the CRAC format. As the C — Conclusion — identify the policy and state that your position promotes it. In the R — Rule/Law section — explain how and why the policy you have identified is valuable using case law, legislative history, law review articles, etc. In the A — Application/Analysis section — tell why and show how your position promotes that policy. In the final C — Conclusion section — again identify the policy and how your position supports it.

Keep in mind in drafting the discussion section that your goal is to persuade a majority of the members of the court that affirming or reversing the decision below is the correct and best thing to do.

XII. Drafting the Components of the Appellate Brief: Order and Timing

The table of contents and the table of authorities should always be finalized last, after the rest of the brief is complete, to ensure the entries and the corresponding page numbers are accurate. *Any* change made in the brief, no matter how small or minor may cause the pagination to change.

The sequence in which the other components are drafted varies from lawyer to lawyer. Some proceed in loose order from beginning to end, starting with the statement of issues, followed by the statement of the case, statement of facts, and the discussion/argument; and then go back and draft the summary of the argument and the headings once the analysis and arguments have gelled. Others begin with the headings as a way of outlining the argument, and then draft the statement of the case and the statement of the facts to set up the argument they have outlined, and then draft the summary of the argument and the discussion/argument section. Some draft the discussion/argument section first. There are risks in drafting the discussion/argument before the statement of facts because the drafter may mistakenly rely on and include facts in her analysis that are not actually in the record. For example, she may be quite certain that a witness made a particular statement, but later be unable to find it in the trial transcript.

No matter what order you choose to draft the appellate brief, approach the process as a series of discrete smaller tasks rather than one giant, looming job. It is best to start drafting as soon as possible and calendar enough time to complete each task well before the filing deadline. Do not wait until you think you have found all the cases and all the answers—because you will not know what additional cases you need and what all the questions may be until you start drafting. Also leave plenty of time to proofread the appellate brief. Once you are sure it is error-free, the tables of contents and authorities can be generated. Generating tables often takes longer than expected and often reveals proofing errors such as alternative spellings of the same case that will need to be corrected.

If you are not sure where to begin—which components to tackle first, start with the one that seems easiest, e.g., a particular subsection of the discussion. For more discussion on the drafting process, see Chapter 8, §IV.

XIII. Appellate Brief Discussion/Argument Drafting and Reviewing Guidelines

Examine your Discussion or Argument section for:

(1) Substance/Analysis

(2) Organization

(3) Sentence Structure, Word Choice, Tone

(4) Paragraph Structure

(5) Technical—Proofing, Grammar, Bluebook, etc.

a. Substance/Analysis

In this category, look at content and persuasiveness. Do you demonstrate that your positions are sound and well supported? Have you addressed the rules, tests, factors, and cases necessary to enable a court to rule in your favor? Are the cases used effectively to highlight and focus the reader's attention on favorable facts? Are the facts used effectively to persuade the court? Is adverse authority effectively distinguished or used to legally assail adverse cases? Are policy arguments used effectively to show that your positions are the better choices? Are the headings informative, compelling, and easy to read? Does the argument promote the theory of the case, theme, or pitch? Have you made it easy for a court to adopt your discussion in its opinion? Do headings clearly identify the issue and main point made in each section and subsection?

The ultimate question is: Would a reader conclude that my positions are (1) sound and well supported, and (2) the better choice?

Also assess your citations to the cases. Every rule, test, factor, and fact you describe must be accompanied by a pinpoint citation to the case from which it came, so that readers can go to the exact page of that case or exact subsection of the statute and see for themselves. In addition, when analogizing or distinguishing the facts of your case with those of a particular judicial opinion, you must pin cite to the exact pages of the opinion where those facts are stated or discussed.

Detractions include:

(A) Omission of important rules, factors, or cases;

(B) Not recognizing or highlighting useful cases, rules, tests, factors, facts from the cases, or client specific facts;

(C) Not distinguishing or critically analyzing flaws in adverse cases;

(D) Spending too much time on weaker points;

(E) Dull, lengthy recitation of the facts in the cases, or dull, lengthy mechanical application of the law;

(F) Sequential analysis and application of the cases — you should synthesize the cases and highlight significant favorable factors and facts;

(G) Policy arguments that are undeveloped, abstract, or hard to quickly grasp.

(H) Headings that are too long or difficult to follow.

b. Organization

First, check to see if you have organized the discussion or argument in a logical manner that is easy to follow. Do the sections/arguments follow the theory of the case? If there is more than one main argument, are the arguments set forth in a compelling and logical order? If the argument(s) is/are divided into subsections, does this help your understanding, or is the flow interrupted? Do the important, general, or overarching rules come first, followed by discussion of factors and facts from the cases? Do the paragraphs logically follow each other, with informative topic or transitional sentences? Are the headings effective signposts that make the discussion section easy to follow?

Next assess whether the arguments are arranged persuasively. Are the most helpful cases in positions of emphasis? Are the client facts placed or woven in strategically, so that the reader can easily see how they meet or fail to meet any applicable test or rule? Are unfavorable facts and cases put in positions of de-emphasis, e.g. in the middle of the argument or paragraph?

The ultimate questions: Will unfamiliar readers understand the discussion or argument? Will they be persuaded by it?

c. Sentence, Word Choice, and Tone

As with any legal document, first, check for sentences that are confusing or hard to read and understand. Then check to see that favorable rules, tests, factors, and cases are set forth using compelling, specific, and descriptive words, in active sentences with concrete subjects and active predicates. Also see if unfavorable facts, tests, factors, or cases are effectively de-emphasized by use of the passive voice and flat general terms.

Assess the tone: is it compelling, persuasive, yet professional? Keep in mind that an overarching goal is for the court to adopt your language in its opinion. Apply the "would readers be likely to roll their eyes?" test. Detractions include an overly emotional, angry, combative, smug, or partisan tone or, conversely, a tone that is too flat, and seemingly uninvolved. Any tone that suggests the lawyer is putting herself in the place of the court or commanding the court is detraction as well.

d. Paragraph Structure

The well-written, persuasive paragraph is the key component of the discussion or argument. Make sure the paragraphs begin with an informative and compelling topic or transition sentence that clearly identifies the point you are advancing. Then every sentence in the paragraph should (1) relate and support the topic/transition sentence and (2) relate to the sentences around it. The second element is accomplished by arranging the sentences in a logical progression, and often, by using with good transition words that signal where you are going with the sentence, e.g., thus, accordingly, moreover, conversely, nevertheless.

Detractions include paragraphs without clear, compelling topic or transition sentences; sentences that do not relate to the topic identified; and paragraphs that are choppy or disconnected because the sentences are not arranged smoothly and/or because transition words are needed. And, of course, paragraphs that fail to effectively emphasize favorable facts or law, or that emphasize or fail to minimize unfavorable facts or law are also detractions.

e. Technical: Proofing, Grammar, *Bluebook*, Etc.

This category assesses attention to detail. Student drafters should avoid leaving points on the table because they have not had time to proofread thoroughly or ensure their cites are in perfect *Bluebook* form. Drafters in the real world should also not let these distractions undermine the substance of their appellate brief and their credibility as an attorney. See Section VI(e)(5) of this chapter for a proofing checklist.

XIV. Heading and Topic Sentence Outline

A good way to test an appellate brief for overall substance and organization is to create a heading and topic sentence outline. After you have completed a first or second draft of the brief, highlight the document's headings and subheading along with the topic (first) sentences of every paragraph, then copy them in order into a separate document and print it out.

First check if the headings and topic sentences identify all the subjects, issues, and points necessary to analyze the problem or matter and persuade the court to rule in your favor. Thus, in the statement of facts, are all the significant categories of facts clearly identified? In the discussion section, are all issues that needed to be addressed, and all points, and arguments that needed to be made, identified? Are the major or overarching applicable laws identified in the topic sentences of the rule/law paragraphs? Are your overall conclusions for each issue and sub issue set forth in the topic sentences of you application paragraphs?

If the outline reveals any ambiguities or omissions in facts or analysis, review your draft. It may be that you have left out subjects, issues, points, or arguments that you intended to address or that you realize need to be addressed, or steps in an analysis or argument may have been omitted — which mean more substantive drafting is needed. Or, you may have fully addressed the necessary subjects and issues, but the headings and topic sentences do not adequately identify them — which means revising or adding headings or topic sentences.

Second, check if the headings and topic sentences are arranged in a logical order that is easy to follow. Pared down to headings and topic sentences, you should be able to tell if the brief provides context before details, puts familiar information before new information, and has an explicit structure. A heading and topic sentence outline also reveals whether the issues and sub issues are logically and persuasively arranged, e.g., threshold issues are addressed first, and issues and sub issues that relate to each other or that follow each other are put one after another, and that, where possible, the strongest arguments are placed first, followed by the next strongest, etc. Also, the subjects and issues may be arranged in logical, persuasive order, but some topic sentences may need transition words to make their relationship explicit.

Third, check if the headings clearly and concisely identify the subject of the section or subsection in the form of a conclusion, and that the topic sentences clearly and concisely identify the subject or point of the paragraph. In other words, check your headings and topic sentences first in isolation to ensure they are clear and strong, and then make sure they are accurate.

XV. Appellate Brief Final Editing Checklist

Overall Tone: Check throughout. Look for an engaged and professional tone. Every articulation of a rule, rule explanation, or case illustration should be put in a way that advances the author's side. Avoid words and sentences that appear bossy, caustic, or over the top, e.g. "obviously," and "clearly."

Overall Sentence/Word Choice: Check throughout. Mark any sentences that are hard to follow. Then note long sentences for unnecessary words—chaff. Watch for jumps between past and present tense. Past tense is usually best, and is required for events, like testimony that has already occurred.

Style: Check for use of full names/titles with a defined term at first reference; record cites, proper citation of authorities.

Identify or Refute Error:

1. Appellant: Have you shown (a) that the decision below was incorrect under the applicable standard of review and (b) that the error was not harmless?

2. Respondent: Have you shown (a) that the decision below was correct or at least not incorrect, under the applicable standard of review and (b) even if there was error, that error was harmless?

Remember: With rare exceptions, an appeal is not about re-trying the case below. It is, at best in terms of the court caring about the particulars of your client's situation, about error correction. In some courts like the United States Supreme Court, it is usually not even that, it is almost solely about policy and the broader ramifications of the ruling to future events and disputes.

Checkpoints

- The purpose of an appellate brief is to persuade a court to reverse or affirm a judgment or order below. An appellate brief should not attempt to retry the case below.

- The audience for the appellate brief will be an intermediate appellate court or a court of last resort. Both these courts include more than one decision maker (judges or justices) and you will need to persuade a majority of them to reverse or affirm.

- The vast majority of appeals are to intermediate appellate courts, whose focus is mainly on error correction. Intermediate appellate courts are much more likely to affirm the judgment or order from the trial court than reverse it. Appeals to intermediate appellate courts are usually heard by three judge panels.

- Courts of last resort also correct errors, but in addition make policy, make new law, and extend or clarify existing law much more than intermediate appellate courts. Courts of last resort are less likely to affirm than intermediate appellate courts. Appeals to courts of last resort may be heard by as many as nine justices, e.g. the United State Supreme Court.

Checkpoints *continued*

- An appellate brief should show:

    - that there was or was not error below—that the decision below was incorrect or correct under the applicable standard of review; and

    - that the error requires reversal because the error was not harmless or does not require reversal because the error was harmless.

- An overarching goal in drafting an appellate brief is for the court to adopt it in large part as its opinion.

- An appellate brief is comprised of separate components, usually prescribed by local rules of procedure. Typical components include a statement of issues on appeal, tables of contents and authorities, a statement of the case, a statement of facts, a summary of the argument, a discussion or argument with headings and subheadings, and a conclusion.

- The tables of contents and authorities should be finalized last. Lawyers vary in the order in which they draft the other components. What is important is to approach the drafting process as a series of discrete tasks rather than one giant job.

- The statement of issues on appeal should specifically identify the alleged error or lack of error below. We recommend using the whether/when format.

- The statement of the case should set out the nature of the case, the relevant procedural history of the case and should also contain the essential reasons why the decision below should be reversed or affirmed. The statement of the case is the drafter's first opportunity to deliver her message. Accurate citations to the record or appendix for each fact or document are essential.

- The statement of facts should tell an accurate story that will make the readers want to adopt your legal positions and that gives them enough information to be able to do so.

- The purpose of the discussion or argument section is to show the readers how to rule in your client's favor and why they should do so. This involves making your points as clearly as possible, which usually means organizing complex information so that the reader can understand it as easily as possible.

- When drafting the discussion section, envision the opinion you would like the court to issue and draft it like that.

- Before you begin to draft, have an idea of what your main arguments are and where they should go. Also have an idea of which arguments should be divided into subsections with their own point headings and CRAC format. This may change as you draft and revise, but it is best to begin with a structure in mind.

- Each separate issue on appeal becomes a main section in the discussion section of both the appellant's and the appellee's brief. Often the issue of reversible versus harmless error gets its own section at the end of the brief.

Checkpoints *continued*

- The discussion section should begin with any threshold issues, e.g. standing to sue or appeal, or whether there is jurisdiction.

- After any threshold issue, the discussion section usually begins with the drafter's strongest argument for reversing or affirming the decision below, and so on.

- An exception would be if the strongest argument has the smallest consequence, e.g. a very strong argument that would reduce the defendant's 25 year sentence by one month.

- The structure of the discussion section is based on the CRAC (Conclusion, Rule/Law, Application, Conclusion) format and is comprised of a series of CRACs. With some issues on appeal the focus will be on the rule/law portion, e.g. if the issue is which law applies, or whether a particular law is valid. On the other hand, other issues on appeal may be factually intensive, such as whether a factual finding is clearly erroneous.

- Persuading the appellate court involves showing that your positions are (1) sound and well supported by authority, and (2) the better choice.

- First and foremost, persuading the court involves drafting arguments that are clear and easy to follow.

- Showing the court that your arguments are sound and well supported requires thorough and sophisticated knowledge of the law and authorities and how they affect the facts in the record.

- Showing that your positions and arguments are the better choice involves:

  - exposing and exploiting the weaknesses of the other side's arguments, and

  - using policy arguments.

- Policy arguments are concrete but larger reasons why the court should adopt a tenable legal position. They show the court that your position advances a particular goal and/or the other side's positions will undermine this goal or cause harm.

- Test your appellate brief for overall substance and organization by creating and reviewing a heading and topic sentence outline.

- Once you have a complete quality draft, thoroughly assess the appellate brief using the statement of facts and discussion/argument guidelines set out in this chapter.

- Make time to print and proofread your appellate brief separately before filing it.

Chapter 12

Oral Argument

Roadmap

- Oral argument is first and foremost for the benefit of the bench.

- There are differences between arguing to an intermediate appellate court and arguing to a court of last resort.

- Counsel's goals in oral argument include: Helping the bench understand the case in a way that benefits their position; determining the bench's concerns and addressing them to their client's benefit; and making their client's case and positions tangible and concrete, and thus more compelling.

- The most important part of oral argument is preparation.

- The essential technique for effective oral argument is the development of talking points, not a scripted argument or memorized speech.

- There are many ways to prepare your material for use in the courtroom. In general, the fewer materials you have with you at the podium, the better. This chapter describes the three panel manila file folder approach to organizing talking points, facts, and record citations.

- You should make sure that you know the court's technical rules for oral argument.

- Your oral argument consists of the opening or introduction, which can be memorized but should be delivered in a genuine, non-mechanical fashion, the main argument, consisting of your favorable talking points, and your conclusion, which can be very brief.

- Rebuttal at oral argument is not the time to reargue your case. It should be used to make one or two incisive points that identify any weaknesses in the other side's positions. In addition, it is an opportunity to address any remaining questions from the court.

- Counsel should welcome questions from the bench and answer them directly, blending in talking points and transitioning back to the presentation.

- When presenting, it is critical to create a good impression, which is accomplished by paying attention to your dress and physical appearance, your manner of delivery, including non-verbal communication, and volume, tone, and pace of your speech.

- Being a good speaker and presenting a good oral argument involve being an observant listener who remembers that the goals of oral argument all point

to being helpful to the panel in a manner that will benefit your position and
your client.

I. Purpose, Audience, and Goals
of Oral Argument

a. Purpose of Oral Argument

Oral argument is first and foremost for the benefit of the bench—the judges
or justices deciding the case. While oral argument presents attorneys with great
opportunities to persuade the court, counsel should always keep in mind that
the bench is above all looking for them to be helpful and useful. This means
being well prepared, answering questions directly and clearly, and remember-
ing that oral argument is about the bench, not you.

Generally the main purposes of oral argument for the bench are:

- to gain or confirm a clear understanding of the case—including its issues, the positions of the parties, the facts and effect of relevant authorities, and the potential impact their decision in this case may have on
  future cases;

- to have their questions and concerns addressed by counsel, and

- to advocate their positions or viewpoints to other members on the bench
  through counsel.

The main purposes of oral argument for counsel are to find out and address the concerns of the bench, while persuading the court that their positions are not only sound, but are, in fact, the better view.

b. Audience

1. Generally

The most obvious audience for oral argument is the bench—those judges
or justices who are deciding the case. The law clerks or court attorneys who have
worked on the case are also likely to be watching or at least listening to oral
argument and may be the ones, besides you, who are most familiar with the
case. Another interested audience member is your opposing counsel, who will
be looking to capitalize on any concerns raised by the bench or other perceived
weakness in your case. But remember, you are not arguing with or to your op-

posing counsel, you are answering questions and conversing with the bench in an effort to have them resolve the case in your client's favor.

The other important audience for oral argument is you. During oral argument pay careful attention to the bench and be ready to stop and answer any questions that the judges may have. Watch for their reactions and body language and try to ascertain their concerns and attitudes regarding your positions as well as the other side's.

2. The Bench — Intermediate Appellate Courts

On intermediate appellate courts, the bench for oral argument is usually comprised of a panel of three decision makers. On most courts, including the United States Circuit Courts of Appeals, these people are called "judges"; however, on some courts, e.g. the California Courts of Appeal, they are called "justices." The time when the identity of the panel members assigned to a case is disclosed varies widely from court to court. For example, in the Seventh and Federal Circuits, the identity of the panel members is not disclosed until the day of oral argument, while in the D.C. Circuit, the identity of the panel is usually included in the notice setting the date of oral argument. The timing is subject to change, thus counsel should regularly check the court's website for any rules or operating procedure changes. Some courts have arranged for Twitter or other social media services to alert attorneys with automatic notice regarding changes in procedure or court operations. The earlier the panel members are known the better; attorneys can then familiarize themselves with the members' background, reputation, general attitudes, demeanor, and recent opinions.

In some intermediate appellate courts, oral argument is scheduled in every case as a matter of course. In others, oral argument is scheduled unless one or all of the parties waive it. In many courts, however, only a portion of the cases are assigned to the oral argument calendar. Simpler cases, generally ones in which the decision below can be affirmed with little discussion, are disposed of without oral argument. In these courts, being calendared for oral argument is a sign to appellants that they have a chance of prevailing. As discussed in Chapter 11, Section I(b), intermediate appellate courts are, statistically speaking, much more likely to affirm than reverse.

Keep in mind during oral argument that your audience is each member of the panel, not just the one or ones that are asking the questions or that appear the most animated. To prevail, you must convince at least two out of the three that your position is sound and a better choice than the other side's. Thus watch, listen, and try to establish eye contact with every member on the panel as you answer questions and make your points. If a bench memo or draft opinion is produced by a particular panel member's chambers attorney or law clerk, that judge is likely to be the most familiar with the case. It is the attorney's mission to ensure all members of the panel gain clear understanding of the case and all their concerns are surfaced and addressed.

For further discussion of intermediate appellate courts see Chapter 11, Section I(b).

3. The Bench — Courts of Last Resort

For oral arguments in front of courts of last resort, the bench is usually comprised of all member of the court — unless a member has recused themself or is otherwise unavailable. Courts of last resort in this country have anywhere from five to nine members. For example, the Tennessee Supreme Court has five justices, the California Supreme Court has seven, and the United States Supreme Court has nine. The members of courts of last resort are usually referred to as "justices," except, for example, The New York Court of Appeals, whose members are called "judges." Since the bench in a court of last resort is typically comprised of all members of the court, attorneys will generally know well in advance who they will be arguing in front of.

In courts of last resort, oral argument is heard in the vast majority of cases. It is also likely that many or most panel members will be interested in the case. Review is discretionary in most cases and thus, a minimum number of judges have voted to take the case. For example, in the United States Supreme Court, by convention, a minimum of four votes is required to grant certiorari. In some state courts of last resort review of certain cases is mandatory, e.g. cases in which the death penalty has been imposed. In those mandatory cases the legislature has determined that the issue presented is of such magnitude that final review must be available in the state's highest court.

Although some justices will likely be more interested in the case than others, you should assume that all members of the court will be well prepared for oral argument — that they have read all of the briefs as well as memos prepared by their law chambers attorneys or law clerks. Thus, it is unlikely that problems or weakness with your or the other side's positions will go unnoticed or unexplored. Thus, with a multitude of well prepared and likely interested justices, counsel arguing before courts of last resort should expect, welcome, and be prepared for a variety of questions — hostile, friendly, and probing.

For further discussion of courts of last resort see Chapter 11, Section I(c).

4. *Goals of Oral Argument*

Your overall goal in oral argument is the same as that in drafting an appellate brief—to persuade the court to affirm or reverse the decision below. Oral argument, however, is your only opportunity to be present "live" before the people deciding your case, thus your focus and specific goals are distinct. Your specific goals in oral argument should be:

- to help the bench understand the case in a way that will make them more inclined to rule in your favor;

- to find out and address the concerns of the bench—concerns that pertain to potential weaknesses or problems with your positions as well as those of the other side,—and, with those concerns in mind, to:

  - focus the court on the main points of your position that are likely to persuade the court to rule in your favor, and

  - respond to the arguments on the other side—which means pointing out and underscoring any weaknesses, as well doing your best to dispel or undermine arguments that appear compelling; and

- to make your client's case and positions tangible and concrete and thus more compelling. During oral argument you will be able to bring life and dimension to your case that is hard to accomplish in an appellate brief.

II. Preparing for Oral Argument

a. Goals

The most important component of oral argument happens outside the court room: Preparation. Your overall goal in preparing for oral argument is to become so conversant in all facets of the case that you can quickly and easily explain your best points, directly address any potential problems or weaknesses, and welcome and answer a wide variety of questions from the bench.

Achieving this goal is a multi-step process that begins with immersing yourself in the case so that you know it better than ever before. Then you are ready to create talking points that highlight your best arguments for reversal or affirmance. The flip side of knowing and being able to easily articulate your best arguments is knowing potential problems or weaknesses in your position and being able to address and dispel them, or at least decrease their impact. At that point you should be able to identify subjects and areas that will likely draw questions from the bench and prepare to address them. Ideally you are discussing the case with colleagues during each stage, testing and practicing points, ideas, and theories. All this preparation will give you the best chance of persuading the court to rule your way.

b. Knowing the Case

To become conversant in the case you need to become readily familiar with everything about it that might bear on the court's decision. A good place to start is with reviewing the appellate appendices and rereading all the briefs with a fresh perspective. Examine your positions and those of the other side and note both the strengths and weaknesses, as well as the facts, rationale, rules, and authorities on which the positions are based. It can be difficult at this stage to objectively examine potential problems in your positions or strengths on the other side, since you likely have become convinced of the superiority of your positions. It is essential, however, that you prepare for any areas of concern so that you can address them at oral argument.

1. Knowing the Law

After reading the briefs, update the cases and authorities to see if they are still good law, as well as to find any cases that have relied on them, distinguished them, criticized them, extended them, clarified them, and the like. Once you are confident that you have all relevant cases on the issues, read any new ones and reread the ones cited in the briefs with a fresh eye. Just as when you are preparing to draft a brief, group and sort the cases according to issue and significance and note which ones are helpful to your position and those that appear more helpful to the other side. Some cases can go either way depending on how they are interpreted or applied. These type of cases are often central to the appeal. To help you remember significant cases think of a short hand description for each—one that describes a unique aspect of the facts, e.g., "amusement park merger"—and write it next to the case's name. Then write out a summary of each case that includes important facts, rules, and rationale. Writing these down and having them at your fingertips help make you conversant with the rules, law, and rationale relevant to the appeal as well as the individual cases themselves.

2. Knowing the Facts

When reading the briefs, also reacquaint yourself with all the facts that might bear on the court's decision and where support for those facts can be found in the appellate appendices or record. For each fact, look up the appendix or record citation both to confirm its accuracy and refamiliarize yourself with the actual documents used to support it. A good way to become conversant with the important facts is to write down the point of every argument made in the briefs, then under each conclusion list the supporting facts in order of significance along with a citation to the appendix or record for each fact. This will help you to remember the facts that support your arguments, as well as critically assess the facts cited in support of arguments on the other side. Either way, you will be able to answer the inevitable question: "Where is that in the record?"

You will also need to be familiar with the pertinent procedural facts in the case — how it has come before the court, who won and who lost what, how, at what stage, etc. The easiest way to keep track of and organize the procedural facts is to make a time-line of the procedural steps leading to the disposition, judgment, or order appealed from until the notice of appeal (and thereafter, if pertinent), along with supporting citations to the appendix or record. This would include the substance of motions and oppositions filed, hearings, trial, court rulings, and the like. If representing the appellant, be sure to note where and how any asserted error was preserved.

3. Knowing the Context

In addition to knowing the law and facts that directly relate to the issues on appeal, it is important to know the field or specialty of law involved, as well as your client's business and the industry, discipline, area, or subject matter involved in the dispute. Thus, for example, if the issues on appeal arise in a bankruptcy case involving a company that operates theme parks, the attorney should be well versed in bankruptcy law and the theme park entertainment industry.

Members of the bench will generally expect the attorneys arguing a case to be familiar with the general body of law involved, including important codes sections and cases that do not appear in any of the briefs. An attorney who does not have this context will not be able to respond to questions that the bench will consider general and basic. An attorney will also need to know how the court's decision might affect the application of other code sections, regulations, rules, and standards in the field of law than the ones directly at issue in the appeal.

Counsel should also be able to explain the factual context from which the appeal arises. This means knowing how a particular business operates, how a product is produced, how an invention works, how a particular type of search is conducted, standard operating procedures, industry norms, etc. Sometimes the bench will ask questions regarding the business, industry, or field involved because they are simply curious. Other times knowing the factual context will help a judge or justice make up his her mind on a particular issue. Either way, counsel will want to have an informed answer, and not have to explain "I don't know; I'm just the lawyer."

Indeed, the United States Supreme Court's *Guide for Counsel* states specifically:

> Know your client's business. One counsel representing a large beer brewing corporation was asked the following by a Justice during argument: "What is the difference between beer and ale?" The question had little to do with the issues, but the case involved the beer brewing business. Counsel gave a brief, simple, and clear answer that was understood by everyone in the courtroom. He knew the business of his client, and it showed. The Justice who posed the question thanked counsel in a warm and gracious manner. [See Rubin v. Coors Brewing Co., 514 U.S. 476 (1995) (holding statute prohibiting displaying the alcohol content on beer labels violated the First Amendment) 1994 WL 714632 (Nov. 30, 1994) (U.S. Sup. Ct. Oral Arg. Tr.)]
>
> For an excellent example of a counsel who was intimately familiar with her client's business, see the transcript of argument in *United States v. Flores-Montano*, 541 U. S. 149 (2004). The case dealt with the searching of vehicle gas tanks by customs agents at an international border. Government counsel had a total grasp of why and how the agents conducted the searches and provided convincing explanations to all questions posed by the Court. [*See* 2004 WL 434141 (Feb. 25, 2004) (U.S. Sup. Ct. Oral Arg. Tr.)]

U.S. Sup. Ct. Guide for Counsel, p. 7 (2010), http://www.supremecourt.gov/oral_arguments/guideforcounsel.pdf.

4. Knowing What You Are Asking the Court to Do and the Possible Effects

An essential part of knowing your case well enough for oral arguments is knowing and understanding what you are asking the court to do and its possible effects on future cases. One aspect is simple — generally, you will be asking the court to reverse or affirm a decision below. However, you may also be asking the court to remand with instructions, or to reverse and enter judgment in your favor. You want to be able to articulate clearly and easily what these extra measures are and why the court should implement them.

Asking the court to reverse or affirm may involve interpreting a statute, rule, or case in a particular way; applying a certain statute, rule, or case and not another; giving an expansive or restrictive reading to a statute, rule, or case; overruling a case or declaring a statute or rule unenforceable; etc., all of which will affect future cases. In that instance, knowing the case means thoroughly examining and analyzing the effects of the ruling you are asking from the court. This means remaining flexible and discussing, asking, and answering a variety of "what if" questions, in preparation for hypotheticals that are likely to be posed from the bench.

c. Developing Talking Points

Oral argument is not the time to summarize your brief or deliver a memorized speech. In other words, do not expect to lecture to the bench. Oral argument is rarely linear. At its best, oral argument is flexible and conversational. Thus, rather than writing out or outlining your presentation, create talking points that you can move to at any time during oral argument.

1. What Talking Points Are and How to Use Them in Oral Argument

Talking points should form the basis of your argument, as well answer the positions of the other side. They are meant to highlight specific conclusions you want the court to make along with the most essential reason(s) in support. While appellate briefs are structured in paragraphs, talking points are structured in bullet points—with the conclusion set out in the main bullet point and the essential legal, factual, or policy reasons in support set out in sub-bullets. Talking points on each issue should generally be limited to one main bullet point and no more than four sub-bullet points. Any more than that and they become unwieldy.

The following is an example of a set of talking points in an appeal involving the admission of the appellant's confession. One of the main arguments in the appellant's brief, requiring many pages of discussion, was that the court erred in admitting the confession at issue under *Miranda v. Arizona*, 384 U.S. 436 (1966), and *Michigan v. Mosley*, 423 U.S. 96, 104 (1975), because after the appellant arguably invoked his right to silence, police did not stop the interview and honor his right to cut off questioning. Here is the discussion in talking points:

- *Miranda* Violation: Police did not "scrupulously honor" Turner's right to cut off questioning.

    - Turner invoked his right to silence when he told police "I think I'm done talking."

- Police were required to "scrupulously honor" that right to cut off questioning.

- Just the opposite—their response was to lie to him to convince him to change his mind.

- So whether or not the confession could be held to be voluntary, the trial court erred in admitting the confession under *Miranda* and *Mosley.*

This set of talking points advances one of the appellant's most important arguments as well as anticipates potential problems. Well prepared appellant's counsel would recognize areas of concern for the bench could be (1) whether appellant effectively invoked his right to silence with the words "I think I'm done talking," (2) if he did, whether the police sufficiently honored his right to cut off questioning, or (3) whether the pertinent question is whether the confession is voluntary—as argued in the appellee's brief. Counsel would expect questions on these issues and should be prepared to answer them.

Counsel should also be prepared to jump to another set of talking points. For example, they may begin with the "scrupulously honor" talking points above, but find that the questions have turned to the issue of whether the confession was voluntary or coerced. Rather than insisting that "isn't the issue," a well prepared attorney would move to their set of talking points regarding why and how the confession was coerced—even if they believe it is not their best position. One of the biggest advantages of building an argument with talking points is flexibility. You are constructing interchangeable blocks of argument that can be moved around to address issues in the order that your primary audience, the court, wants to hear them.

An attorney with talking points that advance their arguments and also address the other side's positions can move seamlessly to the issues the court wants addressed and then back to their stronger points. Basing oral argument on a series of different talking points prepares attorneys to be flexible during oral argument and to expect to move around from point to point advancing their positions, addressing the court's concerns, and answering the other side's contentions.

Talking points are not meant to be read verbatim, or read at all. They are kernels of persuasive conversation that enable an advocate to move from point to point and back again while staying on message. An exception would be if a point or argument depended upon specific language, e.g., from a statute, a contract, a party, etc. If that is the case, the set of talking points should contain that specific language, and counsel should be able to tell the bench where it can find that language for itself.

2. *Deciding on Your Talking Points*

A. Generally

After you have immersed yourself in the case and are well versed in the facts and law surrounding the issues, you will be ready to develop talking points that will form the basis of your argument, as well as answer the arguments of the other side. Although oral argument should not be a summary of your brief, generally, you will select and base your talking points on material in the briefs. You will want talking points for the most significant arguments in your favor, as well as any areas of concern that are likely to engender questions from the bench.

B. Arguments in Your Favor

First, develop a set of talking points that address arguments in your favor. These will form the basis of your presentation, and, in the event of a silent or "dead" bench that asks few questions, will comprise your entire oral argument.

In general, threshold issues, such as standing or jurisdiction, and the *main* arguments in your favor should each get a set of talking points. These will make up the reasons why the court should rule in your favor that you will identify in your opening statement. Do not expect to be able to make every argument set out in your brief. In oral argument you should try to limit the essential reasons why a court should rule in your favor to three. You likely will not have time to address more than three main points, nor will the court be able to easily absorb more than that in the time allotted. Thus, if your brief contains many arguments, you will need to choose your strongest and most easily articulated ones to make into talking points.

Each talking point should be limited to no more than five bullet points in total—one main bullet point and a maximum of four sub-bullet points. This may mean taking a complicated written argument and simplifying it into its essential terms so that you can discuss it quickly and easily. Do not assume this cannot be done—talk through the argument with friends and colleagues until you can explain it in less time than it takes to watch a television commercial. If it is impossible to turn an argument in the brief into five easily explained bullet points, break it down further into multiple sets of talking points.

Ordering your talking points: Generally, talking points that address threshold issues should come first, followed by the set of talking points that address what you believe is your strongest argument, then the set of talking points on the next strongest argument, and so on.

C. Areas of Concern

In addition to your main favorable talking points, it is also important to have talking points for any areas of concern that are likely to garner questions. Having them will prepare you to clearly and directly answer those questions, while advancing your positions.

Ideally, a set of talking points should advance your position as well as anticipate potential problems and answer contentions from the other side — as with the "scrupulously honor" example in Section c(1), above. This is not always possible. For example, covering potential problems or weaknesses in an argument may take too many bullet points — making the talking points for the main argument unwieldy. In that case, create a separate set of talking points that focus on dispelling concerns surrounding the main argument. That way you will be able to move back and forth between the sets of talking points without being stymied or taken off message. Also, in some cases, strong or otherwise problematic arguments from the other side may not be sufficiently related to any of your arguments. Your answers to these arguments should also get their own set of talking points. Just as with talking points for arguments in your favor, each set of "area of concern" talking points should begin with a main bullet point containing the conclusion you want the court to reach, followed by sub-bullets points containing your essential reasons (legal, factual, or policy) in support.

D. Effects of the Court's Ruling

It is essential in oral argument to know exactly what you or the other side is asking the court to do and the effects that may have.

As discussed in Section b(3), at times, in order for the court to rule a certain way, it may have to apply, reject, or strike down a certain rule, interpret a rule in a particular way, or otherwise make a legal decision that may affect future cases. In that instance, you will need a set of talking points on that issue. The main bullet point will contain your overall conclusion regarding the potential impact. For example, that the effects will be minimal and limited to cases with a very similar fact pattern to yours, or, conversely, that the effects will be far reaching with unknown or unintended consequences. The sub-bullet points will contain the essential reasons in support of your conclusion. Having a set of bullet points on the potential effects of a ruling will enable you to better handle hypotheticals posed by the bench. You will not be able to anticipate all the possible hypotheticals on the issue, but having talking points should help you think through the ones that you do get and improve your ability to better stay on message.

On the flip side, the issue may be whether the error below is reversible or harmless—in other words, whether the court's ruling will have any effect at all. Unless it is clear that a finding of error will mandate reversal, counsel for appellant and appellee should have a set of talking points on this issue. As with all sets of talking points, the main bullet point will contain the conclusion counsel wants the court to reach—that an error requires reversal or is harmless—followed by sub-bullet points, one containing the applicable harmless error standards and the others containing the essential reasons why that standard is met or not met. (For further discussion on reversible versus harmless error, see Chapter 10, Section III.)

d. The Introduction and Conclusion

1. *The Introduction*

The introduction to your oral argument is similar to the statement of the case in appellate briefs—it introduces the case to the court from your client's perspective, tells the court the relief you want, and why you are entitled to it. It sets the context and provides a brief road map for your oral argument. The introduction should be short, simple, and concrete, and you should know it by heart. (For discussion regarding the statement of the case in appellate brief, see Chapter 11, Section V).

Generally, an introduction follows this format:

- "May it please the court,"

- The attorney introduces himself or herself:

  "My name is June Smith."

- Then introduces the client, explains the client's status, and the context—including the ruling(s) below:

  "I represent Funsphere, a family theme park operator, the defendant at trial and the appellant on appeal."

  "In this personal injury action, the trial court entered judgment against Funsphere concluding it was negligent per se because it did not comply with State Regulation 1235 by filing yearly tax returns with the secretary of state."

- Provides a brief roadmap by asking for particular relief and stating why the court should grant it:

  "We request that this court reverse the judgment because, (1) Regulation 1235 is inapplicable to licensed theme park operations, and (2) even if 1235 did apply, failing to file tax returns could not have contributed to the accident."

Some attorneys and commentators recommend that counsel begin the introduction with a memorized sentence stating their theme for the case or explaining, theoretically, what the case is about. We recommend against this. First, the bench should know exactly what you want it to do and why you assert it should do so at the earliest opportunity. This request and explanation should be clear and concrete. Moreover, at the very beginning of your oral argument, with little context, the bench may not quickly grasp your stated theme for the case, or they may disagree or quibble with it. Having an underlying theme or message for your arguments is important, but the bench may not appreciate being clubbed over the head with it. Also, do not expect the judges or justices deciding your case to be impressed with you telling them what the case "is about." Weave your theme into your talking points and presentation.

Finally be sure to check the rules and customs of the court you are arguing in front of before finalizing your introduction. For example, in the United States Supreme Court, attorneys begin with "Mr. Chief Justice and may it please the Court" and are not to introduce themselves or their client. *See* U.S. Sup. Ct. Guide for Counsel, p. 5 (2010), available at http://www.supremecourt.gov/oral_arguments/guideforcounsel.pdf.

2. The Conclusion

Your conclusion in oral argument should be quite short and operate essentially as a tag-line. A lengthy, canned conclusion is more likely to irritate than persuade. Thus, to conclude, briefly ask the court for the relief you want, and if there is time, state your essential reasons why you are entitled to it. Often you will be answering a question or in the middle of a talking point when you see that you are running out of time. When that happens, try to finish the point or question to advance your position in some way, add a transition word, and ask for relief. For example: " … therefore we ask this court to reverse the judgment." Even if the conclusion is truncated, that is the better alternative to simply stopping and sitting down.

e. Preparing Your Materials for the Courtroom — The Manila File Folder

In terms of materials you take with you to the podium — less is more. The more documents, binders, legal pads, notes, etc. you bring with you the less prepared and confident in your case you will appear. This impression will be compounded as you shuffle and flip through your materials looking for the answers to question or support for your points. In oral argument we recommend working with a manila file folder that contains your talking points, as well as a list of key facts and their appendix or record citations. It is also a good idea to have available the briefs that were filed and the appendix, or if the appendix is voluminous, a volume containing the pertinent portions.

To ease clutter, we suggest using a three sided, 9 by 11 inch folder that will open up into three panels on the podium. Use one panel for talking points that form the basis of your argument—those that are favorable. After any threshold issues, put what you think is your strongest set of talking points at the top and then set them out in descending order. (This panel will contain your main oral argument). On another panel, set out your talking points for areas of concern, and, if applicable, potential effects of the ruling(s) the court is being asked to make. Then use the last of the three panels to list pertinent facts with appendix or record citations for each.

Which panel to use for which type of material is up to the attorney. Some counsel prefer their talking points to be set out in panels next to each other, so they put their main argument or favorable talking points on the left panel, their areas of concern talking point on the middle panel, and list their key facts and appendix or record citations on the right panel. Other attorneys prefer to set out their key facts on the center panel so that they can be easily referenced regardless of which talking point the attorney is working off of. The talking points and subject areas of the various facts should be clearly labeled so that counsel may move from point to point and provide specific factual support with ease.

In deciding which facts to include, review each set of talking points and, in particular, the sub-bullet points containing factual reasons in support—these could include procedural facts such as certain rulings or conclusions of the trial court. A short bullet point may encompass a series of facts found in various parts of the appendix or record. You will need to be able to describe these facts for the bench with specificity and show where to find support for them in the appendix or record. You will not have space to list the facts in detail, instead you will use shorthand descriptions that trigger your memory, with specific cites. An exception is when an issue turns on particular on a person's or document's specific language—in that case you should quote that language. Finally, if a bullet point sets out a specific fact you may simply add an appendix or record citation to it and not add the fact to your list.

Take for example, in the sample talking points in Section c (1) above:

- *Miranda* Violation: Police did not "scrupulously honor" Turner's right to cut off questioning.

- Turner invoked his right to silence when he told them "I think I'm done talking" (JA 30).

- Police were required to "scrupulously honor" that right to cut off questioning.

- Just the opposite—their response was to lie to him to convince him to change his mind.

- So whether or not the confession could be held to be voluntary, the trial court erred in admitting the confession under *Miranda* and *Mosley*.

Counsel would include an appendix citation for the specific fact in the first sub-bullet point, the appellant's statement to police, "I think I'm done talking." However, the fourth bullet point, indicating police did the opposite of scrupulously honoring the appellant's right to cut off questioning by lying to him to convince him to change his mind, encompasses a series of facts. Counsel would need to specifically describe what the police said and did to support this assertion, as well as cite to supporting documentation in the record. She is likely to know these facts by heart, thus she would list them in very brief short hand followed by supporting citations to the appendix.

Finally, if the attorney knows the pertinent cases thoroughly, as they should in preparing for oral argument, they will not need to bring copies of cases or case briefs up to the podium with them. If the appeal involves many cases, however, and you fear getting them mixed up during oral argument, you should bring a list of short-hand descriptions for each case that include the citation and the holding with important facts, rules, and rationale. Simply putting together this list will help you remember and differentiate among the cases. The list, ideally, will fit on either or both sides of separate a manila panel.

f. Becoming Conversant — Practice

Practice is an essential part of preparing for oral argument. In order to become conversant in the case, and to be able to answer both hostile and friendly questions, you need to talk through the argument with others who will challenge your positions as well as help build them up. You will also need to get comfortable with standing and speaking behind a podium in formal business clothes.

Ideally, in preparing for oral argument you will go through several moot-court-like practice rounds, with colleagues playing the judges or justices asking questions from the bench. Time and budget constraints may make this impractical, however. Still, you can make becoming conversant in a case part of your routine. First, talk through the arguments and potential problems in developing talking points. Then, at the earliest opportunity, create an oral argument folder, described above, and make copies to give to colleagues, friends, and family members who are willing to help you. Practice your introduction and go through talking points with them, while they use the folder to ask you questions—some hostile and some that help your position—and force you to jump among talking points. Also, ask them to pick times, without warning, to ask you nothing at all—to prepare you for the possibility of a quiet or "dead" bench.

In the beginning you may do this in a casual setting, then you will need to go through the process behind a podium or something that acts like a podium while dressed in your suit. Ask someone to video record several of these sessions, even if just on their phone or other portable electronic device. This will allow you to assess "how you come off." Are your words easily understood? Do you appear calm and confident in your case? Do you appear to welcome and directly answer questions? Do you have any distracting mannerisms that need to be eliminated? Many annoying habits are best seen when reviewing a video of yourself performing in "fast forward" mode.

Finally, it is important, if possible, to talk through and work on your argument with others in a back-and-forth, give-and-take answer format. Giving your argument in front of the mirror or in front of a silent audience will not adequately prepare you for the questions and "interruptions" that will likely occur.

g. Knowing the Rules, Procedures, and Format for Oral Argument

Another important part of your preparation is knowing the environment in which you will be arguing. Thus, you will need to make sure you know the court's current rules, procedures, and customs for oral argument beforehand. Things you will want to know include:

- The seating arrangements—at which tables do counsel for the appellant and appellee sit?

- If the time allotted your case is not set out in the notice of oral argument, what is the standard time allotted?

- After counsel is at the podium, how will they know when they may proceed?

- Will counsel be notified as time elapses? How? At what intervals?

- Does counsel for appellant need to reserve time for rebuttal? If so, whom do they ask?

- Is the use of exhibits allowed? If yes, what arrangement needs to be made?

- Are laptops and other portable electronic devices allowed in the courtroom?

- Whom do counsel check in with before oral argument?

- When is the identity of the panel released?

This information is available on many courts' websites. In addition, many courts have put together oral argument guides for counsel. *See, e.g.* U.S. Supreme Court Guide for Counsel (2010), available at http://www.supremecourt.gov/ oral_arguments/guideforcounsel.pdf. Attorneys should check for the most recent of these guides as soon as they learn they have been calendared for oral argument.

Finally, if you have not recently appeared before a particular court, if possible, you should observe a session of oral argument before it to see how the rules, procedures, and customs work in practice.

III. In the Courtroom

a. Remain Flexible and Remember Your Goals

By the time oral argument arrives, counsel may be so focused on themselves and their own arguments that they lose sight of the fact that oral argument is primarily for the benefit of the bench. Thus it is important to keep in mind while in the courtroom that your main goals are to: (1) help the bench understand the case so that it will be inclined to rule your way, and (2) to find out and address the concerns of the bench — concerns that pertain to potential weaknesses or problems with your positions as well as those of the other side.

An important skill in oral argument is, of course, speaking. However, a skill that is just as important, but too often overlooked, is listening — listening to the bench, opposing counsel, and yourself — to how you, your arguments, and your answers are received. At oral argument you should be attuned and attentive to your surroundings and remain flexible at all times. It is not about you. It is about how you and your positions are perceived by your audience.

b. Presenting Your Argument

By "presenting your argument" we mean communicating your main (favorable) talking points as well as your introduction, conclusion, and if applicable, rebuttal. Although you should not expect to present or deliver your argument without interruption or questioning, it is possible, particularly on the intermediate appellate court level, that you may face a quiet or "dead" bench.

1. The Opening

Counsel for both the appellant and appellee should have a brief introduction that they know by heart—meaning it comes across naturally as a short explanation and not a memorized, canned speech. Knowing the introduction by heart means you can be interrupted without becoming flustered, or can alter it to suit the circumstances. Preparing the introduction is discussed above in Section II(d)(1), *supra*.

When the case is called, counsel for the appellant should go stand at the podium and look for the appropriate recognition or other indication that they may proceed. This varies by court. For example, in the United States Supreme Court, the chief justice will recognize counsel by name; in others the presiding judge (the one in the middle) will simple look up or nod. Begin with "May it please the court" or, if in the Supreme Court, "Mr. Chief Justice and may it please the Court," then introduce yourself (if that is the custom), introduce the case from your client's perspective, and tell the court the relief you want and why you are entitled to it. If the oral argument is divided between co-counsel, the first attorney to speak will introduce the other and explain how the argument will be divided. (Splitting up oral argument between counsel is much more common in moot court competitions than it is in real appellate argument.) Finally, if it is the procedure or custom in that court to tell the bench that you would like to reserve a certain amount of time for rebuttal, do so after you introduce yourself. Note that in the United States Supreme Court counsel cannot set aside or reserve time for rebuttal at the beginning of their argument; rather they must preserve it themselves by completing their main argument before the allotted time has run.

When it is counsel for the appellee's turn to argue, they may choose to begin with an introduction similar in form. Or, if they were attuned to the other side's argument and the questions from the bench, they may have discovered a more effecting opening, e.g. answering a question from the bench the appellant had trouble with, or correcting an important misstatement of the law or facts. In that case, appellee's counsel would introduce themselves as necessary and then say, for example, "To answer your earlier question Justice O'Rourke, the answer is _____." Then they would transition into the part of the introduction that asks for the relief they want and explains the essential, or remaining essential reason(s) why the court should grant it.

2. Your Main Argument — The Favorable Talking Points

After their introduction, counsel for both the appellant and the appellee should move directly to their argument, without further introduction or narration. For example, do not say "I will now address the first issue, whether _____" or "I will now move to my main argument." Also, some commentators recommend that attorneys ask the court if it would "like a brief recitation of the facts" or say "Unless the Court would like a brief recitation of the facts, I will go directly to my argument." We disagree. This type of narration wastes time. In the amount of time it would take to go through these lines, the attorney could have set out essential facts she thought the court needed to hear. Also, the talking points themselves should include and address the important facts. If the court wants to hear a factual recitation, it will ask for one.

A one or two word transition from the introduction to the argument is most effective: "First" — then state the overall conclusion of the set of favorable talking points you wish to begin with. Appellant's counsel will usually begin with the set of talking points they decided was most persuasive when preparing for oral argument — the set at the top of their list. Counsel for appellee should remain flexible, listen carefully during the appellant's argument, and begin with the talking points that, in the moment, best highlight the weaknesses of the other side's position.

Talking points are not meant to be read. Rather, they provide you with the essential material to be able to explain your positions to the bench, stay on message, and establish rapport with the bench. You may refer to your talking points to make sure you have covered all the reasons, fact, law, and policy that support the conclusion you want the court to reach. In other words, use your talking points as prompts for all the material you carry in your head.

The quiet bench: While speaking, watch for any reaction or questions from the bench — however, there may be none. If you have a quiet bench this does not mean that they disagree with you, are bored, or do not care. Just the opposite, they may simply understand and agree with your positions. Thus, once you have addressed a set of talking points and well explained and supported your conclusion, move on to the next. Do not belabor a point hoping someone will react or ask a question. This risks boring the bench, or worse, you may create a concern or produce a reaction you did not want. You do not want to snatch defeat out of the jaws of victory. Also, belaboring an argument may make you appear desperate or less than confident in your case. Instead, take solace in the fact that you are able to make your points in the order and manner you had planned. (Handling questions is discussed in Section c, below.)

Finally, as you go through your main argument, pay attention to your time. With five minutes left, you should be thinking of wrapping up you main argument (whether that means nailing down the current set of talking points, or quickly moving to one last set) and concluding.

3. Concluding

In some oral arguments you will have ample time to conclude, in others barely enough. In all cases it is important to watch the bench and keep track of your time to gauge when and how you should conclude.

When you have ample time: If you have well addressed all the talking points in your favor and there are no more questions from the bench, move to your conclusion even if you have significant time left. Do not try to fill up the time with repeating your arguments, or, worse, moving to your talking points regarding areas of concern. Instead finish strong and with confidence—remind the court of the relief you seek and the essential reasons why it should grant it, thank the court, and then sit down. The bench will appreciate your being prudent and efficient with your time as well as theirs.

When you have a few minutes left: If you are in the middle of a set of talking points at the three minute mark, you know that you need to finish them and move to your conclusion. Even if you have kept good track of your time, you may see that you have only one minute left. If that is the case, you need to look for a fast transition to a conclusion. Often this means immediately completing a point and saying "Therefore we ask this Court to reverse/affirm. Thank you."

If time runs out during your argument: If you have run out of time unexpectedly in the middle of an argument, do not keep going and finish your point. Instead, stop, ask the bench to affirm or reverse, thank them, and sit down. Asking for extra time to finish your argument or to give a conclusion will not be well received or leave a favorable impression.

If time runs out during questioning: If time runs out as you are asked a question or in the middle of answering a question, a custom is to ask permission to answer or continue your answer. Note that this is not necessarily required, however. *See, e.g.* U.S. Supreme Court Guide for Counsel, at p. 8, http://www.supremecourt.gov/oral_arguments/guideforcounsel.pdf (when time runs out in the midst of questioning, counsel can answer the pending question and any others that are asked, but are not to return to their argument). In either case, if time runs out during questioning, it is important for counsel to directly and succinctly answer the question at hand, and omit a full conclusion. Ask for your relief, thank the court, and sit down.

4. Rebuttal

Rebuttal should be used to make one or two incisive points that assail or point out weakness in the appellee's arguments or positions. Appellant should never save any main argument points for rebuttal, attempt to make arguments they did not have time to make earlier, or repeat some of their main arguments. Rebuttal should be in response to something that was said during the appellee's arguments. It is a *rebuttal*. It could be a response to a legal, factual, or policy argument by appellee's counsel, a response to the way they answered a question, or a response to a question itself.

Counsel will have laid the ground work for rebuttal in preparing for oral argument. During this process you will have identified the other side's positions and points they are likely to make, as well as potential problems or weaknesses in those positions. Preparing for rebuttal during oral argument itself is a matter of carefully listening to the other side and the questions from the bench and identifying problems and weaknesses you can best exploit in the moment.

Do not use rebuttal to point out de minimus mistakes or misstatements by your opponent—that will only make you seem petty and perhaps desperate. For example, "Your honors, I'd like to point out that my client is 'Funsphere' not 'Funland.'"

Also, remember that even if you have preserved rebuttal time, you do not need to use it. If it appears that all members of the bench favor your positions and disagree with the other side's, it can be very powerful to state: Unless your honors have any questions, I have nothing further."

Be concise in rebuttal, quickly reintroduce yourself, tell the court how many points you have (no more than three), and then make them. For example: "June Smith—I have two points on rebuttal. First,...." Know that the court may ask you a variety of questions during rebuttal and you should continue to welcome and respond to them. Informing the court at the outset how many points you have increases the chance that they will allow you to make them in addition to answering their questions.

c. Answering Questions from the Bench

1. Welcome Questions and Answer Them Immediately and Directly

One of the main purposes of oral argument is to allow the bench to ask the attorneys questions. Unfortunately many attorneys lose sight of this fact, and consider questions from the bench to be annoying interruptions that take away from their argument. This is the absolute wrong view to take. Questions during oral argument show counsel what perceptions and concerns the judges or justices have about the case, and give counsel opportunity to influence perceptions and concerns. Thus lawyers should not only prepare for and expect questions, they should welcome them and make that clear to the bench.

Questions from the bench must be answered, answered immediately, and answered directly. Attorneys should not attempt to duck, evade, or shut down questions from the bench. It is astounding to hear some attorneys brag after an oral argument—"I saw where that question was going and so instead I answered the question I wanted to" or "I kept those judges on a short leash and didn't let them get me off my argument." Evading a question is not only frustrating to the bench, it will heighten their concerns and underscore a potential weakness of your case. In general, the judiciary is made up of intelligent people who can tell when someone is not answering their questions. Attorneys should never avoid an opportunity to address the concern of one of the judges or justices deciding their case. Cutting off, shutting down, or otherwise discouraging questions in favor of "getting through your argument" is always a bad idea. You are at oral arguments to answer the bench's questions and address their concerns, not to lecture to them.

It is important to answer a question immediately—right after it is asked. Counsel who elevate their planned argument over the interests of the bench often respond to a question "I'll get to that later in my argument" Or "I'll answer that questions when I address my second point." In doing that, the attorney has taken a likely favorable question and cast it aside because it was not asked at a convenient time. If a judge or justice asks a question, stop, switch to your applicable set of talking points, and answer it right then, when they are interested. Understand that points usually have more impact when they come in response to a question as opposed to as part of a speech.

Questions from the bench should also be answered as directly as possible. Try to begin each answer with one or two words, e.g., yes or no, it depends, and then follow with an explanation that supports and elaborates on your short answer. Beginning with a yes or no answer is optimal. But this is not always possible. For example, a yes or no response should not be given if either word could be taken as an admission or capitulation on a point that you do not want to make. Also, some questions, e.g., those that ask "why?," cannot be answered yes or no. In either case, begin your answer with a short conclusion — "Because Regulation 1235 did not apply to Funsphere" — then explain and support that conclusion: "Funsphere was a licensed theme park operator, thus...."

Attorneys usually have to train themselves to give a short conclusion first and then elaborate, explain, and support their position. It is easy to launch into a lengthy answer from the beginning that builds to your ultimate conclusion. However, beginning with a short answer is important because (1) it makes it more likely that you will actually address the question asked, and (2) it is important to provide context to the court for your lengthier explanation — the bench should know the point you are making before you make it.

2. Handling Questions: A Multi-Step Process

You will not be able to anticipate every question from the bench. However, during your preparation you will have identified areas of concern likely to elicit questions and developed talking points for those areas. Also, your main talking points will enable you to answer favorable or friendly questions. In other words, you will not have the answer to every conceivable question written down, but your talking points will serve as prompts for the information in your head and help you stay on message. If you think of and treat your argument as all of your talking points — those directly in your favor and those that address areas of concern — then questions from the bench will rarely take you away from your argument. It is a matter of being flexible and determining which talking points to use. That requires keeping a clear head, and carefully listening to each question.

Handling questions at oral argument is a multi-step process, with the majority of steps occurring before you speak. It can be summarized as: Watch, Stop, Listen, Think, Answer, Continue.

Watch: While you are speaking, be attuned to the bench and watch for signs that a judge or justice might want to ask a question. Typical signs are taking a breath, raising their head and looking at you, raising a finger, clearing their throat, uttering something like ah, um, or well. In other words, you want to show the bench you welcome questions and give them ample opportunity to ask them. Some attorneys do just the opposite — preferring to march through their argument and avoid questions. This frustrates the purpose of oral argument and will frustrate the bench. In other words, do not be the waiter in the restaurant that refuses to look at the table with no food and empty water glasses.

Stop: If a judge or justice gives any indication that he or she would like or is about to answer a question, stop your argument and acknowledge them. In other words, stop what you were saying, *look* at the particular judge or justice and say: "Yes, your honor?" Do not attempt to finish your thought. And never, under any circumstances, talk over them.

Listen: It is important to listen carefully to the entire question. The question may have multiple parts, or the judge or justice may be formulating as they go. Resist the urge to anticipate where they are going and jump to an answer. Also do not attempt to "help them along" and suggest what they might be asking. Instead try to clear your head and listen to *their* exact words.

Think: Thinking goes hand and hand with listening. First evaluate the question, then evaluate how to best answer it. As you listen to the entire question, think about the issue or subject it addresses. Then consider which set of talking points you might use to help you answer it—is it a friendly question that brings you to a set of your favorable talking points, or is it a question best addressed with a set of your "areas of concern" talking points. Will you need to identify facts and their appendix citations in answering the question? Is the question multi-faceted such that you will need to answer in parts? Finally, think about how you will answer the question in the most direct and favorable way. What one or two word answer or short conclusion will you begin with? How will you best explain and support that short answer?

Note: While you are listening and thinking it is important to look at the person asking the question. Do not look down at your folder for the answer, do not check how much time you have left, etc.

Answer: After you have watched, stopped, listened, and thought, you are ready to answer the question. If possible, begin with a one or two word answer, or a short conclusion, then use your most apt talking points to explain and support it.

Continue: The final step in the process is continuing your argument. We use the word "continue" rather than "resume," because you will not necessarily go back to exactly where you were when you were asked the questions. Often a question or line of questioning will signify that the bench is more interested in a different point than the one you were making. If that is the case, and you have more to add, stay on the point you went to in answering the question(s). If you moved to an area-of-concern set of talking points to answer a question, think about which favorable talking points are most related and move there after answering the question. If the question(s) did not move you from your talking points, you may keep on them if you have anything to add.

If possible, move seamlessly from answering questions to your talking points. Thus, it is best not to over narrate your transitions. For example, rather than saying "That brings me to my second point," say "Moreover," and then make your second point. Finally, never say anything that might indicate you were interrupted or that the question was an annoyance, e.g., "Okay, getting back to my argument" or "Anyhow,...."

3. Answering Particular Questions

A. Simple Questions

Sometimes after all the preparation for an appeal it is hard to perceive that a question is simple and calls for a quick, easy answer. For example, a judge or justice may ask what case supports one of your arguments or what facts you are relying on and where to find them in the appendix. If that happens, tell them exactly what they want to know—give them the case name and cite or set out the specific facts and say where to find them. It pays to remember the adage: If someone asks you what time it is, tell them the time, not how to make a clock.

B. Hostile Questions

We use the term hostile to mean those questions that get at a potential weakness or problem with your position, whether or not they are asked in a caustic way. It is important to answer hostile questions as calmly and directly as possible. Do not evade or shut down a hostile question—this would be forfeiting your opportunity to address a concern and put your position in the best possible light. Also, the person asking a hostile question may actually agree with your positions but want to test them to be sure. Plus, remember that the one asking a hostile question even if he or she is "against you" is not the only person who is deciding the case. Panel members that favor your position will be watching to see how you handle tough questions.

Although the person asking the question may appear caustic or on the attack, you must never be. You must appear calm and confident even, or particularly, in the face of a barrage from the bench. Do not raise the pitch or volume of your voice or the speed of your delivery to match theirs. In fact it is often best to lower your voice and slow down a bit to interject calm and order to the situation.

Another issue with hostile questions is responding to statements that are not really questions at all, but are posed as arguments. For example, "You client's confession was voluntary, so nothing else matters." In that instance you respond in the same manner as if you were asked a question. "Your honor, if I may, two things in response." Then you would use your talking points regarding the right to cut off police questioning and police coercion. Arguing with the bench will not help your case; giving a calm, reasoned response may.

Be calm and polite in responding to hostile questions, but stay on message and do not admit or agree with anything you are not comfortable with or that might undermine your case. Your goal is to persuade the bench, not please a member of it at the expense of your case.

C. Questions That Ask for a Concession

A particularly dangerous type of hostile question is one that asks or calls for you to admit or concede something. It could be a certain fact, whether a series of facts meet or fail to meet a certain standard, whether an argument on the other side is tenable, etc., or something that appears more minor. Some commentators suggest that attorneys decide beforehand what issues or points they can concede, so they can do so if necessary and move on. However, when pressed to concede or admit to something at oral argument, we caution against it. If a point is truly minor, the court does not need you to concede it, rather, it can address it in one or two lines in the opinion. Generally, counsel is only pressed to concede something minor when they have been quibbling with the bench. (See subsection E, below).

Usually, though, if a member on the bench seeks for you to concede something, it is to get you to help them in ruling against you and your client in the case. No attorney wants to read an opinion that states "Counsel conceded at oral argument that. . . ." and then quickly dispenses with an issue. Given the risk involved in conceding something in the heat of oral argument, we recommend against it. Instead, move on to a different set of talking points. In fact avoiding a concession is one of those times when using narration may be a good idea, e.g., "Your honor, although I cannot concede that, I'll move on. . . ." The idea is to make it look like you are cooperating by moving on to another argument.

D. Questions Posing Hypotheticals

Questions that pose hypotheticals can also be dangerous because they may call for you to agree that a certain set of facts meets or fails to meet a rule or standard — which could be taken as a concession. Thus, attorneys should use great care in responding to hypotheticals, but they should not refuse to answer them. When a judge or justice asks you a question that poses a hypothetical — e.g. "what would happen in this instance . . ." or "How should we rule if . . ." — they are often exploring the potential effects of the ruling they have been asked to make. Some attorneys will rebuff questions with hypotheticals, and simply state: "That's not the case, here." This type of answer is insulting. The bench *knows* their hypothetical is not the case at bar, that's what makes it a hypothetical. Hence, counsel should answer, but be cautions in handling hypotheticals.

Knowing what you are asking the court to do and developing talking points on the potential effects on other cases will help prepare you for questions that pose hypotheticals and keep you on message. In the heat of the moment at oral argument, it is important to listen to the question and hypothetical, assess the ultimate point the judge or justice might be making, determine whether they might be asking you to concede those points, and note any important differences between the hypothetical and your case. Then you should be able to answer the question posed and then explain the significance of these differences between your case and the hypothetical. Also, responding to hypotheticals is one of the rare instances at oral argument where it might be prudent to be slightly equivocal rather than absolute. For example rather than beginning with yes or no, you might state, "In responding to your hypothetical your honor, I do not think...."

E. Questions That Contain Inaccurate Information or Require a Correction

At times questions or statement from the bench may contain inaccurate statements of law or fact or misstate one of your points or arguments. If the misstatement is other than minor you will need to rectify it in your answer, otherwise your silence may be taken as an admission or approval. You do not need to tell the bench directly that they are incorrect. Instead, begin your answer with something like "Your honor, if I may clarify" then make the correction: "At the police station the defendant said 'I think I'm done talking.' He did not request an attorney. That can be found at Appendix 77." It is not necessary tell the judge or justice that they were incorrect or made a misstatement, just simply supply the correction.

If the misstatement is truly minor and will have no consequence on the case, counsel should avoid making a correction, because doing so will waste time and could take the argument off on a tangent. Take, for example, this exchange:

> Court: Okay, you're saying that as a licensed carnival, Funsphere somehow didn't have to comply with State Regulation 1235 and file tax returns with the secretary of state.
>
> Counsel: Your honor, Funsphere is the operator of family theme parks as opposed to a carnival.
>
> Court: It has carnival rides doesn't it?
>
> Counsel: They are much more involved and sophisticated your honor.

Court: Do their parks have a roller coaster? A log flume? A merry-go-round?

Counsel: Well …

Court: Do they, yes or no?

Counsel: Yes.

Court: Glad we could agree. Does it make any difference as far as Regulation 1235 is concerns if Funsphere is called a carnival or a theme park company?

Counsel: I do not believe so, no, your honor.

The point is that making corrections of inconsequential misstatements risks making you look petty, alienating the bench, and diverting the focus of the hearing from your argument.

F. Recognizing Friendly or Favorable Questions

Keep in mind that the bench may also ask you friendly questions that will help or enable you to develop and sell your points. The most important step in dealing with friendly or favorable questions is to recognize them and respond accordingly. This involves an important skill in oral argument: patient listening.

Take, for example, the question "Even if your client did not invoke the right to silence at the police station, his confession was coerced, right?" An attorney who listened and thought about that question would recognize a "friendly" question that invited her to segue to her next point. So, rather than jumping in and arguing at length that her client invoked the right to silence, she would answer:

> Yes, your honor. Here the facts and law demonstrate my client did invoke his right to counsel, but in addition, the police coerced his confession—an independent ground for reversing his conviction.

G. Questions You Are Not Sure You Understand

Even after carefully listening to a question you may not be certain that you understand it. In that instance do not guess or answer the question you hope they asked. Instead ask for clarification while putting the responsibility and work on the questioning judge. For example, say: "I want to make sure I understand you question your honor. Are you asking whether my client invoked his right to silence at the police station or before, in the patrol car?" (or whatever your best guess is). Do not say: "I don't understand the questions, could you clarify it?" or worse: "Your question is confusing, could you clarify?" The only time it is appropriate to ask the court a question during oral argument is when you are seeking clarification.

H. Questions You Believe Are Irrelevant

If asked a question that you think is irrelevant, e.g. because it deals with a rule or subject that is not at issue, treat it like any other question in that you should answer it immediately and directly. However, after your short answer explain how the case and your positions are not affected. For example, "Yes, your honor. Police are required to stop their questioning once a suspect unequivocally invokes his right to counsel. Here, though, there is no contention that the defendant asked for an attorney." Do not say "That question is irrelevant, because the defendant never asked for an attorney."

I. Questions You Do Not Know the Answer To

If you do not know the answer to a question after you have listened, thought, and made sure that you understand the question, say: "I do not know." If you think it is helpful, you may explain, for example, why certain facts were never ascertained, or that you are unfamiliar with a case. If you *are* unfamiliar with a case brought up by the judge, you may offer to review it and prepare further briefing on the subject—an offer that will rarely be accepted. Do not, however, ask the judge or justice to describe the case to you, i.e., do your work for you. Finally, if you clear your head, listen, and think about a question, you may find that you actually can answer it to advance your position and to your client's advantage.

J. Multi-Part Questions

Some questions may contain several questions in one. This is one of the reasons it is important to listen carefully to the whole question, every time. When you get a multi-part question, make sure you understand what the various parts are asking, then decide the best way to tackle the answer. Often this means telling the court that you would like to answer the question in parts, or that you have, e.g., "Three points in response." This puts the work and responsibility on you and gives you more control over the order of your responses. It is better than saying "There are several questions there, which one would you like me to answer first?"

K. Multiple Questions at Once or in Succession

You may also get multiple questions asked in succession by different members of the bench. If this happens, pause to see if they sort out among themselves the order in which to answer the questions. If they do not, you must decide and then let the bench know the order you have chosen. It is often best to preface your explanation with: "I think it would be most helpful if I addressed your questions in[then state the order]."

You may also be in the middle of answering a question from member of the bench and be interrupted with a question from another. Again, pause to see if they sort it out themselves, if one defers, etc. If not, evaluate the questions and the persons asking them and use your best judgment. The new one may be a friendly question designed to help you with the question you are answering. If that is the case, take the help and, in effect, answer both questions at once, e.g., "Yes, in answer to your honors' questions...." Or, you may be interrupted with a question on an entirely different subject. If the new question appears hostile and you were making good points, explain to the interrupting justice that you think it will be helpful in answering their question by completing your answer to the first. If you would prefer to stop and answer the new question, explain to the first judge that you think it would be helpful to do that before coming back to their question.

Note also that if you are answering a question from a person who has only asked a few and are interrupted by one who has asked many, it is best to finish your answer to the first question. Ultimately, it is important to respond to all the questions and make sure each judge feels that their question was recognized as being important.

d. Presentation

1. Creating a Good Impression

At oral argument you want to appear calm and confident in your case. It is a matter of balance, since oral argument is a formal occasion you do not want to look too relaxed or loose. Nor do you want to appear stiff or rigid—which can suggest a lack of confidence. Being confident in your case means being secure in the facts, law, and policy that form the foundation of your talking points—both those that are favorable and those that address areas of concern. Confidence in the case should not be mistaken with being impressed with oneself as an orator. Remember, oral argument is not about you, it is about how you and your case are perceived.

Counsel should be polite at all times during argument. They should never raise their voice to or talk over the bench and, when asked a question by a judge, should immediately stop speaking. Attorneys are usually careful to be polite to members of the bench, although remaining so can be difficult when facing questions or comments from the bench that appear caustic or even abusive. But counsel must remain calm and polite, even when the bench does not. Being polite does not mean being obsequious—which is not only repelling but often portrays a lack of confidence. You are there to persuade the bench, not fawn over the judges. Attorneys must also remember to be polite to opposing counsel and polite while sitting at the counsel table. Thus, do not use derogatory terms or names when referring to opposing counsel or their arguments. Similarly, while seated do not roll your eyes, make faces, or shake your head during their argument.

When it is necessary to address a judge or justice individually, it is best to use the default generic formulation "your honor" unless you are 100% sure that you can identify each judge or justice by their last name, in which case "Judge or Justice [last name]" is fine. Counsel scores few or no points at all with the latter format, and it is just one more thing to keep straight during oral argument. In any event, avoid alternative generic formats like "judge," "ma'am," or "sir."

Finally, counsel should not themselves make jokes or attempt humor during oral argument, but should recognize attempts at humor *from* the bench by smiling or laughing as appropriate.

2. Physical Appearance

Oral argument is not the time to express your individuality. Dress formally and conservatively with very few accent pieces such as jewelry, scarves, pocket squares, etc. Indeed, the Supreme Court's Guide for Counsel states that: "Appropriate attire for counsel is conservative business dress in traditional dark colors (e. g., navy blue or charcoal gray)." U.S. Sup. Ct. Guide for Counsel, at p. 3 (2010), available at http://www.supremecourt.gov/oral_arguments/guide-forcounsel.pdf. Many courts are not that specific, but the advice is well taken. You will be taken more seriously and assumed to be more competent and confident if you are dressed neatly and formally.

Essentially to the extent possible, you want to limit anything in your dress and style that would be worthy of remark—which could be a distraction. Bow ties, amusing ties, short skirts, displays of cleavage, loud jewelry, mutton chops, pony-tails for men, high heels that click-clack all qualify. If you are not used to wearing conservative business clothes, as part of your preparation for oral arguments you should integrate wearing them into your routine.

3. Delivery

A. Non-Verbal Communication

Part of how you and your case are perceived will come from non-verbal communication, which involves your posture, eye contact, facial expressions, and other body language. It helps to keep in mind your goal of projecting calm and confidence. Also, you want to develop rapport with the bench and draw them in.

Posture and hand gestures: Start by standing up straight at the podium with your feet squarely on the ground. Again, it is a balance, you are going for erect and confident, not rigid and terrified. You are not nailed in place, but you need to stay at the podium and avoid peripatetic movement, fidgeting, etc. Similarly you need not and should not clutch the podium throughout oral argument. It is natural for people to use their hands when they talk, and you may do so at oral argument. Make sure that your hand gestures are not distracting, however. Generally, this mean not moving your arms above your shoulders or your hands in front of your face, or moving your hands rapidly, which often makes you appear frantic.

Eye contact: Eye contact is one of the most important ways of gaining rapport with someone. Thus, it is essential that you do not read your argument. Instead look at all the members of the bench when discussing the issue and using your talking points. Avoid looking at a particular judge for a prolonged period of time (which generally makes people uncomfortable), but this can easily be accomplished by looking at another member of the bench. Indeed, it is important to draw in each member of the bench—not just the one(s) who talk the most—and the easiest way to do this is with eye contact. Also, when a judge or justice asks you a question, it is important that you look at them the entire time they are speaking to you. This may seem obvious, but many attorneys will look down at their notes, or at their watch, or other time keeper, during a question. They are not trying to be rude, they may be looking for the answer, or assessing how much time they have to answer, but they are telling the bench that they are distracted. Finally, remember that although you should give eye contact, you may not get it back.

Facial expressions: You want to look calm, confident, and welcoming of questions. This means having facial expressions that are open and pleasant. Although the setting is serious and formal for many people, serious expression can make them look stern or unhappy or as if they are glaring. Many people's "thinking face" can look the same way. In other words, try not to frown, knit your brow, or squint your eyes during oral argument, no matter how tough the question, or how uncomfortable you may feel on the inside. And remember, it is okay to smile.

Other body language: In addition to eye contact, another good way to gain rapport is to nod slightly. Nodding as someone speaks projects interest and attentiveness. Of course you do not want to nod so much that you look like a bobble-head doll. At the opposite end of the spectrum are shaking your head, crossing your arms, pointing your finger at the bench, clenching your fists — all of which project defensiveness or hostility.

Distracting gestures: Preparation for oral arguments should include video recording so that counsel can identify and try to eliminate distracting gestures. These might include tapping your fingers, clicking your pen, biting or folding in your lips, picking at your fingernails, scratching, constant readjustment of glasses, etc. As a general rule to combat distracting gestures, counsel should avoid touching their clothes or themselves at oral argument.

At the counsel table: Non-verbal communication does not stop when an attorney leaves the podium. How you and your case are perceived continue while you are sitting at the counsel table. They should continue to look interested, calm, and confident, and eliminate any rude or distracting facial expressions or gestures. Also, they must be careful to avoid the vacant stare.

For a thorough discussion of non-verbal communication, see Michael J. Higdon, *Oral Argument and Impression Management: Harnessing the Power of Nonverbal Persuasion for a Judicial Audience*, 57 U. Kan. L. Rev. 631 (2009).

B. Speaking

Volume, tone, and pace: First, you want to speak such that all members of the bench can easily hear and understand you. Ideally, as part of your preparation you will have visited the courtroom beforehand to gauge the acoustics and the microphone system, if any. You also need to speak slowly enough so that all your words can be heard, processed, and understood. However, you do not want to go so slowly that you appear to be plodding or talking down to the bench. If the tone or pitch of your voice becomes unnaturally or noticeably high when you speak or are nervous, you must try with practice to keep your pitch lower.

Also, you should vary the volume, tone, and pace of your speech. You will lose your audience with a flat monotone delivery — the bench will start to tune you out. Having talking points, rather than a set speech or rigid outline, helps you to do this naturally. Talking points promote more of a conversation (albeit a formal one), than a lecture. Of course you do not want to go overboard or appear overly dramatic, which would undermine your credibility and generally make the bench uncomfortable.

Your words: At oral argument you want to be direct, concrete, and easily understood. Thus choose words that are precise and accessible — meaning that most people know what they mean. You will not have much time, thus avoid speaking in vague concepts or using complicated analogies. Make sure each conclusion that you want the court to reach is as clear and as simple as possible. Being as direct as possible means eliminating phrases that distance yourself from your client or the case. For example do not preface arguments or responses to questions with "It is my client's position that . . ." or "We would submit that. . . ."

Avoid slang or overly casual terms or terms that are only used in a particular field or industry. Through practice, try to eliminate chaff sounds or words from your delivery, e.g. well, uh, like, you know, um, uh, etc.

Most importantly, being a good speaker means being a good and observant listener. Be watchful for how your words and delivery are being received, and adjust accordingly.

Checkpoints

- Oral argument is first and foremost for the benefit of the bench.

- Counsel should keep in mind the differences between arguing to an intermediate appellate court and arguing to a court of last resort.

  - Intermediate appellate courts usually feature panels made up of less than the full court. As a result, finding out which judges or justices have been appointed to hear your case is important. The earlier you can find this out the better so that you can familiarize yourself with their reputations and prior work.

  - In courts of last resort, generally all the judges or justices hear each case. Thus, it is easy to begin researching the panel and crafting your brief and argument to appeal to the individual members.

- Counsel's goals in oral argument include:

  - Helping the bench understand the case in a way that benefits their position;

  - Determining the bench's concerns and addressing them to their client's benefit; and

  - Making their client's case and positions tangible and concrete, and thus more compelling.

- The most important part of oral argument is preparation, which involves knowing the case, the applicable law, the operative facts, the context, what you are asking the court to do, what the possible ramifications of that relief might be, and how those ramifications can be limited or contained.

Checkpoints *continued*

- The essential technique for effective oral argument is the development of talking points, not a scripted argument that you would feel compelled to "get through" despite the panel's attempts to "throw you off course with their questions."

- Talking points are set out as bullet pointed statements supported by no more than four sub-bullet points that include record citations for any facts that are critical to the talking point.

- Talking points should be prepared for threshold issues (like standing and jurisdiction), the main arguments in your favor — arranged in order of strength, any areas of possible concern, which include the main arguments of opposing counsel.

- The introduction to your argument or presentation should be short and to the point. It should comply with any of the court's particular rules, such as those that require or prohibit particular formats or contents. It should not include a grandiose statement of the theory of your case.

- The conclusion should be short, basically a tag line. It should include a request for the specific relief you are seeking, e.g., "therefore, we ask the court to reverse the judgment below."

- There are many ways to prepare your material for the courtroom. In general, the fewer materials you have with you at the podium, the better. This chapter described the three panel manila file folder approach to organizing talking points, facts, and record citations.

- There is no substitute for practice when preparing for oral argument. Both informal and formal presentations and discussions of your case, using your talking points, help to build familiarity and flexibility in your delivery, which will allow you to adapt your argument to best suit the needs of the bench at the hearing.

- You should make sure that you know the technical rules, procedures, and format for oral argument. This includes things like knowing about the seating arrangements, how time is allotted, how rebuttal time is reserved, what the signal is to begin or end your argument, whether computers and other electronic devices are allowed in the courtroom, and the like.

- When the time for oral argument comes, remain flexible and remember your primary goals:

  - Helping the bench understand the case in a way that benefits your position;

  - Determining the bench's concerns and addressing them to your client's benefit; and

  - Making your client's case and positions tangible and concrete, and thus more compelling.

Checkpoints *continued*

- Your oral argument consists of the opening or introduction, which can be memorized but should be delivered in a genuine, non-mechanical fashion, the main argument, consisting of your talking points, and your conclusion, which can be very brief.

- Rebuttal is not the time to reargue your whole case. Rather, it should be used to make one or two incisive points that identify any weaknesses in the other side's positions. In addition, it is an opportunity to address any questions the court may still have regarding your position.

- Counsel should welcome questions from the bench and answer them immediately and directly. When presenting, counsel should watch and be alert to signs from the bench that a question may be coming. If one is detected, counsel should stop and take the question, looking directly at the questioning judge or justice, while listening carefully to the exact question being asked. Then, think, and answer, framing the answer as much as possible in the terms of one or more of your talking points.

- There are specific techniques for handling simple questions, hostile questions, questions that ask for a concession, hypothetical questions, questions that require a correction, questions you think are irrelevant, questions that you do not know the answer to, multi-part questions, and questions posed simultaneously by multiple judges or justices.

- When presenting, it is critical to create a good impression, which includes paying attention to your dress and physical appearance, your manner of delivery, including non-verbal communication, and volume, tone, and pace of your speech.

- Being a good speaker and presenting a good oral argument involve being an observant listener who remembers that the goals of oral argument all point to being helpful to the panel in a manner that will benefit your position and your client.

Chapter 13

Moot Court

Roadmap

- Moot court competitions are stylized simulated appellate proceedings designed to allow law students to gain in-depth knowledge and experience in legal research, analysis, brief writing, oral advocacy and substantive law.

- The audience in moot court competitions is wider and more varied that in a real-world appeal, and will likely include other students, professors, practitioners, and judges. This broader audience makes it even more important that a moot court brief be all things to all people, be clear, convincing, and easy to follow, and be absolutely free from technical errors.

- There are a wide variety of moot court competitions, each with its own set of rules and timelines. It is very important to note the nuances of each competition's rules and procedures and follow them to the iota; they will most likely be strictly enforced.

- The three main problems that appear in low scoring moot court briefs are: (1) briefs that are cursory or incomplete, (2) briefs that are hard to follow or understand, and (3) briefs that contain technical errors and that appear sloppy.

- Oral argument in moot court is your opportunity to score points in terms of demonstrating thorough knowledge of the issues and the law, and mastery of public speaking and oral advocacy. Convincing the panel to rule in your favor on the merits is of secondary importance.

- Preparation for oral argument is the most important ingredient for success. Organizing one's presentation using a short scripted introduction and a set of fluid talking points is the best method to employ.

- Questions from the bench are not interruptions of your presentation but an opportunity for you to score points and demonstrate your knowledge, public speaking, and advocacy skills. They should be welcomed.

I. Purpose, Audience, and Goals of Moot Court Competitions

a. Purpose

Moot court competitions are interscholastic appellate advocacy competitions between law schools. A wide variety of moot court competitions involving various issues and fields of law are held each year. They are based on a problem designed by the sponsor (often a law school, professional association or both) that simulates a case on appeal—with one or two lower court opinions and usually a short record on appeal. The main purpose of moot court competitions is to enable law students to gain in-depth knowledge and experience in legal research, analysis, brief writing, oral advocacy, and substantive law. Moot court competitions also provide positive publicity and promotion for their sponsors, either schools or professional groups seeking to promote their specialties and expertise.

b. Audience

The audience in moot court competitions is usually wider than that the audience for real-world appeals. First, your brief will likely be read and scored by a wide variety of people rather than the judges on the appellate panel and their clerks and court attorneys. Often, for consistency, moot court briefs are read and scored separately prior to oral argument by a panel of people. They may be scored again by the people who judge you in the oral argument rounds. Or they may be scored only in connection with oral argument. The people scoring them could be lawyers, judges, faculty, or students from the law school hosting the competition, or a combination thereof. Some may be experts in the field of law at issue, while others may know only what your brief explains to them about the subject of the appeal. Therefore, you should expect that the readers and scorers of your brief will have a variety of perspectives, attitudes, and pet-peeves. Also know they will have a limited amount of time to read your brief and all the others in the competition.

Your audience for oral argument is also likely to be wide and varied, especially if and as you advance from the opening toward the final rounds of the competition. In the opening rounds, the judges will often be lawyers—practitioners in the field at issue who have solid knowledge of the law and issues, but often strong ideas of what the "right answer is" or what the result should be. As the competition advances it is more likely that the competition will involve real-world judges in oral argument as the involvement of judges is perceived as raising the stature and importance of the competition. Since, unlike in their day jobs, these judges do not have to actually decide the case, they often enjoy hearing and exploring different views and arguments, even views and arguments that they would never seriously entertain in their real-world tribunals.

Also, although many moot court competitions severely restrict the competitors from receiving any outside assistance or review of the brief, many allow teams to hold practice oral arguments rounds before professors, outside attorneys, and others. These practice rounds will help both in your presentation and your substantive knowledge and understanding or the issues and arguments. They will also provide you with insight on the likely judicial response to your arguments and what kinds of questions you might receive.

An important, but often overlooked, audience for moot court is you and your teammates. You will need to review and assess successive drafts of your brief objectively and incisively. You should assume that a good moot court brief is likely to require ten or more drafts and must be as technically accurate—blue book citations, grammar, spelling—as possible. Objective, technical errors are an easy way to mark down a brief with little thought or attention, and are thus things that busy scoring committees often fixate upon.

Also, you should video record practice rounds and watch, evaluate, and adjust your performance. As you prepare for oral arguments and in the competition itself, you will get a wide variety of comments, criticisms, and suggestions about your presentation, skills, knowledge, analysis, style, habits, etc. These comments may conflict with each other, and you will disagree with many of them. The important thing is learning to sift through and process the comments you receive.

c. Goals

Most students have two main goals in entering and competing in moot court competitions. First, they want to learn and gain practical experience in brief writing, legal research, and analysis, oral advocacy, and the substantive law involved. Second, they hope to do well—ideally, to win.

Accomplishing the first goal means committing yourself to the substantial time and hard work that competing in a moot court competition entails— from analyzing the problem, researching the law, drafting, revising, editing and proofing the brief, to hours and hours of practice rounds, and the oral argument competition itself. Truly, the more you put into it, the more you will get out of the competition, but that comes at a cost—primarily, free time. Many students that we have worked with have said that they learned more competing in moot court than in any other aspect of law school, but that they worked harder than any other time during law school, as well. You should expect to commit at least 10 to 15 hours or more each week to brief preparation and practice before proceeding to the competition itself.

As for the second goal, the harder and smarter that you work and the more committed you are, the more likely you are to do well. The previous chapters in this book, particularly those on legal analysis and drafting, appellate brief writing, and oral argument should also help you succeed in moot court competitions. But doing well or winning in moot court is different than winning in actual real-world appeal. Winning an actual appeal takes convincing the court to affirm or reverse, which means persuading the court that your positions are better than those of the other side. Winning a moot court competition, on the other hand, requires scoring the most points, which may well be different from convincing the court to grant the relief that your client seeks.

In an actual appeal, those deciding the case are most concerned with "the what"—because the facts and law will generally dictate the result. In moot court, those scoring the briefs are largely focused on the technical aspects of writing and how clearly the issues are presented and argued. Similarly, those scoring oral argument, usually those on the bench—first attorneys or professors, later judges—are most focused on "the how"—how well the issues are presented and argued. In oral argument, much rides on your demeanor and presentation. Both in the brief and at orals, arguments that are clear, thorough, and easy to follow are likely to do the best and score the most points.

II. Getting Started

a. Deciding Which Competition to Enter

Deciding which moot court competition to enter depends on many variables. First, your law school must be willing to field a team for the competition. Also, there should be a faculty member, attorney, or student with moot court experience, who is willing and able to coach. Since most competitions require that students compete in teams of a minimum or two to a maximum of three members, there will have to be at least one other student who wants to enter the competition with you. You will want to make sure that your teammates and coach are committed to the project and willing to devote sustained effort to write an excellent brief and develop a winning oral argument. In our view, too much of everyone's time is involved to jeopardize success with insufficient commitment by one member of the team to the team's effort.

Naturally, you should be interested in the area of law involved. In addition, it is optimal to have some knowledge of the subject matter—generally this will be the case if you have already taken the basic course(s) in law school, whether that be tax, constitutional law, bankruptcy, criminal procedure, admiralty, labor law, intellectual property law, etc. To do well and to get the most out of the competition, you will need to be well versed in the area of law involved. Quite simply, in moot court, the more you know and the more you show what you know, the better you will do.

Also familiarize yourself with the basic requirements of the competition and decide if you can commit the time necessary to do well. For example, will each team have to write just one brief, or two—one for each side? When are the briefs due? How much time is there between that date and the first round of oral argument? Is the competition organized by region—where teams will compete in preliminary rounds, with some advancing to a final round? When and where are the oral argument rounds held? Also review the rules regarding outside help. Many competitions greatly limit or forbid any outside assistance in writing the brief. Some prohibit outside assistance of any kind, e.g., oral argument practice rounds with professors or attorneys, until after the brief is filed. A few also prohibit outside assistance in preparing for oral argument at any time, which would eliminate practice rounds with professors and attorneys—often a valuable learning experience.

b. Understanding the Rules and Devising a Timeline

Once you have entered a competition and received the rules, underlying problem, and fact pattern, your first impulse will probably be to jump into the problem. Before you do so, however, carefully review the rules. These rules will dictate much of how you write the brief, when and how you file it, and how best to prepare for the oral arguments rounds.

First read and confirm your understanding of the rules regarding the type of outside assistance the teams may receive. Then note any requirements regarding word or page limits, font size, style, citation (many competitions require cite form to follow the most recent edition of *The Bluebook*), the caption, and what components the brief must contain. Sometimes the competition rules will set out these rules specifically, other times, the competition rules will refer to a particular set of rules of court and direct competitors to follow them, e.g. the Rules of the Supreme Court of the United States.

Also look for information regarding how the briefs and oral argument are scored. For example, each brief may receive a total score of 100 points, with points distributed among categories, e.g. substance, organization, persuasiveness, and writing style, with points subtracted for technical errors. Oral argument scores might be based on a combination of organization, courtroom presence, strength of arguments, answering questions, legal support, etc. The brief and oral arguments scores will likely be weighted, the relative weights changing as oral argument rounds progress. For example, the brief and oral arguments scores may each be weighted 50% in the early rounds, with the brief being worth less and less in the final rounds. Ideally, you will have access to or be able to locate scoring sheets for the competition so that you can focus on performing well in each of the scoring categories.

The rules will also set out requirements for how and when to file and serve copies of the brief and other deadlines. Use these dates to create a timeline for researching, drafting, reviewing, revising, editing, and polishing the brief, as well as preparing for oral argument. Often these dates seem so far off that things are left to the last minute — which results in a moot court brief fire drill and which usually means filing a brief, with, at the very least, costly technical errors. Thus, working backwards from the filing or due date, and allowing at least a day for copying and binding, divide the brief writing process into steps and create early and definite deadlines to complete each step, building in some slack time to account for accidents and illnesses. Also, at the earliest opportunity, set up a schedule for oral arguments practice rounds and begin soliciting volunteers to fill the slots.

It is important that the team members (and not the coach or someone else) take responsibility for knowing and following the rules, creating and sticking to a timeline, and, as much as possible, setting up practice rounds. You will consult your coach if you have any questions about a rule or find a discrepancy that needs resolution. But primarily responsibility for the rules must be the team's, for it is you and your teammates, who are competing and who will be judged.

c. Reviewing and Understanding the Problem

Once you have familiarized yourself with the rules of the competition and created a time line for production of the brief and development of your oral argument, you are ready to delve into the problem. "The problem" will consist of a series of documents including a lower court opinion or two, and a factual record of some sort. Moot court problems are meant to simulate, as best as is reasonably practicable, a case that is on appeal or on review before a court of last resort. Often the case is set in the United States Supreme Court or a state supreme court. Sometimes the problem is patterned after an actual case in which certiorari or review has been granted, or the case is "completely made up" but addresses topical issues in the field. Since many problems are premised on review or certiorari having been granted, the parties are often referred to as the "petitioner" and the "respondent." Usually great efforts are made to design problems that, legally and factually, do not favor one side over the other, but this can be difficult.

Many competitions assign teams to brief either the side of the petitioner or respondent, while some allow the teams to chose. Teams are generally expected to argue each side of the case in the oral argument rounds. If you are assigned a side in the beginning, it is still important to review the problem objectively. Seeing and appreciating all sides of the issues will usually result in a more thorough and sophisticated brief, and will better prepare you to present both sides at oral argument. You should also keep an open mind if you are able to chose the side to brief—try not to quickly latch on to the side you think you agree with or the side you think is the least demanding. Chose the side you think will result in the brief that is the most thorough and yet easy to follow—your brief writing is about scoring the maximum number of points for delivery of the argument, not winning the case on the merits, which can be two different things.

Focus first on the issues raised by the problem. Most problems contain a statement of issues, a notice of appeal, or order granting review or certiorari that specifically states the issues that will be determined. If that is the case, make sure you understand those issues and their parameters before reviewing the rest of the materials that make up the problem. In some cases the issues must be determined by reading the opinions of the lower court.

Generally, two legal questions will be raised in a moot court problem. Often there will be an opinion on the trial court level and another on from an appellate court that affirms or, more likely, reverses the trial court. Read each opinion included in the problem, carefully noting the holdings and the facts and reasoning in support. It is often useful to create a chart. Begin with the opinion from the lowest court and set out its conclusion on each issue as a heading, with two columns underneath each heading. Then, in one column, set out the facts and reasons in support of the conclusion and, in the other column, set out the facts and reasons proffered by the losing side. Do a similar chart for the appellate opinion, if there is one. You may notice that the different courts focused on different facts or rationales, or interpreted the same set of facts differently, etc. Finally, note any authorities that are cited in the opinion(s)—these will become the starting point for your research.

After you have reviewed and analyzed the lower court opinions, turn to the factual record. In some competitions the record is very brief and is essentially a list of facts followed by record citations. In others, the record is a bound volume containing documents and transcripts of testimony—more resembling an appendix filed in a real-life appeal. Whatever type of record you have, go through it in order to get a sense of the factual context of the problem. Then go back through the opinion(s) and find the location in the record for each fact referred to. Also, if the court(s) appeared to have inferred the existence of any facts in reaching a decision, look to see if those facts are in the record. You may find that the problem is missing support for fact(s) relied on by the lower court(s), in which case, the competition administrators will need to be informed as soon as possible. Teams, however, can expect to have to fill in missing contextual or minor facts themselves or work with a gap in the record. In any event, it is important to familiarize yourself and become conversant with the facts and the record early on in the competition. This will make writing the brief easier, and will help you to excel at oral argument.

d. Learning and Understanding the Context

Before or at the same time the team starts to research the specific issues raised in the problem, they need to make sure they are readily familiar with the broader legal subject matter encompassing those issues, e.g., tax, products liability, constitutional law, criminal procedure, admiralty, etc. Ideally all members of the team will have taken the basic course(s) relating to the subject in law school. Even if that is the case, you and your team must ensure that you have sufficient, practical knowledge of the subject matter to be able to write and speak concretely on its issues, and to field a variety or questions on the subject from practicing attorneys—which you are likely to get at oral argument. Thus locate and review secondary sources on the subject aimed both a law students and practicing attorneys. Indeed, a book on topic in Carolina Academic Press's Mastering Series (of which this book is a part) would be a good place to begin. Without sufficient knowledge in the overall subject matter and context you will not understand how the issues raised in the problem fit in the broader scheme of law. This will put you at a disadvantage in both in drafting the brief and at oral argument.

e. Research

The team members should discuss and devise a research plan as a first step. Often teams will divide the research according to the issues, with each team member researching their particular issue—the one they will write up in the brief. If there is a third member, that person might research both, or be on hand to handle specific tasks like finding support for a particular argument, investigating legislative history, etc. Ideally, though, even if the team has divided the issues for brief writing purposes, each member will, at least initially, research all the issues. Then a time can be scheduled to meet and discuss the results, and compare notes, perspectives, ideas, cases, etc. This approach is likely to produce a more thorough brief and prevent "tunnel vision." Whatever approach you and your team decides to take, have a plan and discuss responsibilities and deadlines at the outset.

Logical places to start in researching the issues are with authorities cited in the opinion(s) include with the problem. These would include any statute sections, cases, and secondary authorities. Review those authorities, and note cases or other authorities therein that were relied on, rejected, or distinguished by the court(s). When you have finished you will have a list of authorities, particularly cases, to Sheppardize®, Key Cite® or otherwise update. In the process of updating those cases, you will probably find new cases to review and update. At a certain point, you will keep seeing the same, familiar cases. At that time, it is a good idea to conduct independent searches based on phases and terms you have seen. Also as you update and research independently, note any law review articles that address or touch on the issues in the problem. Law review articles might provide you with additional authorities, or, just as important, discuss various policy reasons and rationale for a particular legal result.

Finally, as you conduct your research, be sure to note and keep track of *all* authorities, points, and arguments that address the issue—those that support the side you will brief, and those that support the other side. This will help you to better understand the strengths and potential weaknesses of your positions and give you more perspective as you draft the brief and prepare for the oral argument rounds.

III. Brief Writing

a. Goals

1. Generally

Your goals in drafting an appellate brief for a moot court competition are: (1) to produce a brief that scores the most possible points, and (2) to gain and master skills in legal analysis and writing—in particular, but not limited to, appellate brief writing. The previous chapters in this book, particularly Chapters 7 through 11 on Appellate Legal Analysis, Appellate Legal Drafting, Citation and Quotation on Appeal, Standards of Review and Harmless versus Reversible Error, and Drafting Appellate Briefs should help you to achieve these goals. In this section we discuss aspects of brief writing that are unique to or more emphasized in moot court competitions than in the real world.

2. Accomplishing Your Goals

A. Overall Focus of the Readers

Briefs in moot court competitions are often styled for the United States Supreme Court, but are read and scored initially by lawyers or law students. In these competitions it is essential that the briefs be easy to read and understand. Readers may have long, multiple-factor scoring sheets. Thus, if possible, your team should obtain a copy of the scoring sheet used in the competition to use as a check-list in drafting, revising, editing, and proofing the brief. Know, however, that although readers may use detailed scoring sheets, most will rank the briefs based on their overall impression, ease of reading experience, and presence of technical errors, and assign scores accordingly. As the rounds advance, it is more likely that actual judges will be involved in reviewing and scoring the briefs, and briefs with the more sophisticated and artful arguments should prevail. However, to make it to the advanced rounds your brief must be easy to read and free from objective errors in grammar, spelling, citation, and compliance with the competition's rules of procedure and format.

B. Addressing the Three Main Problems of Lower Scoring Briefs

There are generally three main problems with appellate briefs that do not score well in moot court competitions: (1) the substance and analysis are cursory or incomplete, (2) the brief is hard to follow or understand, and (3) the brief contains too many technical errors and appears sloppy.

Briefs that are cursory or incomplete: Avoiding the first problem, the cursory or incomplete brief, requires time, planning, dedication, and the use of a check-list. First, the entire team must commit and expend the time and effort it takes to produce a well-researched, thorough brief that addresses and analyses all the sub issues and their permutations. You and your teammates will need to discuss the issues and vet all the potential arguments, then develop the positions and points you will make in the brief. You will need to continue to discuss and evaluate your arguments as you go through several drafts of the brief. Cursory or incomplete briefs are often caused by poor planning, resulting in a rush-job. Thus, get your early drafts done as soon as possible, and critically assess which areas need to be more developed, or what arguments or analyses are missing.

Also, be sure that your brief contains all the components that are described in the rules and that each component is complete and through. Too often the parts of the brief that are not part of the main argument are left to the last minute. Thus, create a check-list of required components and what each entails and be sure to set deadlines for their completion, e.g. the statement of facts, statement of the case, summary of the argument, tables, etc. Finally, be sure to include a statement for the standard of review applicable to each issue. Briefs that omit the standard of review give up needless points.

Briefs that are hard to follow or understand: The second problem, the hard-to-follow brief, can be avoided by (1) using the CRAC structure, (2) talking through the points and arguments, and (3) making time to review, revise and edit successive drafts for clarity and ease of comprehensive. In moot court competitions, CRAC (Conclusion, Rule, Application, Conclusion) should be used to analyze each and every issue and sub issue you have identified. The CRAC structure organizes and delivers a legal discussion in a way that is easiest to understand for the widest variety or readers. Also, it helps the drafters to keep on track and focus their ideas, explanations, and points so that they clearly support their conclusions.

Talking through the issues and arguments with your teammates and others (if allowed) will help you to better understand your points and positions and explain them in writing. In other words, do not write your arguments in quiet isolation and expect others to easily understand them. Finally, drafting a final brief that is easy to follow takes many drafts, critical review sessions, and much revising and editing by different sets of eyes. Use your team's members to leverage each other's efforts and produce better overall work product.

Practice oral argument rounds: Conducting practice oral argument rounds midway during the brief writing process can be very helpful in drafting a thorough and easy to follow brief—combating both the first and second problems. Delivering your arguments or potential arguments in a more formal setting in which you are challenged and questioned will test them and expose weaknesses or areas that need to be more developed or supported. This process will also help you to articulate your position so that they can be most easily understood. If allowed, hold some of these practices with your coach or other knowledgeable volunteers. If the competition rules forbid outside assistance before turning in the brief, formal oral argument practice rounds should be conducted by the team.

Briefs with many technical errors: Avoiding the third problem of the sloppy brief with too many technical error requires (1) being readily familiar with the competition's technical rules, as well as any other applicable rules regarding citation, quotation, style, punctuations etc., and (2) strictly following these rules in the drafting process, and (3) building in enough time to thoroughly proof and polish the brief before turning it in.

From the very beginning, draft with the technical rules in mind and follow them. Do not leave these matters for clean-up at the very end. Thus, for example, put your cites in Bluebook form at the outset and use the full citation up until your are close to taking the brief final. Building in enough time means, for example, having a complete quality draft and creating the table of contents and table of authorities many days before the brief is due. Set the brief aside for a day, and then you and your teammates should review the rules, then comb through the draft looking for and fixing technical errors. Proofreading techniques to use are reading the brief aloud, reading it line-by-line using a straight edge, and reading the brief backwards. When proofing, go through the brief looking for one type of error at a time, then do so again for another type. For example, one pass might be to check all grammar, another for cite form, another for heading uniformity, etc.

b. Working Collaboratively

Another challenge facing teams in moot court competitions is that they must work together collaboratively and effectively. This means recognizing and leveraging different styles, skills, strengths, and work habits.

The first step in working collaboratively is for the team to get together as soon as they receive the problem and create a timeline for accomplishing all the tasks that must be completed in order to produce a quality brief and prepare for oral argument. (Creating a timeline is discussed further in subsection II(b), above). It is not enough to just devise a timeline, however. Every effort must be made by each team member to complete the tasks he or she is responsible for, and to valuably contribute to meetings, discussion, review sessions, etc. If a team member is having problems completing a task or will be unable to make a meeting, he or she must let the others know as soon as possible. Constant communication promoting awareness is the hallmark of successful team work. It allows each member to plan on and deliver their contributions to the project in a timely manner and not be either unprepared when the draft is dropped into their in box or sitting around twiddling their thumbs while waiting for a late handoff of the brief.

Responsibility for drafting various portions of the brief should also be addressed at the outset and divided in a way that leverages interests and talents of the individuals, yet is also considered fair by all the teammates. Many competitions require that all teammates contribute to the brief, while others do not. Regardless, we recommend that all team members participate in drafting the brief, and that each be responsible for drafting a segment or segments. Going through the drafting process is a valuable learning experience and better prepares you for oral argument. All too often, one teammate will not be pulling his weight. The tendency among the other teammates is often to try to take up the slack and ignore the problem rather than confronting it early. This is a mistake. It creates resentment towards the slacking teammate, which grows in intensity while it is unexpressed. The way to handle this situation is to broach the subject as soon as the behavior presents itself, involving the team's coach if necessary, and having a detailed discussion of the rights and responsibilities of each team member—essentially renewing the contract between them and insisting on performance according to its terms.

Team members will also need to review, assist in editing, and comment on each other's work product in a way that is helpful and produces a better brief. This is no time for marginal annotations like "good," "I like this," "awkward" or "this needs work." Rather, comments should be specific line edits as much as possible, supported by comments that explain the thought process behind the changes as needed. The "track changes" and "comments" features of Word™ or similar features of other word processors are helpful in this regard.

It is important that a team's final brief read as a quality, cohesive whole and not like two or more different briefs that have been slapped together. Accomplishing this takes planning, time, and effort, and means that each team member have edited the entire brief repeatedly, so that the resulting brief is the team's collective work product, not the combination of work product produced separately by individuals.

It is important to have early due dates for initial drafts, and for the team to start review and commenting on them in the early stages. In the beginning, the focus will be on the strength and thoroughness of the substantive positions and arguments, then the focus may shift to organization, clarity and ease of comprehension, then to smoothing out style differences.

Chapter 11, Drafting Appellate Briefs, contains drafting and reviewing guidelines for the discussion/argument sections, as well as the statement of facts and the statement of the case. We recommend turning these guidelines into a checklist and then using them to review and comment on drafts of the brief. Using these guidelines should help each team member be more uniform, thorough, and objective in their review and comments their own drafts as well as drafts of their teammates. The team should also take the time to review and discuss each other's comments.

Despite best efforts or good intentions team members may clash during the process, particularly as the due date approaches. If this happens, it is important to step back, cool down, and focus on getting out a quality work product. The focus is on the work product and making it better. In other words, do all that you can to put conflicts or dramas a box and move on in the drafting process. If necessary, involve your coach as a sounding board or counselor to resolve or help you resolve dysfunctional group dynamics.

IV. Oral Argument

a. Goals

Your goals in the oral argument rounds are (1) to score as many points as possible in each round and advance to the next, and (2) to gain and master skills in public speaking and oral appellate advocacy.

As with oral argument in real life, preparation is the most important factor in doing well in the oral argument rounds of a moot court competition. The more you know about the case — its issues, facts, law, and policies in favor and against each side, the better you will do. Unlike real life oral argument, succeeding in moot court is a matter of showing all that you know and sounding persuasive, rather than actually convincing the panel to rule in your favor.

Moot court oral argument involves more "showing off" than does real-world appellate argument. Showing off means much more citation and description of authorities, particularly cases and legislative history, as well as providing record citation for many or most of the facts you bring up. It also involves appearing calm and smooth under pressure, e.g. while facing a barrage of hostile questions from the bench. Of course, you should not look like you are showing off. So, no smiling triumphantly after handing a particularly a difficult question or explaining a series of complicated cases. You should behave as if it all is natural to you.

Most oral argument scoring sheets are designed to assess your argument and performance in a variety of categories, e.g., strength and substance of your arguments; persuasiveness, organization; court room presence and presentation; handing of questions, use of authorities, and a favorite, "ability to transition back to the main argument" or similar description. You should obtain the scoring sheet used by the competition if one is available and use it as a checklist in preparing for the oral argument rounds. However, similar to scoring the brief, oral argument judges will usually rank the competitors in each round based on their overall impression of style and substance and assign scores accordingly.

b. Preparation

Your preparation for the oral arguments rounds starts with a thorough and objective review of the problem and continues during the research phase when you research and examine *all* relevant arguments, positions and supporting authorities—not just those that favor the side you are going to argue in the brief. Each team will be expected to argue both sides in the oral argument rounds, thus, for each issue, the team should build a folder or binder of "off brief" arguments, points, and supporting authorities.

If copies of all the briefs filed in the competition are served on all the other teams, team members should go through them and note the various arguments and support for both sides of each issue. You may find arguments that you did not think of, support you did not have, or novel and persuasive ways of stating a familiar argument, etc. Any new arguments, points, authorities that you think you might use or adapt for oral argument should be verified and further researched. Not only must they be accurate, but you need to become as well versed and familiar with them as you would be if you had used them in your brief.

By the time the briefs have been filed, the oral argument assignments may have been set. For example, on a two person team, each member might argue both sides of the issue he or she briefed. The division is more complicated one a three person team, where for one issue, one team member will argue on brief, and another will argue off-brief, and for the other issue, the third member will argue both sides. The "swing" person is usually the strongest member of the team. However, who is strongest may not emerge until several or more practice rounds. Thus it is a good idea not to pick the swing person too early in the process.

Regardless of the individual assignments, it is best if the entire team participates in developing talking points for each side of each issue to ensure a thorough and well vetted presentation. As with real life oral arguments, you should have sets of favorable talking points as well as sets of talking points that address areas of concern. You should expect to be questioned about how their ruling might affect future cases and have a set of talking points addressing that issue. Also, for each issue and sub issue, know the applicable standard of review and be able to quickly explain how it operates if asked. Questions regarding the standard of review are almost always asked at least once in moot court competitions. For more discussion on developing talking points see Chapter 12, Section II(c).

We recommend that you prepare your materials for the court room by using separate three panel manila file folders for each side. Each file folder should contain sets of favorable talking points and those for areas of concern, as well as a list of relevant facts and their appendix or record citations. To accompany each folder, teams should also prepare a list of holdings, descriptions, and pin cites of the relevant authorities. Remember that moot court oral arguments often involve more discussion of authorities, particularly cases, than oral arguments in the real world. Be prepared to show off your knowledge of how precedents fit together in a synthesized fashion to support your client's side of an issue. For more discussion on developing preparing materials for the courtroom, see Chapter 12, Section II(e).

Finally, the introduction in a moot court oral argument is usually a bit more involved than real life oral argument because the first person to speak needs to introduce their other team members and describe how oral argument is being divided. An example of a moot court oral argument introduction:

"May it please the court"

The team member arguing the first issue introduces himself or herself:

"My name is June Smith."

Then introduces the co-counsel, explains the client's status, and the context — including the ruling(s) below:

"I, along with co-counsel, Mark Brown, represent Funsphere, a family theme park operator, the defendant at trial and the appellant on appeal.

"In this personal injury action, the trial court entered judgment against Funsphere concluding it was negligent per se because it did not comply with State Regulation 1235 by filing yearly tax returns with the secretary of state."

Then provides a brief roadmap by asking for particular relief and stating why the court should grant it, and who will handle each argument:

"We request that this court hold reverse the judgment because, (1) Regulation 1235 is inapplicable to licensed theme park operations, which I will be addressing and (2) even 1235 did apply, failing to file tax returns could not have contributed to the accident, which Mr. Jones will be addressing."

c. Practice Rounds

Practice rounds with other professors, attorneys, and students are a critical component in preparing for moot court oral arguments rounds. First, they will help you become comfortable standing at a podium and discussing your positions in more formal, structured setting. Second, practice rounds will expose you to a wide variety of questions on the issues and allow you to formulate and try out responses. As you progress through practice rounds you will improve on moving back and forth among talking points—those favorable to your position and those that address areas of concern. Moreover, your courtroom presence and speaking style will improve simply with the experience practice rounds will provide.

It is also a good idea to hold some less formal practice rounds—in which time-outs can be taken and potential responses to a question explored, in addition to formal, timed, practice rounds in which comments are given at the end. Indeed, as you prepare for oral argument, you will get a wide variety of comments, criticisms, and suggestions about you presentation, skills, knowledge, analysis, style, habits, etc. These comments may conflict with each other, and you will disagree with many of them. The important things is learning to sift through and process the comments you receive—patterns will likely emerge, and comments that were inartly delivered or that you initially resisted may have merit when discussed or fleshed out with your coach or team mates. You are ultimately responsible for how you present your arguments and which arguments you will highlight. But this should be an informed decision made after considering comments from a wide variety of sources, not a defensive, egotistical, I-did-it-my-way approach.

Also, you should video record practice rounds and watch, evaluate and adjust your performance. A good technique for detecting distracting gestures is to watch the video in fast-motion.

d. Handling Questions

1. Hostile Questioning

You will receive a fair share of aggressive questions at moot court competitions, especially in the early rounds. As in real life oral argument, you should welcome questions from the bench in moot court, because that is how you will show much of what you know and score points. Also, by using the more flexible talking point format of discussion, rather than a scripted argument, you should be able to move back and forth between favorable talking points and to those that address areas of concern, which will score you points in the "transition back to the main argument" category.

Distinguished from aggressive questioning is hostile questioning, which in the moot court context as opposed to the real world means questioning that is overly antagonistic, caustic, bombastic, or abusive. This sort of questioning often comes from practitioners or professors who feel that their role is to "put you through your paces" and really "make you work." Real world judges, in our experience, rarely display this sort of behavior in moot court competitions or practices, or in the real world. This sort of hostile questioning can make you lose your focus, your composure, or your temper. If it happens to you, pause, take a deep breath, and clear your head as best as you can. Know that this hostile questioner is likely making the other members of the bench uncomfortable, and that they are probably rooting for you. If you have attempted to answer their line of questioning to no avail, it is best to disengage rather than let them eat up the rest of your time. Be polite, but confident, and say something like "Judge Small, I see I am not going to persuade you on this point, I will move on to ..." Then, tell the bench what new point you are making. We generally do not recommend narrating oral argument in a manner like this, but to effectively disengage from truly hostile questioning, it is best to tell the bench you are doing so and exactly where you are going. You may not earn points with the aggressive questioner by disengaging, but you may with the other members of the bench.

2. Friendly Questions

On the opposite end of the spectrum from the moot court hostile questioner, is the person who asks friendly questions that will help you develop your positions and gain points. This person may be particularly kind, have a good impression of you, or be testing you to see if you recognize a helpful question. Either way, moot court participants should expect, recognize and be prepared for friendly questions.

3. The Dead Bench

The dead bench, in which the judges ask you few or no questions, is a daunting prospect in moot court. You want the people judging you to be engaged in your presentation, and questions help you to show all that you know. Plus, some competitions require each person to speak for a certain amount of minutes. If you are faced with a dead bench you will need do more all by yourself to show off, while appearing as natural as possible. Thus, as you address your talking points, be more in depth in discussing supporting authorities, pin-cite and describe the facts, rulings, and rationale of cases, be detailed about your supporting facts and provide appendix or record cites for them. Also, as you finish a particular talking point, pause as if expecting or welcoming a question. One of the judges may feel your pain and ask a question; then the others may follow.

Also, if you have completed your favorable talking points, transition into your talking points that cover areas of concern and have an answer for each of them. In effect, you are asking yourself questions and then responding to them. Addressing areas of concern unprompted is very dangerous in real life oral argument, but in moot court it is a way for you to score points.

Finally, unless there is a time minimum you have not yet reached, if you have shown all that you know and addressed all your talking points by the five minute warning that is typical in moot court competitions, you should then move to your conclusion.

e. Courtroom and Competition Demeanor

The conventions and recommendations regarding courtroom presentation and demeanor discussed in Chapter 12, Section III(d) apply in full force in moot court oral argument rounds. In fact, more formalities are usually observed in moot court competitions that in real life oral argument. For example, if you are asked a question as time expires in moot court, it is generally expected that you will state that your time has expired and ask for permission to answer the question, where in real life oral argument, most attorneys would simply answer the question.

Students should keep this formality in mind in how they dress and what they bring to oral argument rounds. Not only should team members wear conservative business suits, but they should consider bringing an inexpensive brief case, versus a backpack, in the courtroom, and remove any stickers or decorations from their books, laptops, etc. Team members also should stay in their business clothes in-between rounds and during other down time. In other words, you may take off your jacket, but do not change into flip-flops. You want to appear as a well prepared, confident professional, both before the bench and your competition.

You should be friendly and polite, but not overly familiar with members of other teams. Quite simply, the tension among competitors during the oral arguments rounds is often palpable, and you do not want to be drawn into it. On the other hand, it is customary to wish the opposing side good luck before the round, and to tell them "well done" or the equivalent afterwards.

Finally, you should remain polite as members of the moot court bench give comments after an oral argument round. Some comments might be useful, either for the competition or later. Some may not be. And if you are lucky, someone might give you substantive tips on answering a tough question. Either way, listen politely or appear to listen politely.

Checkpoints

- Moot court competitions are stylized simulated appellate proceedings designed to allow law students to gain in-depth knowledge and experience in legal research, analysis, brief writing, oral advocacy, and substantive law.

- The audience in moot court competitions is wider and more varied than in a real-world appeal, and will likely include other students, professors, practitioners, and judges, as well as your team members themselves.

- There are a wide variety of moot court competitions, each with its own set of rules and timelines. It is very important to note the nuances of each competition's rules and procedures and follow them to the iota; they will most likely be strictly enforced based upon a perception on the part of the sponsoring organization that it be scrupulously fair and uniform in its dealings with all teams.

- The three main problems that appear in low scoring moot court briefs are: (1) briefs that are cursory or incomplete, (2) briefs that are hard to follow or understand, and (3) briefs that contain technical errors and appear sloppy. The broader audience of moot court makes it even more important that a moot court brief be all things to all people, be complete, clear, and convincing, and be absolutely free from technical errors.

- Before beginning to write the brief, take the time to review and understand the problem thoroughly. Most will have two main issues — make sure that you understand them and their parameters before reviewing the rest of the materials. They should serve to focus and anchor your research, writing, brief, and oral argument.

- After you review the problem and its materials, pull and read every authority cited in the materials. Critically analyze these authorities to see to what extent they actually support the statements for which they are cited. Organize them, issue by issue, into "pro" and "con" categories for both sides. Then do your own supplemental research on the issues, adding them to the accumulating stack of materials. Even before writing the brief and practicing for oral argument, you should become conversant with the facts and holdings of the critical cases involved.

- The skills and techniques described in Chapters 7 to 11 of this book are applicable and important to producing a quality, high-scoring brief.

- Oral argument in moot court is your opportunity to score points in terms of demonstrating your mastery of public speaking and oral advocacy. Convincing the panel to rule in your favor on the merits is of secondary importance.

- Preparation for oral argument is the most important ingredient for success. Organizing one's presentation using a scripted introduction and a set of fluid talking points is the best method to employ.

Checkpoints *continued*

- Holding full practice rounds, both formal and informal, with different people serving as judges is important. You will benefit from being exposed to different personality types, comprehension levels, and conversational patterns. You will also note problems with and questions about your presentation that reappear across many different panels — noting these will provide you with a list of areas for further work and refinement.

- Questions from the bench are not interruptions of your presentation but an opportunity for you to score points and demonstrate your speaking and advocacy skills. They should be welcomed.

- Teams should practice scrupulous professional appearance, behavior, and demeanor in all formal moot court proceedings, including during the waiting time between rounds. "Friendly but not friends" is the professional standard of behavior toward your fellow moot court participants and adversaries.

Mastering Appellate Advocacy and Process Checklist

❏ The federal appellate system consists of intermediate appellate courts called circuit courts, and the nation's court of last resort, the United States Supreme Court.

❏ There are 13 federal intermediate appellate courts. The United States Courts of Appeal for the First through Eleventh, and D.C., Circuits handle appeals from district courts located in their respective geographic regions, as well as the majority of appeals from federal government agencies. The United States Court of Appeals for the Federal Circuit handles appeals from all district courts in patent cases.

❏ The total number of judges appointed to each of the federal circuit courts varies, but in all the circuits, appeals are initially heard and decided by a panel of three judges.

❏ Where an order is final and jurisdiction is proper, appeal to the circuit courts is by right—prior permission is not needed.

❏ The majority of orders and judgment appeals to circuit courts are affirmed.

❏ Procedure in the circuit courts is governed by the Federal Rules of Appellate Procedure and by circuit court local rules.

❏ The United State Supreme Court is the nation's court of last resort. Its review of cases is, with few exceptions, discretionary—granted by writ of certiorari to decisions involving important questions of federal law that are issued by federal circuit courts or by state courts of last resort. U.S. Const. Art. III, § 2; Sup. Ct. R. 10. Nine justices sit on the Court.

❏ In comparison to federal circuit courts, the affirmance rate of the United States Supreme court is relatively low—often less that 50%.

❏ Procedure in the United States Supreme Court is governed by the Rules of the Supreme Court of the United States (http://www.supremecourtus. gov/ctrules/ctrules.html).

❏ 40 of the 50 States have intermediate appellate courts.

❏ The total number of judges sitting on state intermediate courts of appeal varies from state to state, although, as with federal circuit courts, most cases are heard by a panel of three judges.

❏ The focus of state intermediate appellate courts is primarily error correction, *i.e.*, whether the correct law or standard was applied correctly. In contrast, the primary role of state courts of last resort in states with intermediate appellate courts is interpreting or making law, *i.e.*, pronouncing what the law is.

❏ All states have a court of last resort, often called the "Supreme Court." State courts of last resort consist of either 5, 7, or 9 justices.

❏ In states with intermediate appellate courts, review by state courts of last resort is discretionary for many cases, but is by right for certain types of cases. Appeal by right varies from state to state.

❏ State courts of last resort may also decide certified questions from federal courts.

❏ Generally, in order to be addressed on appeal, an error in the trial court must be preserved on appeal. It is up to trial counsel to make sure that both the error and the objection to the error are part of the record.

❏ For evidentiary errors, complaints about the misconduct of opposing counsel, or jury instructions error, counsel should (1) make a timely objection or motion to strike the evidence and (2) state the grounds upon which the objection is made.

❏ Defenses to causes of action must also be preserved. Some must be raised at every juncture in order to be preserved. Others, like subject matter jurisdiction, are automatically preserved and may be raised at any juncture in the proceedings.

❏ Post-trial motions can be critical in preserving issues for appeal.

❏ To preserve the error during the appeal itself, it is necessary to include all supporting material relevant to the error in the record or appendix on appeal and to raise and discuss the error in the appellant's opening brief.

❏ Generally, if an alleged error is supported by the record on appeal and addressed in the appellant's opening brief, it will not be deemed waived if not addressed in oral argument. However, counsel may forfeit issues by conceding them at oral argument.

❏ There are a few exceptions to the general rule that it is counsel's responsibility to preserve error for appeal. These include the "plain" or "fundamental" error rule, lack of subject matter jurisdiction, and lack of standing.

❏ Even if an error is preserved at trial, that error will not be reviewed if the case becomes moot. See Chapter 5, § II(b).

❏ Under the "final judgment rule" an appeal may be taken only from a "final judgment" or "final decision." 28 U.S.C. § 1291.

❏ The final judgment rule requires that all issues in a case be decided by the trial court before any issue may be reviewed by the court of appeals. The rule avoids piecemeal appeals — separate appeals of separate rulings throughout the course of the litigation.

❏ Orders that are not final judgments are generally referred to as "interlocutory orders" and appeals from them, when permitted, are often called "interlocutory appeals."

❏ There are exceptions to the final judgment rule, including:

    ❏ The collateral order doctrine, which allows an appeal from a decision that does not terminate the litigation, but presents an issue completely separate from the merits of the underlying action that cannot be effectively reviewed in an appeal from the final judgment.

    ❏ Where there are multiple claims or parties, partial final judgment as to one or more but fewer that all the claims or parties may be entered under Federal Rule of Civil Procedure 54(b).

    ❏ Appeals of interlocutory orders regarding injunctions, 28 U.S.C. § 1292(a)(1), and appointing a receiver, 28 U.S.C. § 1292(a)(2).

    ❏ Appeals of interlocutory orders involving controlling questions of law under 28 U.S.C. § 1292(b).

    ❏ Interlocutory appeals of class certification decisions under Federal Rule of Civil Procedure 23(f).

    ❏ Review by extraordinary writ under 28 U.S.C. § 1651(a).

    ❏ Pendent Appellate Jurisdiction.

❏ States have their own versions of the final judgment rule, along with exceptions, as well as processes for review by permission or extraordinary writ. Research on this point in the applicable jurisdiction is essential.

❏ The first step in taking an appeal is preparing the notice of appeal. The contents of the notice of appeal are usually simple. *See* Fed. R. App. P. 3. The notice should:

   ❏ Contain the trial court caption and docket number;

   ❏ Specify the party or parties that are appealing;

   ❏ Designate the judgment or order that is being appealed;

   ❏ Name the court to which the appeal is taken; and

   ❏ Be signed by the attorney or the party appealing if pro se.

❏ Many state court notices of appeal involve similar basic information, although some states have additional requirements.

❏ An appeal is initiated by filing a notice of appeal—usually in the trial court or court of original jurisdiction. Although in some states the notice is filed in the appellate court.

❏ Time limits for filing the notice of appeal are usually strictly enforced.

❏ The time within which a notice of appeal must be filed varies not only by jurisdiction, but by type of case, identity of the parties, and the process used in entering the order or judgment and notifying the parties.

❏ Some, but not all, jurisdictions provide that premature notices of appeal shall be deemed timely filed.

❏ In some jurisdictions, including the federal system, relief may be granted for failing to timely file a notice of appeal– but only in limited circumstances.

❏ Filing a notice of appeal generally will not stay execution of the judgment.

❏ Although in some jurisdictions, including the federal system, there is a short automatic stay of certain judgments.

❏ Execution of a money judgment can be stayed by posting a supersedeas bond in an amount to secure the amount of the judgment plus anticipated post-judgment interest. Fed. R. App. P. 62(d).

❏ Appellants who cannot afford to post a bond may apply to the trial court for a stay without bond or with a reduced bond. If granted, the trial court will usually impose conditions to attempt to assure the judgment-creditor will be paid if the judgment is affirmed on appeal.

❏ Non-monetary judgments, e.g., injunctions, generally are not automatically stayed by the posting of a supersedeas bond.

❏ Appellants may apply to the trial court for a stay of an injunction pending appeal, however, as a condition of granting a stay the court may require a bond. Fed. R. App. P. 62(c).

❏ Filing a notice of appeal in many circumstances will divest the trial court of jurisdiction and vest jurisdiction with the appellate court. However, the trial court usually retains jurisdiction to:

   ❏ Rule on motions for attorneys fees and sanctions;

   ❏ Supervise or ensure compliance with injunctions it entered; and

   ❏ Correct clerical errors; see Fed. R. App. P. 60

❏ Generally, only parties to an action that qualify as "persons aggrieved," either original parties, substituted parties, or intervenors, have standing to appeal a decision.

❏ To have standing to appeal, one must have had standing to sue. Standing is part of "case or controversy" requirement in Article III, Section 2, clause 1 of the Constitution.

❏ Constitutional standing requires that the plaintiff's "claimed injury [be] personal, particularized, concrete, and otherwise judicially cognizable." *Raines v. Byrd*, 521 U.S. 811, 817 (1997).

❏ If a case becomes moot while on appeal, generally it will be dismissed. A case becomes moot when the issues are not "live" because an appellate ruling can have no practical effect or the parties no longer have a stake in the outcome. Perhaps the most common cause of mootness is settlement of the case by the parties, in which case the judgment below and any adverse opinions may, but not always, be vacated.

❏ There are three exceptions to the mootness doctrine: (1) cases involving conduct or issues that are capable of repetition yet evade review, (2) when a defendant voluntarily ceases the conduct at issue but may reasonably be expected to engage in that conduct in the future, and (3) when a class action plaintiff/appellant ceases to have a stake and be a member of the class— substitution of another class member cures the mootness problem.

❏ Interested third parties that are not parties to an action may participate in an appeal as amicus curiae (friend of the court) if permitted to do so by the appellate court.

❏ The record on appeal usually consists of the documents filed in the trial court and a record of oral proceedings.

❏ The record on appeal provides the background and foundation for the appellate court's decision.

❏ Any asserted error must appear, and be preserved, in the record.

❏ Generally, in deciding the appeal, the appellate court may consider only what was in the trial court record.

❏ Appellate courts may take judicial notice of facts outside the record that are not subject to reasonable dispute.

❏ A fact may be indisputable because it is "either (1) generally known within the territorial jurisdiction of the trial court or (2) capable of accurate and ready determination by resort to sources whose accuracy cannot reasonably be questioned." Fed. R. Evid. 201(b).

❏ Appellate courts generally have inherent power to supplement the record with information not reviewed by the trial court and not subject to judicial notice, but this power is very rarely used.

❏ The appendix, an abbreviated form of the record, is used in many jurisdictions for the convenience of the court.

❏ A well chosen, well prepared appendix focuses judges, court attorneys, and law clerks on documents pertinent to the appeal and makes those documents easily accessible.

❏ The appendix is usually filed with, or shortly after, the appellate briefs.

❏ It is important for an appellate attorney to analyze the legal and factual issues surrounding the appeal with fresh eyes.

❏ A fresh look for appellate counsel often means revisiting basics techniques and building blocks of legal analysis.

❏ Tools for analyzing and interpreting statutes include:

    ❏ Using tabulation to explode a statute into its constituent parts so that you can identify each element and factor and how they relate.

❏ Viewing the section at issue using the structure and other sections of the same statute. In other words do not read and analyze the section in isolation.

❏ Case law interpreting the statute. Often the applicable statute has been interpreted by the courts. Resist the urge, however, to go directly to reading cases, skipping the first two steps of statutory interpretation. Have a solid understanding of the statute and what it means first.

❏ The plain meaning rule—the wording of the statute at issue. Beware of the plain meaning rule, however, because whether a meaning is plain or what meaning is plain is usually subject to debate.

❏ Legislative history—documents and records created by the various parts of the legislature that enacted the statute. It includes statements of legislators, different versions of the bill as it progressed through the legislative process, and analyses by committees and legislative staff professionals.

❏ Similar statutes in the same jurisdiction that have been addressed by the courts. If courts have not addressed the section at issue, they may have addressed similar ones.

❏ Similar statutes in different jurisdictions that have been addressed by those courts.

❏ Canons of construction—rules of interpretation stated in the abstract. Remember, more than one may apply with conflicting results.

❏ Law review articles and scholarly commentary. Court may use comments from experts in a field to aid in interpreting statutes. Law review articles are also useful for the authorities collected in their footnotes.

❏ A fresh look entails reviewing any new authorities, as well as revisiting the "old," and putting them together into a cohesive, persuasive whole.

❏ In reading a case strategically for how it affects the client and the client's situation use this checklist:

  ❏ Where does the case come from and what level of court decided it?

  ❏ Does the case deal with the same or similar issue as your problem or matter?

  ❏ What laws does the court apply or articulate?

  ❏ What does it say about those laws?

❑ What are the facts of the case?

❑ How does the court apply the laws to the facts?

❑ What is the court's holding? Depending on the client's situation, is it better to describe the holding so that it applies broadly or narrowly?

❑ Does the case contain any useful dicta?

❑ In legal analysis you will need to (1) *distill* the legal principles from multiple cases and explain what they are and how they relate to each other, and (2) *apply* those principles to the facts of your client's situation and advocate the outcome.

❑ In dealing with multiple cases, use this process:

  ❑ Read the cases in the order of most recent to oldest. It is likely that later courts will have synthesized (at least partially) the cases for you— meaning they will have distilled the legal principles from prior cases, fit them together, and explained them.

  ❑ For each case, write out its holding on each issue in a short parenthetical.

  ❑ Sort and group the cases. Create a chart that sets out the issues as categories, then sort the cases based on which issue(s) they address. Then for each issue/category, group the cases by result: those that met the overall standard or requirements and those that did not. Once your chart is complete look for patterns, trends, or factors that point to a result.

  ❑ Distill and synthesize the legal principles from the cases. Once you have sorted, grouped and charted the cases, reread them individually and take down the statements of law and what the court says about them for each issue. Then determine which of the statements of law are elements, and which are factors. Then for each issue fit the statements of law from each case together in as logical and cohesive whole as possible. This usually means going from general statements of law to more specific statements and from broad statements of law to more narrow statements.

❑ Organize and present your legal analysis using the CRAC (Conclusion, Rule/Law, Application, Conclusion) format, which is designed to deliver information in a way that is thorough, comprehensive, persuasive, and easy for the reader to understand.

❑ The key to good appellate legal drafting is ensuring that the audience can easily understand and follow it.

❏ The three key strategies to organizing appellate legal drafting are:

❏ establish the context before discussing the details;

❏ place familiar information before new information and show how new information emerges from or relates to familiar information;

❏ make the structure explicit.

❏ The well-written and organized paragraph is the building block of good appellate legal drafting.

❏ Paragraphs have three essential requirements:

❏ Paragraphs begin with a topic or transition sentence that identifies the point, main idea, or subject of the paragraph.

❏ Every sentence in the paragraph must relate to the topic or transitional sentence.

❏ Every sentence in the paragraph must relate to the sentences around it. This is accomplished by arranging the sentences in a logical sequence, and by using transition words that signal how the sentences relate, e.g., similarly, moreover, however.

❏ Sentences in appellate legal drafting should be clear, direct and concise, and quick and easy to understand. Some tools for accomplishing this:

❏ Where possible, always make your subject a person or entity that can *act*, rather than a concept. In other words, make the subject concrete and put the action in the predicate.

❏ Use plain language — avoid legalese and words that might not be quickly and easily understood by the average reader.

❏ Use fewer words — no more than necessary to clearly and accurately deliver the information or convey your point.

❏ Stamp out narration — eliminate words or sentences that narrate the process of your analysis, e.g. "Guidance is found in several cases."

❏ Avoid nominalizations — unbury your verbs, e.g., write "We represented Ms. Jones" rather than "We provided representation to Ms. Jones."

❏ Avoid intrusive phrases or clauses — do not interrupt the main point of your sentences. Subjects should go close to verbs and verbs close to objects.

❑ Chose the right word—the one that is correct and most accurate.

❑ Use the past tense for events that have already occurred.

❑ Put yourself in the position of the distracted, unfamiliar reader and check if any of your sentences are too long or not easy to follow. Ideally sentences should be between three quarters of a line and two and a half lines.

❑ Keep it as simple as possible.

❑ Appellate legal drafting is a multi step process involving these steps:

   ❑ Organizing your materials into and outline. Before beginning to draft, organize your thoughts and materials into an explicit structure. The structure may change as you draft and revise the document, but it is important to begin with one.

   ❑ Writing the first draft. The first draft is where you get your thoughts and ideas down and where you test them. Writing forces you to think critically. The most important things about the first draft are to just write and get it done.

   ❑ Revising and rewriting. This stage involves distancing yourself from the draft and approaching it as a *reader*. Assess the document's structure and content—does it address all issues and sub issues in a logical way? Then assess how *well* you have addressed the issues and sub issues. This involves critically reviewing any CRACs, paragraphs, clauses, provisions, or sentences and rewriting them as necessary, with the unfamiliar reader in mind.

   ❑ Editing. After your have revised your draft, the editing process involves fine tuning the document for flow and ease of understanding so that it is easily accessible to readers.

   ❑ Proofreading. Once you are satisfied that you have a high quality brief, put it aside. Then print it and go over it with a fine tooth comb ensuring that there *no errors*. Do not combine the editing and proofing steps. Suggested techniques include reading the document aloud and reading with straight edge so that you see only one line at a time. Proofing errors make the brief look shoddy and the drafter look bad.

❑ Citations in legal documents are used to

   ❑ identify and attribute the sources used by drafters in preparing the document and

   ❑ show the readers where to find those sources.

❑ Quotations are

   ❑ used when communicating the exact words of the original source,

   ❑ should be accompanied by a pin point citation, and

   ❑ should be used selectively.

❑ Citations to legal authority are used to support all statements, explanations, and illustrations of the law and to identify the sources from which they come so that readers can look up those sources for themselves.

❑ Citations to legal authority are also used in the application portion of the CRAC format in

   ❑ supporting any conclusions or assertions, and

   ❑ comparing and contrasting the underlying facts with those in the cases used in describing the law.

❑ A key goal in citing legal authority is to show that your legal analyses, discussions, predictions, and assertions are sound and well supported.

❑ Legal authority is not created equally. There is a hierarchy.

❑ First there is primary authority, such as constitutions, statutes and cases. Primary authorities are sources of law.

❑ Within primary authority there is:

   ❑ Binding (sometimes called mandatory) primary authority, which must be followed by the court your case is in. Binding primary authority includes the United State's Constitution, the constitution and statutes of the jurisdiction or state in which the court is situated, and case law rendered by the United States Supreme Court, and higher courts in that state or jurisdiction.

   ❑ Optional (sometimes called persuasive) primary authority, which the court may chose to consider or not. Optional primary authority comes from a state or jurisdiction other than the one in which the court at issue is situated. It also includes case law within the same jurisdiction or state rendered from courts on the same level as the court at issue.

❏ Then there is secondary authority—authorities that are not a source of the law but which comment on and/or describe the law. Secondary authority is always optional, and its persuasiveness depends on the quality and reputation of the source.

❏ Secondary authority includes:

    ❏ Treatises, legal periodicals, encyclopedias and dictionaries, and law reviews.

    ❏ Legislative history.

❏ In most jurisdictions court rules will specify acceptable cite forms for legal authority; often the default format is *The Bluebook*.

❏ The goal of citation to legal authority in an appellate brief is to clearly provide enough information concisely so that readers can easily identify and look up the source.

❏ Citations to the appendix or record are used to support statements and references to procedural and substantive facts in appellate briefs, and allow readers to identify, review, and verify any procedural or factual event described in the brief.

❏ Absent exceptional circumstances, the statement of facts in an appellate brief may contain only facts and evidence that were presented to the court or jury below.

❏ When using another source's words, put quotation marks around those words.

❏ If you have tried to paraphrase a source, but your words are very close to the original, you should quote the source's words and put any changes in brackets, and note omitted words with ellipses.

❏ Do not put quotation marks around your own words.

❏ Your legal drafting and analysis will be judged in part by the quality and correctness of your citation form.

❏ Appellate review involves determining if there was error below and whether it affected the case.

❏ Standards of review define the amount of deference the appellate court will accord the lower court in determining if there was error.

❑ Although there are many different articulations of standards of review, the human mind generally applies one of two: either deferential or non-deferential to the decision or action below.

❑ The four basic standards of review are:

  ❑ De Novo (the decision below must merely be wrong).

  ❑ Clearly Erroneous (the decision below must be very wrong).

  ❑ Substantial Evidence (the decision below must be very wrong).

  ❑ Abuse of Discretion (the decision below must be very, very wrong).

❑ There are many other permutations and articulations of standards of review among the jurisdictions, and it is important to accurately articulate the correct standard.

❑ If the applicable standard of review is not satisfied, the decision or action below will be upheld.

❑ If the appellant successfully convinces the court there was error, the court then determines if the error requires reversal of the judgment or order below.

❑ Certain errors, such as (1) structural errors and (2) errors based on insufficiency of the evidence, require automatic reversal.

❑ Otherwise the court will engage in a harmless error analysis to determine whether and how much the error affected the result at the hearing or trial.

❑ Thus, it is possible to win the battle (convince the court there was error) and lose the war (fail to convince the court that the error requires reversal).

❑ The purpose of an appellate brief is to persuade a court to reverse or affirm a judgment or order below. An appellate brief should not attempt to retry the case.

❑ The audience for the appellate brief will be an intermediate appellate court or a court of last resort. Both these courts include more than one decision maker (judges or justices) and you will need to persuade a majority of them to reverse or affirm.

❑ The vast majority of appeals are to intermediate appellate courts, whose focus is mainly on error correction. Intermediate appellate courts are much more likely to affirm the judgment or order from the trial court than reverse it. Appeals to intermediate appellate courts are usually heard by three-judge panels.

❏ Courts of last resort also correct errors, but in addition make policy, make new law, and extend or clarify existing law much more than intermediate appellate courts. Courts of last resort are less likely to affirm than intermediate appellate courts. Appeals to courts of last resort may be heard by as many as nine justices, e.g. the United States Supreme Court.

❏ An appellate brief should show:

❏ that there was or was not error below—that the decision below was incorrect or correct under the applicable standard of review; and

❏ that the error requires reversal because the error was not harmless, or does not require reversal because the error was harmless.

❏ An overarching goal in drafting an appellate brief is for the court to adopt it in large part as its opinion.

❏ An appellate brief is comprised of separate components, usually prescribed by local rules of procedure. Typical components include a statement of issues on appeal, tables of contents and authorities, statement of the case, statement of facts, summary of the argument, discussion or argument with headings and subheadings, and a conclusion.

❏ The tables of contents and authorities should be finalized last. Lawyers vary in the order in which they draft the other components. What is important is to approach the drafting process as a series of discrete tasks rather than one giant job.

❏ The statement of issues on appeal should specifically identify the alleged error or lack of error below. We recommend using the whether/when format.

❏ The statement of the case should set out the nature of the case, the relevant procedural history of the case and should also contain the essential reasons why the decisions below should be reversed or affirmed. The statement of the case is the drafter's first opportunity to deliver her message. Accurate citations to the record or appendix for each fact or document are essential.

❏ The statement of facts should tell an accurate story that will make the readers want to adopt your legal positions and that gives them enough information to be able to do so.

❏ The purpose of the discussion or argument section is to show the readers how to rule in your client's favor and why they should do so. This involves making your points as clearly as possible, which usually means organizing complex information so that the reader can understand it as easily as possible.

❑ When drafting the discussion section, envision the opinion you would like the court to issue and draft it like that.

❑ Before you begin to draft, have an idea of what your main arguments are and where they should go. Also have an idea of which arguments should be divided into subsections with their own point headings and CRAC format. This may change as you draft and revise, but it is best to begin with a structure in mind.

❑ Each separate issue on appeal becomes a main section in the discussion section of both the appellant's and the appellee's brief. Often the issue of reversible versus harmless error gets its own section at the end of the brief.

❑ The discussion section should begin with any threshold issues, e.g. standing to sue or appeal, or whether there is jurisdiction.

❑ After any threshold issue, the discussion section usually begins with the drafter's strongest argument for reversing or affirming the decision below, and so on.

❑ An exception would be if the strongest argument has the smallest consequence, e.g. a very strong argument that would reduce the defendants 25 year sentence by one month.

❑ The structure of the discussion section is based on the CRAC (Conclusion, Rule/Law, Application, Conclusion) format and is comprised of a series of CRACs. With some issues on appeal the focus will be on the rule/law portion, e.g. if the issue is which law applies, or whether a particular law is valid. On the other hand, other issues on appeal may be factually intensive, such as whether a factual finding is clearly erroneous.

❑ Persuading the appellate court involves showing that your positions are (1) sound and well supported by authority, and (2) the better choice .

❑ First and foremost, persuading the court involves drafting arguments that are clear and easy to follow.

❑ Showing the court that your arguments are sound and well supported requires thorough and sophisticated knowledge of the law and authorities and how they affect the facts in the record.

❏ Showing that your positions and arguments are the better choice involves:

  ❏ exposing and exploiting the weaknesses of the other side's arguments, and

  ❏ using policy arguments.

❏ Policy arguments are concrete but larger reasons why the court should adopt a tenable legal position. They show the court that your position advances a particular goal and/or the other side's positions will undermine this goal or cause harm.

❏ Test your appellate brief for overall substance and organization by creating and reviewing a heading and topic sentence outline.

❏ Once you have a complete quality draft, thoroughly assess the appellate brief using the statement of facts and discussion/argument guidelines set out in Chapter 11.

❏ Make time to print and proofread your appellate brief separately before filing it.

❏ Oral argument is first and foremost for the benefit of the bench.

❏ Counsel should keep in mind the differences between arguing to an intermediate appellate court and arguing to a court of last resort.

  ❏ Intermediate appellate courts usually feature panels made up of less than the full court. As a result, finding out which judges or justices have been appointed to hear your case is important. The earlier you can find this out the better so that you can familiarize yourself with their reputations and prior work.

  ❏ In courts of last resort, generally all the judges or justices hear each case. Thus, it is easy to begin researching the panel and crafting your brief and argument to appeal to the individual members.

❏ Counsel's goals in oral argument include:

  ❏ Helping the bench understand the case in a way that benefits their position;

  ❏ Determining the bench's concerns and addressing them to their client's benefit; and

  ❏ Making their client's case and positions tangible and concrete, and thus more compelling.

❑ The most important part of oral argument is preparation, which involves knowing the case, the applicable law, the operative facts, the context, what you are asking the court to do, what the possible ramifications of that relief might be, and how those ramifications can be limited or contained.

❑ The essential technique for effective oral argument is the development of talking points, not a scripted argument that you would feel compelled to "get through" despite the panel's attempts to "throw you off course with their questions."

❑ Talking points are set out as bullet pointed statements supported by no more than four sub-bullet points that include record citations for any facts that are critical to the talking point.

❑ Talking points should be prepared for threshold issues (like standing and jurisdiction), the main arguments in your favor—arranged in order of strength, any areas of possible concern, which include the main arguments of opposing counsel.

❑ The introduction to your argument or presentation should be short and to the point. It should comply with any of the court's particular rules, such as those that require or prohibit particular formats or contents. It should not include a grandiose statement of the theory of your case.

❑ The conclusion should be short, basically a tag line. It should include a request for the specific relief you are seeking, e.g., "therefore, we ask the court to reverse the judgment below."

❑ There are many ways to prepare your material for the courtroom. In general, the fewer materials you have with you at the podium, the better. Chapter 12 described the three panel manila file folder approach to organizing talking points, facts, and record citations.

❑ There is no substitute for practice when preparing for oral argument. Both informal and formal presentations and discussions of your case, using your talking points, helps to build familiarity and flexibility in your delivery, which will allow you to adapt your argument to best suit the needs of the bench.

❑ Make sure that you know the technical rules, procedures, and format for oral argument. This includes things like knowing about the seating arrangements, how time is allotted, how rebuttal time is reserved, what the signal is to begin or end your argument, whether computers and other electronic devices are allowed in the courtroom, and the like.

❑ When the time for oral argument comes, remain flexible and remember your primary goals:

    ❑ Helping the bench understand the case in a way that benefits your position;

    ❑ Determining the bench's concerns and addressing them to your client's benefit; and

    ❑ Making your client's case and positions tangible and concrete, and thus more compelling.

❑ Your oral argument consists of the opening or introduction, which can be memorized but should be delivered in a genuine, non-mechanical fashion, the main argument, consisting of your talking points, and your conclusion, which can be very brief.

❑ Rebuttal is not the time to reargue your whole case. Rather, it should be used to make one or two incisive points that identify any weaknesses in the other side's positions. In addition, it is also an opportunity to address any questions the court may still have regarding your position.

❑ Counsel should welcome questions from the bench and answer them immediately and directly. When presenting, counsel should watch and be alert to signs from the bench that a question may be coming. If one is detected, counsel should stop and take the question, looking directly at the questioning judge or justice, while listening carefully to the exact question being asked. Then, think, and answer, framing the answer as much as possible in the terms of one or more of your talking points.

❑ There are specific techniques for handling simple questions, hostile questions, questions that ask for a concession, hypothetical questions, questions that require a correction, questions you think are irrelevant, questions that you do not know the answer to, multi-part questions, and questions posed simultaneously by multiple judges or justices.

❑ When presenting, it is critical to create a good impression, which includes paying attention to your dress and physical appearance, your manner of delivery, including non-verbal communication, and volume, tone, and pace of your speech.

❑ Being a good speaker and presenting a good oral argument involve being an observant listener who remembers that the goals of oral argument all point to being helpful to the panel in a manner that will benefit your position and your client.

❏ Moot court competitions are stylized simulated appellate proceedings designed to allow law students to gain in-depth knowledge and experience in legal research, analysis, brief writing, oral advocacy, and substantive law.

❏ The audience in moot court competitions is wider and more varied that in a real-world appeal, and will likely include other students, professors, practitioners, and judges, as well as your team members themselves.

❏ There are a wide variety of moot court competitions, each with its own set of rules and timelines. It is important to note the nuances of each competition's rules and procedures and follow them to the iota; they will most likely be strictly enforced based upon a perception on the part of the sponsoring organization that it be scrupulously fair and uniform in its dealings with all teams.

❏ The three main problems that appear in low scoring moot court briefs are: (1) briefs that are cursory or incomplete, (2) briefs that are hard to follow or understand, and (3) briefs containing technical errors and appear sloppy. The broader audience of moot court makes it even more important that a moot court brief be all things to all people, be complete, clear, and convincing, and be absolutely free from technical errors.

❏ Before beginning to write the brief, take the time to review and understand the problem thoroughly. Most will have two main issues — make sure that you understand them and their parameters before reviewing the rest of the materials. They should serve to focus and anchor your research, writing, brief, and oral argument.

❏ After your review the problem and its materials, pull and read every authority cited in the materials. Critically analyze these authorities to see to what extent they actually support the statements for which they are cited. Organize them, issue by issue, into "pro" and "con" categories for both sides. Then do your own supplemental research on the issues, adding them to the accumulating stack of materials. Even before writing the brief and practicing for oral argument, you should become conversant with the facts and holdings of the critical cases involved.

❏ The skills and techniques described in Chapters 7 to 11 of this book are applicable and important to producing a quality, high-scoring brief.

❏ Oral argument in moot court is your opportunity to score points in terms of demonstrating your mastery of public speaking and oral advocacy.

Convincing the panel to rule in your favor on the merits is of secondary importance.

❏ Preparation for oral argument is the most important ingredient for success. Organizing one's presentation using a scripted introduction and a set of fluid talking points is the best method to employ.

❏ Holding full practice rounds, both formal and informal, with different people serving as judges is important. You will benefit from being exposed to different personality types, comprehension levels, and conversational patterns. You will also note problems with and questions about your presentation that reappear across many different panels — noting these will provide you with a list of areas for further work and refinement.

❏ Questions from the bench are not interruptions of your presentation but an opportunity for you to score points and demonstrate your speaking and advocacy skills. They should be welcomed.

❏ Teams should practice scrupulous professional appearance, behavior, and demeanor in all formal moot court proceedings, including the waiting time between rounds. "Friendly but not friends" is the professional standard of behavior toward your fellow moot court participants and adversaries.

Appendix

Sample Appellate Brief and Resulting Order

No. 07-2787

IN THE UNITED STATES COURT OF APPEALS
FOR THE FIRST CIRCUIT

BAYSTATE TECHNOLOGIES, INC.,
PLAINTIFF

v.

HAROLD BOWERS, D/B/A HLB TECHNOLOGY,
Defendant

—

PROFESSOR GEORGE W. KUNEY,
Movant-Appellant

v.

ROBERT. W. BEAN,
Appellee

*Appeal from the United States District Court
for the District of Massachusetts
in CV-91-40079
Judge Nathaniel M. Gorton*

BRIEF OF THE APPELLANT GEORGE W. KUNEY

George W. Kuney, Professor
University of Tennessee College of Law
1505 W. Cumberland Avenue, Suite 202
Knoxville, Tennessee 37916
(865) 974-2500

TABLE OF CONTENTS

Table of Contents i

Table of Authorities ii

I.   Jurisdictional Statement. 1

II.   Statement of the Issues. 7

III. Statement of the Case. 7

IV.   Statement of Facts. 12

V.   Summary of the Argument 16

VI.   Argument. 17

      A. *The District Court Erred in Finding Moot the Motions to
      Intervene and Dissolve or Modify the Stipulated Protective Order* 17

      B. *The District Court Abused Its Discretion in Denying Kuney's
      Motion to enter the Proposed Stipulated Order* 20

VII. Conclusion 27

ADDENDUM

CERTIFICATE OF COMPLIANCE

CERTIFICATE OF SERVICE

TABLE OF AUTHORITIES

Statutes

28 U.S.C. § 1291 . . . . 4, 5, 6

28 U.S.C. § 1295 1

28 U.S.C. § 1331 . . . . 1, 2

28 U.S.C. § 1338 . . . . 1, 2

Cases

Baystate Technologies v. Bowers, 539 U.S. 928 (2003) 9

Beckman Industry, Inc. v. International Insurance Co.,
    966 F.2d 470 (9th Cir. 1992) 22

Bowers v. Baystate Technologies., Inc.,
    320 F.3d 1317 (Fed. Cir. 2003) 2, 3, 7, 9, 10, 12, 13, 23

Chao v. Hotel Oasis Inc., 493 F.3d 26 (1st Cir. 2007) 23

Cities Service Oil Co. v. Coleman Oil Co.,
    470 F.2d 925 (1st Cir. 1972) 17, 23, 26

FTC v. Standard Financial Management Corp.,
    830 F.2d 404 (1st Cir. 1987) 22, 24

Gowen, Inc. v. F/V Quality One, 244 F.3d 64 (1st Cir. 2001) . . . 16, 17, 19, 20

In re Carp, 340 F.3d 15 (1st Cir. 2003) 16, 17, 21, 23, 26

In re CK Liquidation, No. 03-40097
    (Bankr. D. Mass., filed Aug. 22, 2003) 9, 13

In re Salem Suede, 268 F.3d 42 (1st Cir. 2001) 17, 20, 21, 23, 24, 25

Maine School Administrative District 35 v. Mr. and Mrs. R.,
    321 F.3d 9 (1st Cir. 2003) 17, 18, 20

Morales-Feliciano v. Parole Board of Committee of Puerto Rico,
    887 F.2d 1 (1st Cir. 1989) 6

Oakville Development Corp., v. FDIC, 986 F.2d 611 (1st Cir. 1993) 18

Pansy v. Borough of Stoudsburg, 23 F.3d 771 (3d Cir. 1994) 5, 19

Plymouth Mutual Life Insurance Co. v. Illinois Mid-continent Life
Insurance Co., 378 F.2d 389 (3d Cir. 1967) 7

Poliquin v. Garden Way, 989 F.2d 527 (1st Cir. 1993) 4, 6, 16, 20, 22, 24

Public Citizen v. Liggett Group, Inc.,
    858 F.2d 775 (1st Cir. 1988)................... 1, 4, 17, 19, 20, 22, 25

Ramirez Pomades v. Becton Dickinson & Co., S.A.,
    839 F.2d 1 (1st Cir. 1988) 21

Rhode Island v. United States Environmental Protection Agency,
    378 F.3d 19 (1st Cir. 2004) 5

Shelby v. Subperformance International Inc.,
    435 F.2d. 42 (1st Cir. 2006) 18, 19

Siedle v. Putnam Investments, Inc., 147 F.3d 7
    (1st Cir. 1998)........................ 16, 17, 20, 21, 23, 24, 25, 26

TI Federal Credit Union v. DelBonis, 72 F.3d 921 (1st Cir. 1995)......... 23

United States v. City of Milwaukee, 144 F.3d 524 (7th Cir. 1998).......... 6

Verhoven v. Brunswick School Committee, 207 F.3d 1 (1st Cir. 1999) 17

Xeta, Inc. v. Atex, Inc., 825 F.2d 604 (1st Cir. 1987) 1, 2

I. JURISDICTIONAL STATEMENT

This is an appeal from a postjudgment order (1) finding moot the motions of George W. Kuney ("Kuney") to intervene and to dissolve or modify a stipulated protective order and (2) denying Kuney's motion to enter a proposed stipulated order resulting from a settlement of those motions.[1] The District Court had jurisdiction in the underlying proceeding under 28 U.S.C. §§ 1338 and 1331 because the Stipulated Protective Order was still in effect. *Public Citizen v. Liggett Group, Inc.*, 858 F.2d 775, 782-83 (1st Cir. 1988). Kuney believes the United States Court of Appeals for the Federal Circuit has exclusive jurisdiction over this appeal under 28 U.S.C. § 1295(a)(2) because the underlying litigation arose under patent law. *Xeta, Inc. v. Atex, Inc.*, 825 F.2d 604, 607 (1st Cir. 1987). He originally filed the appeal in this Court, however, and has moved to transfer the appeal to the Federal Circuit. (Motion to Transfer, filed January 4, 2008.) That motion has not yet been heard or decided, and Kuney files this brief in order to comply with local scheduling rules.

The underlying litigation, *Baystate Technologies, Inc. v. Bowers*, No. 91-40079, involved the validity of a patent, patent infringement, copyright infringement, and breach of contract, over which the District Court had subject matter jurisdiction under 28 U.S.C. §§ 1338 and 1331. *Bowers v. Baystate Technologies., Inc.*, 320 F.3d 1317 (Fed. Cir. 2003). The case was dismissed pursuant to stipulation of the parties on May 4, 2006. (Docket No. 546.) On February 21, 2007, Kuney filed his motions to intervene and to dissolve or modify a stipulated protective order entered in 1998 (Stipulated Protective Order) in order to use documents related to the case in a textbook on law and business. (Docket No. 547, Appendix of the Appellant George W. Kuney (Kuney App.), Tab 2, p. 10.) The Stipulated Protective Order provided that " ... this order shall remain in full force and effect after the entry of judgment in this action or after any earlier termination of this litigation." (Docket No. 50, Stipulated Protective Order, ¶ 8, Kuney App., Tab 2, p. 13.) Thus, the District Court had jurisdiction over Kuney's motion to dissolve or modify the order. *Pub-*

---

1. In the Notice of Appeal, the September 17, 2007, order was described as "denying George W. Kuney's Motion to Intervene and Motion to Dissolve or Modify the Stipulated Protective Order...," but this is an understatement. The effect of the order finding moot the motions to intervene and dissolve or modify the stipulated protective order and denying Kuney's motion to enter the proposed stipulated order is to ignore or erase the original motions and Kuney's attempt to access court records. This order has apparently been stripped from the Notice of Appeal filed with the District Court and is no longer listed on the docket. It is attached hereto in the Addendum.

lic Citizen v. Liggett, 858 F.2d at 783 (where a protective order is still in effect, the district court has power to make postjudgment modifications to the order).

Kuney served the motions to intervene and dissolve or modify the Stipulated Protective Order on all parties to *Baystate Technologies, Inc. v. Bowers,* No. 91-40079, and the appeal, *Bowers v. Baystate Technologies., Inc.,* 320 F.3d 1317, as well as their successors and all attorneys involved. (Docket No. 551, Kuney App., Tab 2, p. 10.) Robert Bean ("Bean"), who is not party to the stipulated protective order, filed the only opposition to the motion. (Docket No. 555, Bean's Opposition filed March 21, 2007, Kuney App., Tab 8, p. 129.) Thereafter, Kuney and Bean entered into a settlement providing that Kuney could use the jury exhibits and the confidential and nonconfidential appeal appendixes filed in *Bowers v. Baystate Technologies, Inc.,* 320 F.3d 1317 (Fed. Cir. 2003), Case No. 01-1108-11109. (Docket No. 557, proposed stipulated order signed by Kuney and Bean's counsel, Kuney App., Tab 10, p. 140.) The terms of this settlement are set forth in a proposed stipulated order filed with the District Court on April 2, 2007. (Docket No. 557, Kuney App., Tab 10, p. 140.) No action was taken by the District Court regarding Kuney and Bean's settlement and the proposed stipulated order, however. On August 21, 2007, Kuney filed a motion for entry of the proposed stipulated order serving all interested parties, their successors, and counsel. (Docket No. 559, Kuney App., Tab 12, p. 144.) No opposition was filed to this motion.

On September 17, 2007, the District Court entered an order: (1) "finding as moot" Kuney's motion to intervene and dissolve or modify the stipulated protective order, and (2) denying Kuney's motion to enter the proposed stipulated order "without prejudice; if the defendant, Robert Bean, moves to modify the stipulated protective order, consistent with the provisions of the proposed stipulated order (557, Kuney App., Tab 10, p. 140), serves his motion on all other parties and that motion is unopposed 14 days after service, it will be allowed." (The order was not assigned a docket number in the District Court, and is attached. Interestingly, this order has apparently been stripped from the Notice of Appeal filed with the District Court and is no longer listed on the docket. It is attached hereto in the Addendum.) Bean did not file such a motion.[2] The proposed stipulated order was not entered, and according to the terms of the District Court's September 17, 2007 order, will not be entered.[3]

---

2. Moreover, Bean informed Kuney through his counsel that he would not file or serve such a motion in response to Kuney's offer to fund the costs. (*See* Exhibit A Email from Attorney Louis Ciavarra to Kuney.)

3. There has been no further action in this matter since September 24, 2007, when Kuney's reply to Bean's opposition to the motion to intervene and dissolve or modify the

On October 12, 2007, Kuney timely appealed from the September 17, 2007 order. This postjudgment, postdismissal order finding moot Kuney's motions to intervene and to dissolve or modify the stipulated protective order, and denying his motion for entry of the proposed stipulated order was final and appealable under 28 U.S.C. § 1291. *Public Citizen v. Liggett*, 858 F.2d at 776 (appeal of postjudgment order modifying protective order on the motion of a third party); *see also Poliquin v. Garden Way*, 989 F.2d 527, 530 (1st Cir. 1993) (appeal of orders denying plaintiff's postjudgment motion asking court to rule that certain documents not part of protective order and granting defendant's post judgment motion order to seal documents contained in court files); *see also Pansy v. Borough of Stoudsburg*, 23 F.3d 771, 776 (3d Cir. 1994) (order denying motions to intervene and to reconsider, vacate, or modify confidentiality order is appealable under 28 U.S.C. § 1291). In *Pansy*, 23 F.3d 778, the court, citing *inter alia Public Citizen v. Liggett Group, Inc.*, 858 F.2d at 783-87, noted that "permissive intervention is appropriately used to enable a litigant who was not an original party to an action to challenge protective or confidentiality orders entered in that action."

Although the order stated Kuney's motion to enter the proposed stipulated protective order was denied "without prejudice," this label is inaccurate. Kuney was not invited, given leave, or otherwise allowed to take any action regarding this motion or his original motions—which were found moot. Rather, the District Court, in explaining its use of the term "without prejudice," invited *Bean* to file a motion to modify the stipulated protective order consistent with the terms of the proposed stipulated order. Bean has not done so, and the District Court made clear it would take no further action on the matter. Under these circumstances, courts have not accorded "talismanic significance to a trier of fact's use of the term 'without prejudice.'" *Rhode Island v. United States Environmental Protection Agency*, 378 F.3d 19, 26 (1st Cir. 2004) (discussing an order denying without prejudice a motion to intervene in the underlying proceedings under the collateral order doctrine and declining to rule that the order was not conclusive); *see also United States v. City of Milwaukee*, 144 F.3d 524, 528 n.7, 529 (7th Cir. 1998) *cited in Rhode Island*, 378 F.3d at 26. In *City of Milwaukee*, the district court denied a motion to intervene without prejudice because the motion did not comply with procedural rules, but invited the party seeking intervention to refile the motion, stating: "Scott Culver may, if [he] choose[s] to do so, serve and file a motion to intervene which complies

---

stipulated protective order was filed. (Docket No, 560.) Kuney moved for leave to file this reply on April 3, 2007, and the motion was granted in the District Court's September 17, 2007, order. (Docket No. 556.)

with Rules 5, 7, and 24 of the Federal Rules of Civil Procedure." 144 F.3d at 527-28 & 528 n. 10. The Third Circuit held that, under those circumstances, the order was not final. *Id.* at 529 & 529 n.10. In contrast, the District Court denied Kuney's motion to enter the proposed stipulated order and did not invite or allow him to file anything or otherwise obtain relief. Thus, Kuney's motion was denied with prejudice as to him.

The District Court's September 17, 2007 postjudgment order abrogated the settlement Kuney and Bean had bargained for and leaves Kuney with no other recourse for seeking access to documents that are presumed accessible by the public. *See Poliquin v. Garden Way*, 989 F.2d at 533 (noting evidence admitted at trial and judicial records are presumed accessible). This order is final and appealable. 28 U.S.C. § 1291; *see also Morales-Feliciano v. Parole Board of Committee of Puerto Rico*, 887 F.2d 1, 3-4 (1st Cir. 1989) ("the requirement of finality is to be given a 'practical rather than a technical construction'" (quoting *Cohen v. Beneficial Loan Corp.*, 337 U.S. 541, 546 (1949))); *Plymouth Mutual Life Insurance Co. v. Illinois Mid-continent Life Insurance Co.*, 378 F.2d 389, 391 (3d Cir. 1967) (postjudgment order affecting right bargained for in reaching a settlement is appealable).

II. STATEMENT OF THE ISSUES

(1) Whether the District Court erred as a matter of law in finding moot Kuney's motions to intervene and to dissolve or modify the Stipulated Protective Order.

(2) Whether the District Court abused its discretion in denying Kuney's unopposed motion to enter the proposed stipulated order resulting from a settlement of those motions between Kuney and Bean while indicating it would enter the order if Bean filed a motion to modify the Stipulated Protective order consistent with the terms of the proposed stipulated order.

III. STATEMENT OF THE CASE

The underlying litigation involved patent, copyright, and breach of contract claims relating to computer software developed by Harold Bowers. On May 16, 1991, Baystate filed suit against Bowers in the District Court seeking a declaratory judgment that Baystate's software product did not infringe Bowers's software patent and that the patent was invalid and unenforceable. *Bowers v. Baystate Technologies., Inc.*, 320 F.3d 1317. Bowers counterclaimed for copyright infringement, patent infringement, and breach of contract. *Id.* During discovery in this case, Bowers and Baystate entered into a stipulated protective order that was approved by the District Court on January 27, 1998. (Order Entering Stipulated Protective Order, Jan. 27, 1998, Docket No. 50, Kuney App., Tab 2, p. 13.) The stipulated protective order provides, *inter alia*:

1. Unless otherwise agreed by the parties or their attorneys, any non-public document which is to be produced by the parties in this action in response to the other party's requests pursuant to Rule 34, or by informal agreement or otherwise, and any non-public information supplied in response to Discovery which the responding party reasonably believes is confidential or contains confidential subject matter may be designated "Confidential" by the responding party, and any such document or information shall thereafter be considered confidential. To designate the word "confidential" shall be permanently stamped or written on the materials. For purposes of this Order, all such designated document and information are referred to as Confidential Materials.

· · ·

8.... Unless otherwise agreed by the party producing Confidential Material, this Order shall remain in full force and effect after the entry of a final judgment in this action or after any earlier termination of this litigation. Upon the final determination of this action, all parties shall return any Confidential Material, and all copies thereof, in their possession to the party that produced it unless the parties shall otherwise agree to an alternative method of protecting the confidentiality of all Confidential Material.

(Docket No. 50, Order Entering Stipulated Protective Order, Jan. 27, 1998, Kuney App., Tab 2, p. 13-16.)

On June 7, 2000, after eleven days of trial, a jury returned a verdict in favor of Bowers. (Docket No. 390, Jury Verdict, June 7, 2000.) On September 18, 2000, the District Court entered a judgment in accordance with the jury's verdict in the amount of $5,270,942. (Docket No. 442.) The District Court stayed execution of the judgment pending the resolution of appeals by Baystate. (Docket No. 484.)

Baystate appealed the judgment to the Federal Circuit, which affirmed judgment for breach of contract and copyright infringement, but reversed the judgment on the issue of patent infringement, reducing the jury verdict by $232,977. *Bowers v. Baystate*, 320 F.3d 1317, 1322, 1334 (Fed. Cir. 2003). Baystate filed a petition for Writ of Certiorari with the United States Supreme Court, which the Supreme Court denied on June 16, 2003. *Baystate Technologies v. Bowers*, 539 U.S. 928 (2003). During the course of these appeals, Baystate defaulted on its secured debt. (Docket No. 550, Declaration of George W. Kuney (Kuney Decl.) ¶ 2, Kuney App., Tab 5, p. 41.)

On July 11, 2003, the District Court lifted the stay of execution on the judgment (Docket No. 525) and Bowers sought to execute on his judgment soon thereafter. (Docket No. 527; Docket No. 549 Declaration of Harold L. Bowers. (Bowers Decl.) ¶ 5, Kuney App., Tab 4, p. 31.) However, Cadkey, Corp. (nee Baystate) filed for chapter 11 protection on August 22, 2003, before Bowers could obtain a judgment lien of any sort. *See In re CK Liquidation*, No. 03-40097 (Bankr. D. Mass., Aug. 22, 2003).

On June 14, 2004, over six years after the stipulated protective order was entered on January 27, 1998, Bean was made a party to *Baystate v. Bowers*. (Docket No. 540). On May 4, 2006, the parties to this case stipulated to the dismissal of *Baystate v. Bowers*. (Docket No. 546.) On February 21, 2007, Kuney filed motions to intervene and to dissolve or modify the stipulated protective order entered in January 1998. (Docket No. 547, Kuney App., Tab 2, p. 10.) Kuney served the motions to intervene and dissolve or modify the stipulated protective order on all parties in *Baystate Technologies, Inc. v. Bowers*, No. 91-40079, and the appeal *Bowers v. Baystate Technologies, Inc.*, 320 F.3d 1317 (Fed. Cir. 2003), as well their successors and all attorneys involved. (Docket No. 547, Kuney App., Tab 2, p. 10.) Bean, not party to the stipulated protective order, filed the only opposition. (Docket No. 555, Bean's Opposition filed March 21, 2007, Kuney App., Tab 8, p. 129.) Bean opposed modification of the stipulated protective order, but did not address Kuney's motion to intervene. (Docket No. 555, Kuney App., Tab 8, p. 129.) Thereafter, Kuney and Bean's counsel negotiated a settlement of Kuney's motions that provided Kuney could review and use certain documents used at trial and part of the record filed with the District Court:

> The following documents and any information contained therein, whether stamped or otherwise designated as "Confidential," are not confidential and are no longer subject to the Stipulated Protective Order (Docket No. 50):
>
> a. Jury Notebook Part A (Docket No. 199);
>
> b. Jury Notebook Part B (Docket No. 200);
>
> c. Confidential and Non-Confidential Appeal Appendices, Volumes I, II, III, and IV filed on August 6, 2001, in Case No. 011108, -1109 (Fed. Cir.).

The settlement also provided that " … the parties agree that all source code shall continue to be confidential and not disclosed in violation of the Stipulated Protective Order." (Docket No. 557, proposed stipulated order signed by Kuney and Bean's counsel, ¶¶ 2, 4, Kuney App., Tab 10, p. 141.)

The terms of this settlement were set forth in the proposed stipulated order signed by Kuney and Bean's counsel and filed with the District Court on April 2, 2007. (Docket No. 557, Kuney App., Tab 10, p. 140.) No action was taken by the District Court regarding Kuney and Bean's settlement and proposed stipulated order. On August 21, 2007, Kuney moved for entry of the proposed stipulated order, serving all interested parties, their successors, and counsel. (Docket No. 559, Kuney App., Tab 12, p. 144.) No opposition was filed to this motion. On September 17, 2007, the District Court issued this order:

> Electronic ORDER entered finding as moot [547] Motion to Intervene; granting [556] Motion for Leave to File; Counsel using the Electronic Case Filing System should now file the document for which leave to file was granted in accordance with the CM/ECF Administrative Procedures. Counsel must include—Leave to file granted on (date of order)—in the caption of the document; denying [559] Motion. Motion denied without prejudice; if the defendant, Robert Bean, moves to modify the stipulated protective order, consistent with the provisions of the proposed stipulated order [557], serves his motion on all other parties and that motion is unopposed 14 days after service, it will be allowed.

IV. STATEMENT OF FACTS

This case and ensuing appeals led to the landmark decision by the Federal Circuit Court of Appeals in *Bowers v. Baystate Technologies*, 320 F.3d 1317 (Fed. Cir. 2003), which has had far reaching ramifications for copyright and contract law and has attracted the attention of scholars and other commentators due to its importance in the software and other industries. (Docket No. 560, Kuney's reply to Bean's opposition to motion to dissolve or modify protective order, Kuney App., Tab 13, p. 148.)

Kuney is a Professor of Law at the University of Tennessee College of Law and the Director of the College's Clayton Center for Entrepreneurial Law. He is writing a detailed account of this important case, its appeals, and the chapter 11 and 7 bankruptcy cases that followed. He seeks access to the documents set forth in the proposed stipulated order—trial exhibits and documents filed with the District Court and designated on appeal—to use with the text and to ensure the accuracy and thoroughness of his scholarship. (Kuney Decl. ¶ 2, Kuney App., Tab 5, p. 41.) Not only are the source documents needed to support the text of Kuney's book, but the documents themselves are also intended as concrete examples that will allow students to examine the actual documents that are being summarized in the text. The book will be published in both hard copy and digital form; the digital version will contain links to the underlying documents referenced. Thus, while reading about the trial, students would be able to access electronic copies of the exhibits considered by the jury. This in-depth form of legal study has been impossible until recent years due to the size of case files. Now, however, it is not only possible, but it is fairly easy and allows students a significantly greater opportunity to engage the material. Kuney does not seek disclosure of any computer source codes or trade secrets. (Docket No. 557, proposed stipulated order signed by Kuney and Bean's counsel, ¶¶ 2, 4, Kuney App., Tab 10, p. 140; Docket No. 560; Kuney's reply to Bean's opposition, ¶ 2, Kuney App., Tab 13, p. 148.)

In September 2000, Bowers obtained a $5,270,000 judgment against Baystate (reduced on appeal by $232,977). (Docket No. 442); *Bowers v. Baystate Technologies, Inc.*, 320 F.3d 1317. 1322, 1334 (Fed. Cir. 2003). However, by the time he was permitted to execute this judgment, Cadkey, Corp. (nee Baystate) filed for chapter 11 bankruptcy protection on August 22, 2003, before Bowers could obtain a judgment lien of any sort. *See In re CK Liquidation*, No. 03-40097 (Bankr. D. Mass., filed Aug. 22, 2003).

Because Bowers held 90% of the unsecured claims as a result of his large judgment against Cadkey/Baystate, Bowers was the largest unsecured creditor of Cadkey/Baystate in the Chapter 11 case. (Docket No. 549, Bowers Decl. ¶ 6, Kuney App., Tab 4, p. 31.)

On August 20, 2003, Cadkey/Baystate filed a motion to approve the sale of substantially all its assets free and clear of liens, claims, and encumbrances, including Bowers's judgment. (Docket No. 550, Kuney Decl. ¶ 3, Kuney App., Tab 5, p. 41.) On September 12, 2003, the Bankruptcy Court entered an order approving the sale. (Docket No. 550, Kuney Decl. ¶ 3, Kuney App., Tab 5, p. 41.) Pursuant to the September 12 sale order, Kubotek Corp. (Kubotek) acquired substantially all of Cadkey's assets. (Docket No. 550, Kuney Decl. ¶ 4, Kuney App., Tab 5, p. 42.) The Bankruptcy Court overruled all objections to the sale and entered an order on November 6, 2003, approving the sale to Kubotek for a mere $2,850,000 paid to the bankruptcy estate, effectively wiping out Bowers's $5,000,000+ unsecured judgment. (Docket No. 550, Kuney Decl. ¶ 4, Kuney App., Tab 5, p. 42.) Following the sale, on March 7, 2004, Cadkey/Baystate converted the case to Chapter 7 liquidation. (Docket No. 550, Kuney Decl. ¶ 5, Kuney App., Tab 5, p. 42.)

After the dismissal of *Baystate v. Bowers*, in May 2006, Bowers contacted Kuney to inform him of the underlying details of the litigation and ensuing bankruptcy. (Docket No. 549, Bowers Decl. ¶ 7, Kuney App., Tab 4, p. 32; Docket No. 550, Kuney Decl. ¶ 6, Kuney App., Tab 5, p. 42.) As a result of the litigation in this case, Bowers has possession or control over certain documents and other materials subject to the stipulated protective order, including items in the files of his former counsel, Banner & Witcoff, Ltd. (Docket No. 549, Bowers Decl. ¶ 8, Kuney App., Tab 4, p. 32.) He has indicated that he is willing to share those documents with Kuney but fears he cannot do so as a result of the Stipulated Protective Order. (Docket No. 549, Bowers Decl. ¶ 8, Kuney App., Tab 4, p. 32.) He also lacks the funds or ability to proceed *pro se* to seek modification of the Stipulated Protective Order. (Docket No. 549, Bowers Decl. ¶ 12, Kuney App., Tab 4, p. 33.)

In sum, (1) the trial and appeal in this case are long over; (2) Bowers, a party to the Stipulated Protective Order, has consented to disclosure, and the other party (Baystate/Cadkey) is a corporate shell that has all-but-finally been liquidated in chapter 7 proceedings; (3) Bean, who was not a party to the Stipulated Protective Order, was the only party who opposed Kuney's motion to dissolve or modify the order; (4) Bean entered into a settlement with Kuney that allows access to jury exhibits and appeal appendices, and this agreement was memorialized in a proposed stipulated order filed with the District Court; (5) neither Bean nor any other party opposed Kuney's motion to enter the proposed stipulated order; (6) the District Court indicated it would enter such an order, but only if Bean moved for it; (7) Bean did not, and Kuney has been denied access to trial exhibits and court documents over which no one involved in the case has an objection.

V. SUMMARY OF THE ARGUMENT

The District Court erred as a matter of law in finding moot Kuney's motions to intervene and to dissolve or modify the protective order because the relief requested is capable of being granted. *Gowen, Inc. v. F/V Quality One*, 244 F.3d 64, 66 (1st Cir. 2001). It is possible that the motion to intervene was found moot on the ground that intervention was implicitly allowed. However, Kuney's motion to dissolve or modify the protective order was not granted, explicitly or implicitly; the Stipulated Protective Order is still in place and the documents are still available. Thus, relief is capable of being granted.

The District Court abused its discretion in denying Kuney's unopposed motion to enter the proposed stipulated order while indicating it would enter the order if *Bean* moved for it. *Siedle v. Putnam Investments, Inc.*, 147 F.3d 7, 10 (1st Cir. 1998). In doing so, the District Court ignored "material factor[s] deserv[ing] significant weight," *id.*, and acted in an arbitrary or capricious manner, *In re Carp*, 340 F.3d 15, 24 (1st Cir. 2003). The stipulated order provided for disclosure of judicial records to which there a strong presumption of public access, and "only the most compelling reason can justify [their] non-disclosure...." *Poliquin v. Garden Way*, 989 F.2d 527, 533 (1st Cir. 1993); *see also*

In re Carp, 340 F.3d at 24; *Siedle*, 147 F.3d at 10. The District Court did not consider this presumption of access in denying Kuney's motion, and no reason was submitted by the court or any party to justify nondisclosure of these documents. The District Court also abused its discretion in failing to consider the presumptive right of public access to discovery material under the Federal Rules of Civil Procedure, *Public Citizen*, 858 F.2d at 788, and the strong public policy favoring settlements, *Cities Service Oil Co. v. Coleman Oil Co.*, 470 F.2d 925, 929 (1st Cir. 1972). The District Court had no objection to the substance of the proposed stipulated order and indicated it would enter the order — but only if Bean moved to modify the Stipulated Protective Order consistent with the terms of the proposed stipulated order. This action was arbitrary or capricious and an abuse of discretion. *In re Carp*, 340 F.3d at 24.

Therefore, Kuney requests that the September 17, 2007 order be reversed and the matter remanded with instruction that the proposed stipulated order be entered. *In re Salem Suede*, 268 F.3d 42, 45 (1st Cir. 2001); *Siedle*, 147 F.3d at 12.

VI. ARGUMENT

A. The District Court Erred in Finding Moot the Motions to Intervene and Dissolve or Modify the Stipulated Protective Order

This Court reviews the question of mootness de novo. *Maine School Admin. Dist. 35 v. Mr. and Mrs. R.*, 321 F.3d 9, 17 (1st Cir. 2003); *Verhoven v. Brunswick School Comm.*, 207 F.3d 1, 5 (1st Cir. 1999). A matter becomes moot "[o]nly if it were indisputable that no form of relief could be provided." *Gowen, Inc. v. F/V Quality One*, 244 F.3d 64, 66 (1st Cir. 2001); *see also Mr. and Mrs. R.*, 321 F.3d at 18 (cases filed under the Individual with Disabilities Education Act do not become moot when the child's eligibility for services ends as long as a claim based on past deprivation of services remains). Changed circumstances that make it impossible to grant relief would render a matter moot. *Oakville Dev. Corp., v. FDIC*, 986 F.2d 611, 613 (1st Cir. 1993) (matter became moot where the foreclosure sale that the plaintiff sought to enjoin had occurred and the title to the property passed to third party). A settlement may also render a matter moot. *Shelby v. Subperformance Int'l Inc.*, 435 F.2d. 42, 45-46 (1st Cir. 2006) (appeal rendered moot where a settlement resolved of all the controverted issues between the parties).

Here, the district court erred in finding moot Kuney's motions to intervene and to dissolve or modify the Stipulated Protective Order (Docket No. 547, Kuney App., Tab 2, p. 10). *Mr. and Mrs. R.*, 321 F.3d at 18. None of the circumstances that might render a matter moot are present. *Id.* There have been no changed circumstances that would make it impossible to grant Kuney the relief sought, which is intervention and modification of the stipulated protective order. *Oakville Dev. Corp.*, 986 F.2d at 613. Unlike in *Oakville*, where the property at issue had been sold to a third party at a foreclosure sale, here, the documents Kuney seeks access to still exist and are available to Kuney if the proposed stipulated order is entered. *Id.* Nor is the matter rendered moot due to settlement. *Shelby*, 435 F 2d. at 45-46. Kuney and Bean did negotiate a settlement modifying Stipulated Protective Order, which was embodied in the proposed stipulated order. However, the district court denied Kuney's motion to enter the proposed stipulated order; the order has not been entered and the Stipulated Protected Order remains unmodified. Accordingly, the matter is still in controversy and effective relief can be granted. *Gowen*, 244 F.3d at 66.

Intervention is the appropriate method for a person who was not a party to the original proceedings to seek modification of a protective order, and Kuney sought to intervene to do so. *See Public Citizen v. Liggett*, 858 F.2d at 783-87; *see also Pansy*, 23 F.3d 778 (1994). The September 17, 2006 order is confusing in that it states: "finding as moot [547] Motion to Intervene; ..." Docket No. 547 contains Kuney's "Notice of Motions and Motion to Intervene and Motion to Dissolve or Modify the Stipulated Protective Order...." The District Court's reference to finding moot "the Motion to Intervene" could indicate that Kuney's intervention had been implicitly or tacitly allowed, and thus, at the time of the September 17, 2007 order, the motion to intervene was no longer in controversy. This may be the case because there was no express objection to the Motion to Intervene by any party or interested person in the proceeding, and Kuney had been allowed to file the stipulated proposed order and his motion to enter the proposed stipulated order. (Docket No. 557, Kuney App., Tab 10, p. 140; Docket No. 559, Kuney App., Tab 12, p. 144.)

However, Kuney's motion to dissolve or modify the Stipulated Protective Order — the other motion filed under Docket Number 547 (Kuney App., Tab 2, p. 10) — was not implicitly or tacitly approved, and the relief requested therein and later specified in the proposed stipulated order is capable of being granted. Therefore, that motion is not moot. *Mr. and Mrs. R.*, 321 F.3d at 18; *Gowen*, 244 F.3d at 66.

B. The District Court Abused Its Discretion in Denying Kuney's Motion to enter the Proposed Stipulated Order

Decisions involving modification of protective orders are reviewed for abuse of discretion. *Public Citizen v. Liggett*, 858 F.2d at 790; *see also Poliquin v. Garden Way*, 989 F.2d 527, 532 (1st Cir. 1993). "[A] district court may abuse its discretion by ignoring a material factor that deserves significant weight, relying on an improper factor, or even if it mulls over the proper mix of factors, by making a serious mistake in judgment." *Siedle v. Putnam Investments, Inc.*,

147 F.3d 7, 10 (1st Cir. 1998) ("In this instance, we discern no evidence that the district court identified and balanced the interests at stake, or that the court endeavored to determine whether any information contained in Siedle's filings actually fell within the ambit of the attorney client privilege. In the circumstances at hand, these omissions amounted to an abuse of discretion."); *see also In re Salem Suede*, 268 F.3d 42, 44-45 (1st Cir. 2001) (a court abused its discretion in denying motion to release a sealed transcript hearing, "[g]iven appellant's representation of need, their explanation, and lack of a direct counter"). In both *Siedle* and *Salem Suede*, the court remanded with directions to enter orders granting the relief appellants had requested. *Siedle*, 147 F.3d at 12; *Salem Suede*, 268 F.2d at 45.

A court also abuses its discretion when its actions are arbitrary or capricious. *See In re Carp*, 340 F.3d 15, 24 (1st Cir. 2003); *Ramirez Pomades v. Becton Dickinson & Co., S.A.*, 839 F.2d 1, 3 (1st Cir. 1988).

There are several material factors to be considered in this case. First, there is a strong presumption "favoring public access to judicial proceedings and records." *In re Carp*, 340 F.3d at 245. This presumption "stems from the premise that public monitoring of the judicial system fosters the important values of 'quality honesty and respect for our legal system.'" *Siedle*, 147 F.3d at 9-10 (quoting *FTC v. Standard Financial Management Corp.*, 830 F.2d 404, 410 (1st Cir. 1987). The presumption that the public has a right to see and copy judicial records attaches to those documents which properly come before the court in the course of an adjudicatory proceeding and which are relevant to the adjudication. That presumption, so basic to the maintenance of a fair and open judicial system and to fulfilling the public's right to know, cannot be easily overcome. *Standard Financial Management Corp.*, 830 F.2d at 412 (affirming order unsealing personal financial statements).

Thus, "only the most compelling reason can justify non-disclosure of judicial records," including evidence introduced at trial. *Poliquin v. Garden Way*, 989 F.2d at 533 (quoting *Standard Financial Management Corp.*, 830 F.2d at 410) (holding the district court abused its discretion in denying appellant's motion to release from a protective order a video deposition that had been shown to the jury, as well as interrogatory answers that had been read to the jury).

Second, under the Federal Rules, "the public has a presumptive right of access to discovery materials unless good cause for confidentiality is shown." *Public Citizen*, 858 F.2d at 788. This good cause showing requirement is eviscerated, however, where a stipulated protective order is entered that allows the parties to individually determine and designate documents as confidential and subject to the order. *See Beckman Industry, Inc. v. International Insurance Co.*, 966 F.2d

470, 476 (9th Cir. 1992) (noting that party to a blanket stipulated protective order "never had to make a good cause showing" under Fed.R.Civ. P. 26(c)).

Third, there is a longstanding, "obvious public policy" favoring the amicable settlement of litigation, and agreements accomplishing this result, will be "disregarded only for the strongest of reasons." *Cities Service Oil Co. v. Coleman Oil Co.*, 470 F.2d 925, 929 (1st Cir. 1972). Similarly, "[s]tipulations fairly entered into are favored" and "may not be disregarded or set aside at will." *TI Federal Credit Union v. DelBonis*, 72 F.3d 921, 928 (1st Cir. 1995); *see also Chao v. Hotel Oasis Inc.*, 493 F.3d 26, 31-32 (1st Cir. 2007) (quoting *TI Federal Credit Union v. DelBonis*, 72 F.3d at 928).

Here, the District Court abused its discretion in denying Kuney's motion to enter the proposed stipulated order agreed to by Kuney and Bean while stating that it would grant an identical motion filed by Bean.[4] *Siedle v. Putnam Investments, Inc.*, 147 F.3d at 10; *see also In re Carp*, 340 F.3d at 24; *Salem Suede*, 268 F.2d at 44-45. The District Court ignored "material factor[s] deserv[ing] significant weight," failed to "identify and balance the interests at stake," *Siedle v. Putnam Investments, Inc.*, 147 F.3d at 10, and acted in an arbitrary or capricious manner, *In re Carp*, 340 F.3d at 24.

The documents set forth in the proposed stipulated order—jury exhibits and the appeal appendices filed in *Bowers v. Baystate Technologies, Inc.*, 320 F.3d 1317 (Fed. Cir. 2003)—are judicial records that came before the jury, the District Court, and the Federal Circuit, as the documents were relevant in the adjudication of the case. *Standard Financial Management Corp.*, 830 F.2d at 410. That is the reason Kuney seeks to use them in his text: they enable students to view the actual documents considered by the jury and the courts. There is a strong presumption favoring public access to these judicial records and "only the most compelling reasons can justify [their] non-disclosure...." *Poliquin v. Garden Way*, 989 F.2d at 533 (quoting *Standard Financial Management Corp.*, 830 F.2d at 410).

There has been no showing or reason submitted by *any* party or person involved in this case that would overcome this presumption of public access and justify the nondisclosure of the documents set forth in the proposed stipulated protective order. *In re Salem Suede*, 268 F.3d at 44-45; *Siedle v. Putnam Investments, Inc.*, 147 F.3d at 10. Bean, who was not a party to the Stipulated Protective Order, was the only person who objected to Kuney's motion to dissolve

---

4. The order denied Kuney's motion "without prejudice; if the defendant, Robert Bean, moves to modify the stipulated protective order, consistent with the provisions of the proposed stipulated order (557), serves his motion on all other parties and that motion is unopposed 14 days after service, it will be allowed."

or modify that order. After Kuney and Bean reached a settlement, Kuney filed the proposed stipulated order agreed to by Bean providing access to the jury exhibits and appeal appendices. Kuney's motion to enter this order was unopposed. The District Court denied Kuney's motion without considering the strong presumption in favor of public access to these judicial records and where there was no showing of, or reference to, any reason that would justify their nondisclosure. The court abused its discretion in ignoring this significant factor and failing to identify or weigh Kuney's and the public's interest in access to court proceedings. *Siedle*, 147 F.3d at 10; *see also Salem Suede*, 268 F.2d at 44-45.

There is also no evidence that the District Court considered the public's "presumptive right of access [under the Federal Rules of Civil Procedure] to discovery materials unless good cause for confidentiality is shown." *Public Citizen*, 858 F.2d at 788. The Stipulated Protective Order allowed the parties to designate any document as confidential without making a showing of good cause. (Docket No. 50 ¶ 1, Kuney App., Tab 2, p. 13.) When Kuney filed his motion to dissolve or modify this order, the documents that Bean maintained were confidential were the documents that contain or reveal the source code of Baystate/Cadkey's computer software. Thus, as part of the settlement the proposed stipulated order provided " … the parties agree that all source code shall continue to remain confidential and will not be disclosed in violation of the Stipulated Protective Order." (Docket No. 557 ¶ 4, Kuney App., Tab 10, p. 141.) The District's Court's denial of Kuney's motion to enter the proposed stipulated order, which specifically exempted the source code that Bean maintained was confidential, ignored the presumption of access under the Federal Rules of Civil Procedure and was an abuse of discretion. *Siedle*, 147 F.3d at 10; *Public Citizen*, 858 F.2d at 788.

This District Court also abused its discretion by ignoring public policy favoring settlements and disregarding the proposed stipulated order signed by Kuney and Bean's counsel containing their settlement. *Siedle*, 147 F.3d at 10; *Cities Service Oil Co.*, 470 F.2d at 929. The court took no action on the proposed stipulated order filed in April 2007, and then denied Kuney's unopposed motion to enter the order. The District Court did not state a reason or indicate an objection to the proposed stipulated order. On the contrary, in denying Kuney's motion, the court indicated it would enter a stipulated order containing the exact same terms, but only if *Bean* moved for it. The result was to eviscerate the settlement Bean reached with Kuney and deny access to documents to which the public is entitled.

Furthermore, the District Court's actions in denying Kuney's unopposed motion to enter the proposed stipulated order, while stating that it would grant an identical motion from Bean, were arbitrary or capricious. *In re Carp*, 340

F.3d at 24. The proposed stipulated order designated judicial records to which the public is presumptively entitled access, and no reason has been cited that would compel their nondisclosure — not by the court or any party connected with the case. Bean, the only party to oppose Kuney's motion to dissolve or modify the Stipulated Protective Order, agreed to the disclosure of these judicial records and his counsel signed the proposed stipulated order. Any and all source code was also specifically exempted from disclosure pursuant to Kuney and Bean's settlement.

The proposed stipulated order is fair and proper, and the public is entitled access to the documents designated. The court indicated no objection to the substance of the order, and Kuney's motion to file the proposed stipulated order was unopposed. It was arbitrary and capricious to refuse to enter the order unless *Bean* moved for it. Not only did it call for waste of court resources, but it arbitrarily foreclosed public access to judicial records and proceedings.

VII. CONCLUSION

WHEREFORE, for the reasons discussed above, Kuney respectfully requests that the September 17, 2007 order be reversed and remanded with instruction that the proposed stipulated order be entered.

[Addendum and signature page redacted. The next two pages of the original brief constituted the original Notice of Appeal, along with its Exhibit A, of the District Court order appealed from. This order has apparently been stripped from the Notice of Appeal filed with the District Court and is no longer listed on the docket. Because no other documents are included in this Addendum, a table of contents is not included.]

Dated March 5, 2008   _____

George W. Kuney
The University of Tennessee College of Law
Clayton Center for Entrepreneurial Law
1505 W. Cumberland Avenue, Suite 202
Knoxville, TN 37996-1810

CERTIFICATE OF COMPLIANCE WITH RULE 32(A)

Certificate of Compliance with Type-Volume Limitation,
Typeface Requirements, and Type Style Requirements

1. This brief complies with the type-volume limitation of Fed. R. App. P. 32(a)(7)(B) because:

> This brief contains **6,446** words, excluding the parts of the brief exempted by Fed. R. App. P. 32(a)(7)(B)(iii)

2. This brief complies with the typeface requirements of Fed. R. App. P. 32(a)(5) and the type style requirements of Fed. R. App. P. 32(a)(6) because:

> This brief has been prepared in a proportionally spaced typeface using Microsoft Word 2007 in 14-point Times New Roman font

_____

George W. Kuney

Dated: January 23, 2008

CERTIFICATE OF SERVICE

I hereby certify that on January 23, 2008 I filed the foregoing *Appellant's Brief of George W. Kuney* by United States Mail with the Clerk of the First Circuit Court of Appeals, and I hereby certify that I have mailed these documents to the following parties:

[names and addresses have been redacted]

_____   _____

George W. Kuney   Date

Professor George W. Kuney (Cal # 142777, TN # 021312)
The University of Tennessee College of Law
Clayton Center for Entrepreneurial Law
1505 W. Cumberland Avenue, Suite 202
Knoxville, TN 37996-1810

NOTE: This disposition is nonprecedential.

United States Court of Appeals for the Federal Circuit

2008-1204

BAYSTATE TECHNOLOGIES, INC.,

Plaintiff,

v.

HAROLD L. BOWERS (doing business as HLB Technology),

Defendant.

PROFESSOR GEORGE W KUNEY,

Movant-Appellant

ROBERT W. BEAN and KAREN L. BEAN,

Interested Parties.

George W. Kuney, of Knoxville, Tennessee, pro se.

Appealed from: United States District Court for the District of Massachusetts

Judge Nathaniel M. Gorton

NOTE: This disposition is nonprecedential.

United States Court of Appeals for the Federal Circuit

2008-1204

BAYSTATE TECHNOLOGIES, INC.,

Plaintiff,

v.

HAROLD L. BOWERS (doing business as HLB Technology),

Defendant.

PROFESSOR GEORGE W KUNEY,

Movant-Appellant

ROBERT W. BEAN and KAREN L. BEAN,

Interested Parties.

Appeal from the United States District for the District of Massachusetts in case no. 91CV-40079, Judge Nathaniel M. Gorton.

DECIDED July 10, 2008

Before LOURIE, BRYSON, and PROST, <u>Circuit Judges</u>

PER CURIAM,

Professor George W. Kuney appeals the order of the United States District Court for the District of Massachusetts, denying his motion to intervene and his motion to modify the Stipulated Protective Order. <u>Bay State Techs., Inc. v Bowers</u>, No. 91-CV40079 (D. Mass. Sept. 14, 2007). We <u>vacate</u> and <u>remand</u>.

BACKGROUND

Baystate Technologies, Inc. ("Baystate") filed a declaratory judgment action in the District Court for the District of Massachusetts, seeking a declaration that it did not infringe Harold L, Bowers's software patent. Mr. Bowers counterclaimed for patent infringement, copyright infringement, and breach of contract. Following trial, the jury returned a verdict, and the court granted judgment for Mr. Bowers on his patent Infringement, copyright infringement, and breach of contract claims. <u>Bay State Techs., Inc. v. Bowers</u>, No 91-CV-40079 (D. Mass. Sep. 14, 2000) This court affirmed-in-part and reversed-in-part. <u>Bowers v. Baystate Techs., Inc.</u> 320 F.3d 1317 (Fed. Cir. 2003).Before Mr. Bowers could execute on his judgment, Baystate filed for bankruptcy. <u>In re CK Liquidation</u>, No. 03-44096 (Bankr. D. Mass. Aug. 22, 2003). Thereafter, Robert and Karen Bean, as judgment debtors, were added as interested parties in the case. The case was ultimately dismissed on May 4, 2006.

Professor Kuney is a law professor who is writing a detailed account of the proceedings in this case given its significance to the software industry. He seeks access to trial exhibits and other documents. Early in the litigation, however, the court entered a Stipulated Protective Order, at the request of the parties, which restricts access to those documents, On February 21, 2007, Professor Kuney filed a motion to intervene and motion to modify the Stipulated Protective Order, Mr. Bowers filed a declaration in support of Professor Kuney's motions. Mr. Bean alone opposed Professor Kuney's motion to modify the protective order. Thereafter, Professor Kuney and Mr. Bean agreed on a suitable modification to the protective order, and Professor Kuney submitted a modified Stipulated Protective Order to the court On August 21, 2007, Professor Kuney filed a motion requesting that the court grant his motion to intervene and his motion to modify the Stipulated Protective Order.

On September 14, 2007, the court issued an electronic order, denying Professor Kuney's August 21,2007, motion and finding his February 21, 2007, motion to thus be moot. The court advised that "if defendant, Robert Bean, moves to modify the stipulated protective order, consistent with the provisions of the proposed stipulated order . . . serves his motion on all other parties and that motion is unopposed 14 days after service, It will be allowed," <u>Bay State Techs., Inc. v. Bowers</u>, No 91-CV-40079 (D. Mass. Sept 14, 2007). Mr. Bean did not file a motion to modify the Stipulated Protective Order.

This appeal followed. We have jurisdiction pursuant to 28 U.S.C. § 1295(a)(2).

DISCUSSION

We review a district court's denial of a motion to intervene for abuse of discretion. <u>Geiger v. Foley Haag LLP Retirement Plan</u>, 521 F.3d 60, 64 (1st Cir. 2008). We also review a denial of a motion for modification of a protective order for abuse of discretion. <u>Saldana-Sanchez v. Lopez-Gerena</u>, 256 F.3d 1,8 (1st CiL 2001); <u>Public Citizen v. Liggett Group, Inc.</u>, 858 F.2d 775, 790 (1st Cir. 1988).

The court denied Professor Kuney's motion to intervene and motion to modify the Stipulated Protective Order in a one-paragraph order without explanation, It may be that the court denied Professor Kuney's motion to intervene simply because it considered it more expedient for Mr. Bean, as an interested party in the litigation, to move to modify the protective order. Nevertheless, Mr. Bean never acted in response to the court's order and Professor Kuney was left without access to the documents he sought.

Intervention is the proper means for a non-party to challenge a protective order. <u>Public Citizen</u>, 858 F.2d at 783 Even after judgment, courts have frequently allowed third parties to intervene to challenge a protective order. Id. at 785. Federal Rule of Civil Procedure 26(c); provides that a court may enter a protective order if "good cause" exists to protect discovery information. There is, however, a presumption of public access to judicial records. <u>Siedle v. Putnam Invs., Inc.</u>, 147 F.3d 7, 9 (1st Cir. 1998); <u>Poliquin v. Garden Way Inc.</u>, 989 F.2d 527, 533 (1st Cir. 1993) Thus, in determining whether a protective order should be modified, the court must balance the privacy interests of the parties against the public interest in access to the discovery information. <u>Siedle</u>, 147 F.3d at 10.

Here, it is not apparent whether the court engaged in a balancing and thus it is unclear if the court abused its discretion in denying Professor Kuney's motion to intervene and motion to modify the Stipulated Protective Order. Professor Kuney alleges that no party other than Mr. Bean opposed his motions and that he ultimately agreed to the modified Stipulated Protective Order that was filed with the court, that Mr. Bowers supported his motions, and that Baystate is now a corporate shell. Thus, the parties appear to have little, if any, continued interest in maintaining confidential the documents that Professor Kuney seeks. Further, Professor Kuney alleges that his ability to do scholarly work is dependent on his ability to obtain access to the documents. "[P]ublic monitoring of the judicial system fosters the important values of quality, honesty and respect for the judicial system." Id. (citation and internal quotation marks omitted). We, therefore, deem it proper to return the case to the district court for a balancing of the public and private interests in determining whether to grant or deny Professor Kuney's motions.

CONCLUSION

For the foregoing reasons, we vacate and remand the order of the District Court for the District of Massachusetts denying Professor Kuney's motion to intervene and motion to modify the Stipulated Protective Order.

Each party shall bear its own costs.

Index

Abandonment of Arguments or Issues (see also Conceding Issues or Arguments—avoiding in oral argument, Waiver), 19, 26–30

Abuse of Discretion Standard of Review, 102, 159–167, 169, 173, 194, 195, 206, 207, 257, 261

Active and Passive Voice, use and effect, 121–132, 186, 189, 197, 203

Adjectives and Adverbs, 187

Administrative Agency Decisions
federal circuit jurisdiction over, 5, 16
standards of review, 162–163

Adverse authority, dealing with, 118, 197, 199, 202

Amicus Curiae, 69, 80–82, 274

Ambiguity, Ambiguous, 105, 108, 152

Analogizing and Distinguishing cases, 117, 120–121, 198–199, 202, 279

Analysis, see Appellate Legal Analysis

Appealability, (see also Appeal by Permission, Appeal as of Right, Appellate Court Jurisdiction, Final Judgment Rule and Exceptions)
generally, 33–50, 271

appeals of interlocutory orders under 28 U.S.C. § 1292, 36–39

checkpoints, 49–50, 270–272

class certification decisions under FCRP 23(f), 33, 40–41, 50, 271

collateral order doctrine, 33, 35–36, 46–47, 49, 66, 271

exceptions to the final judgment rule, generally, 33, 35–43, 49–50, 271

final judgment rule, 33–34, 49, 271

independent duty of appellate court to determine finality and appealability of order or judgment, 34

mootness doctrine and exceptions, 30, 69, 77–79, 82, 271, 273

orders involving controlling questions of law, 28 U.S.C. § 1292(b), 39, 50 271

orders regarding injunctions—28 U.S.C. § 1292(a) (1), 38, 50, 271

partial final judgments under FCRP 54(b), 36–38, 50

pendent appellate jurisdiction, 42–43, 50, 271

Appealability, *continued*
  receivership orders—28 U.S.C.
    § 1292(a) (2), 39, 271
  review by extraordinary writ
    (writ of mandamus), 28
    U.S.C. § 1651(a), 41–42, 50,
    271
  review on writ of certiorari, 13
  state systems, 43–49, 272
Appeal as of Right, 6, 13, 15,
  33–34, 43–48
Appeal by Permission, 12–13, 16,
  41–42, 47, 49
Appellate Briefs,
  generally, 169–208, 282–284
  adverse authority, dealing with,
    118, 197, 199, 202
  argument or discussion sections,
    169, 177, 191–200, 202–204,
    207–208, 282–283
  audience, 169–174, 206,
    281–282
  authorities, ranking and using,
    117–118
  checkpoints, 206–208, 281–284
  citations to the appendix or
    record on appeal, 141, 144,
    146–147, 153–154, 157–158,
    180–182, 184, 188, 207,
  citations to factual authority,
    141, 144, 146–147, 153-154,
    157–158, 180–182, 184, 188,
    207,
  citations to legal authority,
    119–120, 141–142, 145–146,
    148–152, 157–158, 194,
    197–198, 202
  components, generally, 169,
    176–177, 207, 282
  conclusion, 169, 177, 207, 282

CRAC (Conclusion, Rule(s), Application, Conclusion) structure, 118–121, 191–192,
  195–199, 2007–28, 283
developing and delivering a message, 174–176
discussion or argument sections,
  169,177, 191–200, 202–204,
  207–208, 282–283
drafting the appellate brief, order
  and timing, 201
error, focus on, 169, 173–174,
  191, 206–207, 282
example, 289–308
drafting and editing guidelines
  and checklists, 182–183,
  188–190, 202–206
formats, 176
goals of appellate briefs, 169,
  173–176, 207, 282
headings and subheadings, 177,
  192, 196, 207, 283
heading and topic sentence outline, 204–205
jurisdictional statement, 126
message, 174–175
moot court competitions, 247,
  255–260, 266, 287
order and organization of arguments, 192–194, 207–208,
  283
persuading the appellate court,
  169, 191, 195–200, 207–208,
  282–283
policy arguments, using policy to
  persuade, 199–200, 208, 283
purpose of appellate briefs, 169,
  173–176, 207, 282
sample appellate brief and resulting order, 289–313

statement of the case, 169, 176, 179–183, 207, 282

statement of facts, 169, 176, 179, 183–190, 207, 282

statement of issues on appeal, 176–179, 207, 282

statement of the standard(s) of review, 194–195

summary of the argument, 177, 190–191,

theme, 174–175

theory of the case, 174–175

Appellate Court Jurisdiction (see also Appealability, Jurisdiction, Final Judgment Rule and Exceptions, Mootness Doctrine and Exceptions, Parties on Appeal, Standing, Subject Matter Jurisdiction)

bankruptcy appeals, 5

case and controversy requirement, 76–78, 273

direct appellate jurisdiction — courts of last resort, 13, 15, 172

diversity jurisdiction, 28-29

effect of filing notice of appeal, 51, 63–67, 272–273

failure to correctly file notice of appeal, 51, 56, 59–60, 66–67, 272

failure to timely file notice of appeal, 51, 60–63, 66–67, 272

federal circuit courts, (United States Courts of Appeals), 5–14

federal question jurisdiction, 28–29

final judgment rule, and exceptions, 28 U.S.C. § 1291, 33–34, 43–49, 271–272

intermediate appellate courts, state, 14, 42–43

jurisdiction of trial court while appeal pending, 66–67

jurisdictional statement of basis for appellate court jurisdiction, 126

mootness, 30, 69, 77–79, 273

patent cases, 5, 12

pendent appellate jurisdiction, 42–43

standing, 29, 76–77, 82, 273

state systems, 14, 43–49

subject matter jurisdiction, 19, 28–31, 76–77, 82, 94, 270–71, 273

threshold issue, 192–193, 219

Appellate Court Systems, (see also Courts of Last Resort, Federal Circuit Courts, Intermediate Appellate Courts, Supreme Courts of the United States, United States Supreme Court)

generally, 3–17

checkpoints, 16–17, 269–270,

courts of last resort, 12–16,

federal courts overview, 3–4

federal district courts, 4–5

federal circuit courts, (United States Courts of Appeals), generally, 5–14

geographic boundaries, federal circuit and district courts, 7

rules governing process and procedure, 6, 14–16,

state intermediate appellate courts, 14–15

Appellate Court Systems, *continued*
  state courts of last resort, 15–16
  United States Court of Appeal
    for the First Circuit, 7
  United States Court of Appeal
    for the Second Circuit, 8
  United States Court of Appeal
    for the Third Circuit, 8
  United States Court of Appeal
    for the Fourth Circuit, 8–9
  United States Court of Appeal
    for the Fifth Circuit, 9
  United States Court of Appeal
    for the Sixth Circuit, 9
  United States Court of Appeal
    for the Seventh Circuit, 9–10
  United States Court of Appeal
    for the Eighth Circuit, 10
  United States Court of Appeal
    for the Ninth Circuit, 10–11
  United States Court of Appeal
    for the Tenth Circuit, 11
  United States Court of Appeal
    for the Eleventh Circuit,
    11–12
  United States Court of Appeal
    for the District of Columbia
    Circuit, 12
  United States Court of Appeal
    for the Federal Circuit, 12
  United States Supreme Court,
    12–14
Appellate Legal Analysis, (see also
  Appellate Brief Writing, Appel-
  late Legal Drafting,
  Authority/Authorities, Cases,
  CRAC, Law, Rule(s), Statutes)
  generally, 101–124, 274–276
  cases, ranking, 117–118

  cases, reviewing and revisiting,
    109–112
  cases, synthesizing, 114–117
  cases, using, 112–114
  checkpoints, 122–124, 274–276
  citations to factual authority,
    141, 144, 146–147,
  153-154, 157–158, 180–182,
    184, 188, 215, 224, 264
  citations to legal authority,
    119–120, 141–142, 145–146,
    148–152,
  157–158, 194, 197–198, 202
  CRAC (Conclusion, Rule(s), Ap-
    plication, Conclusion) struc-
    ture,
  118–121, 191–192, 195–199
  error, focus on, 101
  fresh eyes, 101
  organizing a persuasive legal
    analysis, 118–121, 191–192,
    195–199
  statutes, tools for analyzing and
    interpreting, 102–109
Appellate Legal Drafting, (see also
  Appellate Briefs)
  generally, 125–139, 278
  checkpoints, 138–139, 278
  concrete vs. conceptual, 132-133,
  concision, 131–135
  context before details, 126–128
  CRAC (Conclusion, Rule(s), Ap-
    plication, Conclusion) struc-
    ture, 118–121, 191–192,
    195–199, 207
  drafting guidelines and check-
    lists, 182–183, 188–190,
    202–206
  drafting process, 135–138

editing, 125, 135, 137, 139, 175, 182, 188, 190, 205, 256–257, 259, 278

explicit structure, 129–130

familiar information before new information, 128–129

first draft, 135–136

heading and topic sentence outline, 204–205

headings, 177, 192, 196

long sentences, 134

moot court, 255–260

narration, 133

nominalizations, 133

organization, three key strategies, 125–130, 138

outline, creating an, 135

paragraphs, 130–131, 204

plain language, 132

proofreading, 137

revising and rewriting, 136–137

sentences, 131–135

tenses, 133

topic sentences, 130–131, 196, 198, 204–205

transition words, 129, 131

unfamiliar reader, 134

word choice, 131–135

Appellate Record, see Record on Appeal

Appellate Standards of Review
generally, 159–164, 166–167, 280–81

abuse-of-discretion, 159, 162–163, 167, 281

agency decisions, 163

arbitrary and capricious, 163

bench trials, 162

clearly erroneous, 159, 161–162, 167, 281

de novo, 159, 161, 167, 281

deferential and nondeferential, 160, 167, 281

explained, 159–160

independent, 161

mixed questions of fact and law, 161

other standards of review, 163

plenary, 161

questions of fact, 161–162

questions of law, 161

statements of the standard of review, 194–195

Appendix, (see also Record on Appeal)
generally, 83, 94-99,

citations to, 141, 144, 146–147, 153-154, 157–158, 180–182, 184, 188, 207 223–224, 260, 264

contents, 95–97

explained, 94–95

form, 95, 97–98

in lieu of record on appeal, 94

purpose, 94–95

Application of Law to Facts (see also CRAC), 111, 113, 119–121, 198

Argument, (see also Appellate Briefs, Appellate Legal Analysis, CRAC, Oral Argument)
argument or discussion in appellate briefs, 177, 191–200, 202–204

arguments of opponent, how to address in appellate briefs, 174–175, 197, 199,

arguments of opponent, how to address at oral argument, 220, 222–223, 231–232, 234–236

Argument, *continued*
  CRAC (Conclusion, Rule(s), Ap-
    plication, Conclusion) struc-
    ture, 118–121,
    191–192,195–199
  order and organization of argu-
    ments in appeal briefs,
    192–199, 207–208
  order and organization of argu-
    ments for oral argument,
    217–224
  persuading the appellate court,
    169, 191, 195–200, 207–208,
    282–283
  policy arguments, 199–200, 208,
    283
  summary of the argument, 177,
    190–191
Assistance, limits in moot
  court competitions, 227,
    247–250, 253, 256–258, 261,
    263–266
Audience, appellate briefs
  generally, 169–170, 207,
    281–282
  court or chambers attorneys, 6,
    13, 171–173
  courts of last resort, 13, 15,
    172–173, 206
  intermediate appellate courts, 6,
    14, 171–172, 206
  intermediate appellate courts vs.
    courts of last resort, differ-
    ences, 170
  judges or justices, 5–15, 171–173
  law clerks, 6, 13, 171–173
  panels of decision makers, 6, 14,
    170
Audience, moot court competitions, 248–249, 263–264

Audience, oral argument
  generally, 210–212, 243, 284
  bench, the, 211–212
  counsel (you), 211
  court or chambers attorneys, 6,
    13, 210–211
  courts of last resort, 13, 15, 212
  intermediate appellate courts, 6,
    14, 211–212
  judges or justices, 5–15, 211–212
  law clerks, 6, 13, 210–211
  opposing counsel, 210
  panels of decision makers, 6, 14,
    211
Authority/Authorities (See also Appellate Brief Writing, Appellate
  Legal Analysis, Appendix, Cases,
  Citation, Law(s), Record on Appeal, Rule(s))
  adverse authority, dealing with,
    118, 197, 199, 202
  binding authority, 118, 142–143
  cases, 109-118
  citations to the appendix or
    record, 141, 144, 146–147,
    153-154, 157–158, 180–184,
    188, 223–224, 180–184, 188
  citations to factual authority,
    141, 144, 146–147, 153-154,
    157–158,
    180–182, 184, 188, 223–224,
    260, 264
  citations to legal authority,
    141–142, 145–146, 148–152,
    157–158
  controlling (binding) authority,
    118, 142–143
  CRAC (Conclusion, Rule(s), Ap-
    plication, Conclusion) struc-
    ture,

using authorities with, 118–121, 191–192, 195–199
factual authority, 83–88, 94–98, 141, 144, 146–147, 153–154, 157–158, 180–184, 188, 223–224
hierarchy, 117-118, 142–144
legal authority, 102–118, 141–142, 145–146, 148–152, 157–158
mandatory authority, 118, 142–143
moot court, 254–255, 260–262, 264
nonmandatory authority, 106, 109, 118, 142–143
persuasive authority, 118, 142–143
primary authority, 142–143
optional authority, 106, 109, 118, 142–143
oral argument, 214–215, 223–224
ranking authorities, 117–118, 142–144,
reviewing authorities with a fresh eye, 101–102
secondary authority, 106, 109, 143–144
statutes, 102–109, 117–118,
table of authorities, 176, 201
using authorities, 102–118, 117–118, 145–146, 148–152, 157–158, 214–215, 223–224, 254–255, 260–262, 264
Background (see also Context), 81, 83, 96, 98, 102, 126, 176, 184, 188, 211, 274, 310
Background facts, 184, 188
Background information, 81, 126

Bankruptcy Appeals, 4-5
Bench Trials, standard of review for findings of fact, 162
Bluebooking, 148–156, 158, 204, 251, 258, 280
Briefs, see Appellate Briefs
Broad to Narrow, organization, 116, 119–120, 124, 126, 130–131, 191, 198, 276
Cannons of Construction, 107–109, 122, 275
Captions, 52–53, 66, 96, 109, 123, 251, 272
Case, Statement of the, 176, 179–183, 207
Case law, see Cases
Cases (see also Appellate Briefs, Appellate Legal Analysis, Authority/Authorities, Citation)
generally, 109–117
adverse cases, dealing with, 118, 197, 199, 202
analogizing and distinguishing, 117, 120–121, 198–199
charting, 115–117, 123–124, 276
citations to, 119–120, 141–142, 145–146, 148–152, 157–158, 194, 197–198, 202, 209, 215, 223–224, 233–234, 244, 260, 264
comparing and contrasting, 117, 120–121, 198–199
components, 109–112
CRAC (Conclusion, Rule(s), Application, Conclusion) structure, 118–121, 191–192, 195–199

Cases, *continued*
    descriptions, 115, 119–120,
        141–142, 145–146, 157,
        196–197, 205, 279
    dicta, 112, 114
    distilling rules/law from cases,
        115–117
    examples, use of cases as, 115,
        119–120, 141–142, 145–146,
        157, 196–197, 279
    explaining the rules/law using
        cases, 115–117, 119–120,
        141–142, 157, 197–198,
    facts (procedural and underly-
        ing), 110
    grouping cases, 115
    headnotes, 110, 148
    holdings, 112–113, 115
    illustrations, using cases as illus-
        trations of rules/law, 115,
        119–120,
    141–142, 145–146, 157,
        196–197, 279
    parentheticals, 112–113, 115,
        123, 156, 276
    ranking cases, 117–118, 142–144
    reviewing and revisiting cases,
        109–114
    reviewing case from most recent
        to oldest, 114
    setting out the rules/law using
        cases, 115–117, 119–120,
        141–142, 157, 197–198,
    sorting cases, 115
    summaries, 110
    synthesizing cases to identify and
        explain rules/law, 114–117
    use of cases, whether and how—
        a checklist for deciding,
        112–114, 117–118

Certificate of Compliance, 308
Certificate of Service, 55, 308
Certiorari, 3, 12–14, 16, 40, 106,
    170, 212, 252–253, 269
Charting cases, 115–117, 123–124,
    276
Charts, 7–12,143–144, 253
Checklists, 101–104, 109, 112–114,
    123, 182, 190, 204–205, 256,
    259–260, 269–288
Chronological order, 130–131, 180,
    185–186
Circuit Courts, See Federal Circuit
    Courts, Appellate Court Sys-
    tems)
Citation, Citations, Cites (See also
    Appellate Briefs, Appendix, Au-
    thority/Authorities, Cases,
    Record on Appeal)
    generally, 119–120, 133,
        141–158, 176, 180, 193–194,
        197–198, 202, 204, 206, 215,
        223–224, 234, 251, 258,
        260–261, 264, 266
    appellate briefs, 141–154, 156,
        176, 180–182, 193–194,
        197–198, 202, 204, 206
    appendix, citations to, 144,
        146–147, 153-154, 157–158,
        180–184, 188, 215, 224,
        260–261, 264,
    argument or discussion sections,
        194, 197–198, 202, 204
    Bluebook, 148–156, 158, 204,
        251, 258, 280
    cases, 119–120, 141–142,
        145–146, 148–152,157–158,
        194, 197–198, 202, 258, 260
    checkpoints, 157–158, 279–280

facts, factual authority, information, 141, 144, 146–147, 153-154, 157–158, 180–182, 188, 215, 224, 264, 279–280
 form, 141, 148–154, 158
 headnotes, 148
 how, 148–154
 legal authority, 119–120, 141–142, 145–146, 148–152, 157–158, 194, 197–198, 202, 234, 258, 260, 264
 moot court, 249, 251, 253, 256–258, 260–262, 264
 oral argument, 209, 215, 223–224, 233–234, 244
 pin citation, pin cite, 120, 145, 147, 149, 152–154, 156–157, 169, 197–198, 202, 261, 264, 279
 record on appeal, citations to, 144, 146–147, 153-154, 157–158, 180–184, 188, 215, 224, 260–261, 264
  statement of facts, 184, 188
  statement of the case, 180–182,
  statement of the standard of review, 194
 statutes, 142–143, 148
 summary of the argument, 190
 table of authorities, 176, 201
 when, 141, 145–147
 why, 141–144
Class actions, appealability of class certification orders, 33, 40–41,
Clearly Erroneous Standard of Review, 159, 161–162, 167, 281,
Clerical Errors, correction, 51, 66–67
Cold Bench, 219, 225, 227–229, 264

Collaborative writing, 258–259
Collateral Order Doctrine (see also Appealability, Final Judgment Rule and Exceptions) 33, 35–36, 46–47, 49, 66, 274
Compliance, Certificate of, 308
Concepts, 131–132, 134, 138, 243, 277
Conceding Issues or Arguments, avoiding in oral argument, 26–27, 30, 235–236
Concluding, Conclusion, in Oral Argument, 222, 229–230, 244,
Conclusion Section of Appellate Brief, 169, 177, 207, 282
Conclusion, in the CRAC (Conclusion, Rule(s), Application, Conclusion) Format 195–196, 199, 119–121
Conclusions of Law, appellate standard of review for, 161
Concrete, value of being concrete, 82, 132, 138, 186–187, 189, 197, 200, 203, 209, 213, 221–222, 242–244, 254, 277, 284, 286
Constitutional Provisions (see also Authority, Authorities), 142–143
Constitutional Standing, 29, 76–77, 82, 273
Context, 21–22, 83, 96–97, 104, 107–108, 111, 125–128, 138, 160, 176, 178, 186, 188, 191, 193, 205, 215–216, 221–222, 232, 243, 253–254, 262–263, 277, 285
Context before Details, 125–128, 191, 205
Correcting Errors or Omissions in the Record, 89–90, 273

Court or Chambers Attorneys, 6, 13, 171–173, 210–211

Court Rules, 6, 14–16

Court Websites, 6, 14–16

Courts of Appeals, (see also Appellate Court Systems, Circuit Courts, Intermediate Appellate Courts), 5–12, 14–15, 171–172, 211–212, 206, 269–270, 281

Courts of Last Resort, 13, 15–17, 151, 172–173, 212, 243, 284

CRAC (Conclusion, Rule(s), Application, Conclusion) Structure, 118–121, 191–192, 195–200, 283

Critiquing Teammates' Work, moot court, 259

Cross-Appeal, 76

Current Structure of Federal Appellate Courts, 5–14

Dead or Quiet Bench, 219, 225, 227–229, 264

Deadlines, notice of appeal, 56–59

Deadlines, record on appeal, 25–26, 89–90

Death Penalty, automatic review by courts of last resort, 15, 172, 212

Decision Making, 171–173

Decisions, see Cases, Opinions

De-emphasis, 186–187, 189, 203

Deference, as aspect of appellate standard of review, 159–161

Defined Terms, 134, 153, 190, 206

De Novo Standard of Review, 159, 161, 163, 167, 281

Details, 125–128, 191, 205

Developing and Delivering a Message, appellate briefs, 174–176

Dicta, 112, 114, 123, 276

Differences between Moot Court and Real Life Appeals, 247–248, 250, 255–256, 260, 263–265

Discovery Order, review of, 42, 71

Discussion Sections, Appellate Briefs, 177, 191–200, 202–204, 207–208, 282–283

Distilling Rules/Law from Cases, 115–117

Distinguishing Cases, 117, 120–121, 198–199, 202

District Courts, Federal, 4–5

Dividing the Work of Moot Court Teams, 254–255, 258–261

Docketing Statements, 55

Drafting, generally, see Appellate Legal Drafting

Drafting Guidelines and Checklists, 182–183, 188–190, 202–206

Drafting Process, 135–138

Dress, Moot Court, 265

Dress, Oral Argument, 240

Editing, 125, 135, 137, 139, 175, 182, 188, 190, 205, 256–257, 259, 278

Ejusdem generis, 108

Electronic Filing, 56

Electronic Records, 58, 84, 86, 88

Elements, 65, 102, 104, 107, 111, 116, 119, 124, 127, 186, 194, 276

Emphasis, citations and quotations, 144, 146, 148, 156,

Emphasis of Favorable Facts and Arguments, 185–189, 191, 203–204

En Banc, 6, 14–15

Entry of Judgment, 24, 35–38, 56–62

Error, Errors
  generally, 19–31, 159–166, 207, 282
  appellate briefs, 169, 173–174, 191, 206–207, 282
  appearance in the record, requirement, 83, 98, 270, 274
  clerical errors, 51, 66–67
  correcting errors or omissions in the record, 89–90, 273
  error correction, role of appellate courts, 6, 14–15, 17, 170–172, 206, 270, 281–282
  evidentiary error, 20–22, 163, 270
  focus on error, 101–169, 169, 173–174, 206–207, 280, 282
  fundamental error, 19, 27–28, 31, 271
  harmless error, 164–167, 174, 178, 192–193, 207, 221, 281–282
  issues on appeal, 169, 177–178, 207, 282
  plain error, 19, 27–28, 31, 271
  preservation of error, 19–31, 215, 270–271
  proofing errors, 132, 137, 139, 175, 183, 190, 247, 249, 251–252, 256–258, 206, 278, 287
  refuting error, 169, 173–174, 191, 206–207, 282
  reversible error, 164–167, 174, 178, 192–193, 207, 221, 281–282
  showing error, 169, 173–174, 191, 206–207, 282
  standards of review, 159–164, 167, 174, 194–195, 278
  structural errors, 164–165, 281
  subject matter jurisdiction, error regarding, 19, 28–31, 271
Exhibits, 20–22, 55, 84–86, 96, 145, 184, 226
Explanation of the Law/Rules, Law (See also Appellate Briefs, Appellate Legal Analysis, Appellate Legal Drafting, CRAC), 111, 115–116, 120, 123, 128, 141–142, 145, 157, 197, 205, 257, 279
Explicit, 125–126, 128–130, 135, 138, 191–192, 205, 277–278
Extraordinary Writ, review by, 33, 41–43, 45, 50, 271–272
Eye Contact, importance during oral argument, 232, 241, 245
Factors, 37, 61, 65, 67, 70, 94, 102, 104, 111, 115–116, 119–120, 123–124, 127, 162–163, 186, 197–198, 202–203, 276
Facts (see also Appendix, Appellate Briefs, Appellate Legal Drafting, Statement of Facts)
  analogizing, 117, 120–121, 198–199, 202
  application of law to, 111, 113–114, 120, 127–128, 198, 208, 276
  background or contextual facts, 184, 188
  citations to, 141, 144, 146–147, 153-154, 157–158, 180–182, 188, 215, 224, 264, 279–280
  de-emphasis of unfavorable facts, 186–187, 189, 203
  distinguishing, 117, 120–121, 198–199, 202
  emphasis of favorable facts, 185–189, 191, 203–204

Facts, *continued*
  facts outside the record, judicial
    notice, 83, 89–93, 98, 274
  favorable facts, 185–189, 191,
    203–204
  findings of fact, standards of re-
    view, 162–163
  holdings, 112, 114
  illustrating the law/rules with
    facts from cases, 115,
    119–120,
  141–142, 145–146, 157,
    196–197, 279
  material facts, 83, 184, 187
  mixed questions of law and fact,
    161
  moot court, 252–254, 257–261,
    264, 266, 287
  past tense, use for fact that have
    occurred, 133
  placement of facts, 185–189,
    191, 203–204
  oral argument, 209–210,
    214–216, 223–224, 227–228,
    233–235, 237–239, 243–244,
    284–285
  procedural facts, 110, 123, 176,
    179–183, 207, 282
  review of facts with fresh eyes,
    101
  statement of the case, 176,
    179–183, 207, 282
  statement of facts, 126–127, 130,
    169, 175–176, 183–190, 201,
    205, 207, 282, 284
  statement of issues, essential
    facts raising, 176, 178–179
  underlying facts, 110, 113,
    117–118, 123, 203, 276

Factual Authority, 141, 144–147,
  153-154, 157–158, 180–182,
  188, 215, 223–224, 264,
  279–280
Factual Background, Context, 81,
  178, 188, 215–216, 253, 274
Federal Agencies,
  federal circuit jurisdiction over
    appeals from federal agencies, 5,
    16
  standards of review, 162–163
Federal Circuit Courts (United
  States Courts of Appeals), see
  also Appellate Court Systems
  generally, 5–14
  appeal as of right to circuit
    courts, 6
  geographic boundaries, 7
  en banc hearings, 6
  judges, generally, 5–6
  judges, lifetime tenure, 4
  judges, number per circuit, 5–14
  judges, senior status, 6
  jurisdiction, 5–6, 12, 28–29
  likelihood of affirmance, 6
  panels, 6
  rules of procedure, 6
  United States Court of Appeal
    for the First Circuit, 7
  United States Court of Appeal
    for the Second Circuit, 8
  United States Court of Appeal
    for the Third Circuit, 8
  United States Court of Appeal
    for the Fourth Circuit, 8–9
  United States Court of Appeal
    for the Fifth Circuit, 9
  United States Court of Appeal
    for the Sixth Circuit, 9

United States Court of Appeal
for the Seventh Circuit, 9–10
United States Court of Appeal
for the Eighth Circuit, 10
United States Court of Appeal
for the Ninth Circuit, 10–11
United States Court of Appeal
for the Tenth Circuit, 11
United States Court of Appeal
for the Eleventh Circuit,
11–12
United States Court of Appeal
for the District of Columbia
Circuit, 12
United States Court of Appeal
for the Federal Circuit, 12
Filing the Notice of Appeal, (see
also Initiating an appeal, Notice
of Appeal)
generally, 51, 55–66, 272
effect of filing notice of appeal,
generally, 51, 63–67, 272,
failure to correctly file notice of
appeal, 56, 59–60, 67, 272
failure to timely file notice of appeal, 60–63, 67, 272
jurisdiction of trial court after
filing of notice, 66, 272
location, 55–56, 66, 272
premature notices of appeal,
59–60, 66, 272
stays pending appeal, 63–66,
272
time limits, generally, 56–57, 66,
272
time limits, federal system,
57–58, 66, 272
time limits other jurisdictions,
58–59, 66, 272

Final-Judgment Rule and Exceptions (see also Appealability, Appellate Court Jurisdiction,
Collateral Order Doctrine),
generally, 33–50, 271
appeal as of right, 6, 13, 15,
33–34, 43–48
appeal by permission, 12–13, 16,
41–42, 47, 49
appeals of interlocutory orders
under 28 U.S.C. § 1292, 36–39
checkpoints, 49-50, 270–272
class certification decisions
under FCRP 23(f), 33,
40–41, 50, 271
collateral order doctrine, 33,
35–36, 46–47, 49, 66, 271
exceptions to the final judgment
rule, generally, 35–43, 271
final judgment rule, 33–34, 271
independent duty of appellate
court to determine finality
and appealability of order or
judgment, 34
orders involving controlling
questions of law, 28 U.S.C.
§ 1292(b), 39, 271
orders regarding injunctions—28
U.S.C. § 1292(a)(1), 38, 271
partial final judgments under
FCRP 54(b), 36–38
pendent appellate jurisdiction,
42–43, 271
receivership orders—28 U.S.C.
§ 1292(a)(2), 39, 271
review by extraordinary writ
(writ of mandamus), 28
U.S.C. § 1651(a), 41–42, 271
state systems, 43–49, 272
Findings, 54, 95, 160, 162–163

First Draft, 135–136, 139, 278

Footnotes, 26, 109, 122, 275

Forfeiture (see also, Abandonment of Arguments or Issues, Conceding Issues or Arguments, avoiding in oral Argument, Waiver), 19, 26–30

Fresh Eyes, Look, Perspective, 101–102, 105, 122, 136, 214, 274–275

Friendly Questions, handling in oral argument and moot court, 237, 264

General to Specific, 116, 119, 124, 126, 130–131, 185, 191, 203, 276

Grouping Cases, as part of case synthesis, 115

Habeas Corpus, 94, 165

Harmless Error, 159–160, 164–167, 169, 173–174, 177–178, 182, 185, 192–193, 206–207, 221, 281–283

Heading and Topic Sentence Outline, 204–205, 208, 284

Headings, 119, 130, 169, 175–177, 186, 192, 194, 196, 201–205, 207, 282–283

Headnotes, 110, 123, 148

Hierarchy of Authority, 113, 117–118, 142, 151, 157, 195, 279

Hierarchy of Federal Courts, 4

Holding, 112–115, 118, 123, 276

Hypothetical Questions in Oral Argument, 235–236, 245, 286

Illustrations, Using of Cases as Illustrations of Rules/Law, 115, 119–120, 141–142, 145–146, 157, 196–197, 279

Immunity from Suit, 24, 36, 47

In forma pauperis, 55, 95

Injunction, Injunctive Relief, 13, 38, 43–44, 46, 51, 63–65, 67, 273

Initiating an Appeal, (see also Filing the Notice of Appeal, Notice of Appeal)

generally, 51–67

contents of notice of appeal, 52–55

effect of filing notice of appeal, generally, 51, 63–67, 272,

effect of post-trial motions on time limits for, 57–59

failure to correctly file notice of appeal, 56, 59–60, 67, 272

failure to timely file notice of appeal, 60–63, 67, 272

filing the notice of appeal, generally, 51, 55–63, 67, 272

jurisdiction of trial court after initiating appeal, 66, 272

location for filing notice of appeal, 55–56, 66, 272

premature notices of appeal, 59–60, 66, 272

stays pending appeal, 63–66, 272

time limits, generally, 56–57, 66, 272

time limits, federal system, 57–58, 66, 272

time limits, other jurisdictions, 58–59, 66, 272

Interlocutory Appeals, see also Appealability, Appellate Jurisdiction, Collateral Order Doctrine, Final Judgment Rule and Exceptions

generally, 33, 38–50, 65, 271

appeals of interlocutory orders under 28 U.S.C. § 1292, 36-39
class certification decisions under FCRP 23(f), 33, 40–41, 50, 271
collateral order doctrine, 33, 35–36, 46–47, 49, 66, 271
exceptions to the final judgment rule, generally, 35–43, 271
final judgment rule, 33–34, 271
orders involving controlling questions of law, 28 U.S.C. § 1292(b), 39, 271
orders regarding injunctions—28 U.S.C. § 1292(a)(1), 38, 271
pendent appellate jurisdiction, 42-43, 271
receivership orders—28 U.S.C. § 1292(a)(2), 39, 271
review by extraordinary writ (writ of mandamus), 28 U.S.C. § 1651(a), 41–42, 271
state systems, 43–49, 272
Intermediate Appellate Courts, (see also Appellate Court Systems, Appellate Jurisdiction, Courts of Appeals, Federal Circuit Courts)
appellate jurisdiction in, federal 3, 5–6, 16, 269
appellate jurisdiction in, state 3, 14, 17, 42–43, 269–270
audience for appellate briefs, 169–172, 174, 206, 281
audience for oral argument, 209, 211–212, 227, 243, 284
authority of cases from, 142–143, 152
federal circuit courts, generally, 3, 5–14, 16, 269

focus on error correction, 6, 14, 17, 170–171, 206, 270
judges, federal circuit courts, 3, 5–12, 16
judges, state intermediate appellate courts, 14, 16
likelihood of affirmance, 6, 172, 206, 269,
procedure, rules governing, 3, 6, 14–17, 269
state intermediate appellate courts, generally, 3, 14–15, 270
Intervention, 69–72, 82, 121, 273
Introduction, Oral Argument and Moot Court, 227–228, 262
IRAC, (Issue, Rule, Application, Conclusion) Format101, 118–121
Issues on Appeal (see also Abandonment of Arguments or Issues, Appellate Briefs, Statement of Issues on Appeal, Conceding Issues or Arguments, Avoiding in Oral Argument, Waiver)
appendix, documents pertaining to issues on appeal, 94, 96, 144
CRAC, use of to discuss issues on appeal, 118–121, 191–192, 195–199, 283
drafting process, testing issues on appeal,135–136, 139
facts pertaining to issues on appeal, 184–185, 192
heading and topic sentence outline, testing issues on appeal, 205
issues that become moot, 69, 77, 82, 89, 271, 273

Issues on Appeal, *continued*
  issues raised in amicus briefs, 81
  moot court, in, 247–250,
    252–257, 260, 262, 266, 287
  organization in appellate briefs,
    192–195, 208, 283
  oral argument, at, 210, 214–216,
    218–219, 223, 235–236, 244,
    285
  preserving issues on appeal,
    23–26, 30, 235–236, 270–271
  statement of issues on appeal,
    87, 169, 176–179, 191, 201,
    207, 282
Italics, 148, 150, 196
Joint appendix, 25, 98, 182
Judges, Justices, (see also Appellate
  Court Systems, Federal Circuit
  Courts, Intermediate Appellate
  Courts)
  audience for briefs, courts of last
    resort, 172–173, 206
  audience for briefs, intermediate
    appellate courts, 171–173,
    206
  audience for oral argument,
    courts of last resort, 211–212
  audience for oral argument, in-
    termediate appellate courts,
    210–211
  audience for oral argument,
    non-verbal communication,
    241–243
  federal circuit courts, 3–12, 16
  moot court, 248–249, 256, 260,
    263–264
  state intermediate appellate
    courts, 14, 16
  state courts of last resort, 15, 17
  United States Supreme Court, 13

Judicial Notice,
  generally, 83, 89–94, 98, 274
  facts capable of accurate and
    ready determination 91, 93
  facts generally known, 91–92
Judgment, Judgments (see also Final
  Judgment Rule and Exceptions)
  adverse judgments, 70–71,
    74–76
  developing a message for appel-
    late brief, focus on judgment,
    174
  entry of judgment, 24, 35–39,
    45, 56–64, 72–73, 85, 87
  favorable judgments, 74–76
  judgment below, stays pending
    appeal, 51, 63–67
  judgment as a matter of law, mo-
    tion for, 24–25
  partial judgments, 33, 36–38, 50
  statement of the cases, descrip-
    tion of judgment, 180,
    182–183
  summary judgment, 24, 34
  vacatur of judgment, 58, 60, 79,
    82, 273
Jurisdiction, (see also Appealability,,
  Appellate Court Jurisdiction, Jurisdiction, Final Judgment Rule
  and Exceptions, Mootness Doctrine and Exceptions, Parties on
  Appeal, Standing, Subject Matter
  Jurisdiction
  jurisdiction of trial court while
    appeal pending, 66–67
  effect of notice of appeal on trial
    court jurisdiction, 66–67
  jurisdictional statement, 126
  pendent appellate jurisdiction,
    42, 50

subject matter jurisdiction, 19,
   28–31, 76–77, 82, 94,
   270–71, 273
Jury Instructions, 22–23, 25, 28,
   30, 270
Jury Verdicts, standard of review,
   162,
Law, Laws (see also Appellate Legal
   Analysis, Authority/Authorities,
   Cases, Citations, CRAC, Rule(s),
   Statutes)
   application of law to facts, 111,
      113, 119–121, 198
   cannons of construction,
      107–109, 122, 275
   citation to 119–120, 141–142,
      145–146, 148–152, 157–158,
      194, 197–198, 202, 234, 258,
      260, 264
   constitutional provisions,
      142–143,
   distilling laws from cases,
      115–117
   explanation of the law/rules,
      115–117, 119–120, 123,
      141–142, 157, 197–198, 205,
      237, 279
   illustrations of the law/rules,
      115, 119–120, 141–142,
      145–146, 157, 196–197, 279
   law/rule portion of CRAC,
      119–121, 196–197
   questions of law, 161
   setting out the law/rules, 115,
      117, 119–120
   statements of law, 101–102, 111,
      115–117, 123–124, 141–142,
      145, 157
Legal Analysis, See Appellate Legal
   Analysis

Legal Authority, see Appellate Legal
   Analysis, Authority/Authorities,
   Cases, Citation, CRAC,
   Law/Laws, Rules, Statutes,
Legalese, 132, 134, 138, 277
Legislative History, 101, 106–107,
   122, 142–144, 152, 158, 200,
   254, 260, 275, 280
Logical Order and Organization,
   104, 199, 124, 130–131,
   136–139, 185–186, 189, 192,
   203–205, 276–278
Mandamus, writ of, 41–42, 271
Mandatory and Nonmandatory,
   Authorities, (see also Author-
   ity/Authorities, Citation), 106,
   109, 118, 142–144
Material Facts, 83, 184, 187
Message, developing and delivering
   in appellate briefs, 174–176
Misstatements,
   correcting in the record, 90
   handling at oral Argument, 227,
      230, 236–237
Mixed Questions of Law and Fact,
   standard of review, 161
Moot Court Competitions
   generally, 247–267, 287–288
   audience, 248–249, 256,
      263–264, 266
   brief writing, generally,
      255–260, 266
   brief writing, goals, 255–258
   brief writing, importance of
      proofing, 256–258, 266,
   brief writing, three main prob-
      lems of lower scoring briefs,
      256–258
   brief writing, working collabora-
      tively, 258–260

Moot Court Competitions, *continued*
  checkpoints, 266–267
  context, learning and under-
    standing the context sur-
    rounding the problem, 254
  deciding which competition to
    enter, 247, 250–251, 266
  differences between moot court
    and real life appeals, 247–248,
    250, 255–256, 260, 263–265
  getting started, 250–255
  goals, 249–250
  oral argument, generally,
    260–267
  oral argument, courtroom and
    competition demeanor, 265
  oral argument, dead bench,
    264–265
  oral argument, formality, 265
  oral argument, friendly ques-
    tions, 264
  oral argument goals, 260
  oral argument, handling ques-
    tions, 263–265,
  oral argument, hostile questions,
    263–264
  oral argument,
    introduction/opening, 262
  oral argument, practice rounds,
    262–263
  oral argument, preparation,
    260–263
  oral argument, talking points,
    261
  outside assistance, 251
  purpose, 248
  research, 254–255, 266
  reviewing and understanding the
    problem, 252–254, 266

  understanding the rules and de-
    vising a timeline, 251–252
Mootness Doctrine and Exceptions,
  generally, 30, 77–79, 82, 271,
    273
  case or controversy requirement,
    77, 273
  definition/explanation of the
    mootness doctrine, 77
  dismissal, 82
  exceptions to the mootness doc-
    trine, 78, 82, 273
  legally cognizable interest re-
    quirement, 77–78
  mootness by reason of settle-
    ment, 79, 82, 273
Motions,
  generally, 19, 23–25, 30, 57–59
  judgment as a matter of law
    (JMOL), motion for, 24–25
  new trial, 25,
  post-trial motions, effect on time
    limits to file notice of appeal,
    57–59
  post-trial motions, preserving
    error for appeal, 24–25
  pre-trial motions, preserving
    error for appeal, 23–24
  for stay pending appeal, 64–66
Multiple Drafts, 135–137
Narration, 133, 138, 228, 235, 277
Negative Authorities, 118, 197, 199,
  202
Nominalizations, 133, 138, 277
Notice of Appeal (see also Filing the
  Notice of Appeal, Initiating an
  Appeal)
  generally, 51–67

contents, basic requirements federal and many state systems, 52–53

contents, further requirements — certain state systems, 53–55

filing notice of appeal, generally, 51, 63–67, 272,

effect of filing notice of appeal, 63–66, 272

effect of post-trial motions on time limits for filing notice of appeal, 57–59

failure to correctly file notice of appeal, 56, 59–60, 67, 272

failure to timely file notice of appeal, 60–63, 67, 272

filing the notice of appeal, generally, 51, 55–63, 67, 272

jurisdiction of trial court after filing notice of appeal, 66, 272

location for filing notice of appeal, 55–56, 66, 272

premature notices of appeal, 59–60, 66, 272

stays pending appeal, 63–66, 272

time limits, generally, 56–57, 66, 272

time limits, federal system, 57–58, 66, 272

time limits, other jurisdictions, 58–59, 66, 272

Objections, role in preserving error for appeal

generally, 19–23, 25, 30, 270

evidentiary objections, 20–22

objections to conduct, statements, 22

objections regarding jury instructions, 22–23

Opinions, see Cases

Opponent's Positions and Arguments, preparing for and handling

appellate briefs, 96, 101, 118, 120, 175, 183, 185, 187, 195, 199–200

oral argument, 213–215, 217, 220, 226, 230, 235

Optional Authority, 118, 142–143

Oral argument

generally, 209–245, 284–286

aiding the bench, 209–210, 213, 226, 231, 243–245

answering questions, generally, 209, 231–239, 245 (see also questions)

answering questions, immediately and directly, 231–232, 245

answering questions, a multi-step process, 232–234, 245

appendix, citations to 223–224

audience, generally, 210–212

audience, bench, the, 211–212

audience, counsel (you), 211

audience, court or chambers attorneys, 6, 13, 210–211

audience, courts of last resort, 13, 15, 212

audience, intermediate appellate courts, 6, 14, 211–212

audience, judges or justices, 5–15, 211–212

audience, law clerks, 6, 13, 210–211

audience, opposing counsel, 210

Oral argument, *continued*
  audience, panels of decision
    makers, 6, 14, 211
  authorities and cases, review,
    knowledge and use of, 209,
    215, 223–224, 233–234, 244
  body language, 241–242
  checkpoints, 243–245, 284–286
  citing authorities and cases, 209,
    215, 223–224, 233–234, 244
  concluding, conclusion, 222,
    229–230, 244–245
  conduct at counsel table, 240,
    242
  continuing with your argument,
    218, 233–234
  courtroom decorum and de-
    meanor, 239–243, 245
  creating a good impression,
    239–240
  dead or quiet bench, 227–229
  delivery, 241–243
  distracting gestures, 225, 242
  effects of the court's ruling,
    216–217, 220–221
  eye contact, 241
  facts, knowledge, use, and cita-
    tions to, 209–210, 214–216,
    223–224, 227–228, 233–235,
    237–239, 243–244, 284–285
  flexible, importance of being,
    226, 244
  goals, 209, 213–214, 226, 244
  introduction, opening, 221–222,
    227–228, 244–245
  knowing the case, 214,
  knowing the context, 215–216
  knowing the facts, 214–215
  knowing the law, 214

  knowing the rules, procedures,
    and format, 225–226
  knowing what you are asking the
    court to do and the possible
    effects, 216–217, 220–221
  listening, 226, 243, 245
  materials, preparing for the
    courtroom, 222–224, 244
  manila file folder, use at podium,
    222–224, 244
  non-verbal communication,
    241–242, 245
  organization, 217–224, 227–230,
    244–245
  physical appearance, 240
  practice, becoming conversant,
    224–225
  preparing for oral argument,
    generally, 213–226
  presenting your argument, gen-
    erally, 227–230
  presenting your argument, con-
    cluding, 229–230
  presenting your argument, the
    opening, 227–228
  presenting your argument, main
    argument—the favorable
    talking points, 228–229
  purposes of oral argument, 210,
  questions, generally, 209,
    231–239, 245, 286
  questions asking for a conces-
    sion, 235
  questions containing inaccurate
    information or misstatements,
    236
  questions, favorable, friendly,
    237
  questions, hostile, 234–235
  questions, hypothetical, 235–236

questions, irrelevant, 238
questions, multiple posed at
    once, or in succession,
    238–239
questions, multi-part, 238
questions, simple, 234
questions you do not know the
    answer to, 238
questions you do not under-
    stand, 237–238
rebuttal, 230
returning to your argument, 218,
    233–234
speaking, 242–243
talking points, as basis of your
    argument, generally, 209,
    217–224, 227–229, 233–234,
    244–245
talking points, areas of concern,
    220
talking points, arguments in
    your favor, 219, 228–229
talking points, deciding on,
    219–220,
talking points, developing,
    217–221
talking points, effects of court's
    ruling, 220–221
talking points, explained,
    217–218
talking points, how to use,
    217–218, 223–224, 228–230
talking points, favorable 219,
    228–229
talking points, organization,
    217–220, 223
time limits, 225–226, 229–230
Organization (see also, Appellate
    Briefs, Appellate Legal Drafting,
    CRAC

generally, 125–130, 138,
appellate briefs, 176–177,
    179–180, 182–183, 185–189,
    191–200, 203–205, 207–208
argument/discussion, 192–200,
    203–205, 207–208
context before details, 125–128,
    138
CRAC (Conclusion, Rule(s), Ap-
    plication, Conclusion) Struc-
    ture, 118–121, 191–192,
    195–200, 283
explicit structure, 125, 129–130,
    138
familiar information before new
    information, 128–129, 138
linking information, 128–129
oral argument, 217–224,
    227–230, 244–245
outline, creating an, 135
paragraphs, 125, 130–131, 138
statement of the case, 179–180,
    182–183
statement of facts, 183–189
summary of argument, 190
three key strategies for organiz-
    ing appellate legal drafting,
    125–130, 138
Outline, 135, 204–205, 208, 284
Paragraphs,
    generally, 119, 125, 130–131,
    138, 186, 188–190, 194, 197,
    202–205, 277
    rule paragraphs, 119, 197
    three essential requirements,
    130–131
    topic sentences, 119, 125,
    130–131, 136, 138, 189,
    196–197, 203–205, 208, 277,
    284

Parenthetical Case Descriptions, Parentheticals, 113, 115, 123, 156, 276

Parties on Appeal (see also Constitutional Standing, Mootness Doctrine and Exceptions)
generally, 69–82, 273–274
aggrieved parties, 69–70, 74–76, 82, 273
amicus curiae, 69, 80–82, 274
appeal by non-parties, 70–71
death of a party, 72–73
intervenors, intervention, 69, 71–72, 82, 121, 273
mootness doctrine and exceptions, 69, 77–78, 82, 273
mootness by reason of settlement, 79, 82, 273
parties, 70
standing, 29, 76–77, 82, 273
substitution of parties, 72–74

Passive and Active Voice, use and effect, 121–132, 186, 189, 197, 203

Patent Cases, 5, 12

Pendent Appellate Jurisdiction, Review 42–43

Persuading the Appellate Court, (see also Appellate Briefs, Appellate Legal Analysis, Appellate Legal Drafting, CRAC, Oral Argument, Organization), 118–121, 124, 174–176, 195–200, 203–204, 207–208

Persuasive authority, 118, 142–143

Pinpoint Citations, Pin Cites, importance of, 120, 149, 152, 156–157, 197–198, 202, 261, 264, 279

Plain Error, 19, 27–28, 31, 271

Plain Meaning, 101, 104–105, 108, 122, 275

Plain Language, 132, 138, 277

Plenary Review, 161

Point Headings, 119, 130, 169, 175–177, 186, 192, 194, 196, 201–205, 207, 282–283

Policy Arguments, 199–200, 208, 284

Practice arguments (See also Oral Argument, Moot Court Competitions), 224–225, 244, 262–263, 267

Preservation of Error (see also Objections, Constitutional Standing, Jurisdiction, Mootness Doctrine and Exceptions, Subject Matter Jurisdiction)
generally, 19–31, 270–271
arguments and conduct of counsel and others , 22, 30
briefing the appeal, 26
checkpoints, 30–31, 270–271
evidentiary errors, 20–21, 30
general rule regarding preservation of error, 19–20, 30
general rule, exceptions, 27–31
mootness, 30–31
jury instructions, 22–23, 30
oral argument, 26–27, 30
plain or fundamental error, 27–28, 31
post trial motions, 24–25, 30
preservation of error in the trial court, 20–25, 30
preservation of error during the appeal, 25–27, 30
pre-trial motions, 23–24, 30

record or appendix on appeal,
    25–26, 30
responsive pleadings, 23–25
standing, 29–31
subject matter jurisdiction,
    28–28, 31
Primary authority, 142–143
Proofing, Proofreading, 125, 135,
    137, 139, 175, 185, 188, 190,
    201–202, 204, 208, 249,
    256–258, 278, 284
Pro se parties, 52–53, 66, 272
Questions of Fact, 161–163
Questions of Law, 39, 161
Questions at Oral Argument, See
    Oral Argument: answering ques-
    tions, questions
Quotations,
    generally, 141–142, 144–145,
        147–148, 154–158,
    how, 154–156, 158
    when, 147–148, 158
    why, 141, 144–145, 157
Ranking Authorities and Cases,
    117–118, 142–144,
Reader, Readers,
    court or chambers attorneys, 6,
        13, 171–173
    judges or justices, 5–15, 171–173
    law clerks, 6, 13, 171–173
    panels of decision makers, 6, 14,
        170
    perspective, 134, 137
    unfamiliar reader, 128, 134, 139,
        188, 196, 203, 278
Reading, disfavored at oral argu-
    ment, 241
Reading Aloud, as editing and
    proofing technique, 137

Rebuttal, 226, 230, 245
Receivership Orders, appeals from,
    39, 44–46, 50, 271
Record on Appeal (see also Appen-
    dix, Authorities, Facts, Preserva-
    tion of Error)
    generally, 83–99, 274
    agreed statements, 88
    appendix, (see also Appendix),
        83, 94–99
    background and context for ap-
        pellate review, 83
    certified transcript, 86
    checkpoints, 98–99
    contents, 84–88, 98, 274
    correcting and expanding the
        record on appeal, 89–94
    correcting errors or omissions in
        the record, 89–90, 98
    documents filed with the trial
        court—the clerk's file, 83–86,
        98
    error, requirement that error ap-
        pear in the record, 83
    foundation on which appellate
        court bases its decision, 83
    general rule that an appellate
        court may consider only what
        was in
    the trial court record, 89
    inherent authority of appellate
        courts to supplement record,
        93–94, 98
    judicial notice, generally, 83,
        89–94, 98, 274
    judicial notice, facts capable of
        accurate and ready determina-
        tion 91, 93

Record on Appeal, *continued*
  judicial notice, facts generally
    known, 91–92
  process and procedures for
    preparing, 89–90
  purpose, 83, 98
  record of oral proceedings,
    86–88, 98
  reporter's transcript, 86
  transcript, 86–87, 98
  transcript unavailable, 88
Recusal, 42, 212
Rehearing en banc, 6
Relief Pending Review (see also Filing Notice of Appeal, Initiating an Appeal), 63–66
Reply Briefs, 26, 176
Research
  generally, 50, 59, 104, 109,
    174–175, 200
  moot court, 253–255, 260–261,
    266, 287
Reversible versus Harmless Error,
    159, 164–167, 281
Review as of Right, 3, 6–7, 13,
    15–17, 46–49, 170, 269–270,
Review, Discretionary, 3, 5, 15–17,
    105–106, 160, 170, 172–173,
    212, 269–270
Review, Standards of, see Standards
    of Review
Reviewing Authorities and Cases,
    109–114, 123–124, 209, 215,
    223–224, 233–234, 244
Revising, (see also, Appellate Legal
    Drafting), 125, 135–137, 139,
    278
Rewriting, 125, 135–137, 139, 278
Right of Appeal (See Review as of
    Right, Discretionary Appeal, Appealability, Appellate Court Jurisdiction, Final Judgment Rule and Exceptions)
Roadmaps, 3, 19, 33, 51, 69, 83,
    101, 125, 141, 159, 169–170,
    209–210, 247
Rule, Rules, (see also Appellate
    Legal Analysis, Authority/Authorities, Cases, Citation, CRAC, Statutes)
  application of rules to facts, 111,
    113, 119–121, 198
  cannons of construction,
    107–109, 122, 275
  citation to 119–120, 141–142,
    145–146, 148–152, 157–158,
    194, 197–198, 202, 234, 258,
    260, 264
  constitutional provisions,
    142–143,
  distilling rules from cases,
    115–117
  explanation of the rules,
    115–117, 119–120, 123,
    141–142, 157, 197–198, 205,
    237, 279
  illustrations of the rules, 115,
    119–120, 141–142, 145–146,
    157, 196–197, 279
  rule/law portion of CRAC,
    119–121, 196–197
  setting out rules, 115, 117,
    119–120
  statutes, 102–109
  statements of law, 101–102, 111,
    115–117, 123–124, 141–142,
    145, 157
Rules of Interpretation, 107–109,
    122, 275

citation to 119–120, 141–142, 145–146, 148–152, 157–158, 194, 197–198, 202, 234, 258, 260, 264

Secondary Authority, 106, 109, 143–144

Sentences, (see also Appellate Legal Drafting, Paragraphs, Topic Sentences, Word Choice), 125, 130–135, 138–139, 175, 186, 189, 192, 203–205, 277–278

Standards of Review
    generally, 159–164, 166–167, 280–81
    abuse-of-discretion, 159, 162–163, 167, 281
    agency decisions, 163
    arbitrary and capricious, 163
    bench trials, 162
    clearly erroneous, 159, 161–162, 167, 281
    de novo, 159, 161, 167, 281
    deferential and nondeferential, 160, 167, 281
    explained, 159–160
    independent, 161
    mixed questions of fact and law, 161
    other standards of review, 163
    plenary, 161
    questions of fact, 161–162
    questions of law, 161
    statements of the standard of review, 194–195
    substantial evidence, 159, 162, 165, 167, 181
    unwritten presumption of correctness, 160

Statement of the Case, (see also Appellate Briefs)
    generally, 169, 176, 179–183, 207, 282
    drafting and editing checklist, 182–183
    examples, 181–182

Statement of Facts, (see also Appellate Briefs, Facts)
    generally, 169, 176, 183–190, 207, 282
    drafting and editing guidelines, 188–190
    goals, 183–184
    material facts in the record, 184–185
    organization, 185–187

Statement of Issues on Appeal, 169, 176–179,

Statutes, analyzing and interpreting, 101–109, 122, 274–275

Subject Matter Jurisdiction, 19, 28–31, 76–77, 82, 94, 270–71, 273

Substantial Evidence Standard of Review, 159, 162, 165, 167, 181, 207

Sufficiency of the Evidence, harmless error analysis, 159, 165, 167

Summary of Argument, 169, 190–191, 207

Summary Judgment, 24, 34, 39

Supersedeas Bonds, 51, 64–65, 67, 272–273

Supreme Court of the United States (see also Appellate Court Systems, Appellate Court Jurisdiction, United States Supreme Court) 3–4, 12–14, 16, 38, 41,

Supreme Court of the United
    States, *continued*
    142–143, 151, 157, 172–173,
    206, 212, 216, 222, 226–227,
    229, 240, 252, 269–270, 279,
    282
Synthesizing Cases, Synthesis, 101,
    114–117, 123–124
Table of Authorities, 169, 176, 201
Table of Contents, 169, 176, 201
Tabulation, use in analyzing and in-
    terpreting Statutes, 102–104
Tax Court, 4
Theme, 174–175, 177, 188, 198,
    202, 222
Theory, 174–175, 177, 188, 202,
    222
Tools for Analyzing and Interpret-
    ing Statutes, 102–109, 122
Topic Sentences, 119, 125,
    130–131, 136, 138, 189,
    196–197, 203–205, 208, 277,
    284
Transition Sentences, 130–131, 138,
    189, 203–204
Transition Words, 128–129, 131,
    189, 199, 204–205
Trial Court
    bench Trials, standard of review
        for findings of fact, 162
    deference accorded, 160
    documents filed with the trial
        court—the clerk's file, 83–86,
        98

expanding the trial court record,
    89–94
jurisdiction of trial court while
    appeal pending, 66–67
preservation of error in the trial
    court, 20–25, 30
Unfavorable Facts, 185–187, 189,
    203–204
United States Supreme Court, (see
    also Appellate Court Systems,
    Appellate Court Jurisdiction,
    Supreme Court of the United
    States) 3–4, 12–14, 16, 38, 41,
    142–143, 151, 157, 172–173,
    206, 212, 216, 222, 226–227,
    229, 240, 252, 269–270, 279,
    282
United States Supreme Court Guide
    for Counsel, 216, 222, 226, 229,
    240
Vacatur, 79, 82
Vague, Vagueness, 187, 243
Verb Tense in Case Descriptions,
    133
Waiver (see also Abandonment,
    Forfeiture, Preservation of
    Error), 19, 26–30
Whether/When, Format for
    Statement of Issues on Appeal,
    178–179,
Word Choice, 129, 131–135,
    186–187, 189
Writing process, 135–138